Rick Steves'®

PORTUGAL

P9-DMM-200

CONTENTS

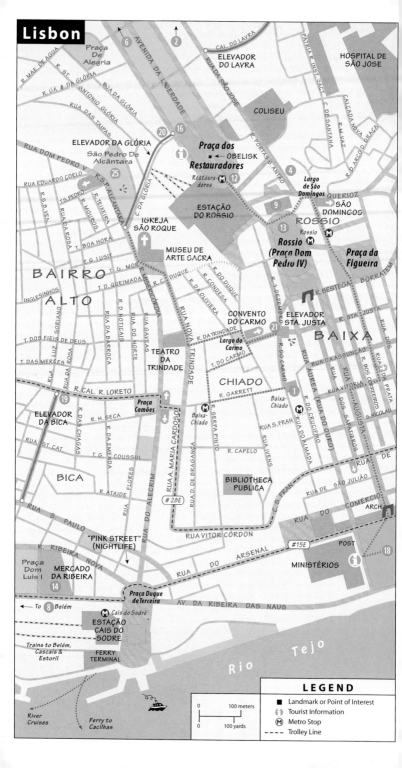

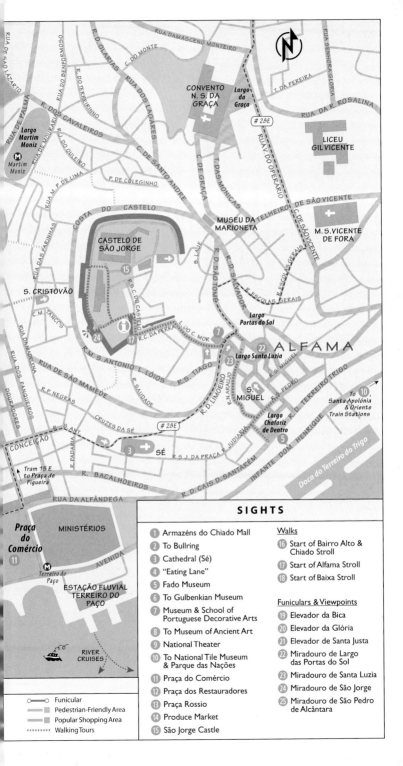

SIGHTS

1. Armazéns do Chiado Mall
2. To Bullring
3. Cathedral (Sé)
4. "Eating Lane"
5. Fado Museum
6. To Gulbenkian Museum
7. Museum & School of Portuguese Decorative Arts
8. To Museum of Ancient Art
9. National Theater
10. To National Tile Museum & Parque das Nações
11. Praça do Comércio
12. Praça dos Restauradores
13. Praça Rossio
14. Produce Market
15. São Jorge Castle

Walks

16. Start of Bairro Alto & Chiado Stroll
17. Start of Alfama Stroll
18. Start of Baixa Stroll

Funiculars & Viewpoints

19. Elevador da Bica
20. Elevador da Glória
21. Elevador de Santa Justa
22. Miradouro de Largo das Portas do Sol
23. Miradouro de Santa Luzia
24. Miradouro de São Jorge
25. Miradouro de São Pedro de Alcântara

Funicular
Pedestrian-Friendly Area
Popular Shopping Area
Walking Tours

Lisbon at night

Market vendor

Futebol on Nazaré's beach

Terraced vineyards in the Douro Valley

Fado — songs of sadness & hope

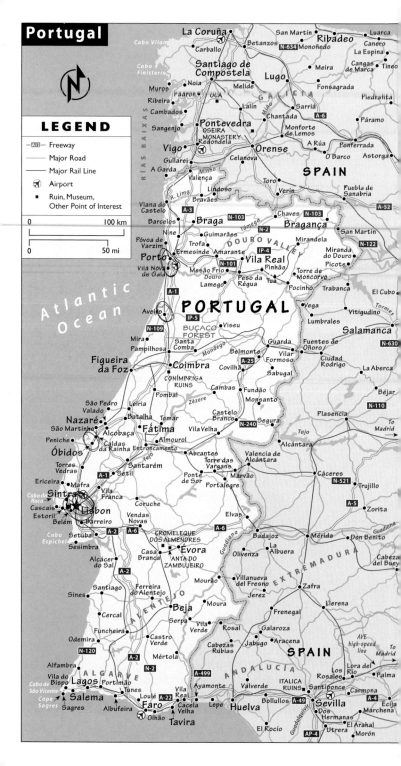

Rick Steves'

PORTUGAL

Top Destinations in Portugal

INTRODUCTION

Tucked into a far corner of the Continent, Portugal is Western Europe's least-touristed country. Its relative isolation preserves a traditional culture of widows in black and fishermen mending nets. Along with the old, you'll find the modern, especially in the culturally rich capital of Lisbon and in the resort towns that rival Spain's (but feel more authentic). If your idea of travel includes friendly locals (who speak a bit of English), exotic architecture, windswept castles, and fresh seafood with chilled wine on a beach at sunset... you've chosen the right destination.

In recent years, Portugal has experienced some economic success, thanks to its membership in the European Union. While Portugal is no longer a bargain basement for travelers, it's still a good budget option compared to the tourist-mobbed destinations of Northern Europe.

This book breaks Portugal into its top big-city, small-town, and rural destinations, giving you all the information and opinions necessary to wring the maximum value out of your limited time and money. Experiencing Portugal's culture, people, and natural wonders economically and hassle-free has been my goal for more than three decades of traveling, guiding tours, and travel writing. With this new edition, I pass on to you the lessons I've learned.

While including the predictable biggies, this book also mixes in a healthy dose of Back Door intimacy. You'll eat barnacles with green wine, recharge your solar cells in an Algarve fishing village, and wax nostalgic over bluesy fado singing. This book is selective. For example, while there are plenty of Algarve beach towns, I recommend only the top stops: Salema and Tavira.

The best is, of course, only my opinion. But after spending half my adult life exploring and researching Europe, I've developed a

Key to This Book

Updates

This book is updated regularly, but things change. For the latest, visit www.ricksteves.com/update, and for a valuable list of reports and experiences—good and bad—from fellow travelers, check www.ricksteves.com/feedback.

Abbreviations and Times

I use the following symbols and abbreviations in this book:
Sights are rated:

▲▲▲	**Don't miss**
▲▲	**Try hard to see**
▲	**Worthwhile if you can make it**
No rating	**Worth knowing about**

Tourist information offices are abbreviated as **TI,** and bathrooms are **WC**s. To categorize accommodations, I use a **Sleep Code** (described on page 18).

Like Portugal, this book uses the **24-hour clock** for schedules. It's the same through 12:00 noon, then keep going: 13:00, 14:00, and so on. For anything over 12, subtract 12 and add p.m. (14:00 is 2:00 p.m.).

When giving **opening times,** I include both peak season and off-season hours if they differ. So, if a museum is listed as "May-Oct daily 9:00-16:00," it should be open from 9 a.m. until 4 p.m. from the first day of May until the last day of October (but expect exceptions).

For **transit** or **tour departures,** I first list the frequency, then the duration. So, a train connection listed as "2/hour, 1.5 hours" departs twice each hour, and the journey lasts an hour and a half.

sixth sense for what travelers enjoy. Just thinking about the places featured in this book makes me want to hang out in a fado bar.

About This Book

Rick Steves' Portugal is a personal tour guide in your pocket. This book is organized by destinations. Each destination is a mini-vacation on its own, filled with exciting sights, strollable neighborhoods, affordable places to stay, and memorable places to eat. In the following chapters, you'll find these sections:

Planning Your Time suggests a schedule with thoughts on how to best use your limited time.

Orientation includes specifics on public transportation, helpful hints, local tour options, easy-to-read maps, and tourist information.

Sights describes the top attractions and includes their cost and hours.

Self-Guided Walks take you through interesting neighborhoods, with a personal tour guide in hand.

Sleeping describes my favorite hotels, from good-value deals to cushy splurges.

Eating serves up a range of options, from inexpensive eateries to fancy restaurants.

Connections outlines your options for traveling to destinations by train, bus, or plane, plus route tips for drivers.

Portugal: Past and Present gives you a quick overview of Portugal, from its prehistoric beginnings to the issues it faces today.

The **appendix** is a traveler's tool kit, with telephone tips, useful phone numbers, transportation basics (on trains, buses, car rentals, driving, and flights), recommended books and films, a festival list, a climate chart, a handy packing checklist, a hotel reservation form, and Portuguese survival phrases.

Browse through this book and select your favorite sights. Then have a great trip! Traveling like a temporary local, you'll get the absolute most of every mile, minute, and dollar. I'm happy that you'll be visiting places I know and love, and meeting my favorite Portuguese people.

Planning

This section will help you get started on planning your trip—with advice on trip costs, when to go, and what you should know before you take off.

Travel Smart

Your trip to Portugal is like a complex play—easier to follow and really appreciate on a second viewing. While no one does the same trip twice to gain that advantage, reading this book in its entirety before your trip accomplishes much the same thing.

Design an itinerary that enables you to visit sights at the best possible times. Note holidays, festivals, seasonal closures, and days when sights are closed. For example, many museums and sights close on Mondays. Hotels are most crowded on Fridays and Saturdays, especially in resort towns. To get between destinations smoothly, read the tips in this book's appendix on taking trains and buses, and renting a car and driving. A smart trip is a puzzle—a fun, doable, and worthwhile challenge.

Be sure to mix intense and relaxed periods in your itinerary. To maximize rootedness, minimize one-night stands. It's worth taking a long drive after dinner (or a train ride with a dinner picnic) to get settled in a town for two nights. People renting out private rooms are more likely to give a good price to someone staying more than one night. Every trip—and every traveler—needs slack time

INTRODUCTION

Portugal's Best Two-Week Trip by Car

DayPlan		Sleep in
1	Arrive in Lisbon	Lisbon
2	Lisbon	Lisbon
3	More time in Lisbon, or side-trip to Sintra by train; pick up car and drive to Salema in evening	Salema
4	Salema	Salema
5	Salema, side-trip to Cape Sagres	Salema
6	To Tavira via Lagos	Tavira
7	To Évora	Évora
8	More time in Évora, then to Nazaré via Óbidos in the afternoon	Nazaré
9	Nazaré	Nazaré
10	Near Nazaré (Alcobaça, Batalha, and Fátima), continue to Coimbra	Coimbra
11	Coimbra	Coimbra
12	To Douro Valley	Douro Valley
13	Douro Valley, end in Porto (could drop off car)	Porto
14	Porto	Porto
15	Drive or take the train back to Lisbon; or drive north to Santiago, Spain	

Notes: Try to avoid being in Lisbon (or Porto) on a Monday, when many major sights are closed (including Lisbon's Gulbenkian Museum, Museum of Ancient Art, National Tile Museum, and Fado Museum, as well as Belém's Monastery of Jerónimos, Coach Museum, Maritime Museum, Monument to the Discoveries—except open daily May-Sept, and Belém Tower). If you end up in Lisbon on a Monday, take a walking tour, a trolley ride, any of my self-guided neighborhood walks, or a side-trip to Sintra, where the major sights are open.

Lisbon is worth an extra day if you like big cities. But if you're a beach lover, leave Lisbon early and drive to Salema.

If, after touring Portugal, you're continuing to the Spanish destinations of Salamanca or Madrid, it's better to visit Porto and the Douro Valley before Coimbra.

By Train and Bus: While this itinerary is designed to be done

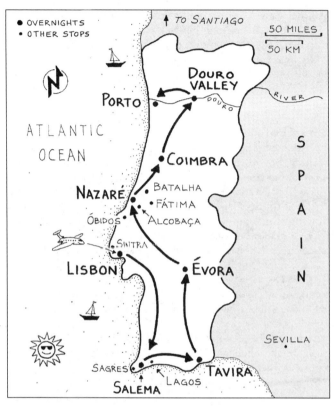

by car, it can also be done by train and bus. If you're taking public transportation, stay three nights in Lisbon and catch a bus to Salema on the morning of the fourth day. Skip Tavira. From the Algarve, take the bus to Évora (via Lagos) and spend a day and night, then take a bus to Nazaré (there's no direct service, so you have to go via Lisbon). See the sights near Nazaré by bus, using Nazaré as your home base. Take the bus to Coimbra. Catch the bus or train to Porto, and using Porto as a home base, see the Douro Valley on a combination boat/train tour (or, with extra time, spend the night).

(for laundry, picnics, people-watching, and so on). Pace yourself. Assume you will return.

Reread this book as you travel, and visit local TIs. Upon arrival in a new town, lay the groundwork for a smooth departure; get the schedule for the train or bus that you'll take when you depart. Drivers can study the best route to their next destination.

Get online at your hotel or at Internet cafés. Carry a mobile phone (or use a phone card) to make travel plans: You can find tourist information, learn the latest on sights (special events, tour schedules, etc.), book tickets and tours, make reservations, reconfirm hotels, research transportation connections, and keep in touch with your loved ones.

Enjoy the hospitality of the Portuguese people. Connect with the culture. Set up your own quest for the best cod dish, cloister, fado bar, or custard tart. Slow down and be open to unexpected experiences. Ask questions—most locals are eager to point you toward their idea of the right direction. Keep a notepad in your pocket for confirming prices, noting directions, and organizing your thoughts. Wear your money belt, learn the currency, and figure out how to estimate prices in dollars. Those who expect to travel smart, do.

Trip Costs

Five components make up your trip costs: airfare, surface transportation, room and board, sightseeing and entertainment, and shopping and miscellany.

Airfare: A basic round-trip flight from the US to Lisbon can cost, on average, about $900-1,500 total, depending on where you fly from and when (cheaper in winter). Smaller budget airlines provide bargain service from several European capitals to Lisbon (see "Cheap Flights" on page 347). Consider saving time and money in Europe by flying into one city and out of another; for instance, into Lisbon and out of Barcelona.

Surface Transportation: For a two-week whirlwind trip of all of my recommended Portuguese destinations, allow $300 per person for public transportation (trains and buses). For a two-week car rental, parking, gas, and insurance, allow $675 per person (based on two people sharing the car and expenses). Leasing is worth considering for trips of three weeks or more. Car rental and leases are cheapest when arranged from the US. Train passes, normally available only outside Europe, are a waste of money for a Portugal-only trip. It's cheaper to simply buy bus and train tickets as you go. For more on public transportation and car rental, see "Transportation" in the appendix.

Room and Board: You can thrive in Portugal on $100 a day per person for room and board (less in villages). A $100-a-day budget allows $15 for lunch, $5 for snacks, $30 for dinner, and $50 for

Portugal at a Glance

▲▲▲**Lisbon** Lively, hilly port and capital, with historic trolleys, grand squares, fado clubs, fine art, and a salty sailors' quarter topped by a castle.

▲▲**Sintra** A striking town, within easy day-tripping distance from Lisbon, known for its fairy-tale castles, verdant hills, and beautiful gardens.

▲▲▲**The Algarve** Portugal's sunny southern coast, strung with the simple fishing village of Salema, the historic "end of the road" of Cape Sagres, the beach-party town of Lagos, and the laid-back resort of Tavira.

▲▲**Évora** Whitewashed little college town with big Roman, Moorish, and Portuguese history encircled by its medieval wall.

▲▲**Nazaré and Nearby** Traditional fishing village turned small-town resort, and jumping off point for day trips to the monastery at Batalha, the pilgrimage site of Fátima, Portugal's largest church in Alcobaça, and the photogenic walled town of Óbidos.

▲▲**Coimbra** Portugal's Oxford, home to an Arab-influenced old town and bustling with students from its prestigious university.

▲▲**Porto** Gritty, urban second city with picturesque riverfront, charming old town, and museums sporting modern architecture.

▲**Douro Valley** Terraced farming valley and birthplace of port wine, with home bases in modern Peso da Régua and workaday Pinhão.

lodging (based on two people splitting a $100 double room that includes breakfast). If you have more money, I've listed great ways to spend it. Students and tightwads can do it on $60 ($30 for a bed, $30 for meals).

Sightseeing and Entertainment: You'll pay about $6-8 per major sight (museums, churches), $4-5 for minor ones (climbing towers), and $30 for splurge experiences (fado concerts, bullfights). An overall average of $15 a day works in most places. Don't skimp here. After all, this category is the driving force behind your trip—you came to sightsee, enjoy, and experience Portugal.

Shopping and Miscellany: Figure roughly $1-2 per postcard (including postage), coffee, beer, and ice-cream cone. Shopping can vary in cost from nearly nothing to a small fortune. Good budget travelers find that this category has little to do with assembling a trip full of lifelong and wonderful memories.

Sightseeing Priorities

Depending on the length of your trip, assuming you're using public transportation, and taking geographic proximity into account, here are my recommended priorities.

3 days:	Lisbon, Sintra
6 days, add:	The Algarve (Salema and Tavira)
9 days, add:	Évora, Nazaré
11 days, add:	Sights near Nazaré, Coimbra
14 days, add:	Porto, Douro Valley

When to Go

In peak season, May through September, sightseeing attractions are wide open. While it's not nearly as hot in Portugal as it is in Spain (except in the Alentejo region), an air-conditioned room is worth the splurge in summer. Book ahead if your stay coincides with a holiday or festival (see the list in the appendix).

Spring and fall offer the best combination of good weather, light crowds, long days, and plenty of tourist and cultural activities. In the off-season, roughly October through April, expect shorter hours, more lunchtime breaks at sights, and fewer activities. Confirm your sightseeing plans locally, especially when traveling off-season.

For weather specifics, see the climate chart in the appendix.

Know Before You Go

Your trip is more likely to go smoothly if you plan ahead. Check this list of things to arrange while you're still at home.

You need a **passport**—but no visa or shots—to travel in Portugal. You may be denied entry into certain European countries if your passport is due to expire within three to six months of your ticketed date of return. Get it renewed if you'll be cutting it close. It can take up to six weeks to get or renew a passport (for more on passports, see www.travel.state.gov). Pack a photocopy of your passport in your luggage in case the original is lost or stolen.

Book rooms well in advance if you'll be traveling during peak season (May-Sept) or any major holidays (see page 352).

Call your **debit and credit card companies** to let them know which countries you'll be visiting, to ask about fees, to request your PIN (it will be mailed to you), and more. See page 13 for details.

Do your homework if you want to buy **travel insurance.**

Compare the cost of the insurance to the likelihood of your using it and your potential loss if something goes wrong. Also, check whether your existing insurance (health, homeowners, or renters) covers you and your possessions overseas. For more information, see www.ricksteves.com/insurance.

If you're planning on **renting a car** in Portugal, you'll need your driver's license. Be aware that Portugal has one of the highest rates of automobile accidents in Europe.

If you plan to hire a **local guide,** reserve ahead by email. Popular guides can get booked up.

If you're bringing a **mobile device,** download any apps you might want to use on the road, such as translators, maps, and transit schedules. Check out **Rick Steves Audio Europe,** featuring hours of travel interviews and other audio content about Portugal (via www.ricksteves.com/audioeurope, iTunes, Google Play, or the Rick Steves Audio Europe free smartphone app; for details, see page 348).

Check the **Rick Steves guidebook updates** page for any recent changes to this book (www.ricksteves.com/update).

Because **airline carry-on restrictions** are always changing, visit the Transportation Security Administration's website (www.tsa.gov) for an up-to-date list of what you can bring on the plane with you...and what you have to check.

Practicalities

Emergency and Medical Help: In Portugal, dial 112 for police or medical emergencies. If you get sick, do as the Portuguese do and go to a pharmacist for advice. Or ask at your hotel for help—they'll know the nearest medical and emergency services.

Theft Alert: Thieves target tourists throughout Portugal, especially in Lisbon. While hotel rooms are generally safe, thieves snatch purses, pick pockets, and break into cars. Keep your passport, credit and debit cards, and cash in a money belt (a pouch with a strap that you buckle around your waist like a belt and wear under your clothes). Be on guard, especially on the Metro and trolleys, and treat any disturbance around you as a smoke screen for theft. Don't believe any "police officers" looking for counterfeit bills. When traveling by train, keep your backpack nearby and in sight. For tips for drivers, see the appendix.

Dealing with Theft or Loss: To replace a passport, you'll need to go in person to a US embassy or consulate (see page 338). If your credit and debit cards disappear, cancel and replace them (see "Damage Control for Lost Cards" on page 13). File a police report either on the spot or within a day or two; it's required if you submit an insurance claim for lost or stolen railpasses or travel gear, and can help with replacing your passport or credit and debit cards. For more information, see www.ricksteves.com/help. Precautionary measures can minimize the effects of loss: back up your photos and other files frequently.

Time Zones: Though Portugal and Spain are neighbors, Portugal sets its clock one hour earlier than Spain and most of continental Europe. (This is always true, even during Daylight Saving Time.) Portugal's time zone is the same as Great Britain's: five/eight hours ahead of the East/West coasts of the US. The exceptions are the beginning and end of Daylight Saving Time: Europe "springs forward" the last Sunday in March (two weeks after most of North America) and "falls back" the last Sunday in October (one week before North America). For a handy online time converter, try www.timeanddate.com/worldclock.

Business Hours: In Portugal, some businesses take an afternoon break (about 13:00-15:00). When it's 100 degrees in the shade, you'll understand why. The biggest museums stay open all day. Smaller ones often close for lunch. Banks are generally open Monday through Friday from 8:30 to 15:00. Small shops are usually open on Saturday only in the morning and are closed all day Sunday.

Saturdays are virtually weekdays, though places may close earlier and transportation connections can be less frequent. Sundays have the same pros and cons as they do for travelers in the US: Sightseeing attractions are generally open and street markets are lively with shoppers, but public transportation is limited. Popular destinations are even busier on weekends.

Watt's Up? Europe's electrical system is 220 volts, instead of North America's 110 volts. Most newer electronics (such as laptops, battery chargers, and hair dryers) convert automatically, so you won't need a converter, but you will need an adapter plug with two round prongs, sold inexpensively at travel stores in the US. Avoid bringing older appliances that don't automatically convert voltage; instead, buy a cheap replacement in Europe.

Discounts: Discounts aren't listed in this book. However, many Portuguese sights offer discounts for seniors (loosely defined as those who are retired or willing to call themselves a senior), youths (under age 18), and students or teachers with proper identification cards (www.isic.org). Always ask. Some discounts are available only for EU citizens.

Exchange Rate

1 euro (€) = about $1.30

To roughly convert prices in euros to dollars, add about 30 percent: €20 = about $26, €50 = about $65. (Check www. oanda.com for the latest exchange rates.) Just like the dollar, one euro (€) is broken down into 100 cents. Coins range from €0.01 to €2, and bills from €5 to €500.

Money

This section offers advice on how to pay for purchases on your trip (including getting cash from ATMs and paying with plastic), dealing with lost or stolen cards, VAT (sales tax) refunds, and tipping.

What to Bring

Bring both a credit card and a debit card. You'll use the debit card at cash machines (ATMs) to withdraw local cash for most purchases, and the credit card to pay for larger items. Some travelers carry a third card, in case one gets demagnetized or eaten by a temperamental machine.

As an emergency reserve, bring several hundred dollars in hard cash in easy-to-exchange $20 bills. Be aware that most Portuguese banks won't exchange foreign currency; instead you will need to go to a *casa de cambio* (currency exchange booth). These booths are found throughout large towns, especially near tourist areas, but generally have lousy rates and/or outrageous fees. Smart travelers use their ATM card rather than exchanging currency.

Cash

Cash is just as desirable in Europe as it is at home. Small businesses (hotels, restaurants, shops, etc.) prefer that you pay your bills with cash. Some vendors will charge you extra for using a credit card, and some won't take credit cards at all. Cash is the best—and sometimes only—way to pay for bus fare, taxis, and local guides.

Throughout Europe, ATMs are the standard way for travelers to get cash. Stay away from "independent" ATMs such as Travelex, Euronet, and Forex, which charge huge commissions and have terrible exchange rates.

To withdraw money from an ATM, you'll need a debit card, plus a PIN code. Know your PIN code in numbers; there are only numbers—no letters on European keypads. For security, it's best to shield the keypad when entering your PIN code at an ATM.

Although you can use a credit card for ATM transactions, it's generally more expensive (and only makes sense in an emergency), because it's considered a cash advance rather than a withdrawal. Try to withdraw large sums of money to reduce the number of per-transaction bank fees you'll pay.

Some readers report having difficulty using MasterCard-brand debit cards in Portugal (at hotels, restaurants, and ATMs), even when they've notified their bank ahead of time. For the best chances of accessing money from your US bank account, look for an ATM that uses a network whose logo is on the back of your ATM card (for example, Cirrus or Accel).

Pickpockets target tourists; be alert and follow my tips on page 9.

Credit and Debit Cards

For purchases, Visa and MasterCard are more commonly accepted than American Express, though many merchants in Portugal, especially outside the main tourist areas, take only MultiBanco credit cards (issued by a Portuguese bank). Just like at home, credit and debit cards work easily at larger hotels, restaurants, and shops. I typically use my debit card to withdraw cash to pay for most purchases. I use my credit card only in a few specific situations: to book hotel reservations by phone, to cover major expenses (such as car rentals, plane tickets, and hotel stays), and to pay for things near the end of my trip (to avoid another visit to the ATM). While you could use a debit card to make most large purchases, using a credit card offers a greater degree of fraud protection (because debit cards draw funds directly from your account).

Ask Your Credit- or Debit-Card Company: Before your trip, contact the company that issued your debit or credit cards.

• Confirm that your card will work overseas, and alert them that you'll be using it in Europe; otherwise, they may deny transactions if they perceive unusual spending patterns.

• Ask for the specifics on transaction **fees.** When you use your credit or debit card—either for purchases or ATM withdrawals—you'll often be charged additional "international transaction" fees of up to 3 percent (1 percent is normal) plus $5 per transaction. If your card's fees seem high, consider getting a different card just for your trip: Capital One (www.capitalone.com) and most credit unions have low-to-no international fees.

• If you plan to withdraw cash from ATMs, confirm your daily **withdrawal limit,** and if necessary, ask your bank to adjust it. Some travelers prefer a high limit that allows them to take out more cash at each ATM stop (saving on bank fees), while others prefer to set a lower limit in case their card is stolen. Note that foreign banks also set maximum withdrawal amounts for their ATMs.

• Get your bank's emergency **phone number** in the US (but not its 800 number, which isn't accessible from overseas) to call collect if you have a problem.

• Ask for your credit card's **PIN** in case you need to make an emergency cash withdrawal or encounter Europe's chip-and-PIN system; the bank won't tell you your PIN over the phone, so allow time for it to be mailed to you.

Chip and PIN: If your card is declined for a purchase in Europe, it may be because Europeans are increasingly using chip-and-PIN cards, which are embedded with an electronic chip (rather than the magnetic stripe used on our American-style cards). Much of Europe is adopting this system, and some merchants rely on it exclusively. You're most likely to encounter chip-and-PIN problems at automated payment machines, such as those at train and subway stations, toll roads, parking garages, luggage lockers, and self-serve gas pumps. If a machine won't take your card, find a cashier who can make your card work (they can print a receipt for you to sign), or find a machine that takes cash.

Don't panic. Most travelers who are carrying only magnetic-stripe cards never encounter any problems. Still, it pays to carry plenty of euros (you can always use an ATM with your magnetic-stripe debit card). Memorizing the PIN lets you use it at some chip-and-PIN machines—just enter your PIN when prompted.

If you're still concerned, you can apply for a chip card in the US (though I think it's overkill). While big US banks offer these cards with high annual fees, a better option is the no-annual-fee GlobeTrek Visa, offered by Andrews Federal Credit Union in Maryland (open to all US residents; see www.andrewsfcu.org).

Dynamic Currency Conversion: If merchants offer to convert your purchase price into dollars (called dynamic currency conversion, or DCC), refuse this "service." You'll pay even more in fees for the expensive convenience of seeing your charge in dollars.

Damage Control for Lost Cards

If you lose your credit, debit, or ATM card, you can stop people from using it by reporting the loss immediately to the respective global customer-assistance centers. Call these 24-hour US numbers collect: Visa (tel. 303/967-1096), MasterCard (tel. 636/722-7111), and American Express (tel. 336/393-1111). European toll-free numbers (listed by country) can be found at the websites for Visa and MasterCard.

At a minimum, you'll need to know the name of the financial institution that issued you the card, along with the type of card (classic, platinum, or whatever). Providing the following information will allow for a quicker cancellation of your missing card: full card number, whether you are the primary or secondary cardholder, the cardholder's name exactly as printed on the card, billing address, home phone number, circumstances of the loss or theft, and identification verification (your birth date, your mother's maiden name, or your Social Security number— memorize this, don't carry a copy). If you are the secondary cardholder, you'll also need to provide the primary cardholder's identification-verification details. You can generally receive a temporary card within two or three business days in Europe (see www.ricksteves.com/help).

If you report your loss within two days, you typically won't be responsible for any unauthorized transactions on your account, although many banks charge a liability fee of $50.

Tipping

Tipping in Portugal isn't as automatic and generous as it is in the US, but for special service, tips are appreciated, if not expected. As in the US, the proper amount depends on your resources, tipping philosophy, and the circumstances, but some general guidelines apply.

Restaurants: Tipping is an issue only at restaurants that have table service. If you order your food at a counter, don't tip.

In most restaurants, service is included—your menu typically will indicate this by noting *serviço incluido*. Still, if you are pleased with the service, it's customary to leave up to 5 percent. If service is not included *(serviço não incluido)*, tip up to 10 percent. Leave the tip on the table. It's best to tip in cash, even if you pay with your credit card. Otherwise, the tip may never reach your server.

Taxis: To tip a cabbie, round up. For a typical ride, 5-10 percent is about right (for instance, if the fare is €13, pay €14). If the cabbie hauls your bags and zips you to the airport to help you catch your flight, you might want to toss in a little more. But if you feel like you're being driven in circles or otherwise ripped off, skip the tip.

Services: In general, if someone in the service industry does a super job for you, a small tip of a euro or two is appropriate...but not required. If you're not sure whether (or how much) to tip for a service, ask your hotelier or the TI.

Getting a VAT Refund

Wrapped into the purchase price of your souvenirs is a Value-Added Tax (VAT, called IVA or *Imposto sobre o Valor Acrescentado* in Portuguese) of about 20 percent. You're entitled to get most of that tax back if you purchase more than €60 (about $78) worth of goods at a store that participates in the VAT-refund scheme. Typically, you must ring up the minimum at a single retailer—you can't add up your purchases from various shops to reach the required amount.

Getting your refund is usually straightforward and, if you buy a substantial amount of souvenirs, well worth the hassle. If you're lucky, the merchant will subtract the tax when you make your purchase. (This is more likely to occur if the store ships the goods to your home.) Otherwise, you'll need to:

Get the paperwork. Have the merchant completely fill out the necessary refund document, called a "cheque." You'll have to present your passport at the store. Get the paperwork done before you leave the store to ensure you'll have everything you need (including your original sales receipt).

Get your stamp at the border or airport. Process your VAT document at your last stop in the EU (such as at the airport) with the customs agent who deals with VAT refunds. Before checking in for your flight, find the local customs office, and be prepared to stand in line. Keep your purchases readily available for viewing by the customs agent (ideally in your carry-on bag—don't make the mistake of checking the bag with your purchases before you've seen the agent). You're not supposed to use your purchased goods before you leave. If you show up at customs wearing your hand-knit Portuguese sweater, officials might look the other way—or deny you a refund.

Collect your refund. You'll need to return your stamped documents to the retailer or its representative. Many merchants work with a service, such as Global Blue or Premier Tax Free, that has offices at major airports, ports, or border crossings (either before or after security, probably strategically located near a duty-free shop). These services, which extract a 4 percent fee, can refund your money immediately in cash or credit your card (within two billing cycles). If the retailer handles VAT refunds directly, it's up to you to contact the merchant for your refund. You can mail the documents from home, or more quickly, from your point of departure (using an envelope you've prepared in advance or one that's been provided by the merchant). You'll then have to wait—it can take months.

Customs for American Shoppers

You are allowed to take home $800 worth of items per person duty-free, once every 30 days. You can also bring in a liter of alcohol duty-free. As for food, you can take home many processed and packaged foods: vacuum-packed cheeses, dried herbs, jams, baked goods, candy, chocolate, oil, vinegar, mustard, and honey. Fresh fruits and vegetables and most meats are not allowed. Any liquid-containing foods must be packed in your checked luggage, a potential recipe for disaster. To check customs rules and duty rates, visit www.cbp.gov.

Sightseeing

Sightseeing can be hard work. Use these tips to make your visits to Portugal's finest sights meaningful, fun, efficient, and painless.

Plan Ahead

Set up an itinerary that allows you to fit in all your must-see sights. For a one-stop look at opening hours in the bigger cities—Lisbon and Porto—see the "At a Glance" sidebars. Most sights keep stable hours, but you can easily confirm the latest by checking with the TI or visiting museum websites.

Don't put off visiting a must-see sight—you never know when a place will close unexpectedly for a holiday, strike, or restoration. On holidays (see list on page 352), expect reduced hours or closures. In summer, some sights may stay open late. Off-season, many museums have shorter hours.

When possible, visit major sights in the morning (when your energy is best) and save other activities for the afternoon. Hit the museum highlights first, then see the rest if you have the stamina and time.

Study up. To get the most out of the sight descriptions in this book, read them before you visit.

At Sights

Here's what you can typically expect:

Some important sights require you to check daypacks and coats. To avoid checking a small backpack, carry it under your arm like a purse as you enter. From a guard's point of view, a backpack is generally a problem, while a purse is not.

At churches—which offer interesting art (usually free) and a cool, welcome seat—a modest dress code (no bare shoulders or shorts) is encouraged.

Flash photography is sometimes banned, but taking photos without a flash is usually allowed. Flashes damage oil paintings and distract others in the room. Even without a flash, a handheld camera will take a decent picture (or buy postcards or posters at the museum bookstore).

Museums may have special exhibits in addition to their permanent collection. Some exhibits are included in the entry price, while others come at an extra cost (which you may have to pay even if you don't want to see the exhibit).

Expect changes—artwork can be on tour, on loan, out sick, or shifted at the whim of the curator. To adapt, pick up any available free floor plans as you enter, and ask museum staff if you can't find a particular item.

Many sights rent audioguides, which generally offer sometimes dry-but-useful recorded descriptions in English (about €5). If you bring along your earbuds, you can enjoy better sound and avoid holding the device to your ear. To save money, bring a Y-jack and share one audioguide with your travel partner.

Important sights may have an on-site café or cafeteria (usually a good place to rejuvenate during a long visit). The WCs at sights are free and generally clean.

Many sights sell postcards that highlight their attractions. Before you leave a sight, scan the postcards and thumb through the biggest guidebook (or skim its index) to be sure you haven't overlooked something that you'd like to see.

Most sights stop admitting people 30-60 minutes before closing time, and some rooms may close early (often about 45 minutes before the actual closing time). Guards usher people out, so don't save the best for last.

Every sight or museum offers more than what is covered in this book. Use this information as an introduction—not the final word.

Sleeping

Portugal offers some of the best accommodations values in Western Europe. Most places are government-regulated, with posted prices. While prices are low, street noise can be high. Always ask to see your room first. Check the price posted on the door, consider potential night-noise problems, ask for another room, or bargain down the price. You can request *com vista* (with a view) or *tranquilo* (quiet). In most cases, the view comes with street noise. Especially in resort areas, prices go way up in July and August. Most of the year, prices are soft.

I favor accommodations and restaurants that are handy to your sightseeing activities. Rather than list lodgings scattered throughout a city, I describe two or three favorite neighborhoods and recommend the best accommodations values in each, from simple dorm beds to fancy doubles with all of the comforts.

A major feature of this book is its extensive listing of good-value rooms. I like places that are clean, central, relatively quiet at night, reasonably priced, friendly, small enough to have a hands-on owner and stable staff, run with a respect for Portuguese traditions, and not listed in other guidebooks. (In Portugal, for me, six out of these eight criteria means it's a keeper.) I'm more impressed by a convenient location and a fun-loving philosophy than flat-screen TVs and shoeshine machines.

Book your accommodations well in advance if you'll be traveling during busy times. See page 352 for a list of major holidays and festivals in Portugal; for tips on making reservations, see page 20.

Sleep Code

(€1 = about $1.30, country code: 351)

Price Rankings
To help you easily sort through the listings, I've divided the accommodations into three categories, based on the price for a standard double room with bath:

$$$ **Higher Priced**
$$ **Moderately Priced**
$ **Lower Priced**

I always rate hostels as $, whether or not they have double rooms, because they have the cheapest beds in town.

Prices can change without notice; verify the hotel's current rates online or by email.

Abbreviations
To pack maximum information into minimum space, I use the following code to describe accommodations in this book. Prices listed are per room, not per person. When a price range is given for a type of room (such as double rooms listing for "Db-€100-150"), it means the price fluctuates with the season, size of room, or length of stay; expect to pay the upper end for peak-season stays.

S = Single room (or price for one person in a double).
D = Double or twin room. "Double beds" can be two twins sheeted together and are usually big enough for nonromantic couples.
T = Triple (generally a double bed with a single).
Q = Quad (usually two double beds; adding an extra child's bed to a T is usually cheaper).
b = Private bathroom with toilet and shower or tub.
s = Private shower or tub only (the toilet is down the hall).

According to this code, a couple staying at a "Db-€100" hotel would pay a total of €100 (about $130) for a double room with a private bathroom. Unless otherwise noted, breakfast is included, hotel staff speak basic English, and credit cards are accepted.

There's almost always Wi-Fi and/or Internet access available, either free or for a fee.

Rates and Deals

I've described my recommended accommodations using a Sleep Code (see sidebar). Prices listed are for one-night stays in peak season, include breakfast, and assume you're booking directly (not through a TI or online hotel-booking engine). Using an online booking service costs the hotel about 20 percent and logically closes the door on special deals. Book direct.

These days, many hotels change prices from day to day according to demand. Given the economic downturn, hoteliers are often willing and eager to make a deal. I'd suggest emailing several hotels to ask for their best price. Comparison-shop and make your choice.

As you look over the listings, you'll notice that some accommodations promise special prices to my readers who book direct (without using a room-finding service or hotel-booking website, which take a commission). To get these rates, you must mention this book when you reserve, and then show the book upon arrival. Rick Steves discounts apply to readers with ebooks as well as printed books. Discounts may not apply to promotional rates.

In general, prices can soften up if you do any of the following: offer to pay cash, stay at least three nights, or mention this book. You can also try asking for a cheaper room or a discount, or offer to skip breakfast.

Types of Accommodations

Hotels

Double rooms listed in this book range from $60 (very simple, toilet and shower down the hall) to $400 suites (maximum plumbing and more), with most clustering around $100. Hotel rooms are generally pleasant by American standards. Don't judge hotels by their bleak and dirty entryways. Landlords, stuck with rent control, often stand firmly in the way of hardworking hoteliers who'd like to brighten up their buildings.

All rooms have sinks with hot and cold water. Rooms with private bathrooms are often bigger and renovated, while the cheaper rooms without bathrooms often will be dingier and/or on the top floor. Any room without a bathroom has access to a bathroom in the corridor. Hotel elevators, while becoming more common, are often very small, forcing you to send your bags up separately—pack light.

Prepare for cool evenings if you travel in spring and fall. Summer can be extremely hot. Consider air-conditioning, fans, and noise (since you'll want your window open), and don't be shy about asking for ice at the fancier hotels. Many rooms come with mini-refrigerators (if it's noisy at night, unplug it).

Most hotel rooms with air conditioners come with control

INTRODUCTION

Making Hotel Reservations

Given the good value of the accommodations I've found for this book, reserve your rooms several weeks in advance—or as soon as you've pinned down your travel dates, particularly for Lisbon. Note that some national holidays jam things up and merit your making reservations far in advance (see page 352).

Requesting a Reservation: It's usually easiest to book your room through the hotel's website; many have a reservation-request form built right in. (For the best rates, be sure to use the hotel's official site and not a booking agency's site.) Just type in your preferred dates and the website will automatically display a list of available rooms and prices. Simpler websites will generate an email to the hotelier with your request. If there's no reservation form, or for complicated requests, send an email from your personal address. Other options include calling (see "Phoning" below, and be mindful of time zones) or faxing.

The hotelier wants to know these key pieces of information (also included in the sample request form in the appendix):

- number and type of rooms
- number of nights
- date of arrival
- date of departure
- any special needs (such as bathroom in the room or down the hall, twin beds vs. double bed, air-conditioning, quiet, view, ground floor, etc.)

When you request a room, use the European style for writing dates: day/month/year. For example, for a two-night stay in July of 2014, I would request: "1 double room for 2 nights, arrive 16/07/14, depart 18/07/14." Consider in advance how long you'll stay; don't just assume you can tack on extra days once you arrive. Mention any discounts offered—for Rick Steves readers or otherwise—when you make the reservation.

If you don't get a response to your email, it usually means the hotel is already fully booked—but try sending the message again or call to follow up.

Confirming a Reservation: Most places will request your credit-card number to hold the room. To confirm a room using a hotel's secure online reservation form, enter your contact information and credit-card number; the hotel will email a confirmation.

If you sent an email to request a reservation, the hotel will reply with its room availability and rates. This is not a confirmation. You must email back to say that you want the room at the given rate. While you can email your credit-card information (I do), it's safer to share that confidential info via phone call, two emails (splitting your number between them), or the hotel's secure online reservation form.

Canceling a Reservation: If you must cancel your reservation, it's courteous to do so with as much notice as possible. Simply make a quick phone call or send an email. Hoteliers and *pensão* hosts lose money if they turn away customers while holding a room for someone who doesn't show up. Understandably, many places bill no-shows for one night.

Cancellation policies can be strict: For example, you might lose a deposit if you cancel within two weeks of your reserved stay, or you might be billed for the entire visit if you leave early. Internet deals may require prepayment, with no refunds for cancellations. Ask about cancellation policies before you book.

If canceling via email, request confirmation that your cancellation was received to avoid being billed accidentally.

Reconfirming Your Reservation: Always call to reconfirm your room reservation a day or two in advance from the road. Smaller places appreciate knowing your estimated time of arrival. If you'll be arriving late (after 17:00), let them know. On the small chance that a hotel loses track of your reservation, bring along a hard copy of their confirmation.

Reserving Rooms as You Travel: You can make reservations as you travel, calling places a few days to a week before your arrival. If everything's full, don't despair. Call a day or two in advance and fill in a cancellation. If you'd rather travel without any reservations at all, you'll have greater success snaring rooms if you arrive at your destination early in the day. When you anticipate crowds (weekends are worst), call hotels at about 9:00 or 10:00 on the day you plan to arrive, when the receptionist knows who'll be checking out and just which rooms will be available. If you encounter a language barrier, ask the fluent receptionist at your current hotel to call for you.

Phoning: To call Portugal from the US or Canada, dial 011-351-local number. The 011 is our international access code, and 351 is Portugal's country code. If you're calling Portugal from another European country, dial 00-351-local number. The 00 is Europe's international access code. To make calls within Portugal, dial the local number.

For more tips on calling, see page 331.

sticks (like TV remotes, sometimes require a deposit) that generally have similar symbols: fan icon (adjust wind power); louver icon (choose steady flow or waves); snowflake and sunshine icons (heat or cold); clock ("O" setting: run X hours before turning off; "I" setting: wait X hours to start); and temperature control (20 degrees Celsius is comfortable).

If you're arriving early in the morning, your room probably won't be ready. You can drop your bag safely at the hotel and dive right into sightseeing.

Hoteliers can be a great help and source of advice. Most know their city well and can assist you with everything from public transit and airport connections to finding a good restaurant, the nearest launderette, or an Internet café.

Even at the best places, mechanical breakdowns occur: Air-conditioning malfunctions, sinks leak, hot water turns cold, and toilets gurgle and smell. Report your concerns clearly and calmly at the front desk. For more complicated problems, don't expect instant results. Any regulated hotel will have a complaint book *(livro de reclamações)*, which is checked by authorities. A request for this book will generally prompt the hotelier to solve your problem to keep you from writing a complaint.

If you suspect night noise will be a problem (if, for instance, your room is over a nightclub), ask for a quieter room in the back or on an upper floor. To guard against theft in your room, keep valuables out of sight. Some rooms come with a safe, and others have safes at the front desk. Use them if you're concerned. I've never bothered using one.

For environmental reasons, towels are often replaced in hotels only when you leave them on the floor. In private accommodations and some cheap hotels, they aren't replaced at all, so hang them up to dry and reuse.

Checkout can pose problems if surprise charges pop up on your bill. If you settle your bill the afternoon before you leave, you'll have time to discuss and address any points of contention (before 19:00, when the night shift usually arrives).

Above all, keep a positive attitude. Remember, you're on vacation. If your hotel is a disappointment, spend more time out enjoying the city you came to see.

Historic Inns

Portugal has luxurious, government-sponsored historic inns. These *pousadas* are often renovated castles, palaces, or monasteries, many with great views and stately atmospheres. While full of Old World character, they often are run in a very sterile, bureaucratic way. These are pricey ($225-450 doubles), but can be a good deal for younger people (30 and under) and seniors (55 and over), who often get discounted rates; for details, bonus packages, and family deals, see www.pousadas.pt.

Rooms in Private Homes *(Quartos)*
In touristy areas, you'll typically find locals who've opened up a spare room to make a little money on the side. These rooms are usually as private as hotel rooms, often with separate entries. Especially in resort towns, the rooms might be in small, apartment-type buildings. Ask for a *quarto* (KWAR-too). They're less expensive than hotels ($45-75 for a double without breakfast). Given that the boss changes the sheets, people staying several nights are most desirable; one-night stays sometimes cost extra. *Quartos* usually offer a good experience.

Hostels and Campgrounds
Portugal has plenty of youth hostels and campgrounds, but considering the great bargains on other accommodations, I don't think they're worth the trouble and barely cover them in this book. Instead, I prefer simple, family-run hotels (listed as a *pensão* or *residencial*); they're easy to find, inexpensive, and, when chosen properly, a fun part of the Portuguese cultural experience. If you're on a starvation budget or just prefer camping or hosteling, plenty of information is available in the *Let's Go Spain & Portugal* guidebook, through the national TI, and at local TIs.

Eating

The Portuguese meal schedule is slightly later than in the US. Lunch *(almoço)* is the big meal, served between 12:30 and 14:00, while supper *(jantar)* is from about 19:30 to 21:30. You'll eat well in mom-and-pop restaurants for €10. For tips on tipping, see page 14. One of the most important things to remember when eating in Portugal is that if appetizers (olives, bread, butter, pâtés, and a veritable mini-buffet of other tasty temptations) are brought to your table before you order, they are not free. If you don't want them, push them to the side—you won't be charged for what you don't touch. But taking just one olive means you pay for the whole dish. Simple appetizers usually cost about €1 each, so it won't break the budget—just don't be surprised at extra charges on your bill. Most mom-and-pop restaurateurs will figure the bill in front of you, so everyone agrees on the final amount to be paid. All restaurants are now smoke-free to meet EU regulations.

Eat seafood in Portugal (except on Monday, when the fish isn't fresh). Fish soup *(sopa de peixe)* and shellfish soup *(sopa de mariscos)* are worth seeking out. *Caldo verde* is a popular vegetable soup. *Frango assado* is roast chicken; ask for *piri-piri* sauce if you like it hot and spicy. *Porco á Alentejana* is an interesting combination of pork and clams. Potatoes and greens are popular side dishes. Carbs never went out of style in Portugal—it's common to get both potatoes and rice with a meal. As in Spain, garlic and olive oil are big.

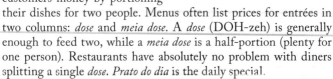

Many restaurants save their customers money by portioning their dishes for two people. Menus often list prices for entrées in two columns: *dose* and *meia dose.* A *dose* (DOH-zeh) is generally enough to feed two, while a *meia dose* is a half-portion (plenty for one person). Restaurants have absolutely no problem with diners splitting a single *dose. Prato do dia* is the daily special.

For a quick snack, cafés are usually cheaper than bars. Many cafés also double as lunch joints, which locals frequent. If you see a menu written on a paper tablecloth and taped in the window, you can be assured of a quick, home-cooked meal. Just don't expect fancy presentation (and be willing to sit at a table with someone— don't worry, it makes for great conversation).

Bars have an enticing selection of savory treats on display for a quick cheap snack, such as codfish cakes *(pastel de bacalhau)* in northern Portugal, or deep-fried pastries with flaked cod *(pastéis de bacalhau)* near Lisbon.

Sandwiches *(sandes)* are everywhere. The Portuguese breakfast *(pequeno almoço)* is just coffee and a sweet roll. A standard, wonderful local pastry is the custard tart, *pastel de nata* (called *pastel de Belém* in Lisbon's fancy suburb of the same name).

When you want the bill, say, *"Conta, por favor."*

Portuguese Drinks

Despite its small size, Portugal is the world's seventh-largest wine producer—150 million gallons in a good year. And Portuguese wines are cheap, decent, and distinctively fruity.

Vinho verde (VEEN-yoo VAIR-day) is light, refreshing, almost always white, and slightly fizzy. This "green wine" is actually golden in color, but "green" (young) in age—picked, made, and drunk within a year. *Alvarinho* grapes, from the northern Minho region, are low-sugar and high-acid. After the initial fermentation, winemakers introduce a second fermentation, whose by-product is carbon dioxide—the light fizz. The wines are somewhat bitter alone, but great with meals, especially seafood. The best are from Monaco Amarante and Aveleda, but the one on every menu is the perfectly acceptable Casal Garcia. If you like white *vinho verde,* you might enjoy the

Typical Portuguese Foods

bacalhau	dried and salted cod, served a reputed 365 different ways (arguably the national dish, but definitely an acquired taste)
frango assado	roast chicken, commonly served with *piri-piri* hot sauce
porco á Alentejana	diced pork covered with clams, Portugal's unique contribution to world cuisine
sardinhas grelhadas	fresh sardines, grilled or barbecued

Soups and Stews *(Sopas)*

caldo verde	"green" soup of kale greens and potato puree
cataplana	seafood and potatoes cooked in a copper clamshell dish
caldeirada de peixe	like *cataplana,* but cooked in a casserole
sopa de mariscos	thick seafood soup
feijoada	pork and beans
arroz de mariscos	rice and mixed seafood stew (the "Portuguese paella")
sopa Alentejana	garlic soup with a poached egg, cilantro, and bread crumbs dropped in

Snacks

pastel de bacalhau	fried codfish cakes
prego	steak sandwich
tosta mista	grilled ham and cheese sandwich
batatas fritas	potato chips

Desserts

You'll find various concoctions made from egg yolk and sugar, such *abarrigas de freiras* ("nuns' bellies") and *papo de anjo* ("angel's double chin").

pudim	flan
arroz doce	rice pudding with cinnamon
salame de chocolate	cookies and chocolate pressed together to look like salami when sliced
queque	muffin

How Was Your Trip?

Were your travels fun, smooth, and meaningful? If you'd like to share your tips, concerns, and discoveries, please fill out the survey at www.ricksteves.com/feedback. I value your feedback. Thanks in advance—it helps a lot.

harder-to-find red version. It's dark in color, like a cabernet, but still fizzy and light in flavor, like a rosé—a unique combination.

The Dão region also produces fine red wines, mostly from the Mondego Valley between Coimbra, Guarda, and Viseu. They should sit for a year or two in the bottle before drinking. The Alentejo region (look for bottles labeled "Borba") is known for its high-quality red.

Madeira, made from grapes grown in volcanic soil in the Madeira Islands, is fortified and blended (as is port), and usually served as a sweet dessert wine. The English and George Washington both liked it ("Have some Madeira, m'dear"), though today's version is drier and less syrupy. A Madeira called *Sercial* is served chilled (like sherry) with almonds. If you find yourself drowning in choices, simply try a glass of the house wine *(vinho da casa)*. Beer *(cerveja)* is also popular—for a small draft beer, ask for *uma imperial*.

If you like port wine, what better place to sample it than its birthplace, Port-ugal? (For a crash course on port wine, see page 290.) *Reserva* on the label means it's the best-quality port (and the most expensive). All bottles of port should have a *selo de garantia* (a seal of guarantee) issued by the Port Wine Institute.

Freshly squeezed orange juice *(sumo de laranja),* mineral water *(água mineral),* and soft drinks are widely available. When ordering water, fizzy or not, you will always be asked, *"Fresco o natural?"* *Fresco* is chilled, and *natural* is room temperature.

Coffee lovers enjoy a *bica,* the very aromatic shot of espresso so popular in Portugal. For an espresso with a little milk (like a macchiato), ask for a *café pingado.*

Here are more words to help quench your thirst:

água da torneira	tap water
água com/sem gás	water with/without bubbles
meia de leite	coffee with warm milk
galão	¼ coffee, ¾ warm milk served in a tall glass

chá	tea
vinho tinto	red wine
vinho branco	white wine
cerveja	beer
imperial	small draft beer
aguardente	firewater distilled from grape seeds, stems, and skins, with a kick like a mule
ginjinha	cherry liqueur, served at special bars in Lisbon and Óbidos

Traveling as a Temporary Local

We travel all the way to Europe to enjoy differences—to become temporary locals. You'll experience frustrations. Certain truths that we find "God-given" or "self-evident," such as cold beer, ice in drinks, bottomless cups of coffee, hot showers, and bigger being better, are suddenly not so true. One of the benefits of travel is the eye-opening realization that there are logical, civil, and even better alternatives.

Europeans generally like Americans. But if there is a negative aspect to the European image of Americans, it's that we are loud, wasteful, ethnocentric, too informal (which can seem disrespectful), and a bit naive.

While the Portuguese look bemusedly at some of our Yankee excesses—and worriedly at others—they nearly always afford us individual travelers all the warmth we deserve.

Judging from all the happy feedback I receive from travelers who have used this book, it's safe to assume you'll enjoy a great, affordable vacation—with the finesse of an independent, experienced traveler.

Thanks, and happy travels! *Boa-viagem!*

Back Door Travel Philosophy

From *Rick Steves' Europe Through the Back Door*

Travel is intensified living—maximum thrills per minute and one of the last great sources of legal adventure. Travel is freedom. It's recess, and we need it.

Experiencing the real Europe requires catching it by surprise, going casual..."through the Back Door."

Affording travel is a matter of priorities. (Make do with the old car.) You can eat and sleep—simply, safely, and enjoyably— anywhere in Europe for $120 a day plus transportation costs. In many ways, spending more money only builds a thicker wall be- tween you and what you traveled so far to see. Europe is a cultural carnival, and time after time, you'll find that its best acts are free and the best seats are the cheap ones.

A tight budget forces you to travel close to the ground, meeting and communicating with the people. Never sacrifice sleep, nutrition, safety, or cleanliness to save money. Simply enjoy the local-style alternatives to expensive hotels and restaurants.

Connecting with people carbonates your experience. Extro- verts have more fun. If your trip is low on magic moments, kick yourself and make things happen. If you don't enjoy a place, maybe you don't know enough about it. Seek the truth. Recognize tourist traps. Give a culture the benefit of your open mind. See things as different, but not better or worse. Any culture has plenty to share.

Of course, travel, like the world, is a series of hills and valleys. Be fanatically positive and militantly optimistic. If something's not to your liking, change your liking.

Travel can make you a happier American, as well as a citizen of the world. Our Earth is home to seven billion equally precious people. It's humbling to travel and find that other people don't have the "American Dream"—they have their own dreams. Europeans like us, but with all due respect, they wouldn't trade passports.

Thoughtful travel engages us with the world. In tough eco- nomic times, it reminds us what is truly important. By broadening perspectives, travel teaches new ways to measure quality of life.

Globetrotting destroys ethnocentricity, helping us understand and appreciate other cultures. Rather than fear the diversity on this planet, celebrate it. Among your most prized souvenirs will be the strands of different cultures you choose to knit into your own char- acter. The world is a cultural yarn shop, and Back Door travelers are weaving the ultimate tapestry. Join in!

PORTUGAL

Portugal is underrated. The country seems somewhere just beyond Europe—prices are a bit cheaper, and the pace of life is noticeably slower than in Spain. While the unification of Europe is bringing sweeping changes to Portugal, the traditional economy is still based on fishing, cork, wine, and textiles.

Portugal isn't touristy—even its coastal towns lack glitzy attractions. The beach and the sea are enough, as they have been for centuries. They were the source of Portugal's seafaring wealth long ago, and are the draw for tourists today.

The locals, not jaded by tourists, will meet you with warmth—especially if you learn at least a few words of Portuguese, instead of launching into Spanish (see "Portuguese Survival Phrases" in the appendix).

Over the centuries, Portugal and Spain have had a love-hate, on-again-off-again relationship, but they have almost always remained separate, each with their own distinct language and culture. The Portuguese seem humbler and friendlier than the Spanish. In Spain, if you ever feel like you can't do anything right, you'll find it's just the opposite in Portugal—you can't do anything wrong. Portugal is also more ethnically diverse than Spain, as it's inhabited by many people from its former colonies in Brazil, Africa, and Asia. The Portuguese continue to have a special affinity for their Brazilian cousins.

Portugal bucked the Moors before Spain did, establishing its present-day borders 800 years ago. A couple of centuries later, the Age of Discovery (1500-1700) made Portugal one of the world's richest nations.

Portugal's Prince Henry the Navigator sponsored the voyages of explorers who traveled to Africa seeking a trade route to India. Bartolomeu Dias and Vasco da Gama, building upon the knowl-

PORTUGAL

Portugal Almanac

Official Name: It's República Portuguesa, but locals just say "Portugal."

Population: 11 million people. Most Portuguese are Roman Catholic (85 percent), with indigenous Mediterranean roots; there are a few black Africans from former colonies and some Eastern Europeans.

Latitude and Longitude: 39°N and 8°W (similar latitude to Washington, D.C. or San Francisco).

Area: 35,000 square miles, which includes the Azores and Madeira, two island groups in the Atlantic.

Geography: Portugal is rectangular, 325 miles long and 125 miles wide. (It's roughly the size and shape of Indiana.) The half of the country north of Lisbon is more mountainous, cool, and rainy. The south consists of rolling plains, where it's hot and dry. Portugal has 350 miles of coastline.

Rivers: The major rivers, most notably the Tejo (or Tagus) River (600 miles long, spilling into the Atlantic at Lisbon) and the Douro (100 miles, flowing through wine country, ending at Porto), run east-west from Spain.

Mountains: Serra da Estrela, at 6,500 feet, is the highest point on the mainland, but Portugal's highest peak is Mt. Pico (7,713 feet) in the Azores.

Biggest Cities: Lisbon (the capital, 564,000 in the core, with more than 3 million in greater Lisbon), Porto (238,000 in the core, with 1.7 million total), and Coimbra (168,000 in the core and 435,000 in the greater metropolitan area).

Economy: The Gross Domestic Product is $230 billion (slightly more than Louisiana's). The GDP per capita is $22,700 (Loui-

edge of previous generations, actually found the way. Portuguese-born Ferdinand Magellan, sailing under the auspices of Spain, was the first to undertake a voyage that successfully circumnavigated the globe (though he himself died en route).

A naval superpower for a century, Portugal established trading posts that eventually became colonies in Brazil and throughout Africa. The wealth that flowed into the country led to an explosion of the arts back home. The finest architecture from this era (now named the Manueline period, after King Manuel I) is in Lisbon, represent-

ed by Belém's tower and monastery. But no country can corner the market on trade for long, and as with Spain, Portugal underwent a long decline.

siana's is $23,100). Some major money-makers for Portugal are fish (canned sardines), cork, budget clothes and shoes, port wine, and tourism. A quarter of Portugal's foreign trade is with Spain. Portugal's outlook has improved considerably since joining the European Union in 1986 (then called the European Community), thanks to EU subsidies, but it's still struggling, with unemployment in 2011 hovering around 15 percent. One in 10 Portuguese works in agriculture, 60 percent work in service jobs, and 30 percent in industry.

Government: The prime minister—currently the center-right Social Democrat Pedro Passos Coelho—is the chief executive, having assumed power as the head of the leading vote-getting party in legislative elections. President Aníbal Cavaco Silva, re-elected in 2011 to a second five-year term, commands the military and can dissolve the Parliament when he sees fit (it's rarely done, but he has the power). There are 230 legislators, elected to four-year terms, making up the single-house Assembly. Regionally, Portugal is divided into 20 districts (Lisbon, Coimbra, Porto, etc.).

Flag: The flag is two-fifths green and three-fifths red, united by the Portuguese coat of arms—a shield atop a navigator's armillary sphere.

Soccer: The three most popular teams are Sporting CP Lisbon, Benfica (also from Lisbon), and FC Porto.

***Senhor* and *Senhora* Average:** The average Portuguese is 40 years old and will live 78 years. One in three Portuguese uses the Internet, two in five live near either Lisbon or Porto, and slightly less than two in three own a car.

Portugal endured the repressive regime of António de Oliveira Salazar and his successor Marcello Caetano, from 1932-1974—the longest dictatorship in Western European history. Salazar pumped money into fighting wars to hang on to the last of the country's African colonies. When Portuguese military officers staged a coup in 1974, the locals were on their side (see sidebar on the Carnation Revolution, page 88). Portugal lost its colonies, but those former holdings—as well as the Portuguese people—won their freedom.

Once the poorest European Union country in Western Europe, Portugal has worked hard to meet EU standards...and has enjoyed heavy EU investment. The major issues facing the country are how to tame its rising national debt, continue providing generous social services, keep taxes reasonable, and reduce unemployment. Poverty still exists in Portugal, particularly in rural areas, but overall, the country has become more prosperous since joining the EU. New products are on the market, the infrastructure has improved, and Portugal is participating more in international politico.

With a rich culture, friendly people, affordable prices, and a salty setting on the edge of Europe, Portugal understandably remains a rewarding destination for travelers.

LISBON

Lisboa

Lisbon is a ramshackle but charming mix of now and then. Vintage trolleys shiver up and down its hills, bird-stained statues mark grand squares, taxis rattle and screech through cobbled lanes, and well-worn people sip coffee in Art Nouveau cafés. It's a city of faded ironwork balconies, multicolored tiles, and mosaic sidewalks, of bougainvillea and red-tiled roofs with antique TV antennas. Men in suits and billed caps offer to "plastify" your documents, and Africans in traditional garb sell gemstones from handkerchiefs spread on sidewalks.

Lisbon, Portugal's capital, is the country's banking and manufacturing center. A port city on the yawning mouth of the Rio Tejo (Tagus River), Lisbon welcomes large ships to its waters and state-of-the-art dry docks. Residents call their city Lisboa (leezh-BOH-ah), which comes from the Phoenician term *Alis Ubbo* ("calm port").

Romans and Moors originally populated Lisbon, but the city's glory days were in the 15th and 16th centuries, when explorers such as Vasco da Gama opened new trade routes around Africa to India, making Lisbon one of Europe's richest cities. Portugal's Age of Discovery fueled rapid economic growth, which sparked the flamboyant art boom called the Manueline period—named after King Manuel I (r. 1495-1521). In the 17th and 18th centuries, the gold, diamonds, and sugarcane of Brazil (one of Portugal's colonies) made Lisbon even wealthier.

Then, on the morning of All Saints' Day in 1755, while most of the population was at church, a tremendous underwater earthquake occurred off the Portuguese coast. The violent series of tremors were felt throughout Europe—as far away as Finland.

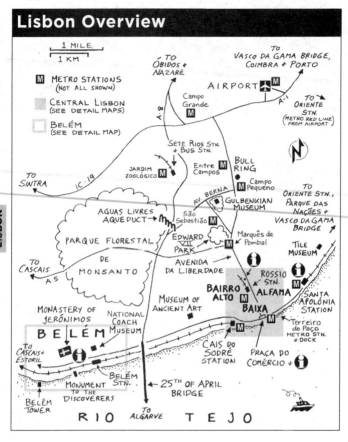

Lisbon Overview

Two-thirds of Lisbon was leveled. Fires—started by cooking flames and church candles—raged through the city, and a huge tsunami caused by the earthquake blasted the waterfront. Imagine a disaster similar to 2004's Indian Ocean earthquake and tsunami, devastating Portugal's capital city. The earthquake's impact was profound, not only on Portugal, but on all of Europe. (For more on this tragic event, see page 70.)

Under the energetic and eventually dictatorial leadership of Prime Minister Marquês de Pombal—who had the new city planned within a month of the quake—downtown Lisbon was re-built on a progressive grid plan, with broad boulevards and square squares. Remnants of Lisbon's pre-earthquake charm survive in Belém, the Alfama, and the Bairro Alto district. The bulk of your sightseeing will likely be in these neighborhoods.

As the Paris of the Portuguese-speaking world, Lisbon (pop. 564,000 in the core) is the Old World capital of its former

Pronunciation Guide to Lisbon

Lisboa	leezh-BOH-ah
Rossio (main square)	roh-SEE-oo
Praça da Figueira (major square)	PRAH-sah dah fee-GAY-rah
Baixa (lower town)	BYE-shah
Alfama (hilly neighborhood)	al-FAH-mah
Bairro Alto (high town)	BYE-roh AHL-toh
Chiado (part of Bairro Alto)	shee-AH-doo
Belém (suburb with sights)	bay-LEHM
Rio Tejo (Tagus River)	REE-oo TAY-zhoo
rua (street)	ROO-ah

LISBON

empire—for some 100 million people stretching from Europe to Brazil to Africa to China. Immigrants from former colonies such as Mozambique and Angola have added diversity and flavor to the city, making it as likely that you'll hear African music as Portuguese fado these days.

And Lisbon's heritage survives. With its elegant outdoor cafés, exciting art, stunning vistas, entertaining museums, a salty sailors' quarter, and a hill-capping castle, Lisbon is a world-class city.

Planning Your Time

For a two-week tour of Portugal, Lisbon is worth three days, including perhaps a day for a side-trip to Sintra. If you have an extra day, Lisbon has plenty to offer. Many top sights are closed on Monday, particularly in Belém. That'd be a good day to choose among the following options: Take my self-guided neighborhood walks; day-trip to Sintra (where all of the major sights are open); go on a guided walking tour with Lisbon Walker or Inside Lisbon (see page 49); or head to Parque das Nações for a dose of modern Lisbon.

Day 1: See Lisbon's three downtown neighborhoods (following the self-guided walks described in this chapter). Kick off your visit to the Bairro Alto with a ride up the Elevador da Glória funicular. After a downhill stroll through the neighborhood, catch a trolley for a joyride to the Alfama. Start your Alfama visit at the highest point in town, São Jorge Castle, and survey the city from the castle's viewpoint. Hike down to another fine viewpoint (Miradouro de Largo das Portas do Sol), then descend into the Alfama. Explore. Walk, bus, or taxi to the Baixa ("lower town"), and wander through the shops on your way to the major squares, Praça da Figueira and Rossio. Art-lovers can then hop a taxi to the Gulbenkian Museum (closed Mon). Consider dinner at a fado show in the Bairro Alto or the Alfama. For more evening options, see "Entertainment in Lisbon" (see page 101) and "Shopping in Lisbon" (malls/cinemas are open late, page 100).

Day 2: Trolley to Belém and tour the monastery, tower, and National Coach Museum. Have lunch in Belém, then tour the Museum of Ancient Art on your way back to Lisbon.

Day 3: Side-trip to Sintra to tour the Pena Palace and explore the ruined Moorish castle.

Orientation to Lisbon

Downtown Lisbon fills a valley flanked by two hills along the banks of the Rio Tejo. At the heart sits the main square, **Rossio,** in the center of the valley (with Praça dos Restauradores and Praça da Figueira nearby). The **Baixa,** or lower town, stretches from Rossio to the waterfront. It's a flat, pleasant shopping area of grid-patterned streets and the pedestrian-only Rua Augusta. The **Alfama,** the hill to the east, is a colorful tangle of medieval streets, topped by São Jorge Castle. The **Bairro Alto** ("high town"), the hill to the west, has characteristic old lanes on the top and high-fashion stores along Rua Garrett (in the lower section called **Chiado**).

From Rossio, the **modern city** stretches north (sloping uphill) along wide Avenida da Liberdade and beyond (way beyond), where you find Edward VII Park, breezy botanical gardens, the bullring, and the airport. To the east is **Parque das Nações,** site of the 1998 World Expo and now a modern shopping complex and riverfront promenade. The suburb of Belém, home to several Age of Discovery sights, is three miles west of the city, along the waterfront.

Greater Lisbon has more than three million people and some frightening sprawl, but for the visitor, the old city center is your target—a delightful series of parks, boulevards, and squares in a crusty, well-preserved architectural shell. Focus on the three characteristic neighborhoods that line the downtown harborfront: the Bairro Alto, the Alfama, and the Baixa.

Tourist Information

Lisbon has several tourist offices, and additional information kiosks sprout around town late each spring. The main TIs are: on **Praça dos Restauradores** at Palacio Foz (daily 9:00-20:00, tel. 213-463-314; TI for rest of Portugal in same office, tel. 218-494-323 or 213-463-658); on **Praça do Comércio** at the "Ask Me Lisbon" center (daily 9:00-20:00, tel. 210-312-810); and at the **airport** (daily 7:00-24:00, especially helpful, tel. 218-450-660). TI kiosks are at the **Santa Apolónia train station** (Tue-Sat 8:00-13:00, closed Sun-Mon, at the far end, by the lockers) and in front of the monastery in **Belém** (Tue-Sat 10:00-13:00 & 14:00-18:00, closed Sun-Mon, tel. 213-658-435).

Each TI offers handy freebies including a Lisbon city map (with helpful inset of town center), an in-depth *Public Transport Guide* (showing bus, Metro, and trolley lines in detail), and the monthly *Follow Me Lisboa* magazine (mainly cultural and museum listings). *Agenda Cultural* lists current exhibits, musical events, and hip new bars and restaurants in Portuguese only (monthly, free at TI, €0.50 at newsstands). If you want a LisboaCard (described next), buy it at a TI. Good websites for information are www.inside lisbon.com, www.visitlisboa.com, and www.visitportugal.com.

LisboaCard: This card covers all public transportation (as well as trains to Sintra and Cascais) and free entry to many museums (including the Museum of Ancient Art, National Tile Museum, National Coach Museum, Monastery of Jerónimos, and Bélem Tower, plus some Sintra sights). It also provides discounts on many museums, city tours, and the AeroBus airport buses.

You can buy the card only at Lisbon's TIs (including the airport TI), not at participating sights. If you plan to museum-hop, the card is a good value, particularly for a day in Belém (covers your transportation and most sightseeing). Don't get the card for Sunday, when many sights are free until 14:00, or for Monday, when many sights are closed. The card is also unnecessary if you're a student or senior, for whom most sights are free or half-price.

The LisboaCard is straightforward and can save you €25 if you do everything suggested in my three-day plan for Lisbon. Carry the LisboaCard booklet with you when you sightsee; some discounts require coupons contained inside, plus it serves as a proof of purchase (€19/24 hours, €32/48 hours, €39/72 hours, kids 5-11 half-price, includes excellent explanatory guidebook).

Arrival in Lisbon

Information on arriving in Lisbon by plane, train, bus, cruise ship, and car follows. A helpful website is www.golisbon.com/transport. If you have a little money and/or are traveling with a group, simply hop in a taxi upon arrival—they're plentiful and cheap (except at the cruise terminals; see warning on page 40).

By Plane

Lisbon's easy-to-manage Portela Airport is five miles northeast of downtown. While you're at the airport, get info on Lisbon and all of Portugal at the helpful TI (daily 7:00-24:00, tel. 218-450-660). For airport info, call 218-413-700 or TAP tel. 707-205-700 (airport code: LIS). Construction of a huge new airport across the Rio Tejo has been shelved due to the economic crisis.

Getting downtown from Lisbon's very central airport is a snap. There are three options: taxi, shuttle bus, and Metro.

Taxis line up on the curb (if there's a long line, go upstairs to the departure level and snare one as they are dropping their passengers). Rides into town cost about €10. There's a legitimate €1.60 fee for your luggage (not per bag, but to use the trunk). In the past it was tough to get cabbies to use their meter for airport pickups, but these days that rule is more strictly enforced. If the meter starts at €2 and is set to *Tarifa 1* (or *Tarifa 2* for nights, weekends, and holidays; €2.50 drop rate), relax—you should be fine. There is no "airport fee" supplement. To return to the airport by taxi from downtown to the airport is easy, fast, and cheap. Simply hail one on the street (€10). Skip the €23 taxi vouchers sold by the airport TI—these are for rides outside the center and double your cost.

While dirt-cheap **public buses** leave from the airport curb, these are not really intended for people with luggage. The **AeroBus** is faster and nearly as cheap. You likely want their city center route #1 (€3.50, 3/hour, runs 7:00-23:00, departs outside of arrival level), which stops at Marquês de Pombal, Avenida da Liberdade, Restauradores, Rossio, and Praça do Comércio. Route #2 goes to Oriente, a train station with Metro connections. Aerobus tickets are sold at the airport TI or on the bus, and double as a 24-hour pass for all of the public transit in the city except the Metro.

To take the **Metro**'s red line into Lisbon, exit the airport arrivals hall and turn right to find the Aeroporto stop. Before boarding, buy a reloadable Viva Viagem card at the ticket machine; you can get a 24-hour pass and have Lisbon by the tail for just €5.50 (includes €0.50 start-up fee; see details under "Getting Around Lisbon," later).

By Train

Lisbon has four primary train stations—Santa Apolónia (to Spain and most points north), Oriente (for the Algarve and Évora), Rossio (for Sintra, Óbidos, and Nazaré), and Cais do Sodré (for Cascais and Estoril).

Santa Apolónia Station covers international trains and nearly all of Portugal. It's located just east of the Alfama. It has ATMs, a TI, and good Metro and bus connections to the town center. A taxi from Santa Apolónia Station to any of my recommended hotels costs roughly €8. Bus #794 goes downtown to Praça do Comércio (leaving the station, bus stop is on the right across the street). Bus #759 goes to Rossio and

LISBON

Praça dos Restauradores, and buses #9, #90, and #746 continue up Avenida da Liberdade. As you leave the station, bus stops are on the left along busy Avenida Infante Dom Henrique. Most trains using Santa Apolónia Station also stop at **Oriente Station** (Metro: Oriente; for more on this architecturally interesting station, see page 80).

Rossio Station, which handles trains to Sintra (direct, 4/hour, 40 minutes, buy tickets from machines at track level), is in the town center and an easy walk from most recommended hotels. It also handles trains to Óbidos and Nazaré, but since both destinations require a transfer at Cacém, the bus is a better option. Its all-Portugal ticket office on the ground floor (next to Starbucks) sells long-distance and international train tickets (Mon-Fri 7:00-20:00, closed Sat-Sun, cash only).

Cais do Sodré Station, on the waterfront just west of Praça do Comércio (Metro: Cais do Sodré), serves Cascais and Estoril (30 minutes).

By Bus

Lisbon's efficient Sete Rios bus station is in the modern part of the city, several miles inland from the harbor. It has ATMs, a rack of schedules (near entrance), a nifty computer that displays routes and ticket prices, and two information offices—one for buses within Portugal, the other for international routes (Intercentro booth). While you can buy bus tickets up to a week in advance, you can almost always buy a ticket just a few minutes before departure. The EVA company covers the south of Portugal (Lisbon bus info tel. 808-224-488, www.eva-bus.com), while Rede Nacional de Expressos does the rest of the country (bus info tel. 707-223-344, www.rede-expressos.pt).

The bus station is across the street from the small Sete Rios train station, which sits above the Jardim Zoológico Metro stop. To get from the bus station to downtown Lisbon, it's a €5 taxi ride or a short Metro trip on the blue line (from bus station, walk down and across to Sete Rios train station, then follow signs for *Metro: Jardim Zoológico*).

By Cruise Ship

Lisbon's port is the busiest on Europe's Atlantic coast, with most cruise ships docking at one of two terminals: Alcântara (about two miles west of downtown) or Santa Apolónia (near the train station of the same name).

Both terminals have taxi stands, public phones, ATMs, and WCs. Most cruise lines offer inexpensive shuttle service from either terminal to Praça do Comércio. If you're taking public transit from the Alcântara terminal, you can reach central Lisbon on trolley

#15E (use pedestrian underpass to reach trolley stop, 5/hour, 15 minutes, €3, coins only) or on any bus (direction: Centro, pay the driver). From the Santa Apolónia cruise-ship terminal, it's a short walk to the Santa Apolónia train station, described above under "By Train." From this terminal, bus #714 goes to Praça da Figueira and out to Belém.

The taxis that wait at either terminal are notoriously dishonest. For a fair, metered rate, you might have better luck walking across the big street and hailing one as it drives by.

By Car

It makes absolutely no sense to drive in Lisbon. If you're starting your trip in Lisbon, don't rent a car until you're on your way out of town.

If you enter Lisbon from the north, a series of boulevards takes you into the center. Navigate by following signs to *Centro, Avenida da República, Marquês de Pombal, Avenidu da Liberdade, Praçu dos Restauradores, Rossio,* and *Praça do Comércio.* If coming from the east over the Vasco da Gama Bridge and heading for the airport, take the first exit after the bridge.

If you're returning in your car in Lisbon, consider dropping it at the airport (rental-car turn-in clearly signposted, no extra expense to drop it here, very helpful TI open late) and riding a sweat-free taxi for €10 to your hotel. Or, if you must drive into town, consider hiring a taxi and following it to your hotel.

There are many safe underground pay parking lots in Lisbon (follow blue *P* signs), but they discourage anything but short stays by getting more expensive by the hour. They can cost €40 per day (at the most central Praça dos Restauradores).

Helpful Hints

Theft Alert: Lisbon has piles of people doing illegal business on the street. While the city is generally safe, if you're looking for trouble—especially after dark—you may find it. Pickpockets (mostly Romanian) target tourists on the trolleys (especially #12E, #15E, and #28E) and on the Metro. Enjoy the sightseeing, but also be aware of your surroundings—wear your money belt and keep your pack zipped up. Many thieves pose as tourists by wearing cameras and toting maps. Be on guard whenever you're in a crush of people, or jostled as you enter or leave a tram or bus.

Pedestrian Warning: Sidewalks can be narrow in certain neighborhoods, and drivers are daring; cross the street with care. Warnings at crosswalks alert pedestrians to "stop to look and to be seen" and graphically show the consequences of ignoring this advice.

Calendar Concerns: Tuesdays and Saturdays are flea- and food-market days in the Alfama's Campo de Santa Clara. National museums are free on Sunday (all day or until 14:00) and closed all day Monday. Bullfights take place irregularly throughout the summer, mainly on Thursdays (see page 105).

Laundry: Drop off clothes at centrally located **5àSec Lavandaria** (€7.50/kilo, same-day wash-and-dry service, Mon-Fri 8:00-20:00, Sat and Sun 10:00-20:00, near Baixa-Chiado Metro stop at Rua do Crucifixo 99, tel. 504-622-030). Hostels and shopping malls generally have laundry services, or your hotelier can recommend a place nearby.

Internet Access: Each downtown square has an Internet café: Rossio (**PTComunicações,** corner nearest Rossio Station, daily 9:00-21:00, 25 terminals, €1.50/30 minutes, €2/unlimited access) and Praça da Figueira **(Western Union)** are particularly good. There are many cheap hole-in-the-wall shops catering to immigrants' need for cheap Internet access.

Post Office and Telephones: The post offices *(correios)* on Praça do Comércio (Mon-Fri only) and at Praça dos Restauradores 58 are modern and user-friendly (Mon-Fri 8:00-22:00, Sat-Sun 9:00-18:00). The **Portugal Telecom** office on Rossio sells phone cards, and has metered phones and card-operated pay phones (daily 8:00-23:00).

Travel Agency: Agencies line the Avenida da Liberdade. For flights (and train tickets in Portugal only—same price as at station, no fee), **GeoStar** is handy and helpful (€15 booking fee for flights, Mon-Fri 9:30-18:30, closed Sat-Sun, Praça dos Restauradores 14, tel. 213-245-240).

Updates to this Book: For news about changes to this book's coverage since it was published, see www.ricksteves.com/update.

Getting Around Lisbon

To use Lisbon's transit economically, take advantage of the reloadable **Viva Viagem** card (which works much like London's Oyster Card). The card works on the Metro, funiculars, trolleys, and buses.

Viva Viagem cards are sold at smart machines at any Metro stop for a one-time €0.50 fee and loaded with your choice of options: single ride (€1.25, good for one hour of travel within Zone 1); 24-hour pass (€5); or "zapping" (pre-load the card with whatever amount you'd like, and credit is deducted at the single-ride rate as you use it—you can "top it up" when the credit runs out). For intense users, the 24-hour pass is best. If using the system more sparingly, the "zapping" method may be smartest (www.carris.pt).

To buy or top up your Viva Viagem card at a smart machine, touch the screen to begin, press the British flag for English, then

Lisbon's Public Transportation

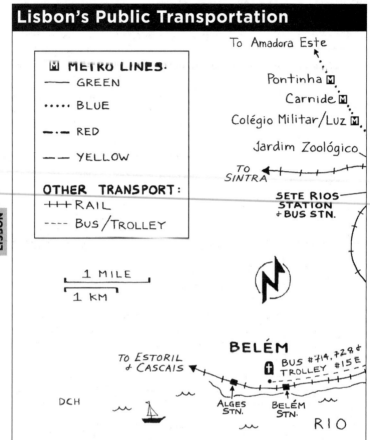

make your selection according to what you need to do. You can pay with coins or bills (but not with magnetic-stripe American credit cards). To buy a card without using the machine—or to get information on the system—drop by the Casa da Sorte office (see blue sign from Rossio and Praça da Figueira, Mon-Fri 8:00-20:00, closed Sat-Sun).

Hang onto your Viva Viagem card, as you'll need to swipe it entering and leaving the system, and to avoid paying an extra €0.50 each time you buy a ticket.

Note that the **LisboaCard** (see page 37) also covers Lisbon's public transportation and many museums, plus train rides to Sintra and Cascais.

By Metro

Lisbon's simple, fast, and color-coded subway system is a delight to use (runs daily 6:30-1:00 in the morning). Though it's not nec-

essary for getting around the historic downtown, the Metro is handy for trips to or from Rossio (Metro: Rossio or Restauradores), Praça do Comércio (Metro: Terreiro do Paço), the Gulbenkian Museum (Metro: São Sebastião), the Chiado neighborhood (Metro: Baixa-Chiado), Centro Colombo shopping mall (Metro: Colégio Militar/ Luz), Parque das Nações and the Oriente train station (both at Metro: Oriente), Sete Rios bus and train stations (Metro: Jardim Zoológico), and the airport (Metro: Aeroporto).

With the Viva Viagem card (described above), a Metro ride costs €1.25 within Zone 1 (which includes everything of interest to most tourists). Scan the card as you enter, and keep the card handy until your trip is over—you'll need it to exit the sliding doors.

Metro stops are marked above ground with a red "M." *Saída* means exit. You can find a Metro map at any Metro stop, on most city maps, and in the TI's in-depth *Public Transport Guide* (www. metrolisboa.pt).

By Trolley, Funicular, and Bus

For fun and practical public transportation, use the trolleys and funiculars. Buy your ticket from the driver (€3, no transfers), or use your Viva Viagem card (€1.25/ride if "zapping" or covered by €5 24-hour pass). Like San Francisco, Lisbon sees its trolleys as part of its heritage, and has kept a few in use. Trolleys #12E (circling the Alfama) and #28E (a scenic ride across the old town) use vintage cars; #15E (to Belém) uses a modern version. Buy a ticket, have a pass, or risk a big fine on the spot. Also see "By Trolley" under "Tours in Lisbon," below.

By Taxi

Lisbon is a great taxi town. Cabbies are good-humored and (except for crooked ones at the cruise terminals) willing to use their meters. Rides start at €2, and you can go anywhere in the center for around €5. Decals on the window clearly spell out all charges in English. The most typical scam is the cabbie setting his meter at the high-price tariff. The meter should be at about €2 at the start and set to *Tarifa 1* (Mon-Fri 6:00-21:00, including the airport) or *Tarifa 2* (€2.50 drop rate; for nights, weekends, and holidays). If the meter reads *Tarifa 3, 4,* or *5,* simply ask the cabbie to change it, unless you're going to Belém, which is considered outside the city limits of Lisbon (and has corresponding *Tarifa 3* rates). *Tarifa 5* is only for round-trips.

Cabs are generally easy to hail on the street (green light means available, lit number on the roof indicates it's taken). If you're having a hard time flagging one down, ask a passerby for the location of the nearest taxi stand: *praça de taxi* (PRAH-sah duh taxi). They're all over the town center.

Especially if you're with a companion, Lisbon's cabs are a cheap time-saver. For an average trip, couples save less than a dollar by taking public transportation, but spend an extra 15 minutes getting there—bad economics. If you're traveling with a companion and your time is limited, taxi everywhere.

Tours in Lisbon

▲▲By Trolley

Lisbon's trolleys, many vintage models from the 1920s, shake and shiver through the old parts of town, somehow safely weaving within inches of parked cars, climbing steep hills, and offering sightseers breezy views of the city (rubberneck

out the window and you die). As you board, pay the driver (€3) or swipe your Viva Viagem card (much cheaper), take a seat, and watch the pensioners as they lurch by. Buses and trolleys usually share the same stops and routes. Signs for bus stops list the bus number, while signs for trolley stops include an E (for *eléctrico*) before or after the route number. Remember that most pickpocketing in Lisbon takes place on trolleys, so enjoy the ride, but keep an eye on your belongings.

Trolley #28E is a Rice-A-Roni-style Lisbon joyride. Trolley stops from west to east include Estrela (the 18th-century, late Baroque Estrela Basilica and Estrela Park—cozy neighborhood scene with pondside café and a "garden library kiosk"); the top of the Elevador da Bica funicular (which drops steeply through a rough-and-tumble neighborhood to the riverfront); Chiado's main square (the café and "Latin Quarter"); Baixa (on Rua da Conceição between Augusta and Prata); the cathedral (Sé); Miradouro de Largo das Portas do Sol (the Alfama viewpoint); Campo de Santa Clara (flea market on Tue and Sat); and the pleasant and untouristy Graça district (with another excellent viewpoint).

Trolley #15E, while not usually vintage or pickpocket-free, whisks you efficiently to Belém from Praça da Figueira or Praça do Comércio.

Trolley #12E (Circular Tour): For a colorful, 20-minute loop around the castle and the Alfama, catch this trolley on Praça da Figueira (departs every few minutes from the stop at corner of square closest to castle). The driver can tell you when to get out for the Miradouro de Largo das Portas do Sol (viewpoint) near the castle (about three-quarters of the way up the hill), or stay on the trolley and you'll be dropped back where you started.

Here's what you'll see on your self-guided trolley tour: Leaving Praça da Figueira, you enter Largo de Martim Moniz—named for a knight who died heroically while using his body as a doorjamb

Lisbon's Best Viewpoints
(*Miradouros* and *Belvederes*)

The first three viewpoints are included in the self-guided walks described in this chapter:

- Miradouro de São Pedro de Alcântara (view terrace in Bairro Alto, at top of Elevador da Glória funicular; see "The Bairro Alto and Chiado Stroll," page 51)
- São Jorge Castle (on top of the Alfama; see photo above and "The Alfama Stroll," page 59)
- Miradouro de Largo das Portas do Sol (south slope of Alfama; see "The Alfama Stroll," page 59)
- Elevador de Santa Justa (in the Baixa, page 55)
- Cristo Rei (statue on hillside across the Rio Tejo, page 85)
- Edward VII Park (at north end of Avenida da Liberdade)
- Bica Miradouro (atop the Elevador da Bica funicular)

to pry open the castle gate, allowing his Christian Portuguese comrades to get in and capture Lisbon from the Moors in 1147. The big, maroon-colored building capping the hill on the left was a Jesuit monastery until 1769, when the dictatorial Marquês de Pombal booted the pesky order out of Portugal and turned the building into the Hospital São Jose. Today, this is an immigrant neighborhood with lots of cheap import shops.

Turning right onto Rua de Cavaleiros, you climb through the atmospheric Mouraria neighborhood on a street so narrow that a single trolley track is all that fits. Notice how the colorful mix of neighbors who fill the trolley all seem to know each other. If the trolley's path is blocked and can't pass, lots of horn-honking and shouts from passengers ensue until your journey resumes. Look up the skinny side streets. Marvel at the creative parking and classic laundry scenes. This was the area given to the Moors after they were driven out of the castle and Alfama. Natives know it as the home of the legendary fado singer Maria Severa. The majority of residents these days are immigrants from Asia, making this Lisbon's version of Chinatown.

At the crest of the hill (Largo Rodrigues de Freitas), you can get out to explore, eat at a cheap restaurant (see "Eating in Lisbon," later), or follow Rua de Santa Marinha to the Campo de Santa Clara flea market (Tue and Sat).

When you see the river, you're at Largo das Portas do Sol (Gates of the Sun), where you'll also see the remains of one of the seven old Moorish gates of Lisbon. The driver usually announces *"castelo"* (cahzh-TAY-loo) at this point. Hop out here if you want to visit the Museum and School of Portuguese Decorative Arts (see page 64), enjoy the most scenic cup of coffee in town, explore the Alfama, or tour the castle.

The trolley continues downhill past the fortress-like cathedral (Sé, on left—see page 74) and into the Baixa (grid-planned Pombaline city—get off here to take my self-guided Baixa walk—see page 66). After a few blocks, you're back where you started—Praça da Figueira.

By Bus and Tram

Carris City Bus and Tram Tours—Carris Tours offers three different downtown tours (all hop-on, hop-off). While uninspiring and not cheap, they're handy and run daily year-round. Tram tours start and end at Praça do Comércio. Bus tours start and end at Praça da Figueira (look for yellow bus and tram signs at stops, buy tickets from driver). For more information, stop by their info trolley in the northeast corner of Praça do Comércio (tel. 966-298-558, www.carristur.pt). Tickets for their hop-on, hop-off tours do double-duty as a 24-hour public transit pass, covering Lisbon's trolleys, buses, and funiculars (but not the Metro, which is owned by a different company).

Hop-on, Hop-off Bus Tours: Two tours on yellow, double-decker buses make overlapping loops around Lisbon, starting from Praça da Figueira (€15 apiece, includes audioguide). You can get off, tour a sight, and catch a later bus. The **Tagus Tour** covers west Lisbon, stopping at major sights such as the Museum of Ancient Art and Belém (runs twice hourly April-Oct 9:15-19:45, fewer in winter). The **Olisipo Tour** covers east Lisbon, with stops at Parque das Nações, the National Tile Museum, and more (runs hourly April-Oct 10:00-19:00, less in winter). You cannot hop on and hop off between the two different tours without buying a second ticket.

Hills Tram Tour: This hop-on, hop-off tour takes you on a shiny red 1900s tramcar through the Alfama, Bairro Alto, and other Lisbon hills (€18, 1.5-hour tour with five stops, recorded narration available in English, runs twice hourly July-Aug 10:00-19:00, fewer off-season).

Sintra Day Trip: Carris also offers a day trip to Sintra and its Pena Palace, making a swing around the scenic and historic peninsula. Option 1 includes entry to the Pena Palace (otherwise €13) and gives you 1.5 hours to tour the palace and 20 minutes in Sintra, while Option 2 skips the palace and gives you two hours in Sintra (Option 1-€42, Option 2-€29; both depart daily from Praça do Comércio at 14:00, 5 hours, live guide switches between 3-5 languages). Both options include Cabo da Roca (20-minute stop, frustrating to reach on your own, even with a car), Guincho, Boca de Inferno, and Cascais (10-minute stop). If you want to see the peninsula beyond Sintra, this is your most economical and efficient bet.

Gray Line/Cityrama Tours—Another option for hop-on, hop-off tours are the red Gray Line/Cityrama buses, which offer four different routes: The **Castle** line covers the city center; the **Belém** line gets you to that district; the **Oriente** line includes Parque das Nações; and the **Cascais** line heads west along the coast past the charming beach towns of Estoril and Cascais to the scenic beaches near Guincho. Buses have free on-board Wi-Fi, making multi-tasking a snap (one line-€12, two lines-€18, four lines-€25, ticket valid 48 hours, recorded English narration available; Castle and Belém lines run 2/hour April-Oct 9:30-18:00, Oriente line runs every 45 minutes, Cascais line departs 4/day but doesn't run Nov-March; main info kiosk at north side of Marquês de Pombal roundabout but you can catch buses at any stop, tel. 800-208-513, www.cityrama.pt).

By Boat

Rio Tejo Cruise—**Cruzeiros no Tejo** runs two river tours daily. Their longer tour does a big east-west loop to the Vasco da Gama Bridge and Parque das Nações, then to Belém and back (€20, daily at 15:00, 2.5 hours, departs from Terreiro do Paço dock off Praça do Comércio). Their shorter tour makes a loop downtown to Belém and back (€15, daily at 16:15, one hour, departs from Cais do Sodré ferry terminal). Each operates April through October and comes with a four-language narration (free drinks and WC on board, tel. 210-422-417, www.transtejo.pt). If you take the longer cruise, you can ask to get off at Belém (skipping the last half-hour of the cruise) and visit that neighborhood on your own, returning to the center by trolley.

Another outfit, cleverly called **River Cruises,** runs tours from Cais do Sodré to the Belém Tower (at 11:45 and 15:15) and vice versa (at 14:00 and 16:30). Trips are narrated in Portuguese and English (€12 one-way, €16 round-trip, April-Oct, no Mon tours, one hour each way, tel. 213-913-030, www.lvt.pt).

Cheap River Ferry Ride to Cacilhas—For a quick, cheap trip

Ways to Get from the Baixa up to the Bairro Alto and Chiado

- Ride the Elevador da Glória funicular (a few blocks north of Rossio on Avenida da Liberdade) or walk alongside the tracks if the funicular isn't running.
- Walk up lots of stairs from Rossio (due west of the central column).
- Taxi to the Miradouro de São Pedro de Alcântara.
- Take the escalator at the Baixa-Chiado Metro stop.
- Catch trolley #28E from Rua da Conceição.
- Hike up Rua do Carmo from Rossio to Rua Garrett.
- Take escalators or elevators from the Armazéns mall to Rua Garrett.
- Take the Elevador de Santa Justa, which goes right by the Convento do Carmo and the Chiado.

across the river with great city and bridge views in the company of Lisbon commuters rather than tourists, hop the ferry to Cacilhas (kah-SEE-lahsh) from the Cais do Sodré Station (a 10-minute walk from Praça do Comércio). At the terminal, follow signs to *Cacilhas*, not *Montigo* (€2 each way, 4/hour, signs say *next partida* and *destino*). Either hop out for a look at the rough little industrial port, or stay on for a 25-minute round-trip.

On Foot

Walking Tours—Two walking-tour companies—**Lisbon Walker** and **Inside Lisbon**—offer excellent, affordable tours led by young, top-notch guides with a passion for sharing insights to their hometown. Well-priced to start with, both companies give my readers their discounted student prices. Tour groups are small (generally 2-12 people) and given in English only. Each company has a helpful website explaining their tours and has an easygoing style—just show up at the meeting point (no reservations needed) and you'll get started in moments. With either company, you'll likely feel like you've made a friend in your guide (a great way to get to know a local). Especially with the substantial discount given to readers of this book, these tours are time and money very well spent.

Lisbon Walker: Standard tours include: "Revelation" (best 3-hour overview with good coverage of the Baixa and the main squares, a quick look at the Bairro Alto, and a trolley ride across town to the Graça viewpoint); "Old Town" (2-hour walk through Alfama that examines the origins of Lisbon—Romans, Moors, and its castle); and "Downtown" (2-3 hours, covers the 1755 earthquake and the rebirth of Lisbon). Other more-focused tours are: "Legends & Mysteries," "City of Spies," "Castle Hill" (including the tangled, multi-ethnic Mouraria neighborhood), and "Uptown Lisbon" (€15/person; €10 for youth, seniors, and those with this book; daily year-round at 10:00 and often at 14:30, meet at northwest corner of Praça do Comércio near Rua do Arsenal, in front of the TI—see map on page 110, tel. 218-861-840, www.lisbonwalker. com).

Inside Lisbon: Tours include: "Original Lisbon Walk" (a good highlights tour of the main squares, the Chiado, and the Alfama; €15, daily year-round at 10:00); "Old Lisbon Walk" (takes you through the oldest parts of the city, including Graça and the Alfama; €15, April-Oct Tue and Sat at 10:00, Nov-March Sat at 10:00); the "Gourmet Walk" (with stops at traditional eateries and bars in the Baixa, Chiado, and Bairro Alto for lots of fun things to eat and drink; €25, April-Oct Tue, Thu, and Sat at 16:30); and the "Lisbon Experience Walk" (a walking-and-eating tour from Praça dos Restauradores to Mouraria, ending with a ferry to Cacilhas for seafood; €26, year-round Mon, Wed, Fri, and Sat at 10:30). Most tours meet at the statue of Dom Pedro IV in the center of Rossio, except for the Lisbon Experience Walk, which starts on Praça dos Restauradores. All last about three hours and offer €4 discounts for those with this book. Except for the Gourmet Walk, no reservations are required in summer. Reservations are required in the off-season and always for the Gourmet Walk (reserve before noon on the day of the tour via website or phone, tel. 968-412-612, www.insidelisbon.com). They also offer private tours and day trips by minivan to Sintra/Cascais and Obidos/Fátima. You can also organize a private city tour with them, or use their helpful website as a resource for seeing Lisbon on your own.

Local Guides—Hiring a private local guide in Lisbon can be a wonderful luxury. They'll meet you at your hotel and tailor your tour to your interests. Especially with a small group, this can be a fine value. And, as audioguides are rare in Lisbon and the history can be tough to figure out on your own, having your own guide can really help. Guides charge the about the same rates (Mon-Fri €115/half-day, €180/day; Sat-Sun €140/half-day, €230/day). **Cristina Duarte** leads tours for my company and knows Lisbon well (mobile 919-316-242, acrismduarte@gmail.com). **Claudia da Costa**, who you may have seen with me on my Lisbon TV show, is also excellent (mobile 965-560-216, claudiadacosta@hotmail.com). **Cristina Quental** is another fine local guide (mobile 919-922-480, anacristinaquental@hotmail.com).

Self-Guided Walks in Lisbon

While Lisbon had its famous quake, there's nothing earthshaking about most of its downtown sights. Lisbon's charms are its people and the city itself, with hilltop views, ramshackle neighborhoods, and entertaining slices of urban life. The best way to explore Lisbon is like a local: on foot.

The "Three Neighborhoods" Walk

You can see Lisbon's three downtown neighborhoods—the Bairro Alto, the Alfama, and the Baixa—in a single four- to five-hour walk, linking together my three walks, which are described next.

Start with "The Bairro Alto and Chiado Stroll": From north of Rossio Station, take the Elevador da Glória funicular (or walk) up to the Bairro Alto and walk downhill to Café A Brasileira and Rua Garrett. From there, you can get to the beginning of "The Alfama Stroll" by catching trolley #28E across the Baixa and up the Alfama. At the Largo das Portas do Sol viewpoint (third stop past the cathedral), walk five minutes uphill to São Jorge Castle, where you can start the Alfama walk back down the hill to the Baixa. (To avoid the walk up to the castle altogether, catch a taxi or take minibus #37 from Praça da Figueira, which stops just a few feet in front of the castle gate.) The Alfama walk leaves you near the base of the Baixa (Praça do Comércio). From here, you can finish with "The Baixa Stroll: Lisbon's Historic Downtown" through Lisbon's lower town.

▲▲▲The Bairro Alto and Chiado Stroll

Rise above the Baixa on the funicular, Elevador da Glória, located near the obelisk at Praça dos Restauradores (€3 if you pay driver, cheaper with Viva Viagem card, 6/hour); you can also hike up alongside the tracks.

• *Leaving the funicular on top, turn right (go 100 yards, up into a park) to enjoy the city view from the...*

❶ **Miradouro de São Pedro de Alcântara (San Pedro Belvedere):** The tile map guides you through the view, stretching from the twin towers of the cathedral (Sé, far right behind trees), to the ramparts of the castle birthplace of Lisbon (right), to another quaint, tree-topped viewpoint in Graça (directly across, end of trolley #28E), to the skyscraper towers of the new city in the distance (on far left). Note that whenever you see a big old building in Lisbon, it's often a former convent or monastery, nationalized by the state, and now occupied by a hospital, school, or the military.

In the park, a bust honors a 19th-century local journalist (founder of Lisbon's first daily newspaper) and a charming, barefooted delivery boy. This district is famous for its writers, poets,

The Bairro Alto & Chiado Stroll

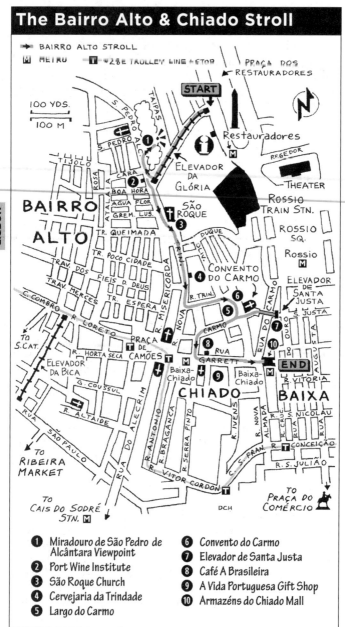

➡️ BAIRRO ALTO STROLL
Ⓜ️ METRO ▬▬ #28E TROLLEY LINE + STOP

1 Miradouro de São Pedro de Alcântara Viewpoint
2 Port Wine Institute
3 São Roque Church
4 Cervejaria da Trindade
5 Largo do Carmo
6 Convento do Carmo
7 Elevador de Santa Justa
8 Café A Brasileira
9 A Vida Portuguesa Gift Shop
10 Armazéns do Chiado Mall

publishers, and bohemians. (The walk continues downhill from here.)

• *Directly across the street from where you got off the Elevador da Glória is the...*

❼ **Port Wine Institute:** If you're into port (the fortified wine that takes its name from the city of Porto, covered later in this book), you'll find the world's greatest selection at **Solar do Vinho do Porto** (run by the Port Wine Institute, Mon-Sat 11:00-24:00, closed Sun, WCs, Rua São Pedro de Alcântara 45, tel. 213-475-707, www.ivdp.pt). You're welcome to go in to simply browse even if you're not drinking. The plush, air-conditioned, Old World living room is furnished with leather chairs (this is not a shorts-and-T-shirt kind of place). You can order from a selection of over 150 different ports, €1.50-22 per glass, generally poured by an English-speaking bartender. (You might want to try only 50 or so, and save the rest for the next night.) Read the very instructive menu for an education in port. Fans of port describe it as "a liquid symphony playing on the palate." Browse through the easy menu. Start white and sweet (cheapest), taste your way through spicy and ruby, and finish mellow and tawny. A *colheita* (single harvest) is particularly good. Appetizers *(aperitivos)* are listed in the menu with small photographs. Seated service can be slow and disinterested when it's busy. To be served without a long wait, go to the bar. Enjoy the Douro Valley photos, maps, and models of traditional boats that add to the port-industry ambience of the place. For more on port, see page 290.

• *Follow the main street (Rua São Pedro de Alcântara) downhill a couple of blocks. Throughout this walk, look up and notice the fine tile work—both old and modern—on the buildings. When you reach the small square, Largo Trindade Coelho, on your left you'll see...*

❽ **São Roque Church:** Step inside, and then sit on a pew in the middle to take it all in (free, Tue-Sun 9:00-18:00, closed Mon, tiles explained in English leaflet available near the door). Built in the 16th century, the church of St. Roque is one of Portugal's first Jesuit churches. The painted wood, false-domed ceiling is perfectly flat. The acoustics here are top-notch, important in a Jesuit church, where the emphasis is on the sermon (given from twin pulpits mid-nave). The numbered panels on the floor are tombs, nameless because they were for lots of people. They're empty now—the practice was stopped in the 19th century when parishioners didn't want plague victims rotting under their feet.

Survey the rich side chapels. The highlight is the Chapel of St. John the Baptist (left of altar, gold and blue lapis lazuli columns). It looks like it came right out of the Vatican—and that's because it did. Made in Rome out of the most precious materials, the chapel was the site of one papal Mass; then it was disassembled

Portugal's Two Greatest Poets

The Portuguese are justifiably proud of their two most famous poets, whose names, works, and memorials you may encounter in your travels.

Portugal's most important poet, **Luís de Camões** (1524-1580), was a Renaissance-age equivalent of the ancient Greek poet, Homer. Camões' masterpiece, *The Lusiads (Os Lusíadas)* tells the story of an explorer far from home. But instead of Odysseus, this epic poem describes the journey of Vasco da Gama, the man who found the route from Europe to India. Camões—who had sailed to Morocco to fight the Moors (where he lost an eye), to Goa (where he was imprisoned for debt), and to China (where he was shipwrecked)—was uniquely qualified to write about Portugal's pursuit of empire on the high seas. For more on Camões, see page 93.

Fernando Pessoa (1888-1935) used multiple personas in his poetry. He'd take on the voice of a simple countryman and express his love of nature in free verse. Or he'd write as an erudite scholar, sharing philosophical thoughts in a more formal style. By varying his voice, he was able to more easily explore different viewpoints and truths. While Pessoa loved the classics—reading Milton, Byron, Shelley, and Poe—he was a true 20th-century bohemian at heart. Café A Brasileira, where he'd often meet with friends, has a statue of Pessoa outside. Today, fado musicians still remember Pessoa, paying homage to him by putting his poetry into the Portuguese version of the blues.

and shipped to Lisbon. Per square inch, it was the most costly chapel ever constructed in Portugal. Notice the mosaic floor (with the spherical symbol of Portugal) and the three "paintings" that are actually intricate, beautiful mosaics—a Vatican specialty, designed to avoid damage from candle smoke that would darken real paintings. To the right, a glass case is filled with relics trying to grab your attention. The next chapel to the left features a riot of babies. Individual chapels—each for a different noble family—seem to be in competition. Keep in mind that the tiles are considered as extravagant as the gold leaf and silver.

To the right of the altar is the sacristy where, along with huge chests of drawers for vestments, you can see a series of 17th-century paintings illustrating scenes from the life of St. Frances Xavier—founder of the Jesuit order.

The São Roque Museum, with some old paintings and church

riches, is not as interesting as the church itself (€2.50, Tue-Sun 10:00-18:00, closed Mon).

• *Back outside in the church square (rustic WC underground), visit the statue of a friendly lottery-ticket salesman. Two lottery kiosks are nearby. Locals who buy into the* totoloto *rub the statue's ticket for good luck. Continue (kitty-corner across the square) downhill along Rua Nova da Trindade. At #20, pop into...*

❹ **Cervejaria da Trindade:** The famous and recommended "oldest beer hall in Lisbon" is worth a visit for a look at its 19th-century tiles. While its circa-1860 tiles are more beer hall than Christian in theme, this was once the refectory (dining hall) of a monastery. It became a brewery after the monks were expelled in 1834. If you're tired of all this history, continue downhill to Livraria Barateira at #16, Lisbon's biggest used bookstore, where you can sell this book.

• *Continue down the hill, where at the next intersection, signs point left to the ruined Convento do Carmo. Follow the inside trolley tracks downhill and to the left to the next square...*

❺ **Largo do Carmo:** On this square decorated with an old fountain, lots of pigeons, and jacaranda trees from South America (with purple blossoms in April), police officers guard the headquarters of the National Guard. Famous among residents, this was the last refuge of the fascist dictator António Salazar's successor. The Portuguese people won their revolution in 1974, in a peaceful uprising called the Carnation Revolution. The name came when revolutionaries placed flowers in the guns of the soldiers, making it clear it was time for democracy here. For more history, see the sidebar on page 88.

• *On Largo do Carmo, check out the ruins of...*

❻ **Convento do Carmo:** After the convent was destroyed by the 1755 earthquake, the Marquês de Pombal directed that the delicate Gothic arches of its church be left standing—supporting nothing but open sky—as a permanent reminder of that disastrous event. If you pay to enter, you'll see a fine memorial park in what was the nave, and a simple museum with Bronze Age and Roman artifacts, medieval sarcophagi, and a couple of mummies unearthed by the quake—all explained in English (€3.50—cheapskates can do a deep knee-bend at the ticket desk, sneak a peek, and then crawl away; April-Sept Mon-Sat 10:00-19:00, Oct-May until 18:00, closed Sun year-round).

• *Just past the convent, a lane with trolley tracks leads out to a fine city viewpoint from the top of the Elevador de Santa Justa.*

❼ **Elevador de Santa Justa:** In 1902, an architect—perhaps inspired by Gustav Eiffel's tower in Paris—completed this 150-foot-tall iron elevator, connecting the lower and upper parts of town. The elevator's Neo-Gothic motifs are an attempt to match

Lisbon at a Glance

In Lisbon

▲▲▲**The Bairro Alto and Chiado Stroll** The high town's views, churches, and Chiado fashion district. See page 51.

▲▲▲**The Alfama Stroll** Tangled medieval streets topped by São Jorge Castle. See page 59.

▲▲▲**The Baixa Stroll: Lisbon's Historic Downtown** The lower town, gridded with streets and dotted with major squares. See page 66.

▲▲▲**Gulbenkian Museum** Lisbon's best museum, featuring an art collection spanning 2,000 years, from ancient Egyptian to Impressionist to Art Nouveau. **Hours:** Tue-Sun 10:00-18:00, closed Mon. See page 75.

▲▲**Museum of Ancient Art** Portuguese paintings from the 15th- and 16th-century glory days. **Hours:** Tue 14:00-18:00, Wed-Sun 10:00-18:00, closed Mon. See page 79.

▲▲ **Parque das Nações** Inviting waterfront park with a long promenade (and rental bikes), a modern mall, the Expo '98 fairgrounds, and an aquarium. **Hours:** Park always open. See page 81.

▲**Fado Museum** The story of Portuguese folk music. **Hours:** Tue-Sun 10:00-18:00, closed Mon. See page 65.

▲**National Tile Museum** Tons of artistic tiles, including a panorama of pre-earthquake Lisbon. **Hours:** Tue 14:00-18:00, Wed-Sun 10:00-18:00, closed Mon. See page 83.

Port Wine Institute Plush place selling tastes of the world's greatest selection of ports. **Hours:** Mon-Sat 11:00-24:00, closed Sun. See page 53.

São Roque Church Fine 16th-century Jesuit church with false dome ceiling, chapel made of precious stones, and a less interesting museum. **Hours:** Tue-Sun 9:00-18:00, closed Mon. See page 53.

São Jorge Castle Eighth-century bastion, first built by the Moors, with kingly views at the highest point in town. **Hours:** Daily March-Oct 9:00-21:00, Nov-Feb 9:00-18:00. See page 62.

Museum and School of Portuguese Decorative Arts A stroll through aristocratic households richly decorated in 16th- to 19th-century styles. **Hours:** Wed-Mon 10:00-17:00, closed Tue. See page 64.

Elevador de Santa Justa A 150-foot-tall iron elevator offering a glittering city vista. **Hours:** Daily 7:00-21:00. See page 75.

Cathedral (Sé) From the outside, an impressive Romanesque fortress of God; inside, not much. **Hours:** Church—daily 9:00-19:00; cloisters—Mon-Sat 14:00-19:00, until 18:00 off-season, closed Sun; treasury—Mon-Sat 10:00-17:00, closed Sun. See page 74.

In Belém

Note that all of these sights—except the Monument to the Discoveries—are closed on Monday year-round.

▲▲▲Monastery of Jerónimos King Manuel's giant 16th-century, white limestone church and monastery, with remarkable cloisters and the explorer Vasco da Gama's tomb. **Hours:** May-Sept Tue-Sun 10:00-18:30, off-season until 17:30, closed Mon. See page 89.

▲▲National Coach Museum Dozens of carriages, from simple to opulent, displaying the evolution of coaches from 1600 on. **Hours:** Tue-Sun 10:00-18:00, closed Mon. See page 87.

▲Maritime Museum A salty selection of exhibits on the ships and navigational tools of the Age of Discovery. **Hours:** April-Sept Tue-Sun 10:00-18:00, off-season until 17:00, closed Mon. See page 94.

▲Monument to the Discoveries Giant riverside monument honoring the explorers who brought Portugal great power and riches centuries ago. **Hours:** May-Sept daily 10:00-19:00; Oct-April Tue-Sun 10:00-18:00, closed Mon. See page 95.

▲Belém Tower Consummate Manueline building with a worthwhile view up 120 steps. **Hours:** May-Sept Tue-Sun 10:00-18:30, off-season until 17:30, closed Mon. See page 97.

LISBON

the ruined church near its top. While you'll need to pay extra to go to the very top floor lookout for a fine city view, the view from the entry-ramp level is nearly as good—and free (€5 round-trip ticket, free with Via Viagem card loaded with 24-hour pass—if "zapping," it'll cost you €5, daily 7:00-21:00).

Stroll around this celebration of the Industrial Age, enjoy the view, and retrace your steps to the square in front of the convent. (The nearby Leitaria Académica, a venerable little working-class eatery with tables spilling onto the delightful square, can be handy for a snack or drink.)

• *Leave Largo do Carmo, walking a block slightly uphill on Travessa do Carmo. At the next square, take a left on Rua Serpa Pinto, walking downhill to Rua Garrett, where—in the little pedestrian zone 50 yards uphill on the right—you'll find a famous old café across from the Baixa-Chiado Metro stop.*

❽ **Café A Brasileira:** Reeking of smoke and slinky with Art Nouveau decor, this café is a 100-year-old institution for coffeehouse junkies. Drop in for a *bica* (Lisbon slang for an espresso, €0.70 at the bar) and a €1.30 *pastel de nata* custard tart—a Lisbon specialty. (WCs are down the stairs near the entrance.) This café was the literary and creative soul of Lisbon in the 1920s and 1930s, when the country's avant-garde poets, writers, and painters would hang out here. The statue outside is of the poet Fernando Pessoa (see sidebar), making him a perpetual regular at this café. A Brasileira was originally a shop selling Brazilian products, a reminder that this has long been the city's shopping zone.

At the neighboring Baixa-Chiado (shee-AH-doo) Metro stop, a slick series of escalators whisks people effortlessly between Chiado Square and the Baixa (the lower town). It's a free and fun way to survey a long, long line of Portuguese—but for now, we'll stay in the Chiado neighborhood. (If you'll be coming for fado in the evening—recommended places are nearby—consider getting here by zipping up the escalator.)

The Chiado District is popular for its shopping and theaters. Browse downhill on Rua Garrett and notice its mosaic sidewalks, ironwork balconies, and fine shops. Peek into classy stores, such as the fabric-lover's paradise Paris em Lisboa (at #77, with a heavy dose of French style) or the venerable Bertrand bookstore (at #73, English books and a good guidebook selection in Room 5). My favorite shop for traditional Portuguese gifts is behind the bookstore: ❾ **A Vida Portuguesa** (Mon-Sat 10:00-20:00, closed Sun, Rua Anchieta 11). The street lamps you see are decorated with the symbol of Lisbon: a ship, carrying the remains of St. Vincent, guarded by two ravens. In 1988, much of this area was destroyed in a fire.

• *Rua Garrett ends abruptly at the entrance of the big vertical mall. For*

Italian-style gelato, locals like Santini em Casa, *a few steps downhill to the left (at #9, 30 meters below mall entry). Step into the fancy...*

⓾ **Armazéns do Chiado Mall:** This grand, six-floor shopping center connects Lisbon's lower and upper towns with a world of ways to spend money (daily 10:00-22:00, lively food court on sixth floor open daily about 12:00-23:00—see page 101).

• *This walk is over. To get from the mall to the Baixa—the lower town— take the elevator (press 1) or the escalators down (to exit on the ground level, you'll pass through the Sports Zone shop). To get from the mall to the Metro, exit through the lowest floor of the mall, turn right, and walk 50 yards to the Baixa-Chiado Metro stop.*

You can connect to the following Alfama walk by hopping on trolley #28E; to get from the mall to the trolley stop, leave the mall at the lowest level, and turn right down Rua do Crucifixo to Rua da Conceição, where you'll catch the trolley going left.

LISBON

▲▲▲The Alfama Stroll

Explore the Alfama, the colorful sailors' quarter that dates back to the age of Visigoth occupation, from the sixth to eighth centuries A.D. This was a bustling district during the Moorish period, and eventually became the home of Lisbon's fishermen and mariners (and of the poet Luís de Camões, who wrote, "Our lips meet easily, high across the narrow street"). The Alfama's tangled street plan is one of the few features of Lisbon to survive the 1755 earthquake. It helps make the neighborhood a cobbled playground of Old World color. Visit at the best time, during the busy mid-morning market, or in the cooler hours in the late afternoon or early evening, when the streets teem with residents. While much of its grittiness has been cleaned up in recent years (as traditional residents have been replaced by immigrant laborers), the Alfama remains one of the most photogenic neighborhoods in all of Europe.

• *Start your walk at the highest point in town, São Jorge Castle. Get to the castle gate by taxi (€4) or by minibus #37 from Praça da Figueira. (Trolleys #28E and #12E go to Largo Santa Luzia and Largo das Portas do Sol, respectively, a few blocks below.)*

❶ **São Jorge Castle Gate:** Just inside the castle gate (on left) is a little statue of George, named for a popular saint in the 14th century. St. George (São Jorge; pronounced "sow ZHOR-zh") hailed from Turkey and was known for fighting valiantly (he's often portrayed slaying a dragon). When the Christian noble Afonso Henriques called for help to eliminate the Moors from his newly founded country of Portugal, the Crusaders who helped him prayed to St. George...and won. If you're on a budget, this place is skippable—at €7, it has the steepest admission in town, and offers only a hill-capping park with a commanding city view and the stark ruins of a rebuilt medieval castle (daily March-Oct

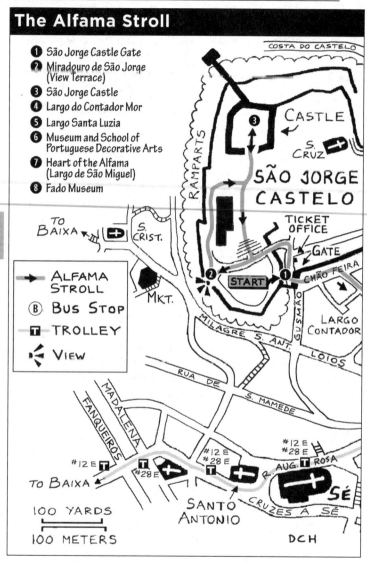

The Alfama Stroll

1. São Jorge Castle Gate
2. Miradouro de São Jorge (View Terrace)
3. São Jorge Castle
4. Largo do Contador Mor
5. Largo Santa Luzia
6. Museum and School of Portuguese Decorative Arts
7. Heart of the Alfama (Largo de São Miguel)
8. Fado Museum

➡ ALFAMA STROLL
Ⓑ BUS STOP
🚊 TROLLEY
◄ VIEW

100 YARDS
100 METERS

9:00–21:00, Nov-Feb 9:00–18:00). Along with your classic big-city viewpoint, there's a café and a WC in the park.

• *If you decide to go in, pick up your ticket and then follow the cobbles uphill past the first lanes of old Lisbon into the Miradouro de São Jorge. Otherwise, skip ahead to* 4.

2 **Miradouro de São Jorge (View Terrace):** Enjoy the grand view. The Rio Tejo is one of five main rivers in Portugal, four of which come from Spain. (Only the Mondego River, which passes by Coimbra, originates inside Portuguese territory, in the Serra de

LISBON

Estrela.) While Portugal and Spain generally have very good relations, a major sore point is the control of all this water. From here, you have a good view of the 25th of April Bridge, which leads south to the Cristo Rei statue (described on page 85). Past the bridge, you can barely see the Monument to the Discoveries and the Belém Tower on a clear day.

Stroll inland along the **ramparts** for a more extensive view of Pombal's Lisbon, described in a circa-1963 tile-panorama chart (which lacks the big 25th of April Bridge—it was built in 1969).

From Praça do Comércio on the water, the grid streets of the Baixa lead up to the tree-lined Avenida da Liberdade and the big Edward VII Park, capped with a large Portuguese flag on the far right. Locate places you know, such as the Elevador de Santa Justa (the Eiffel-style elevator in front

of the ruined Convento do Carmo) and the sloping white roof of Rossio Station. After walking farther inland under the second arch, take a right and then a left to wander the grounds. Then enter the inner castle (which usually only offers a chance to climb up for more views, although sometimes exhibitions are housed here). The strolling peacocks remind visitors that exotic birds like these came to Lisbon originally as trophies of the great 16th-century voyages and discoveries.

❸ São Jorge Castle: This much-renovated structure was first built by the Moors in the 11th century. After Portugal's first king, Afonso Henriques (whose statue stands on the view terrace), beat the Moors in the 12th century, the castle began its three-century-long stint as a royal residence. (The sloping walls—typical of castles from this period—were designed to withstand 14th-century cannonballs.) In the 16th century, the kings moved to their palace on Praça do Comércio—where they lived until the 1755 earthquake—and this castle fell into ruins. What you see today was mostly rebuilt by the dictator Salazar in the 1960s (for more on Salazar, see the sidebar on page 84).

As you explore the castle's inner sanctum, imagine it lined with simple wooden huts. The imposing part of the castle is the exterior. The builders' strategy was to focus on making the castle appear so formidable that its very existence was enough to discourage any attack. If you know where to look, you can still see stones laid by ancient Romans, Visigoths, and Moors. The Portuguese made the most substantial contribution, with a wall reaching all the way to the river to withstand anticipated Spanish attacks. The humble museum shows off a few Moorish tiles and some old pottery.

• *Leave the castle. Across the ramp from the castle entrance (20 yards ahead, on the left) is a tidy little castle district with cute shops and cafés, worth a wander for its peaceful lanes and a chance to enjoy the Manueline architecture. Notice how the tiny balconies are limited to "one-and-a-half hands" in width. A strictly enforced health initiative kept the town open and well-ventilated. When you finally leave the castle complex grounds (at the little statue of St. George), jog to the left 50 yards past the gate, turn right on Travessa do Chão da Feira, and follow the striped lane downhill through...*

❹ Largo do Contador Mor: This small, car-clogged square

Pombal's Lisbon

In 1750, lazy King José I (r. 1750-1777) turned the government over to a minor noble, the Marquês de Pombal (1699-1782). Talented, ambitious, and handsome, Pombal was praised as a reformer, but reviled for his ruthless tactics. Having learned modern ways as the ambassador to Britain, he battled Church repression and promoted the democratic ideals of the Enlightenment, but enforced his policies with arrests, torture, and executions. He expelled the Jesuits to keep them from monopolizing the education system, put the bishop of Coimbra in prison, and broke off relations with the pope. When the earthquake of 1755 leveled the city, within a month Pombal had kicked off major rebuilding in much of today's historic downtown—featuring a grid plan for the world's first quake-proof buildings. In 1777, the king died and the controversial Pombal was dismissed.

with a Parisian ambience has two handy outdoor restaurants, with grilled sardines as their specialty.

• *Continue downhill 50 yards farther, passing the trolley tracks, to reach a superb Alfama viewpoint at...*

❺ **Largo Santa Luzia:** From this square (a stop for trolleys #12E and #28E), admire the panoramic view from the small terrace, Miradouro de Santa Luzia, where old-timers play cards amid lots of tiles.

In the distance to the left, the **Vasco da Gama Bridge** (opened in 1998, described on page 83) connects Lisbon with new, modern bedroom communities south of the river. Below, the purple building with the green shades marks the square called Largo de São Miguel—the center of the Alfama. Where the Alfama neighborhood hits the river, notice the relatively new embankment. It reclaimed 100 yards of land from the river to make a modern port, used these days by large cruise ships. The huge building dominating the neighborhood on the far left is the Monastery of São Vicente, constructed around 1600 by the Spanish king, Philip II, who wanted to leave his mark with this tribute to St. Vincent.

Look at the church on the square you're on; find the wall of 18th-century tiles on the riverside façade that show Praça do Comércio before the 1755 earthquake. The 16th-century royal palace (shown on the left of the tilework, where the king went after abandoning the castle) was completely destroyed in the quake. Farther on, another tile panel depicts the reconquest of Lisbon from the Moors by Afonso Henriques, described earlier. For an even better city view, hike around the church and walk out to the seaside end of the Miradouro de Largo das Portas do Sol catwalk. At the kiosk café on the terrace, you can have the most scenic cup of coffee in town (daily 10:00-18:00).

• *Across the street from the café, you'll find the...*

❻ **Museum and School of Portuguese Decorative Arts (Museu Escola de Artes Decorativas Portuguesas):** This museum offers a unique stroll through an aristocratic household, richly decorated in 16th- to 19th-century styles. In 1947, Ricardo do Espirito Santo Silva restored this Azurura Palace to house his collection of 15th- to 18th-century fine art, and then willed it to the state. He created perhaps the best chance for visitors to experience what an aristocratic home looked like during Lisbon's glory days. The coach at the ground level is "Berlin style," with a state-of-the-art suspension system. The grand stairway leads past 18th-century glazed tiles (Chinese-style blue-and-white was in vogue) upstairs into a world rich in colonial riches. Portuguese aristocrats had a flair for "Indo-Portuguese" decorative arts: exotic woods, shells, and Oriental porcelain (€4, Wed-Mon 10:00-17:00, closed Tue, Largo das Portas do Sol 2, tel. 218-814-640, www.fress.pt).

• *From here, it's downhill all the way. From Largo das Portas do Sol (the plaza with the statue of local patron St. Vincent, near the kiosk café on the terrace), go down the stairs (Rua Norberto de Araújo, between the church and the catwalk). The old fortified wall (on the right) once marked the boundary of Moorish Lisbon. Consider that the great stones on your right were stacked here a thousand years ago. At the bottom of the wall, continue downhill, then turn left at the railing...and go down more stairs. Explore downhill from here. The main thoroughfare, a concrete stepped lane called Escadinhas de São Miguel, leads to the Alfama's main square, and...*

❼ **The Heart of the Alfama:** This square, Largo de São Miquel, is the best place to observe a slice of Alfama life. While city leaders rebuilt the rest of Lisbon after the 1755 quake, this neighborhood was left out and consequently retains its tangled medieval street plan.

If you've got the time, explore the Alfama. Its urban-jungle roads are squeezed into confusing alleys—the labyrinthine street plan was designed to frustrate invaders and guidebook researchers trying to get up to the castle. What was defensive then is atmospheric now. Bent houses comfort each other in their romantic shabbiness, and the air drips with laundry and the smell of clams. Get lost. Poke aimlessly, peek through windows, buy a fish. Locals hang plastic water bags from windows to try to keep away the flies. Favorite saints decorate doors to protect families. St. Peter, protector of fisher-

men, is big in the Alfama. Churches are generally closed, since they share a priest. As children have very little usable land for a good soccer game, goalposts are painted onto the stairs.

If you see carpets hanging out to dry, it means a laundry is nearby. Because few homes have their own, every neighborhood has a public laundry and bathroom. (There's actually a public bath and laundry on the uphill side of Largo de São Miguel). Until recently, in the early morning hours, the streets were busy with residents in pajamas, heading for these public baths. Today, young people are choosing to live elsewhere, lured by modern conveniences unavailable here, and the old flats are congested with immigrant laborers (mostly Ukrainian and Brazilian) who came during the construction boom a decade ago. In just a couple of generations, the demographics have changed—from fishermen's families to immigrants and young bohemians.

Traditionally the neighborhood here was tightly knit, with families routinely sitting down to communal dinners in the streets. Feuds, friendships, and gossip were all intense. Historically, when a woman's husband died, she wore black for the rest of her life—a tradition that's just about gone.

The Alfama hosts Lisbon's most popular outdoor party on St. Anthony's Day (June 13). Imagine tables set up everywhere, bands playing, bright plastic flowers strung across the squares, and all the grilled sardines *(sardinhas grelhadas)* you can eat. The strings and wires overhead await future festival dates when the neighborhood will again be festooned with colorful streamers.

While there are plenty of traditional festivals here, the most action on the Alfama calendar is the insane, annual mountain-bike street race from the castle to the sea (which you can see hurtle by in under two minutes on YouTube; search "Lisboa downtown race").

• *Continue exploring downhill from here. You'll see a trendy little restaurant (the recommended Restaurante Santo Antonio de Alfama) and the recommended amateur fado restaurant (A Baiuca). Then, a few steps below the square, you'll hit Rua São Pedro. This darkest of the Alfama's streets, in nearly perpetual shade, was the logical choice for the neighborhood's fish market. Modern hygiene requirements (which forbid outdoor stalls) killed the market, but it's still a characteristic lane to explore. Turn left and follow Rua São Pedro out of the Alfama to the square called Largo do Chafariz de Dentro and the...*

❽ **Fado Museum:** This museum, rated ▲, tells the story of fado in English—with a great chance to hear these wailing fisherwomen's blues. Three levels of wall murals show three generations of local fado stars, and the audioguide lets you hear the Billie Holidays of Portugal (€5, includes audioguide, Tue-Sun 10:00-18:00, closed Mon, last entry 30 minutes before closing, Largo do Chafariz de Dentro, tel. 218-823-470, www.museudofado.pt).

• *This walk is over. To get back downtown (or to Praça do Comércio, where the next walk starts) from the Fado Museum, walk a block to the main waterfront drag (facing museum, go left around it) where busy Avenida Infante Dom Henrique leads back to Praça do Comércio downtown (a 15-minute walk, plenty of taxis, bus stop to your left, all buses except #728 go to Praça do Comércio, bus #759 goes to Praça dos Restauradores; #9, #90, and #746 continue up Avenida da Liberdade).*

▲▲▲The Baixa Stroll: Lisbon's Historic Downtown

This walk covers the highlights of Lisbon's downtown, the Baixa, which fills the flat valley between two hills, sloping gently from the waterfront up to the Rossio, Praça dos Restauradores, Avenida da Liberdade, and the newer town. The walk starts at Praça do Comércio and ends at Praça dos Restauradores.

After the disastrous 1755 earthquake, the Baixa district was rebuilt on a grid street plan. The uniform and utilitarian Pombaline architecture (named after the Marquês de Pombal, the prime minister who rebuilt the city—see sidebar, earlier) feels almost military. That's because it is. The Baixa was built by military engineers who had experience building garrison towns overseas. The new Lisbon featured the architecture of conquest—simple to assemble, economical, with all the pieces easy to ship. The 18th-century buildings you'd see in Mozambique and Brazil are interchangeable with those in Lisbon.

The buildings are all uniform, with the same number of floors and standard facades. They were designed to survive the next earthquake, with stone firewalls and wooden frameworks featuring crisscross beams that flexed. The priorities were to rebuild fast, cheap, and earthquake-proof.

If it were left up to the people, who believed the earthquake was a punishment from God, they would have rebuilt their churches bigger and more impressive than ever. But Pombal was a practical military man with a budget, a timeline, and an awareness of his society's limits. He didn't want church-building to compromise the needs of the people. In those austere post-earthquake days, Pombal got his way.

The Baixa has three squares: two pre-earthquake (Comércio and Rossio) and one added later (Figueira), and three main streets: Prata (silver), Aurea (gold), and Augusta (relating the Portuguese king to a Roman emperor). The former maze of the Jewish Quarter was eliminated, but the area has many streets named for the crafts and shops once found there. The Baixa's pedestrian streets, inviting

LISBON

cafés, bustling shops, and elegant old storefronts give the district a certain charm. City-government subsidies make sure the old businesses stay around, but modern ones find a way to creep in. I find myself doing laps up and down Rua Augusta in a people-watching stupor. Its delightful ambience is perfect for strolling and reminiscent of the Ramblas in Barcelona.

• *Start your walk under the statue of King José I in the center of Praça do Comércio.*

❶ **Praça do Comércio ("Trade Square"):** At this riverfront square bordering the Baixa, ships used to dock and sell their goods. Nicknamed "Palace Square" by locals, it was the site of Portugal's royal palace for 200 pre-earthquake years. After the 1755 earthquake/tsunami/fire, the jittery king fled, never to return (he lived out his life in a wooden palace in the more-stable Belém district). These days, government ministries ring Praça do Comércio. It's also the departure point for city bus and tram tours, and boats that cruise along the Rio Tejo. The area opposite the harbor was conceived as a residential neighborhood for the upper class, but they chose the suburbs. Today, the square has two names ("Palace Square" and "Commercial Square") and no real life. Locals consider it just a big place to pass through.

The statue is of King José I, the man who gave control of the government to Pombal, who rebuilt the city after the earthquake. Built 20 years after the quake, it shows the king on his horse, with Pombal (on the medallion), looking at their port. The horse (symbolic of triumph) stomps on snakes (symbolic of evil—perhaps Protestants...or trouble-making noble families), while the elephant represents the Portuguese empire's colonies in India and Africa.

The big arch marking the inland side of the square is Lisbon's Arch of Triumph (with Vasco da Gama on the left and Pombal on the right). Disregarding his usual austerity, Pombal restored some of the city's Parisian-style grandeur at this central approach into downtown.

• *With your back to the harbor (facing the Arch of Triumph), the tour bus departure point is ahead on the right; the TI, Vini Portugal wine-tasting center, and meeting point for walking tours are on your left; and the Terreiro do Paço Metro stop is behind you (in the southeast corner of the square).*

❷ **Wine-Tasting Center:** At **Vini Portugal** (mid-arcade), Portugal's vintners sponsor a non-profit wine-appreciation venue. Three regions are always represented, and there are generally 20

The Baixa Stroll

TO ⑬ (AVENIDA DA LIBERDADE)

PRAÇA DOS RESTAURADORES

ELEVADOR DA GLÓRIA

Post

TR. S. ANT.

⑫ END

Restaur-adores

Rossio Train Stn.

CHIADO

RUA GARRETT

Baixa-Chiado

Mall

S. JUSTA ELEVADOR

RUA SERPA PINTO

VITOR CORDON

RUA DO ARSENAL

TO CAIS DO SODRÉ STN. (FERRIES TO CACILHAS)

AV. RIBEIRA DAS NAUS

RIO TEJO

Post

PRAÇA

LISBON WALKER MTG. PT.

ARCH

PRAÇA DO COMÉRCIO

① START

②

BUS TOURS

Terreiro do Paço

TERREIRO DO PAÇO RIVER CRUISES

BAIXA STROLL

M METRO

T TROLLEY LINE & STOP

100 YDS.
100 M

"EATING LANE"

LARGO DE SÃO DOMINGOS

Martim Moniz

TO ALFAMA

#12 E

TEATRO

PRAÇA DO ROSSIO

Rossio

PRAÇA DA FIGUEIRA

#12 E
#15 E

R. BETESGA

S. CRIST

TO ALFAMA

RUA DE CONCEIÇÃO

JULIÃO

COMÉRCIO

TO SÉ & ALFAMA

RUA ALFANDEGA

LISBON

The Baixa Stroll Key

① Praça do Comércio	⑧ Largo de São Domingos
② Wine-Tasting Center	⑨ Ginjinha Bars (2)
③ Rua do Comércio	⑩ Rossio Square
④ Rua São Julião	⑪ Rossio Station
⑤ Church of St. Nicola	⑫ Praça dos Restauradores
⑥ Praça da Figueira	⑬ To Avenida da Liberdade
⑦ Church of São Domingos	

Portuguese wines available for tasting (your choice of four). It's entirely free, but they do ask you to fill out a survey to help them know what consumers like best (tastings on the hour Tue-Sat 11:00-19:00, closed Sun-Mon, next to TI).

• *Pass through the big arch and walk down Rua Augusta into the Baixa district. The next three stops along this walk take you straight down Rua Augusta, stopping at three cross streets.*

❸ **Rua do Comércio:** Look right to see the old cathedral with its Romanesque fortress-like crenellations (described on page 74). Notice that many of the surrounding buildings are austere, with no tiles—this was the architectural style adopted immediately after the earthquake, when only the interiors of buildings were tiled. In the Portuguese colony of Brazil, people found that tiles protected against humidity, and eventually (by the 19th century), tilework was adopted as a form of exterior decoration here in Lisbon. The characteristic black-and-white cobbled sidewalk *(calçada)* is uniquely Portuguese. These mosaic cobbles were first cut and laid by 19th-century prison laborers. Later on this walk, you'll see a monument to the many generations of *calceteiros,* the men who made Lisbon's traditional sidewalks. On the right you'll pass the Museum la Mode, Lisbon's museum of design (a.k.a. MUDE; free to enter). Filling the Art Deco ground floor of a former bank, it offers a quick, one-floor stroll through 20th-century fashion.

• *At Rua São Julião, look left about 30 yards and try to find the church—it's hiding.*

❹ **Rua São Julião:** Churches are scarce in the post-earthquake Baixa. Only a few of the churches destroyed by the quake were permitted to be rebuilt. The replacement churches were incorporated into the no-nonsense military style, with facades that match the rest of the street. You'll notice that the Baixa district is struggling to stay vital, with many buildings now mostly empty (especially the upper floors). Look up for evidence of how downtown's Lisbon's population is shrinking, as more people move to the suburbs.

At the next block, the handy trolley #28E stops at Rua da Conceição. Ahead on the right (in the windows of the Millennium

The Lisbon Earthquake of 1755

At 9:40 in the morning on Sunday, November 1—All Saints' Day—an earthquake estimated to be close to 9.0 in magnitude rumbled through the city, punctuated by three main jolts. Its arrival came midway through Mass. Ten minutes later, thousands lay dead under the rubble.

Along the waterfront, shaken survivors scrambled aboard boats to sail to safety. They were met by a 20-foot wall of water, the first wave of a tsunami that rushed up the Rio Tejo. The ravaging water capsized ships, swept people off the docks, crested over the seawall, and crashed 800 feet inland.

After the quake, the city turned into an inferno, as overturned cooking fires and fallen candles ignited raging fires. The fires blazed for five days, ravaging the downtown from the Bairro Alto across Rossio to the castle atop the Alfama.

Of Lisbon's 270,000 citizens, up to 90,000 may have perished. Besides leveling the city, the quake shook conservative Portugal's moral and spiritual underpinnings. Had God punished Lisbon for the Inquisition killings carried out on nearby Praça do Comércio?

King José I was so affected by the earthquake that he moved his entire court to an elaborate complex of tents in the foothills of Belém and resisted living indoors for the rest of his life.

This earthquake, one of the most violent in recorded history, was the first one to be studied methodically, marking the beginning of the science of seismology.

Bank) are Roman artifacts—a reminder that Lisbon's history goes way back.

• *At Rua da Vitoria, turn right and walk to Rua da Prata, where you'll see the camouflaged...*

❺ Church of St. Nicola (Igreja de São Nicolau): Notice how its church-like facade was allowed, but the entire green-tiled side is disguised as just another stretch of post-earthquake Baixa architecture. The monument in front of the church honors the city's tile-makers.

• *Head left down Rua da Prata toward the statue marking Praça da Figueira. At Rua de Santa Justa, look left for a good view of Elevador de Santa Justa before continuing straight to the square.*

❻ Praça da Figueira ("Fig Tree Square"): This was the site of a huge hospital destroyed in the earthquake. With no money to replace the hospital, the space was left open until the late 1880s, when it was filled with a big iron-framed market (similar to Barcelona's La Boqueria). That structure was torn down decades ago, leaving the square you see today. The big building on the left is run-down—after 50 years of rent control, many landowners are demoralized and do nothing to fix up their property. Buildings are often either vacant or occupied by old pensioners living out their lives amid increasingly decrepit conditions. By contrast, the right side (under the castle) is more lived-in and vibrant.

The nearby **Confit Nacional** shop is a venerable palace of sweets little changed since the 19th century. In the window is a display of *"conventuel* sweets"—special nun-made treats often consisting of sugar and egg yolks (historically, the nuns used the egg whites to starch their laundry). For a great budget snack or meal in a classic local scene, find the recommended **Casa Brasileira** (100 yards from the square at Rua Augusta 265, daily 7:00-24:00). Their fast, cheap lunch deals are served only at the bar. And their *pastel de nata* (custard tart pastries) are as tasty as those that people line up for in Belém.

The square is a transportation hub, with stops for the minibus #37 and the old trolley #12E going to the castle (see page 45 for a self-guided trolley tour), the modern trolley #15E and bus #714 heading out to Belém, and the touristic hop-on, hop-off buses.

• *Walk to the far left corner of the square, past skateboarders oblivious to its historical statue—Portugal's King John I on a horse. Leave the square down the Rua Dom Antão de Almada. This lane has several characteristic shops. Pop into the classic cod shop (on the left at #1C—you'll smell it). Cod is part of Portugal's heritage as a nation of seafaring explorers: It was salted and could keep for a year on a ship. Just soak in water to rinse out the salt and enjoy. The adjacent ham counter serves* pata negra (presunto ibérico) *from acorn-fed pigs—the very best. The non-pork* alheira *sausage is made with game and was a favorite among Lisbon's Jews back when they needed to fake being Christians. At the end of the lane stands a big church facing another square.*

❼ **Church of São Domingos:** A center of the Inquisition in the 1600s, this is now one of Lisbon's most active churches (daily 7:30-19:00). The evocative interior—more or less rebuilt from the ruins left by the 1755 earthquake—reminds visitors of that horrible All Saints' Day Sunday, when most of the city was at Mass and the earth rolled. Across the city, heavy stone church walls like these collapsed on their congregations. Standing at the back of the nave, you can see which parts of the pre-1755 stone walls remained standing after that tragic day. The black soot on the walls and the charred stonework at the altar recalls the horrible fires that followed the earthquake. Our Lady of Fátima is Portugal's most popular saint. Her chapel (in the left rear of the church) always has the most candles. She's accompanied by two of the three children who saw the miraculous apparition (the third was still alive when this chapel was made and so is not shown in heaven with the saint).

• *Step into the square just beyond the church.*

❽ Largo de São Domingos: This area was just outside of the old town walls—long a place where people gathered to keep watering holes busy and enjoy bohemian entertainment. Today, this square is busy with immigrants from Portugal's former African colonies. They hang out, trade news from home, and watch tourists go by. The square is home to classic old bars (a *ginjinha* bar is described next) and a busy "eating lane," Rua das Portas de Santo Antao (to the right of the National Theater). The square once held a palace that functioned as the headquarters of the Inquisition. It was demolished, and in an attempt to erase its memory, the National Theater (far side of the square) was built in its place. The city massacred the town's Jews on this square in 1506. A stone monument, unveiled in 2008, remembers this sad event.

• *Find the colorful little hole-in-the-wall tavern facing the square and serving the traditional* ginjinha *drink.*

❾ Liquid Sightseeing: *Ginjinha* (zheen-ZHEEN-yah) is a favorite Lisbon drink. While nuns baked sweets, the monks took care of quenching thirsts with this sweet liquor, made from the sour cherry-like *ginja* berry, sugar, cinnamon, and brandy. It's now sold for €1.10 a shot in funky old shops throughout down-

town. Buy it with or without berries (*com elas* or *sem elas*—that's "with them" or "without them") and *gelada* (if you want it poured from a chilled bottle). In Portugal, when people are impressed by the taste of something, they say, *"Sabe que nem ginjas"*—"It tastes like *ginja*." The oldest *ginjinha* joint in town is a colorful hole-in-the-wall at Largo de São Domingos 8. If you hang around the bar long enough, you'll see them refill the bottle from an enormous vat. (Another *ginjinha* bar, named for Eduardino the clown and consid-

ered the most authentic, is a block away on the restaurant row, Rua das Portas de Santo Antão, next to #59; daily 7:00-24:00.)

• *The big square around the corner (fronting the National Theater) is Rossio.*

❿ Rossio: Lisbon's historic center, Rossio, is still the city's bustling cultural heart. Given its elongated shape, historians believe it was a Roman racetrack 2,000 years ago; these days, cars circle the loop instead of chariots. It's home to the colonnaded National Theater, a McDonald's, and street vendors who can shine your shoes, laminate your documents, and sell you cheap watches, autumn chestnuts, and lottery tickets. The column in the square's center honors Pedro IV—king of Portugal and emperor of Brazil. (Many maps refer to the square as Praça Dom Pedro IV, but residents always just call it Rossio, referring to the train station at one corner.)

Rossio, once the site of Lisbon's 16th-century slave market, is now a meeting point for the city's black community—immigrants from former Portuguese colonies such as Angola, Mozambique, and Portuguese Guinea. From here you can see the Elevador de Santa Justa and the ruined convent breaking the city skyline. Notice the fine stone patterns in the pavement—evoking waves encountered by the great explorers—which once upon a time made locals seasick.

• *Crossing the square in front of the National Theater, you see Rossio Station.*

⓫ Rossio Station: The circa-1900 facade of Rossio Station is Neo-Manueline. You can read the words *Central Station* printed on its striking horseshoe arches. Find the statue of King Sebastian in the center of two arches. This romantic, dashing, and young soldier king was lost in 1580 in an ill-fated crusade in Africa. As Sebastian left no direct heir, the crown ended up with Philip II of Spain, who became Philip I of Portugal. The Spanish king promised to give back the throne if Sebastian ever turned up—and ever since, the Portuguese have dreamed that Sebastian will return, restoring their national greatness. Even today, in a crisis, the Portuguese like to think that their Sebastian will save the day—he's the symbol of being ridiculously hopeful.

• *Just uphill from Rossio Station is Praça dos Restauradores, at the bottom of Lisbon's long and grand Avenida da Liberdade.*

⓬ Praça dos Restauradores: This monumental square connects Rossio with Avenida da Liberdade (listed next). Its centerpiece, an obelisk, celebrates the restoration of Portuguese independence from Spain in 1640 (without any help from the still-missing Sebastian mentioned earlier).

Just off the square is Lisbon's oldest hotel (the Hotel Avenida Palace, built as a terminus hotel at the same time as Rossio Station), the 1920s Art Deco facade of the Eden Theater, a TI, a green ABEP kiosk (selling tickets for concerts, movies, bullfights, and sports events; schedules of upcoming events posted in windows) at the southern end, the Elevador da Glória funicular that climbs to the Bairro Alto, and a Metro station. A block to the east is Lisbon's "eating lane" (Rua das Portas de Santo Antão), the restaurant-lined street mentioned earlier.

• *While this walk ends here, stroll up Avenida da Liberdade for a good look at another facet of this fine city.*

® **Avenida da Liberdade:** This tree-lined grand boulevard, running north from Rossio, connects the old town (where most of the sightseeing action is) with the newer upper town. Before the great earthquake, this was the city's royal promenade. After 1755, it was the grand boulevard of Pombal's new Lisbon—originally limited to the aristocracy. The present street, built in the 1880s and inspired by Paris' Champs-Elysées, is lined with banks, airline offices, nondescript office buildings...and eight noisy lanes of traffic. The grand "rotunda"—as the roundabout formally known as Marquês de Pombal is called—tops off the Avenida da Liberdade with a commanding statue of Pombal. Allegorical symbols of his impressive accomplishments decorate the statue. (A single-minded dictator can do a lot in 27 years.) Beyond that lies the fine Edward VII Park. From the Rotunda (Metro: Marquês de Pombal), it's an enjoyable 20-minute downhill walk along the mile-long avenue back to the Baixa.

Sights in Lisbon

Central Lisbon

To get a full picture of the best of central Lisbon, take the three neighborhood strolls (the Bairro Alto, Alfama, and Baixa) covered earlier.

Cathedral (Sé)—The cathedral, just a few blocks east of Praça do Comércio, is not much on the inside, but its fortress-like exterior—solid enough to survive the 1755 earthquake—is a textbook example of the stark and powerful Romanesque "fortress of God" so typical of its age. Twin, castle-like, crenellated towers solidly frame an impressive rose window.

Cost and Hours: Church—free, daily 9:00-19:00; cloisters—€2.50, Mon-Sat 14:00-19:00, until 18:00 off-season, closed Sun; treasury—€2.50, Mon-Sat 10:00-17:00, closed Sun; on Largo da Sé, several blocks east of Baixa—take Rua da Conceição east, which turns into Rua de Santo António da Sé.

Visiting the Church: Started in 1150, this was the first place of worship that Christians built after they retook Lisbon from the Moors. Located on the former site of a mosque, it made a powerful statement: The Reconquista was here to stay. The church is also the site of the 1195 baptism of St. Anthony—a favorite saint of Portugal (locals appeal to him for help in finding a parking spot, true love, and lost objects). Also, some of St. Vincent is buried here—legend has it that in the 12th century, his remains were brought to Lisbon on a ship guarded by two sacred black ravens, the symbol of the city.

The **cloisters** are peaceful and an archaeological work-in-progress—they're currently uncovering Roman ruins. The humble **treasury** is worth its fee only if you want to support the church and climb some stairs.

Elevador de Santa Justa—This 150-foot-tall iron tower, built in 1902, connects the flat Baixa district with the Barrio Alto/Chiado districts up above. You can ride the elevator for a fine city view, while getting a sweat-free connection to the upper town (€5 round-trip tickets only, covered by Viva Viagem card, but only worthwhile with 24-hour card—which makes it free; note that if "zapping," it'll cost you €5; daily 7:00-21:00).

North Lisbon

▲▲▲**Gulbenkian Museum**—This is the best of Lisbon's 40 museums. It's two miles north of the city center, but worth the trip for art lovers. Calouste Gulbenkian (1869-1955), an Armenian oil tycoon, gave Portugal his art collection (or "harem," as he called it). His gift was an act of gratitude for the hospitable asylum granted him during World War II (he lived in Lisbon from 1942 until he died in 1955). The Portuguese consider Gulbenkian—whose billion-dollar estate is still a growing and vital arts foundation promoting culture in Portugal—an inspirational model of how to be thoughtfully wealthy. (He made a habit of "tithing for art," spending 10 percent of his income on things of beauty.) The foundation often hosts classical music concerts in the museum's auditoriums.

Gulbenkian's collection, spanning 5,000 years and housed in a classy modern building, offers the most purely enjoyable museum experience in Iberia—it's both educational and just plain beautiful. The museum is cool, uncrowded, gorgeously lit, and easy to grasp, displaying only a few select and exquisite works from each epoch. Walk through five millennia of human history, appreciating our ancestors by seeing objects they treasured.

Cost and Hours: €6, free on Sun; open Tue-Sun 10:00-18:00, closed Mon; good 1.5-hour audioguide-€4, pleasant gardens, good air-conditioned cafeteria, Berna 45, tel. 217-823-000, www.museu.gulbenkian.pt.

Getting There: From downtown, hop a cab (€6) or take the Metro from Restauradores to the São Sebastião stop and exit the station following signs to *Avenida de Aguiar (norte)*. Once at street level, walk a long block down Avenida de Aguiar with the massive El Corte Inglés department store behind you. Just before the roundabout (across from the funky, pink Spanish embassy on the left), you'll see a small sign pointing right to the *fundação*—the museum entrance is straight ahead through this park, past an office building, about 100 yards away. (It's also possible to use the Praça de Espanha Metro stop, which is the same distance from the museum, but the São Sebastião stop will save you from having to cross several busy streets.)

Nearby: A fine modern art gallery (CAMJAP) is next door. And Belém is a quick €8 taxi ride away.

➲ Self-Guided Tour: From the entrance lobby, there are two wings, covering roughly pre-1500 and post-1500. Following the museum's layout, you'll see...

LISBON

❶ Egypt (2,500-500 B.C.): Ancient Egyptians, believing that life really began after death, carved statues to preserve the memory of the deceased, whether it be a prince (Statue of the Courtier Bes, 664-610 B.C., with an inscription calling him "the king's friend") or a likeness of the family pet. The cat statue nurses her kittens atop a coffin that once held the cat's mummy, preserved for the afterlife. Egyptians honored cats—even giving them gold earrings like those on the statue. They believed cats helped the goddess Bastet keep watch over the household. Now, more than 2,500 years later, we remember the Egyptians for these sturdy, dignified statues, built for eternity.

❷ Greece and Rome (500 B.C.-A.D. 500): The black-and-red Greek vase (calyx-crater), decorated with scenes of half-human satyrs chasing human women, reminds us of the rational Greeks' struggle to overcome their barbarian, animal-like urges as they invented Western civilization. Alexander the Great (r. 336-323 B.C., seen on a coin) used war to spread Greek culture throughout the Mediterranean, creating a cultural empire that would soon be taken over by Roman emperors (seen on medallions).

Journey even further back in time to the very roots of civilization: Mesopotamia (modern Iraq), where writing was invented. Five thousand years ago, the cylinder seals were used to roll an impression in sealing wax or clay.

❸ Islamic World (700-1500): The Muslims who lived in Portugal—as far west of Mecca as you could get back then—might have decorated their homes with furnishings from all over the Islamic world. Imagine a Moorish sultan, dressed in a shirt from Syria, sitting on a carpet from Persia in a courtyard with Moroccan tiles. By a bubbling fountain, he puffs on a hookah.

The culture of Moorish Iberia (711-1492) was among Europe's most sophisticated after the Fall of Rome. The intricate patterns on the glass lanterns are not only beautiful...they're actually quotes (in

Gulbenkian Museum

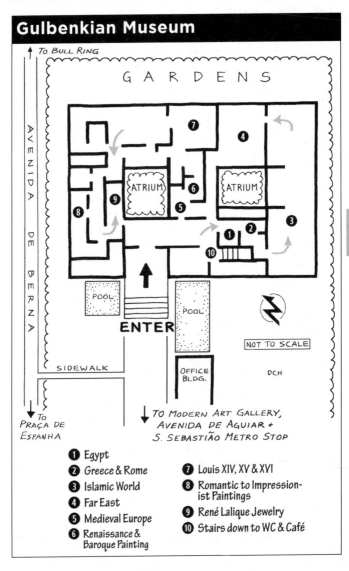

To Bull Ring

GARDENS

AVENIDA DE BERNA

ATRIUM

ATRIUM

NOT TO SCALE

POOL

POOL

ENTER

SIDEWALK

OFFICE BLDG.

DCH

To PRAÇA DE ESPANHA

To MODERN ART GALLERY,
AVENIDA DE AGUIAR +
S. SEBASTIÃO METRO STOP

LISBON

❶ Egypt
❷ Greece & Rome
❸ Islamic World
❹ Far East
❺ Medieval Europe
❻ Renaissance & Baroque Painting

❼ Louis XIV, XV & XVI
❽ Romantic to Impressionist Paintings
❾ René Lalique Jewelry
❿ Stairs down to WC & Café

Arabic) from the Quran, such as "Allah (God) is the light of the world, shining like a flame in a glass lamp, as bright as a star."

❹ **Far East (1368-1644):** For almost 300 years, the Ming dynasty ruled China, having reclaimed the country from Genghis Khan and his sons. When Portuguese traders reached the Orient, they brought back blue-and-white ceramics such as these. They became all the rage, inspiring the creation of both Portuguese tiles and Dutch Delftware. Writing utensils fill elaborately decorated boxes from Japan. Another type of box was the ultimate picnic basket—*bento* was the best way to enjoy the Japanese countryside.

In the other wing, look for the art of

❺ **Medieval Europe (500-1500):** While China was thriving and inventing, Europe was stuck in a thousand-year medieval funk (with the exception of Muslim Arab-ruled Iberia). Most Europeans from the "Age of Faith" channeled their spirituality into objects of Christian devotion. A priest on a business trip could pack a portable altarpiece in his backpack, travel to a remote village that had no church, and deliver a sermon carved in ivory. In monasteries, the monks with the best penmanship laboriously copied books (illuminated manuscripts) and decorated them with scenes from the text—and wacky doodles in the margins. These books were virtual time capsules, preserving the knowledge of Greece and Rome until it could emerge again, a thousand years later, in the Renaissance.

❻ **Renaissance and Baroque Painting (1500-1700):** Around 1500, a cultural revolution was taking place—the birth of humanism. Painters saw God in the faces of ordinary people, whether in Domenico Ghirlandaio's fresh-faced maiden, Frans Hals' wrinkled old woman, or Rembrandt's portrait of an old man, whose crease-lined hands tell the story of his life.

❼ **Louis XIV, XV, XVI (1700-1800):** After the Italian-born Renaissance, Europe's focus shifted northward to the luxurious court of France, where a new secular culture was blossoming. In one tapestry, love is in the air (see cupids flying overhead) as Venus frolics in a landscaped garden. Powder-wigged nobles in their palaces enjoyed the luxury of viewing art like this pagan scene, while relaxing in chairs like the kind you see here. This furniture, once owned by French kings (and Marie-Antoinette and Madame de Pompadour), is a royal home show. Anything heavy, ornate, and gilded (or that includes curved legs and animal-clawed feet) is from the time of Louis XIV. The Louis XV style is lighter and daintier, with Oriental motifs, while furniture from the Louis XVI era is stripped-down, straight-legged, tapered, and more modern. Listen to find out which clocks still work.

❽ **Romantic to Impressionist Paintings (1700-2000):** Europe ruled the world, and art became increasingly refined. Young British aristocrats (Thomas Gainsborough portrait) traveled Europe on the Grand Tour to see great sights like Venice (Guardi landscape). Follow the progression in styles from stormy Romanticism (J. M. W. Turner's tumultuous shipwreck) to Pre-Raphaelite dreamscapes *(Mirror of Venus)* to Realism's breath-of-fresh-air simplicity (Manet's bubble-blower) to the glinting, shimmering Impressionism of Monet...Renoir...and John Singer Sargent.

❾ **René Lalique Jewelry:** Finish your visit with the stunning, sumptuous Art Nouveau glasswork and jewelry of French designer

René Lalique (1860-1945). Fragile beauty like this, from the elegant turn-of-the-century belle époque, was about to be shattered by the tumultuous 20th century. Art Nouveau emphasized forms from nature and valued the organic and artisan over cold, calculated mass production. Ordinary dragonflies, orchids, and beetles become breathtaking when transformed into jewelry. The work of Lalique—just another of Gulbenkian's circle of friends—is a fitting finale to a museum that features both history and beauty.

East Lisbon

▲▲Museum of Ancient Art (Museu Nacional de Arte Antiga)—This is Portugal's finest museum for paintings from its glory days, the 15th and 16th centuries. (Most of these works were gathered from Lisbon's abbeys and convents after their dissolution in 1834.) You'll also find a rich collection of furniture, as well as art by renowned European masters such as Hieronymus Bosch, Jan van Eyck, and Raphael—all in a grand palace. Pick up the free informative pamphlet at the entrance.

Cost and Hours: €5, free Sun until 14:00; open Tue 14:00-18:00, Wed-Sun 10:00-18:00, closed Mon; tel. 213-912-800.

Getting There: It's located about a mile west of downtown Lisbon (from Praça da Figueira, take trolley #15E to Cais Rocha, cross the street and walk up a lot of steps; or take bus #760 to Rua das Janeles Verdes 9).

Services: The museum has a good cafeteria with seating in a shaded garden overlooking the river.

❍ Self-Guided Tour: Here are some of the museum's highlights, starting on the top floor.

Third Floor—Portuguese Paintings: The *Adoration of St. Vincent* is a multi-paneled altarpiece by the late-15th-century master Nuno Gonçalves. A gang of 60 real people—everyone from royalty to sailors and beggars—surrounds Lisbon's patron saint. In Room 1, if you've visited the sights in Belém, you'll recognize the Monastery of Jerónimos before it was fully decorated (painting by Felipe Lobo). Room 2 contains a small collection of paintings that depict Lisbon after the horrific 1755 earthquake.

Second Floor—Japanese Screen and Jewels: Find the enchanting Namban screen painting (Namban means "barbarians from the south"). It shows the Portuguese from a 16th-century Japanese perspective—with long noses as well as great skill at climbing rigging, like acrobats. The Portuguese, the first Europeans to make contact with Japan, gave the Japanese guns, Catholicism (Nagasaki was founded by Portuguese Jesuits), and a new deep-frying technique we now know as tempura.

On the same floor, have a quick look at the impressive jewelry collection decorated with the red cross of the Order of Christ,

LISBON

responsible for funding Portuguese explorations. Make your way to a freestanding glass case to see the Monstrance of Belém, made for Manuel I from the first gold brought back by Vasco da Gama. Squint at the fine enamel creatures filling a tide pool on the base, the 12 apostles gathered around the glass case for the Communion wafer (the fancy top pops off), and the white dove hanging like a mobile under the all-powerful God bidding us peace on earth. There is another notable monstrance nearby, as well as more jewels and fine porcelain on the rest of this floor.

First Floor—European Paintings: Pass through the gift shop and look for Bosch's *Temptations of St. Anthony* (a three-paneled altarpiece fantasy, c. 1500, in Room 57) and Albrecht Dürer's *St. Jerome* (just opposite). Note the complete collection of the larger-than-life *Twelve Apostles* by the Spanish master Zurburán.

Modern Lisbon: Oriente, Parque das Nações, and More

To get out of the quaint, Pombal-esque old town and enjoy a peek at the modern side of Lisbon, ride the Metro east to Oriente Station. Nearby you can stroll through a light and airy shopping mall, bike across the sprawling site of the 1998 World Expo, and promenade with locals along the Rio Tejo riverfront park. It's worth a visit any day, especially on Monday (when most museums in town are closed). It's a particularly vibrant scene when the people are out early on summer evenings.

Oriente Train Station (Gare do Oriente)—*Oriente* means "facing east." This impressive hub ties together trains (to the Algarve and Évora), the Metro, and buses under a swooping concrete roof designed by the Spanish architect, Santiago Calatrava. From the Oriente Metro station, you'll notice right away that the theme here is the sea. That was the theme of the 1998 Expo. And just about everything in this area is named for the great Portuguese explorer Vasco da Gama.

Vasco da Gama Mall—Facing Oriente Station is the inviting, soaring glass facade of Lisbon's top shopping mall, also designed by Calatrava (daily 9:00-24:00). Originally the grand entrance to the 1998 World Expo, the city has done a good job of turning the remains of that fair into useful infrastructure. Stepping into the mall, you'll see that its design seems to have been inspired by the main shopping hall of a luxury cruise ship. Notice the water cascading down the glass roof—a clever and fun-to-look-at way to keep things cool and avoid any greenhouse effect. From the mall's entrance, climb the stairs to a small outdoor terrace for a good view back at the train station. Then stroll through the upper level of the mall to the opposite end, where you can step out to another outdoor terrace—giving you yet again the feeling that you're vacationing

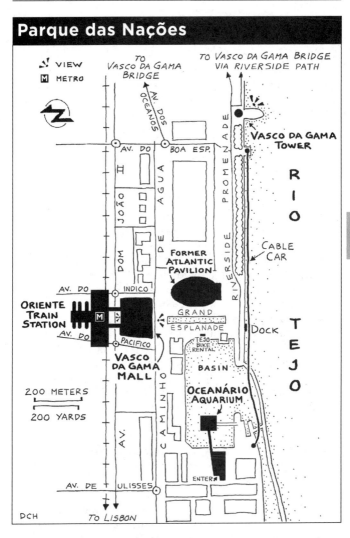

Parque das Nações

LISBON

on a cruise ship. Survey the scene. With your back to the river, look up at the two skyscraping luxury condo buildings. With fine transportation connections and modern office space, this area holds lots of promise, both for residences and businesses. Microsoft just set up its Portuguese headquarters here, and the Portuguese national court recently relocated to contemporary new buildings nearby. From here you can also look toward the river and survey Parque das Nações—the grounds of Portugal's 1998 World Expo (described next).

▲▲ **Parque das Nações**—Lisbon celebrated the 500th anniversary of Vasco da Gama's voyage to India by hosting Expo '98 here at Parque das Nações. The theme was "The Ocean and the Seas," emphasizing the global importance of healthy, clean waters.

To get the lay of the land, climb to the outdoor terrace at the Vasco de Gama Mall (see previous listing), or stand at the top of the Grand Esplanade (Rossio Olivais). Ahead of you, lining the esplanade, are 155 flags—one for each country represented at the fair. The flags are arranged in alphabetical order, so the first ones are South Africa (Africa dul Sul), Albania, and Germany (Alemanha). In the middle you'll find the US (Estados Unidos), Spain (Espanha), and Estonia side-by-side. The striped oval dome to the left, once the Atlantic Pavilion (Pavilhão Atlântico), is now an 18,000 seat concert hall. The oil refinery tower far to the right marks the west end of the park and stands as a reminder of the industrial wasteland that was here before the fair.

The basin in front of you pre dates the fair. Back before World War II it was a watery "parking lot" (just 1.5 yards deep) for seaplanes. Across the basin to your right, the blocky building that resembles an aircraft carrier with a spiky rooftop is the Oceanário aquarium (described below)—the big hit of the fair and still the park's major attraction. From behind that the cable car (€4 one-way, €6 round-trip, nothing special) drifts east to the Vasco da Gama Tower, which marks that end of the park. Directly ahead, the red shipping container is the bike-rental place (see next listing). Two miles away, built as part of the 1998 celebrations, is the Vasco da Gama Bridge (described later). A delightful promenade (Caminho dos Pinheiros; "The Way of the Pine Trees") runs along the riverfront from the marina all the way to a park at the base of the Vasco de Gama Bridge.

Parque das Nações Bike Ride—The most enjoyable way to explore the sprawling park is by bike. Simply enjoy a big loop pedaling around modern art, under fancy eaves, along the riverside promenade, and past local lovers enjoying a little *"marmalade"* (local slang for heavy petting). **Tejo Bike Rental,** which operates out of a red shipping container on the Grand Esplanade, rents simple one-speed bikes (€3/30 minutes, €5/hour, daily in summer 10:00-20:00, off-season 12:00-18:00, no locks, www.tejobike.pt).

Oceanário—Europe's largest aquarium simulates four different oceanic underwater and shoreline environments. Built in a modern version of a ship at sea, the aquarium's enormous centerpiece is a central tank with lots of fish and the occasional hungry shark. Penguins, sea otters, and weekday-morning school groups are all happily on display.

Cost and Hours: €12, daily April-Oct 10:00-19:00, off-season until 18:00, last entry 45 minutes before closing, tel. 218-917-002, www.oceanario.pt.

Vasco da Gama Bridge—Europe's longest bridge (10.7 miles) was opened in 1998 to connect the Expo grounds with the south side of the Rio Tejo, and to alleviate the traffic jams on Lisbon's only other bridge over the river, the 25th of April Bridge. The Vasco de Gama Bridge helped connect north and south Portugal, back when a freeway was a big deal in this late-to-develop European nation. Built low to the water, the bridge's towers and cables are meant to suggest the sails of a caravel ship.

West Lisbon

▲National Tile Museum (Museu Nacional do Azulejo)—Filling the Convento da Madre de Deus, the museum features piles of tiles, which, as you've probably noticed, are an art form in Portu-

gal. They've tried to showcase the tiles as they would have originally appeared (note the diamond-shaped staircase tiles). While the presentation is low-tech, the church is sumptuous, and the tile panorama of pre-earthquake Lisbon (upstairs) is fascinating.

Cost and Hours: €5, free Sun until 14:00; open Tue 14:00-18:00, Wed-Sun 10:00-18:00, closed Mon; located about a mile east of Praça do Comércio—10 minutes on bus #794 from Praça do Comércio (in front of TI) or bus #759 from Praça dos Restauradores, buses stop at museum entrance on Rua da Madre de Deus 4, tel. 218-100-340, http://mnazulejo.imc-ip.pt.

▲25th of April Bridge (25 de Abril)—At 1.5 miles (3,280 feet between the towers), this is one of the longest suspension bridges in the world. The foundations are sunk 260 feet below the surface into the riverbed, making it the world's deepest bridge. It was built in 1966 by the same company that made its famous San Francisco cousin (but notice the lower deck for train tracks). Originally named for the dictator Salazar, the bridge was renamed for the date of Portugal's 1974 revolution and liberation. For a generation, natives have shown their political colors by choosing which name to use. While conservative Portuguese still call it the "Salazar Bridge," liberals refer to it as the "25th of April Bridge" (just as Washington, D.C.'s airport is called "National" by some and "Reagan" by others). Imagine that before 1966, there was no way across the Rio Tejo except by ferry.

António Salazar

Q: *What do you get when you cross a lawyer, an economist, and a dictator?*
A: *António Salazar, who was all three—a dictator who ruled Portugal through harsh laws and a strict budget that hurt the poor.*

Shortly after a 1926 military coup "saved" Portugal's floundering democracy from itself, General Oscar Carmona appointed António de Oliveira Salazar (1889-1970) as finance minister. A former professor of economics and law at the University of Coimbra, Salazar balanced the budget and the interests of the country's often-warring factions. His skill and his reputation as a clean-living, fair-minded patriot earned him a promotion. In 1932, he became prime minister, and he set about creating his New State *(Estado Novo)*.

For nearly four decades, Salazar ruled a stable but isolated nation based on harmony between the traditional power blocs of the ruling class—the military, big business, large landowners, and the Catholic Church. This Christian fascism, backed by the military and secret police, was ratified repeatedly in elections by the country's voters—the richest 20 percent of the populace.

As a person, Salazar was respected, but not loved. The son of a farm manager, he originally studied to be a priest before going on to become a scholar and writer. He never married. Quiet, low-key, and unassuming, he attended church regularly and lived a nonmaterialistic existence. But when faced with opposition, he was ruthless, and his secret police became an object of fear and hatred.

Salazar steered Portugal through the turmoil of Spain's Civil War (1936-1939), remaining officially neutral while secretly supporting Franco's fascists. He detested Nazi Germany's "pagan" leaders, but respected Mussolini for reconciling with the pope. In World War II, Portugal was officially neutral, but was often friendly with longtime ally Britain and used as a base for espionage. After the war, it benefited greatly from the United States' Marshall Plan for economic recovery (which Spain missed out on during Franco's rule), and the country joined NATO in 1949.

Salazar distracted his poor and isolated masses with a cynical credo: *"Fado, Fátima, and Futebol"* (the three "Fs"). Salazar's regime was undone by two factors: the liberal 1960s and the unpopular, draining wars Portugal fought abroad to try to keep its colonial empire intact. When Salazar died in 1970, the regime that followed became increasingly less credible, leading to the liberating events of the Carnation Revolution in 1974.

South of Lisbon, Across the River

Cristo Rei (Christ of Majesty)—A huge, 330-foot concrete statue of Christ (à la Rio de Janeiro) overlooks Lisbon from across the
Rio Tejo, stretching its arms wide to symbolically bless the city (or
as less reverent Portuguese say, "to dive into the river"). Lisbon's
cardinal, inspired by a visit to Rio de Janeiro in 1936, wanted a replica built back home. Increased support came after an appeal was
made to Our Lady of Fátima in 1940 to keep Portugal out of World
War II. Portugal survived the war relatively unscathed, and funds
were collected to build this statue in appreciation. After 10 years
of construction, it opened to the public in 1959. It's now a sanctuary and pilgrimage site, and the chapel inside holds regular Sunday Mass. The statue was designed to be seen from a distance, and
there's little reason to go to the trouble of actually visiting it. If you
do visit, an elevator will take you to the top for a panoramic view:
From left to right, see Belém, the 25th of April Bridge, downtown
Lisbon (Praça do Comércio and the green Alfama hilltop with the
castle), and the long Vasco da Gama Bridge.

LISBON

Cost and Hours: €4, daily 9:30-18:00, tel. 212-751-000.

Getting There: To get to Cristo Rei, catch the 10-minute
ferry from downtown Lisbon to Cacilhas (€2, 4/hour, more during
rush hour, from Cais do Sodré Metro/train station follow signs to
Terminal Fluvial, which serves many destinations). The bus marked
101 Cristo Rei takes you to the base of the statue in 15 minutes (3/
hour, exit ferry dock left into the maze of bus stops to find the
#20 stop with the "101 Cristo Rei" schedule under the awning).
Because of bridge tolls to enter Lisbon, taxis from the site are expensive. Consider taking a late-morning ferry to Cristo Rei; catch
a taxi from the statue to Porto Brandão and have lunch there (see
page 100); and ferry direct to Belém and see the sights. Ferries also
go direct from Cacilhas to Belém. For drivers, the most efficient
visit is a quick stop on your way to or from the Algarve.

Belém District

Three miles west of downtown Lisbon, the Belém district is a
stately pincushion of important sights from Portugal's Golden
Age, when Vasco da Gama and company turned the country into
Europe's richest power. Belém was the send-off point for voyages
in the Age of Discovery. Sailors would stay and pray here before
embarking. The tower welcomed them home. The grand buildings
of Belém survived the great 1755 earthquake, so this is the best
place to experience the grandeur of pre-earthquake Lisbon. After
the earthquake, safety-conscious (and rattled) royalty chose to live
here—in wooden rather than stone buildings. The modern-day
president of Portugal calls Belém home.

To celebrate the 300th anniversary of independence from

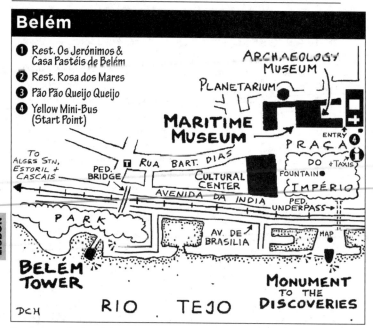

Belém

1. Rest. Os Jerónimos & Casa Pastéis de Belém
2. Rest. Rosa dos Mares
3. Pão Pão Queijo Queijo
4. Yellow Mini-Bus (Start Point)

Spain, a grand exhibition was held here in 1940, resulting in the fine parks, fountains, and monuments. Nearly all of Belém's museums are closed on Monday (though the Monument to the Discoveries is open Mon May-Sept).

Getting to Belém

You'll get here quickest by taxi (€15 from downtown). Buses #714 and #728 serve Belém, but I prefer riding the slower and cheaper trolley #15E (30 minutes, catch at Praça da Figueira or Praça do Comércio). In Belém, the first trolley stop is at the National Coach Museum, the second is at the Monastery of Jerónimos, and another is two blocks inland from the Belém Tower. Even if you miss the first stop (subtly named "Belém"), you can't miss the second stop at the massive monastery.

Consider doing Belém in this order: the National Coach Museum, pastry and coffee break, Monastery of Jerónimos, Maritime Museum (if interested) and/or lunch at its cafeteria (public access, museum entry not required), Monument to the Discoveries, and Belém Tower. If arriving by taxi, start at Belém Tower, the farthest point, and do the recommended lineup in reverse, ending at the National Coach Museum. Belém also has a cultural center, a children's museum, and a planetarium—not priorities for a quick visit. For recommended eateries in this area, see page 99.

When you're through, hop on trolley #15E or bus #714 to return to Praça da Figueira or Praça do Comércio. Bus #728 takes

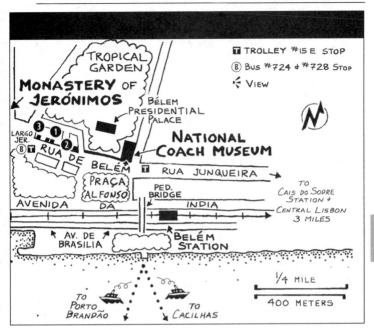

you to Santa Apolónia Station, and continues to Parque das Nações and Oriente Station.

Tourist Information

The little TI kiosk is directly across the street from the entrance to the monastery (Tue-Sat 10:00-13:00 & 14:00-18:00, closed Sun-Mon, tel. 213-658-437).

A little **Yellow Bus Tour** mini-bus offers a handy hop-on, hop-off tour around the Belém sights—which can feel far-flung if you're tired—departing every hour from the monastery entrance (€5, includes multi-language audioguide; Mon-Fri hourly 9:30-12:30 & 14:00-17:00, exact pickup times listed at each stop; you can get off to explore a sight and catch the next mini-bus).

▲▲National Coach Museum

In 1905, the last Queen of Portugal saw that cars would soon obliterate horse-drawn carriages as a form of transportation. She decided to use the palace's riding-school building to preserve her fine collection of royal coaches, which became today's National Coach Museum (Museu dos Coches). A new, larger museum is being built kitty-corner from the present location and is expected to open sometime in 2013. The following description is based on the current configuration; if you visit after the new building opens, request a map as you enter.

Cost and Hours: €5, free Sun until 14:00, Tue-Sun 10:00-

The Carnation Revolution

António Salazar, who ruled Portugal from 1926 to 1968, was modern Europe's longest-ruling dictator (he died in 1970). Salazar's authoritarian regime, the Estado Novo, continued in power under Prime Minister Marcelo Caetano until 1974.

By the 1970s, all the fighting in Portugal's far-flung colonies over the past decade had demoralized much of Salazar's military, and at home, there was a growing appetite for a modern democracy. On April 25, 1974, several prominent members of the military reluctantly sided with a growing popular movement to oust the government. Their withdrawal of support spelled the end of the Salazar era. Only five people died that April day, in a well-planned, relatively bloodless coup. Citizens spilled into the streets to cheer and put flowers in soldiers' rifle barrels, giving the event its name: the Carnation Revolution. Suddenly, people were free to speak aloud what they formerly could only whisper in private.

In the revolution's aftermath, the country struggled to get the hang of modern democracy. Their economy suffered as overseas colonies fell to nationalist uprisings, flooding the country with some 800,000 emigrants. For colonial overlords, life went from "shrimp day and night" to a sudden collapse of the empire; for their own safety, they fled back to Portugal. A good number of these "returnees" didn't fit into their newly democratic old country—feeling like people without a homeland, many ultimately left Portugal (joining Salazar's henchmen, who took refuge in Brazil). Even those who stayed were generally pro-dictator and angry about the revolution, contributing to a polarization of modern Portuguese society that exists to this day.

In 1976, the Portuguese adopted a constitution that separated church and state. These changes helped to break down the almost-medieval class system and establish parliamentary law. Mario Soares, a former enemy of the Salazar regime, became the new prime minister, ruling as a stabilizing presence through much of the next two decades. Today, Portugal is enthusiastically democratic.

18:00, closed Mon, last entry 30 minutes before closing, tel. 213-610-850, www.museudoscoches.pt.

Visiting the Museum: The collection is impressive, with more than 70 dazzling carriages (described in English) lining the elegant old riding room. Check out the ceiling, which is as remarkable as the carriages, and look for coach #1 (from around 1600). This crude and simple coach was once used by Philip II, king of Spain and Portugal, to shuttle between Madrid and Lisbon. Notice that the coach has no driver's seat—its drivers would actually ride the horses. You'll have to trust me on this, but if you lift up the cushion from the passengers' seat, you'll find a potty hole—also handy for road sickness. Imagine how slow and rough the ride would be with bad roads and a crude leather-strap suspension.

Study the evolution of suspension technology, starting with the first coach, or "Kotze," made in the 15th century in a Hungarian town of that name. Trace the improvement of coaches through the next century, noticing that as the decoration increases, so does the comfort. A Portuguese coat of arms indicates that a carriage was part of the royal fleet. Ornamentation often includes a folk festival of exotic faces from Portugal's distant colonies. Examples of period riding costumes are displayed in cases between many of the coaches.

At the far end of the first room, the lumbering Ocean Coach, as ornate as it is long, stands shining. At the stern, gold figures symbolize the Atlantic and Indian Oceans holding hands, a reminder of Portugal's mastery of the sea. The Ocean Coach is flanked by two equally stunning coaches with similar symbols of ocean exploration.

The second room shows sedan chairs and traces the development of carriages as a common means of transportation. They got lighter and faster, culminating in a sporty, horse-drawn Lisbon taxi.

Wander upstairs to get a glimpse of velvet-covered saddles and special riding gear designed for the royal kids. A spectacular view of the entire building interior is picture-perfect (no flash). The portrait gallery of most Portuguese royalty is handy for putting a face to all the movers and shakers you've read about so far.

Nearby: A taxi stand is across the street. The National Coach Museum is on Rua de Belém, which is also home to the monastery, the guarded entry to Portugal's presidential palace, some fine pre-earthquake buildings, and a famous pastry shop—an obligatory stop for those with a sweet tooth (see page 99).

▲▲▲Monastery of Jerónimos

King Manuel (who ruled from 1495) erected this giant, white limestone church and monastery—which stretches 300 yards along the Lisbon waterfront—as a "thank you" for the discoveries made by early Portuguese explorers. It was financed in part with "pepper money," a 5 percent tax on spices brought back from India. Manuel built the church on the

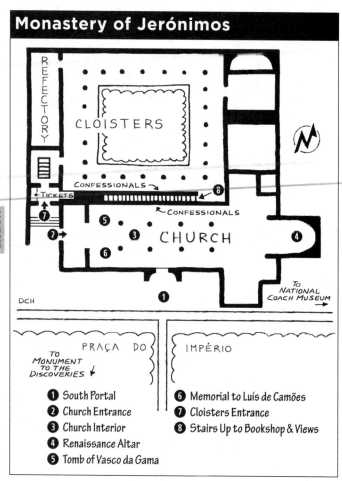

Monastery of Jerónimos

REFECTORY

CLOISTERS

CONFESSIONALS →

TICKETS

← CONFESSIONALS

8 Stairs Up to Bookshop & Views

7 Cloisters Entrance

CHURCH

5 Tomb of Vasco da Gama

3 Church Interior

4 Renaissance Altar

6 Memorial to Luís de Camões

2 Church Entrance

1 South Portal

To NATIONAL COACH MUSEUM

DCH

PRAÇA DO   IMPÉRIO

TO MONUMENT TO THE DISCOVERIES ↓

1 South Portal
2 Church Entrance
3 Church Interior
4 Renaissance Altar
5 Tomb of Vasco da Gama
6 Memorial to Luís de Camões
7 Cloisters Entrance
8 Stairs Up to Bookshop & Views

LISBON

site of a humble chapel where sailors spent their last night ashore in prayer before embarking on frightening voyages. What is the style of Manuel's church? Manueline.

Cost and Hours: The church is free, but the cloisters cost €7. A €10 combo-ticket saves you €2 if you also visit the Tower of Belém (both free Sun until 14:00, hours for both: May-Sept Tue-Sun 10:00-18:30, off-season until 17:30, closed Mon, last entry 30 minutes before closing, www.mosteirojeronimos.pt).

❷ **Self-Guided Tour:** Here's a tour, starting outside the monastery:

❶ **South Portal:** The fancy portal, facing the street, is textbook Manueline. Henry the Navigator stands between the doors with the king's patron saint, St. Jerome (above on the left, with the lion). Henry (Manuel's uncle) built the original sailors' chapel on this site. This door is only used when Mass lets out or for Saturday weddings. (The electronic snapping sound you hear is designed to keep the pigeons away.)

❷ **Church Entrance:** As you approach the main entrance, the church is on your right and the cloisters are straight ahead. Flanking the church door are kneeling statues of King Manuel I, the Fortunate (left of door, with St. Jerome), and his wife, Maria (right, with John the Baptist).

❸ **Church Interior:** The Manueline style is on the cusp of the Renaissance. The space is more open than earlier medieval churches. Slender, palm tree-like columns don't break the interior space (as Gothic columns would), and the ceiling is all one height. Motifs from the sea hide in the decor. The sea brought Portugal 16th-century wealth and power, making this art possible. You'll see rope-like arches, ships, and monsters that evoke the mystery of undiscovered lands. Artichokes, eaten for their vitamin C to fend off scurvy, remind us of the hardships sailors faced at sea.

❹ **Renaissance Altar:** Nearly everything here survived the 1755 earthquake, except for the stained glass (the replacement glass is from 1940). In the main altar, elephants—the Oriental symbol of power, which dethroned lions as the most powerful and kingly of beasts—support two kings and two queens (King Manuel I is front-left). Many Portuguese churches (such as the cathedrals in downtown Lisbon and Évora) were renovated in Renaissance and Baroque times, resulting in an odd mix of dark, older naves and pretty pastel altars. Walk back on the side with the seven wooden confessional doors (on your right). Notice the ornamental carving around the second one: a festival of faces from newly discovered corners of the world. Ahead of you (near the entry, under a ceiling that's a veritable *Boy Scout's Handbook* of rope and knots) is the...

❺ **Tomb of Vasco da Gama:** On the night of July 7, 1497, da Gama (1460-1524) prayed for a safe voyage, in the small chapel that stood here before the current church was built. The next day, he set sail from Belém with four ships (see the caravel carved in the middle of the tomb's side) and 150 men. He was armed with state-of-the-art maps and sailing technology, such as the carved armillary sphere, a globe surrounded by movable rings designed to determine the positions of the sun or other stars to help sailors track their location on earth. (Some say its diagonal slash is symbolic of the unwritten pact and ambition of Spain and Portugal to split the world evenly, but it actually represents the path of the planets as they move across the heavens.)

Da Gama's mission? To confirm what earlier navigators had hypothesized—that the ocean recently discovered when Bartolomeu Dias rounded Africa was the same one seen by overland

Manueline Architecture (c. 1480-1580)

Portugal's unique style (from its peak of power under King Manuel I, the Fortunate, r. 1495-1521) reflects the wealth of the times and the many cultural influences of the Age of Discovery. The purpose is decorative, not structural. Whether the building uses pointed Gothic or round Renaissance arches, it can be embellished with elaborate Manueline carved stonework, particularly around windows and doors.

Manueline aesthetic is ornate, elaborate, and intertwined, often featuring symbols from a family's coat of arms (shields with castles, crosses, lions, banners, and crowns) or motifs from the sea (rope-like columns or borders, knots, shells, coral, anchors, and nets). Manuel's personal symbol was the armillary sphere—a globe of the earth surrounded by movable rings—which was an indispensable navigational aid for sailors. You'll also see imports of the age from opium poppies to strange animals.

Architecture students will recognize elements from Gothic's elaborate tracery, the abstract designs of Moorish culture, similarities to Spain's intricate Plateresque style (which dates from the same time), and the elongated excesses of Italian Mannerism.

travelers to India. Hopefully, da Gama would find a direct sea route to the vast, untapped wealth of Asia. The symbols on the tomb show the icons of the period—the cross (symbolizing the religious military order of the soldier monks who funded these voyages), the caravel (representing the method of travel), and Portugal's trading power around the globe (the result).

By Christmas, da Gama rounded the Cape of Good Hope. After battling hostile Arabs in Mozambique, he hired an Arab guide to pilot the ships to India, arriving on the southwest coast in Calicut (from which we get the word "calico") in May of 1498. He traded for spices, networked with the locals for future outposts, battled belligerent chiefs, and then headed back home. Da Gama and his crew arrived home to Lisbon in September of 1499 (after two years and two months on the seas), and were greeted with all-out Vasco-mania. The few spices he'd returned with (many were lost in transit) were worth a staggering fortune. Portugal's Golden Age was launched.

King Manuel dubbed da Gama "Admiral of the Sea of India" and sent him out again, this time to subdue the Indian people, establish more trade outposts, and again return home to wealth and honor. Da Gama died on Christmas Eve 1524, in India. His memory lives on due to the tribute of two men: Manuel, who built this large church, and Luís de Camões (honored opposite Vasco), who turned da Gama's history-making voyage into an epic poem.

❻ Memorial to Luís de Camões: Camões (kah-MOISH, 1524-1580) is Portugal's Shakespeare and Casanova rolled into one, an adventurer and writer whose heroic poems glorifying the nation's sailing exploits live on today. It was Camões who described Portugal as the place "where land ends and the sea begins."

After college at Coimbra, Camões was banished from the court (1546) for flirting with the noble lady Dona Caterina. He lost an eye soldiering in Morocco (he's always portrayed squinting), served jail time for brawling with a bureaucrat, and then caught a ship to India and China, surviving a shipwreck on the way. While serving as a colonial administrator in India, he plugged away at the epic poem that would become his masterpiece. Returning to Portugal, he published *The Lusiads* (*Os Lusíadas*, 1572), winning minor recognition and a small pension.

The long poem describes Vasco da Gama's first voyage to India in heroic terms, on the scale of Homer's *Odyssey*. *The Lusiads* begins:

> *Arms and the heroes, from Lisbon's shore,*
> *sailed through seas never dared before,*
> *with awesome courage, forging their way*
> *to the glorious kingdoms of the rising day.*

The poem goes on to recite many events in Portuguese history, from the time of the Lusiads (the original pre-Roman natives) onward. Even today, Camões' words are quoted by modern Portuguese politicians in search of a heroic sound bite. And Portugal's national holiday, June 10, is known as Camões Day, remembering the day in 1580 when the great poet died. The stone monument here—with literary rather than maritime motifs—is a cenotaph (his actual burial spot is unknown).

❼ Cloisters: Leave the church (turn right), purchase your ticket, and enter the cloisters. These restored cloisters are the architectural highlight of Belém. The lacy arcade is Manueline; the simpler diamond and decorative rose frieze above the top floor is Renaissance. Study the carvings, especially the gargoyles above the lower set of arches. Among these functioning rainspouts, find a monkey,

a kitten, and a cricket. The small basin in the corner (where the monks washed up before meals) marks the entrance to the refectory, or dining hall—today an occasional concert venue lined with fine 18th-century tiles. The tiles are considered textbook Rococo (from the French word for "shell," as you can see). Rococo ignores the parameters set by the architecture, unlike Baroque, which works within the structure.

To the left of the refectory is the burial spot of Portugal's most revered modern poet, Fernando Pessoa (see sidebar on page 54). Continuing around, a large room contains an exhibit of the lengthy restoration process, as well as the tomb of Alexandre Herculano, a Romantic 19th-century poet. Quotes from Herculano adorn his tomb: "Sleep? Only the cold cadaver that doesn't feel sleeps. The soul flies and wraps itself around the feet of the All-Powerful."

Heads of state are often received in the cloisters with a warm welcome. This is also the site of many important treaty signings, such as Portugal's admittance to the European Union in 1986.

❽ **Upstairs:** You'll find a bookshop, WCs (women's upstairs, men's downstairs—guys, watch your head), and better views of the church and the cloisters, along with exhibits about the monastery's history.

Monks often accompanied the sailor-pirates on their trading/pillaging trips, hoping to convert the heathens to Christianity. Many expeditions were financed by the Knights of Christ, a brotherhood of soldier monks. (The monks who inhabited these cloisters were Hieronymites—followers of St. Jerome, hence the monastery name of Jerónimos.)

King Manuel, who did so much to promote exploration, was also the man who forcibly expelled all Jews from the country. (In 1497, the Church agreed to allow him to marry a Spanish princess on the condition that he deport the Jews.) Francis Xavier, a Spanish Jesuit, did much of his missionary work traveling in Asia in the service of Portugal.

It was a time of extreme Christian faith. The sheer size of this religious complex is a testament to the zealous motivation that—along with money—propelled the Age of Discovery.

Age of Discovery Sights

▲**Maritime Museum (Museu de Marinha)**—If you're interested in Portugal's historic ships and navigational tools, this museum, which fills the west wing of the Monastery of Jerónimos (listed earlier) and has good English descriptions, is worth a look. Sailors love it.

Cost and Hours: €5, free Sun 10:00-14:00; open April-Sept Tue-Sun 10:00-18:00, off-season until 17:00, closed Mon; facing

Portugal Explores the Sea

VOYAGES
1 ..... DIAS 1488
2 ••• DA GAMA 1498
3 —·— CABRAL 1500
4 --- MAGELLAN 1522

the planetarium from the square, a cafeteria—open to the public—
is to your left and the museum entrance is to your right.

▲**Monument to the Discoveries (Padrão dos Descobrimentos)**—In 1960, the city honored the 500th anniversary of the death of Prince Henry the Navigator by rebuilding this giant riverside monument, which had originally been constructed for the 1940 World Expo (see photo on page 98; reached from the monastery via a pedestrian tunnel under the busy boulevard). The elevator inside takes you up to a tingly view.

Cost and Hours: €3; May-Sept daily 10:00-19:00; Oct-April Tue-Sun 10:00-18:00, closed Mon; last entry 30 minutes before closing, tel. 213-031-950.

Visiting the Monument: Walk around the huge monument. The 170-foot concrete structure shows that exploring the world was a team effort. The men who braved the unknown stand on the pointed, raised prow of a caravel, about to be launched into the Rio Tejo.

Leading the charge is Prince Henry the Navigator (for more about him, see page 158), holding a model of a caravel and a map, followed by kneeling kings and soldiers who Christianized foreign lands with the sword. Behind Henry (on the west side, away from bridge), find the men who financed the voyages (King Manuel I, holding an armillary sphere, his personal symbol), those who glorified it in poems and paintings (like Luís de Camões, holding a

Caravels

These easily maneuverable trading ships were fast, small (80 feet), and light (100 tons), with few guns and three triangular-shaped sails (called lateen-rigged sails) that could pivot quickly to catch the wind. They were ideal for sailing along coastlines. Many oceangoing caravels were also rigged with a square foresail to make them more stable. (This photo shows the model held by Prince Henry on Belém's Monument to the Discoveries.) Columbus' *Niña* and *Pinta* were re-rigged caravels.

poem), and, at the very end, the only woman, Philippa of Lancaster, Henry's British mother.

On the east side (closest to bridge—as you walk, notice the optical illusion of waves on the flat cobbled surface), Vasco da Gama stands with his eyes on the horizon and his hand on his sword. Magellan holds a circle, representing the round earth his ship circumnavigated, while in front of him, Pedro Cabral puts his hand to his heart, thankful to have (perhaps accidentally) discovered Brazil. Various monks, navigators with maps, and crusaders with flags complete the crew. Check out the pillory, decorated with the Portuguese coat of arms and a cross, erected in each place discovered by the Portuguese—leaving no doubt as to who was in charge.

In the **marble map in the pavement** (a gift from South Africa) in front of the Monument to the Discoveries, follow Portugal's explorers as they inched out into monster-infested waters at the edge of the world. From their tiny, isolated nation in Europe, the Portuguese first headed south to the coast of Morocco, conquering the Muslims of Ceuta in God's name (1415), and gaining strategic control of the mouth of the Mediterranean. They braved the open Atlantic to the west and southwest, stumbling on the Madeiras (1420), which Prince Henry planted with vineyards, and the remote Azore Islands (1427).

Meanwhile, the Portuguese slowly moved southward, hugging the African coast, each voyage building on the knowledge from previous expeditions. They cleared the biggest psychological hump when Gil Eanes sailed around Cape Bojador (Western Sahara, 1434)—the border of the known world—and into the equatorial seas where it was thought that sea monsters lurked, no winds blew, and ships would be incinerated in the hot sun. Eanes survived, returning home with 200 Africans in chains, the first of what would become a lucrative, abhorrent commodity. Two generations later, Bartolomeu Dias rounded the southern tip of Africa (1488), discovering the sea route to Asia that Vasco da Gama (1498) and others would exploit to colonize India, Indonesia, Japan, and China (Macao in 1557, on the south coast).

In 1500, Pedro Cabral (along with Dias and 1,200 men) took a wi-i-i-ide right turn on the way down the African coast, hoping to avoid windless seas, and landed on the tip of Brazil. Brazil proved to be an agricultural goldmine for Portugal, which profited from sugar plantations worked by African slaves. Two hundred years later, gold and gemstones were discovered in Brazil, jumpstarting the Portuguese economy again.

In 1520, Portuguese Ferdinand Magellan, employed by Spain, sailed west with five ships and 270 men, broke for R&R in Rio, continued through the Straits of Magellan (tip of South America), and suffered through mutinies, scurvy, and dinners of sawdust and ship rats before touching land in Guam. Magellan was killed in battle in the Philippines, but one remaining ship continued west and arrived back in Europe, having circumnavigated the globe after 30 months at sea.

By 1560, Portugal's global empire had peaked. Tiny-but-filthy-rich Portugal claimed (though they didn't actually occupy) the entire coastline of Africa, Arabia, India, the Philippines, and south China—a continuous stretch from Lisbon to Macao—plus Brazil. The Treaty of Tordesillas (1494) with Spain divvied up the colonial world between the two nations, split at 45 degrees west longitude (bisecting South America—and explaining why Brazil speaks Portuguese and the rest of the continent speaks Spanish) and 135 degrees east longitude (bisecting the Philippines and Australia).

But all of the wealth was wasted on Portugal's ruling class, who neglected to reinvest it in the future. Easy money ruined the traditional economy and stunted industry, hurting the poor. Over the next four centuries, one by one, Portugal's colonies were lost to other European nations or to local revolutions. Today, only the (largely autonomous) islands of the Azores and Madeiras remain from the once-global empire.

▲**Belém Tower**—Perhaps the purest Manueline building in Portugal (built 1515-1520), this white tower protected Lisbon's harbor. Today it symbolizes the voyages that made Lisbon powerful, with carved stone representing ropes, Manuel's coat of arms, armillary spheres, and shields with the cross of Manuel's military, called the Order of the Cross.

Cost and Hours: €5, €10 combo-ticket saves you €2 if you also visit the cloisters at the Monastery of Jerónimos, free Sun until 14:00, May-Sept Tue-Sun 10:00-18:30, off-season until 17:30, closed Mon, last entry 30 minutes before closing, tel. 213-620-034.

The Age of Discovery

In 1660, you could sail from Lisbon to China without ever losing sight of land explored by Portugal. The riches of the world poured into the tiny nation—spices from India and Java (black pepper, cinnamon, and curry powder); ivory, diamonds, and slaves (sold to New World plantations) from Africa; sugarcane, gold, and diamonds from Brazil; and, from everywhere, knowledge of new plants, animals, and customs. How did tiny Portugal pull this off?

First, its people were motivated by greed, hoping to break the Arab and Venetian monopoly on Eastern luxury goods (the price of pepper was jacked up 1,000 percent by the time it reached European dinner tables). They were also driven by a crusading Christian spirit, a love of science, and a spirit of adventure. An entire 15th-century generation was obsessed with finding the legendary kingdom of the fabulously wealthy Christian named "Prester John," supposedly located in either India or Africa. (The legend may be based on a historical figure from around 1120 who visited the pope in Rome as "patriarch of India.")

Portugal also had certain natural advantages. Its Atlantic location led to a strong maritime tradition. A unified nation-state (one of Europe's first) financed and coordinated expeditions. And a core of technology-savvy men used and developed their expansive knowledge of navigational devices, astronomy, maps, shipbuilding, and languages.

Visiting the Tower: This was the last sight sailors saw as they left, and the first as they returned, loaded with gold, spices, and social diseases. When the tower was built, the river went nearly to the walls of the monastery, and the tower was mid-river. Its interior is pretty bare, but the views of the bridge, river, and Cristo Rei statue are worth the 120 steps.

The floatplane on the grassy lawn is a monument to the first flight across the South Atlantic (Portugal to Brazil) in 1922. The original plane (which beat Charles Lindbergh's *Spirit of Saint Louis* across the North Atlantic by five years) is in Belém's Maritime Museum.

If you're choosing between towers, the Monument to the Discoveries is probably the better choice, because it offers a better view of the monastery. Both towers are interesting to see from the outside, whether or not you go up.

Eating in Belém

You'll find snack bars at Belém Tower, a cafeteria at the Maritime Museum, and fun little restaurants along Rua de Belém, between the National Coach Museum and the monastery.

Restaurante Os Jerónimos is a busy little place good for fresh fish. Hardworking Carlos treats his customers well and serves fine €12 meals including drinks. Trust him for suggestions (Sun-Fri 12:00-22:30, closed Sat, Rua de Belém 74, tel. 213-638-423, next to pastry place described below).

Restaurante Rosa dos Mares is an old favorite in a new location, and a good option for tasty, fresh fish. Try the grilled codfish with cream sauce (€14) or the *arroz marisco* (seafood rice, €36) for two people (€10-12 fish-and-meat plates, Tue-Sat 12:00-22:30, Sun 12:00-18:00, closed Mon, Rua de Belém 2-4, tel. 213-621-811).

Pão Pão Queijo Queijo ("Bread Bread Cheese Cheese") serves quick and tasty sandwiches, salads, kebabs, and shawarma sandwiches for less than €5. Eat at tables outside, in the crowded upstairs dining room, or better yet, get it to go and picnic in the park across the street (€8 combo plates, Tue-Sat 10:00-24:00, Sun 10:00-20:00, closed Mon, Rua de Belém 124-126). Many more fine places with outdoor seating are in the restaurant row behind the McDonald's that faces the park.

The **Casa Pastéis de Belém** café is the birthplace of the wonderful custard tart that's called *pastel de nata* throughout Portugal, but here is dubbed *pastel de Belém*. Since 1837, residents have come to this café to get their tarts warm out of the oven (€1.05 each, daily 8:00-24:00, Rua de Belém 84-92, tel. 213-637-423). This place's popularity stems mainly from the fact that their recipe is a closely guarded secret—supposedly only three people know the exact proportions of ingredients. While the recipe is fine, my hunch is that the explanation for their undeniable goodness is simply that, because they crank out 20,000 or so a day, you get them fresh and crunchy, literally hot out of the oven. (Take one back to your hotel and eat it tonight and it tastes about like any other in town.) Sit down and enjoy one with a *café com leite*. Sprinkle on as much cinnamon and powdered sugar as you like. If the to-go line is too long, there's plenty of seating in the café and perhaps faster service (if you need a WC, this is an easy choice). You can also often save time by lining up not at the front counter but on the backside of the counter.

Ferry from Belém to Porto Brandão

For a delightfully untouristy little adventure, consider having lunch across the river in **Porto Brandão.** The ferry terminal is immediately in front of the National Coach Museum, across a busy road and train tracks (€1.65 each way, 8-minute cruise, ferries depart on the hour and half hour except hourly from 13:30-15:30, last ferry departs 23:00 weekdays and 22:00 weekends; for a memorable Tejo experience, tall men can use the urinal while sticking their head out the porthole). Boats continue to Trafaria before returning to Belém via Porto Brandão. Upon arrival, carefully confirm return times.

Porto Brandão is a tiny (and dead) three-street town whose harborfront square has several good fish restaurants. I like cozy, blue-and-white-tiled **Restaurante Porto Brandão** (€10-20 fish meals, daily 12:00-15:00 & 18:00-23:00, Rua Bento Jesus Caraça 25, tel. 212-959-145). Their *bacalhau à lagareiro* is for garlic lovers. The *cataplana* (a traditional fish-and-veggie stew) and seafood fondue meals are made for two but stuff three (€15-20/person).

Shopping in Lisbon

Lisbon—Portugal's capital city—has shopping opportunities that run the gamut from flea markets to the country's biggest shopping mall.

Produce Market—The market closest to downtown is Mercado da Ribeira (Mon-Sat 6:00-14:00, closed for produce on Sun but open for a coin collectors' market, Metro: Cais do Sodré).

Flea Markets—On Tuesdays and Saturdays, the Feira da Ladra flea market attracts bargain hunters to Campo de Santa Clara in the Alfama (8:00-15:00, best in morning). A coin market jingles at Mercado da Ribeira, listed above, on Cais do Sodré (Sun 9:00-13:00).

Vasco da Gama Mall—This finest shopping mall in town fills the grand entryway to the 1998 World Expo site at the Oriente train/Metro station. It's well worth a trip out here to feel the pulse of today's Portuguese society, enjoy **Parque das Nações,** and take in the modern architecture (daily 9:00-24:00, mall described on page 80).

Centro Colombo Shopping Mall—This is the largest shopping center in Spain or Portugal. More than 400 shops—including FNAC's biggest department store, 10 cinemas, 60 restaurants, and a health club—sit atop what they claim is Europe's biggest underground parking lot and under a vast, entertaining play center. There's plenty to amuse children here, and the place offers a fine look at workaday Lisbon (shops open daily 10:00-22:00, food court and cinemas remain open until 24:00, pick up a map at info desk,

Metro: Colégio Militar/Luz takes you right there, tel. 217-113-636).

Armazéns do Chiado—This shopping center's six luxurious floors connect Lisbon's lower and upper towns. It's a stop on "The Bairro Alto and Chiado Stroll" described earlier in this chapter, and has a lively food court on the sixth floor. The FNAC department store hides behind an old facade and is known for its helpful English-speaking staff.

Here's how to find the mall: If you approach from Chiado, take Rua Garrett, which dead-ends at the main entrance. If coming from the Baixa, head up Rua Assunção toward the mall, where you'll find three subtle entrances on Rua do Crucifixo—through the Sports Zone store (take their escalators up into the mall), at #113, or at #89 (where small, simple, unmarked doorways lead to elevators). The mall is open daily 10:00-22:00 (eateries about 12:00-23:00, www.armazensdochiado.com).

A Vida Portuguesa—Located just two blocks from the Armazéns do Chiado shopping center, this is the best shop I found for genuine traditional Portuguese products, from stationery and toiletries to toys and jewelry (Mon-Sat 10:00-20:00, closed Sun, Rua Anchieta 11, tel. 213-465-073, www.avidaportuguesa.com).

El Corte Inglés—The Spanish mega-department store has arrived in Lisbon with a huge store at the top of Edward VII Park. Inside, there's an enormous supermarket with great picnic supplies, a food court, and a cinema (Mon-Sat 10:00-22:00, closed Sun, Avenida António Augusto de Aguiar 31, Metro: São Sebastião, near Gulbenkian Museum, tel. 213-711-700).

Entertainment in Lisbon

Nightlife

Nightlife in the Baixa seems to be little more than loitering prostitutes and litter stirred by the wind. Head instead up to the Bairro Alto for fado halls, bars, and the Miradouro de São Pedro de Alcântara (view terrace), a pleasant place to hang out. Nearby Rua Diario de Noticias is lined with busy bars and fun crowds spilling onto the street.

The Docas—The trendy hot spot for Lisbon's young people is the dock district under the 25th of April Bridge. The Docas (DOH-kash) is a 400-yard-long strip of warehouses turned into pricey restaurants and nightclubs (particularly Doca de Alcântara and Doca de Santo Amaro). Popular places include Hawaii, Buddha, Havana, and Doca 6 (catch a taxi or trolley #15E from Praça da Figueira to the Avenida Infante Santo stop, take overpass, then a 10-minute walk toward bridge; or bus #714 from Praça da Figueira, ask driver for *"Paragem Docas"*). If you're returning late, night bus

#201 starts at 1:00 in the morning, and runs every 30 minutes to Cais do Sodré, where you can walk 15 minutes or connect with night bus #205 or #207 to Rossio.

Pink Street—This happening, crazy street (much easier to get to than the Docas) is a block inland from Praça Duque da Terceira in the Cais do Sodré neighborhood. Rua Nova do Carvalho, otherwise known as "Pink Street," was once notorious as the sailors' red-light zone. Now the prostitutes are just painted onto the walls and the made-over street is painted a bright pink. After the bars in other neighborhoods close, late-night revelers hike 10 minutes from Chiado down Rua do Alecrim to reach Pink Street. Surrounded by largely uninhabited Pombaline buildings, Pink Street's four bars are lively late each night.

Pensão Amor ("House of Love"), wallpapered with sexy memories of the days when it was a brothel, is a grungy tangle of corners to hang out in and enjoy a drink (or just stare at the wallpaper), often against a backdrop of live jazz (Rua Nova do Carvalho 38, also possible to enter from top at Rua do Alecrim 19, tel. 213-143-399).

Sol e Pesca Bar, a nostalgic reminder of the sailor-and-fisherman heritage of this street, sells drinks and preserved food in tins. Just browse the shelves of classic €1-6 tinned seafood—from pâté and sardines to caviar—and wash down your salty seafood tapas with a glass of wine amid the lures and nets (Rua Nova do Carvalho 44, tel. 213-467-203).

Bar de Velha Senhora ("The Old Lady") is a dark bar with a busy little stage where you're likely to hear jazz or classical music, or even see a burlesque show (no cover, Rua Nova do Carvalho 38, tel. 213-468-479).

Povo Lisboa is a simple bar with fado most nights from 21:30 (no cover, just buy a drink, light food, Rua Nova do Carvalho 32, tel. 213-473-403).

Evening Stroll—While not as big a deal as in Spain, the people of Lisbon enjoy an early evening stroll after work and before dinner when the weather is balmy. When it comes to weather, Lisboners are pretty spoiled. If it's even a little blustery, they'll likely stay in. But when it's nice, in the summer, you'll find lots of people out strolling. Three good places: Rua Augusta through the heart of the Baixa district; along the seaside promenade near the Belém Tower; and along the fine riverfront promenade at Parque das Nações.

▲▲Fado

Fado is the folk music of Lisbon's back streets. Since the mid-1800s, it's been the Lisbon blues—mournfully beautiful and haunting ballads about lost sailors, broken hearts, and bittersweet romance.

While generally sad, fado can also be jaunty...but in a nostalgic way.

Fado has become one of Lisbon's favorite late-night tourist traps, but it's easy to find a convivial and rustic bar without the high prices and tour groups. Both the Bairro Alto and the Alfama have small, informal fado restaurants. Go either for a late dinner (after 21:00) or an even later evening of drinks and music. Homemade "fado tonight" *(fado esta noite)* signs in Portuguese are good news, but even a restaurant filled with tourists can come with good food and fine fado. Prices for a fado performance vary greatly. Many have a steep cover charge, while others just bring out a late-night menu (with prices double those at lunch) and expect you to buy a meal. Appetizers, bread, or cheese that appear on your table aren't free—if you nibble, you'll pay. Send them back if you don't want to be charged. Assume any place recommended by a hotel has prices bloated by kickbacks.

Fado in the Bairro Alto
In the Bairro Alto, wander around Rua Diario de Noticias and neighboring streets. **Canto do Camões,** run by friendly, English-speaking Gabriel, is easy to reserve and has good music and tasty food. Call ahead to assure a seat (open at 20:00, music from 20:30 until around 1:00 in the morning; €27 meal required—includes appetizer, 3 courses, water, and wine; after 22:00 €11 minimum for two drinks; from Rua da Misericordia, go 2.5 blocks uphill on Travessa da Espera to #38, see map on page 119; tel. 213-465-464). When it's busy, the room feels like a stage show, with 25 or 30 tables filled mostly with tourists, all enjoying classic fado. Relax, spend some time, and close your eyes, or make eye contact with the singer. Let the music and wine collaborate.

Restaurante Adega do Ribatejo is a dark, homey place crowded with locals who enjoy open-mike fado *(fado vadio)* nightly (except Sun) from around 20:30 to 24:00. Just around the corner from Canto do Camões and less touristy (almost anti-touristy), you can sit down here and just pay for whatever you want to eat or drink with no required minimum (€15 meals, Mon-Sat from 19:00, closed Sun, Rua Diario de Noticias 23, see map on page 119, tel. 213-468-343).

Fado in the Alfama
While pretty lonely and dead after dark, the Alfama has several bars offering fado with their meals—just head uphill from the Fado Museum. Some bars are geared for tourists and tour groups, but others feel organic, spontaneous, and part of the neighborhood culture. While schedules at any particular place can be inconsistent, if you hike up Rua São Pedro de Alcântara to the Church of São

Fado

Fado songs reflect Portugal's bittersweet relationship with the sea. Fado means "fate"—how fate deals with Portugal's adventurers...and the women they leave behind. These are songs of both sadness and hope, a bittersweet emotion called *saudade* (meaning yearning or nostalgia). The lyrics reflect the pining for a loved one across the water, hopes for a future reunion, remembrances of a rosy past or dreams of a better future, and the yearning for what might have been if fate had not intervened. (Fado can also be bright and happy when the song is about the virtues of cities such as Lisbon or Coimbra, or of the warmth of a typical *casa portuguesa*.)

The songs are often in a minor key. The singer *(fadista)* is accompanied by a 12-string Portuguese *guitarra* (with a round body like a mandolin) or other stringed instruments unique to Portugal. Many singers crescendo into the first word of the verse, like a moan emerging from deep inside. Though the songs are often sad, the singers rarely overact—they plant themselves firmly and sing stoically in the face of fate.

A verse from a typical fado song goes:

O waves of the salty sea,
where do you get your salt?
From the tears shed by the women in black
on the beaches of Portugal.

Miguel, you'll hear the music wafting out from hole-in-the-wall eateries and be greeted by men hustling business for their fado restaurants. Generally you simply pay for the meal and enjoy the music as included entertainment.

My favorite Alfama fado experience is at a tiny, fun-loving restaurant called **A Baiuca.** It serves up spirited fado with traditional home-cooking. The menu and wine list are straightforward, but the pre-dinner munchies are costly—turn them away (€25 minimum for meal and fado, best singing Thu-Mon 20:00-24:00; reservations smart, in the heart of the Alfama, just off Rua São Pedro up the hill from Fado Museum, at Rua de São Miguel 20, see map on page 116, tel. 218-867-284, abaiuca@sapo.pt). This intimate place is a neighborhood affair—grandma dances with a bottle on her head, and the cooks gaze out of their steamy hole in the wall to catch the musical action. It's surround sound, as everyone seems to get into the music. If seats are still available after 22:30, English-speaking manager Henrique and his singer-wife Lydia welcome fado enthusiasts to grab a spot for simply the price of a drink (no cover). When the metal door is closed, they're full—but you can peek at the action through the window around to the left. If you like, sweet-talk the doorman and wait for someone to leave. The name *baiuca* (bay-YOO-kah) means a very rough tavern...the lowest grade of pub.

Clube de Fado is considered the launching pad for each generation's new fado stars, and the best place in town to hear quality fado. While a bit pricey, it just feels great, and there's not a bad seat in the house. Music plays every night in this formal yet intimate setting. When very busy, the musicians switch from between two adjacent halls, giving waiters time to serve between sets. Plan on spending €50 for dinner with wine, plus a €7.50 per-person cover charge for the music (meals from 20:00, dinner reservations required, music 21:30-2:00 in the morning; after 23:00, pay just a €10 cover charge plus cost of your drink; around corner from cathedral at Rua São João da Praça 94, see map on page 116, tel. 218-852-704).

Bullfights, Soccer, Concerts, and Movies

Tickets to all bullfights, soccer games, concerts, and other events are sold at the green **ABEP kiosk** at the southern end of Praça dos Restauradores (also posts a schedule of upcoming events in its windows).

▲▲▲**Portuguese Bullfight**—If you always felt sorry for the bull, this is Toro's Revenge: In a Portuguese bullfight, the matador is brutalized along with the bull. Lisbon hosts only about a dozen fights a year, but if you're in town for one, it's an unforgettable experience.

In Act I, the horseman *(cavaleiro)* skillfully plants four beribboned barbs in the bull's back while trying to avoid the leather-padded horns. The horses are the short, stocky Lusitano breed, with excellent balance. In Act II, a colorfully clad eight-man suicide squad (called *forçados*) enters the ring and lines up single file facing the bull. With testosterone sloshing everywhere, the leader taunts the bull—slapping his knees and yelling, *"touro!"*—then braces himself for a collision that can be heard all the way up in the cheap seats. As he hangs onto the bull's head, his buddies pile on, trying to wrestle the bull to a standstill. Finally, one guy hangs on to o *touro*'s tail and "water-skis" behind him. (In Act III, the *ambulância* arrives.)

Unlike the Spanish *corrida de toros*, the bull is not killed in front of the crowd at the Portuguese *tourada*...but it is killed later. (Some brave bulls with only superficial wounds are spared to fight another day.) Spanish aficionados insist that Portuguese fights are actually crueler, since they humiliate the bull, rather than fight him as a fellow warrior. Animal-rights groups enliven the scene before each fight.

The ring is small, so there are no bad seats. To sit nearly at ringside, try the cheapest *bancada* seats, on the generally half-empty and unmonitored main floor (Metro: Campo Pequeno). The ring is a spectacular, Moorish-domed brick structure that bears a resemblance to Madrid's bullring. After five years of remodeling, it reopened with a shopping mall underneath and a retractable roof overhead for concerts. It hosts a variety of restaurants inside, oddly including an Argentine steak restaurant. Maybe the beef served was in the ring earlier?

Fights are generally held on Thursday at 20:00 and on Sunday afternoons from Easter through September. Important note: Half the fights are simply Spanish-type *corridas* without the killing. For the real slam-bam Portuguese-style fight, confirm that there will be *grupo de forçados* ("bull grabbers"). Tickets are always available at the door (€20-50, no surcharge, tel. 217-932-143 to confirm; tickets sold at the ABEP kiosk on Praça dos Restauradores add a 10 percent surcharge).

Soccer—Lisbon is home to two *futebol* teams, Benfica and Sporting CP, which means there are lots of games (1-2/week Aug-May, tickets €20 and up) and lots of team spirit. Benfica, with the red jerseys, plays at the 65,400-seat Stadium of Light near the Centro Colombo mall (Estádio da Luz; Metro: Colegio Militar/Luz, www.slbenfica.pt). Sporting CP, with the green-and-white jerseys, plays at the 50,000-seat Estádio José Alvalade to the north of Lisbon's center (Metro: Campo Grande, www.sporting.pt). Tickets are generally available at the stadium or at the ABEP kiosk on Praça dos Restauradores.

Concerts—You can hear classical music by national and city orchestras at the Gulbenkian Museum (see page 75) and at the cultural center in Belém (www.ccb.pt). Traditional Portuguese theater plays in the National Theater on Rossio and in theaters along Rua das Portas de Santo Antão (the "eating lane"—see page 120) stretching north from Rossio. For popular music, these days you're more likely to find rock, jazz, Brazilian, and African music than traditional fado. The monthly *Agenda Cultural* provides the most up-to-date listing of world music, arts, and entertainment (free at TI, €0.50 at newsstands, in Portuguese only).

Movies—In Lisbon, unlike in Spain, most films are shown in the original language with subtitles. (That's one reason the Portuguese speak better English than the Spanish.) Many of Lisbon's theaters are classy, complete with assigned seats, ushers, and intermissions. Check the newspaper to see what's playing, or drop by the ABEP kiosk at Praça dos Restauradores, where a list of all the movies playing in town is taped to a side window (on the left). São Jorge Theater (midway up Avenida da Liberdade) is a grand old Art Deco movie palace showing choice cinema selected by the same cultural organization that runs the São Jorge Castle and the Monument to the Discoveries. More modern options are in malls or at the Monumental complex in the ritzy Saldanha neighborhood (Metro: Saldanha).

Sleeping in Lisbon

With a few exceptions, cheaper hotels downtown feel tired and well-worn. Singles cost nearly the same as doubles. If you're on a tight budget and want to stay in the center, consider Lisbon's famously classy hostels, which welcome travelers of all ages. Addresses such as 26-3 stand for building #26, third floor (which is the fourth floor in American terms). For locations of accommodations, see the map on page 110.

Be sure to book in advance if you'll be in Lisbon during its festival—Festas de Lisboa—the last three weeks of June, when parades, street parties, concerts, and fireworks draw crowds to the city. Conventions can clog Lisbon at any time.

In the Center
Central as can be, the Baixa district bustles with lots of shops, traffic, people, street musicians, pedestrian areas, and urban intensity.

On Rossio
$$$ Internacional Design Hotel has 55 hip, ultra-modern double rooms centrally located at the southeast corner of Rossio. Each of its four floors has a different theme—pop, Zen, tribal, and urban. I've listed its expensive rack rates, but you can often get a room for half-price by booking ahead online (Db-€120-400 depending on size, Db with pull-out child's bed-€500, buffet breakfast in bright room overlooking Rossio, air-con, elevator, free Wi-Fi, underground parking nearby-€15/day, Rue da Betesga 3, tel. 213-240-990, fax 213-240-999, www.idesignhotel.com, book@idesign hotel.com).

$$$ Hotel Métropole keeps its elegant 1920s style throughout 36 carefully appointed but slightly worn rooms. It's overpriced, but you're paying for the prime location. The quieter back rooms are

Sleep Code

(€1 = about $1.30, country code: 351)
S = Single, **D** = Double/Twin, **T** = Triple, **Q** = Quad, **b** = bathroom, **s** = shower only. Unless otherwise noted, credit cards
are accepted, English is spoken, and breakfast is included.

To help you easily sort through these listings, I've divided
the accommodations into three categories, based on the price
for a standard double room with bath during high season:

$$$ Higher Priced—Most rooms €115 or more.
$$ Moderately Priced—Most rooms between €65-115.
$ Lower Priced—Most rooms €65 or less.

Prices can change without notice; verify the hotel's current rates online or by email.

smaller, but cost the same unless you ask for a break. Prices drop
by a third in slow times. Don't be shy; ask for a 10 percent Rick
Steves discount when you reserve (Sb-€110-200, Db-€130-200,
extra bed-€50, check website for discounts, buffet breakfast, air-
con, elevator, Internet access, free Wi-Fi in lobby, Rossio 30, tel.
213-219-030, fax 213-469-166, www.almeidahotels.com, metro
pole@almeidahotels.com).

On Praça dos Restauradores

$$$ Hotel Avenida Palace, the most characteristic five-star
splurge in town, was built with Rossio Station in 1892 to greet big-
shot travelers. Back then, trains were new, and Rossio was the only
station in town. The lounges are sumptuous, dripping with chan-
deliers, and the 82 rooms mix elegance with 21st-century com-
forts (Sb-€190, Db-€215, 15 percent less July-Aug, more expensive
suites available, reserve on website for substantial discounts, air-
con, elevator, free in-room Wi-Fi, laundry service, free parking,
hotel's sign is on Praça dos Restauradores but entrance is at Rua 1
de Dezembro 123, tel. 213-218-115, fax 213-422-884, www.hotel
avenidapalace.pt, reservas@hotelavenidapalace.pt).

**$$$ VIP Executive Suites
Eden** rents 134 slick and contempo-
rary compact apartments (with small
kitchens). It has a rooftop swimming
pool and breakfast terrace with commanding city, castle, and river views.
The building used to be a 1930s cinema, hence the Art Deco architecture
and the slightly pie-shaped rooms.

Perfectly located at the Rossio end of Avenida da Liberdade, this is a clean, quiet pool of modernity amid the ramshackle charm of Lisbon. It's also an intriguing option for groups or families of four (Db studio-€95-129, 2-bedroom apartment with bed-and-sofa combo that can sleep 4 people-€139-189, breakfast-€9, includes taxes, check website for deals, air-con, elevator, Praça dos Restauradores 24, tel. 213-216-600, fax 213-216-666, www.viphotels. com, res.eden@viphotels.com).

Near Praça da Figueira

$$$ Hotel Lisboa Tejo (leezh-BO-ah TAY-zhoo) is an oasis of 58 comfy ocean-blue rooms with hardwood floors (Sb-€113, Db-€131, includes crowded buffet breakfast, 10 percent discount with this book when reserved direct through hotel, air-con, elevator, Internet access and Wi-Fi; from southeast corner of Praça da Figueira, walk one block down Rua dos Condes de Monsanto and turn left to Condes de Monsanto 2; tel. 218-866-182, fax 218-865-163, http://lisboatejohotel.com, reservas@lisboatejohotel.com).

$$ Grande Pensão Alcobia opened in 2006 with 44 crisp rooms. It offers a comfortable alternative to higher-priced hotels located in the same part of town, and some upper-floor rooms have views of São Jorge Castle (Sb-€45-60, Db-€50-80, Tb-€90-105, higher prices apply April-Oct, 10 percent discount with this book when reserved direct through hotel, air-con, small elevator, Internet access and Wi-Fi, Poço do Borratem 15, tel. 218-844-150, fax 218-864-201, www.pensaoalcobia.com, residencial.alcobia@mail. ptprime.pt).

$ Pensão Praça da Figueira is a backpacker place on a dreary but central street with youth hostel prices, a kitchen on every floor, and 30 clean, basic rooms. A little street noise is a minor downside (D-€28-38, Ds-€38-48, Db-€48-58, singles-€7 less, extra bed-€20, no breakfast, 2 flights up with no elevator, Internet access, entrance is at Travessa Nova de São Domingos 9, behind Praça da Figueira, tel. 213-426-757, fax 213-424-323, www.pensaopraca dafigueira.com, pensaofigueira@clix.pt).

Near Rossio

$$ Pensão Residencial Gerês rents 20 bright, basic, cozy rooms with older plumbing but without the dingy smokiness that pervades Lisbon's cheaper hotels. Double-paned windows keep out much of the street noise (S-€45, Sb-€55, Db-€60, Tb-€85-100, 10 percent discount Nov-March with cash and this book, no breakfast, Internet access and Wi-Fi, uphill a block off northeast corner of Rossio, Calçada do Garcia 6, tel. 218-810-497, fax 218-882-006, www.pensaogeres.net, info@pensaogeres.net). The Nogueira family speaks some English.

Central Lisbon Hotels

Central Lisbon Hotels Key

❶	Internacional Design Hotel	⓫	Pensão Norte
❷	Hotel Métropole	⓬	To Avenida da Liberdade Area
❸	Hotel Avenida Palace		Hotels & Ibis Hotels
❹	VIP Executive Suites Eden	⓭	Lisbon Destination Hostal
❺	Hotel Lisboa Tejo	⓮	Home Lisbon Hotel
❻	Grande Pensão Alcobia	⓯	Living Lounge Hostel
❼	Pensão Praça da Figueira	⓰	Lisbon Lounge Hostel
❽	Pensão Residencial Gerês	⓱	To Hotel As Janelas Verdes
❾	Residencial Florescente	⓲	Laundry
❿	Pensão Duas Nações		

$ Residencial Florescente rents 68 rooms on the "eating lane," a thriving pedestrian street a block off Praça dos Restauradores. (Sb-€40-45, Db-€65, bigger twin Db-€65-85, Tb-€85-95, higher prices apply July-Sept, air-con, free Wi-Fi, Rua das Portas de Santo Antão 99, tel. 213-426-609, fax 213-427-733, www.residencialflorescente.com, geral@residencialflorescente.com).

$ Pensão Duas Nações offers 70 small rooms in a great location (Db-€65, air-con, Rua Augusta and Rua da Victoria 41, tel. 213-460-710, fax 213-470-206, www.duasnacoes.com, reservas@duasnacoes.com).

$ Pensão Norte rents 24 small, linoleum-floored rooms. It beats a youth hostel—barely (Ds-€30-35, Db-€50, Tb/Qb-€65, higher prices apply July-Sept, no breakfast, a bit smoky, Rua dos Douradores 161, tel. 218-878-941, fax 218-868-462, norte.douradores@gmail.com).

Along Avenida da Liberdade
These listings are a 10-minute walk or short Metro ride from the center.

Near Metro: Avenida
$$$ Hotel Lisboa Plaza, a large, plush four-star gem, mixes traditional style with bright-pastel classiness. With 112 rooms, it offers snappy and polite service, all the amenities, and a free glass of port when you check in (Sb-€150-190, Db-€160-200, extra bed-€47, higher prices apply March-June and Sept-Oct, larger "superior" rooms cost 25 percent more, buffet breakfast-€14, air-con, one allergen-free floor, Wi-Fi, parking-€10/day; well-located on a quiet street off busy Avenida da Liberdade, a block from Metro: Avenida, Travessa do Salitre 7; tel. 213-218-218, fax 213-471-630, www.heritage.pt, plaza@heritage.pt). Hotel Lisboa Plaza and its sister, Hotel Britania (listed below), offer a deal in July and August:

free entrance to Lisbon's museums for guests who stay at least three nights.

$$ Hotel Botânico, in a blocky, modern building on a characteristic street a steep five-minute walk above Avenida da Liberdade, is quiet—unless there's a demonstration at the Planned Parenthood clinic across the street. The hotel rents 30 modern, business-class rooms; street-side rooms on the top floor have a view of São Jorge Castle (Sb-€45-90, Db-€50-95, Tb-€60-95, air-con, elevator, free Wi-Fi, parking, Rua Mãe d'Água 16, tel. 213-420-392, fax 213-420-125, www.hotelbotanico.pt, hotelbotanico@netcabo.pt).

$$ Residêncial Roma, a stark little place, rents 40 simple rooms. It's tucked away on a side street, 50 yards off the big Avenida da Liberdade (Sb-€45-60, Db-€50-70, extra bed-€10-15, air-con, no elevator, Travessa da Glória 22, tel. 213-460-558, fax 213-460-557, www.residenciaroma.com, res.roma@cyclopnet.pt). They also rent apartments (Db-€75, €10/extra person).

$$ Hotel Alegria, a fine old establishment with 35 rooms, faces a quiet, inviting park in a peaceful neighborhood 200 yards from the Avenida Metro station. Varnished like a ship, it has sloping hardwood floors and solid furniture (Db-€60-70, third person-€15 extra, breakfast-€6, air-con, elevator, Praca da Alegria 12, tel. 213-220-670, www.alegrianet.com, mail@alegrianet.com).

Others near Avenida da Liberdade

$$$ Hotel Britania maintains its 1940s Art Deco charm throughout its 33 spacious rooms, offering a clean and professional haven on a tranquil street one block off Avenida da Liberdade. Three new top-floor suites are decorated in a luxurious Mod Deco style. Run by the Hotel Lisboa Plaza folks (listed earlier), it offers the same four-star standards for the same prices (air-con, elevator, laundry service, non-smoking floor, Wi-Fi, free street parking or €10/day in next-door garage; from Metro: Avenida stop, walk uphill on boulevard, turn right on Rua Manuel de Jesus Coelho and take first left to Rua Rodrigues Sampaio 17; tel. 213-155-016, fax 213-155-021, www.heritage.pt, britania.hotel@heritage.pt).

$ Lisbon Dreams Guesthouse has 18 fresh, relaxing, Ikea-esque rooms, occupying three apartments and sharing seven bathrooms (S-€50, D-€60, T-€80, includes breakfast, discounts often available on their website, free Wi-Fi and loaner laptops, laundry service-€6, two shared terraces, kitchen for guest use; Metro: Marquês de Pombal, take Rua Alexandre Herculano uphill a few blocks, then left on Rua Rodrigo da Fonesca to #29; tel. & fax. 213-872-393, www.lisbondreamsguesthouse.com, info@lisbondreams guesthouse.com).

$ Lisbon Centre Hostel has 31 dorm rooms and some private rooms in a 19th-century building (bed in 3- to 6-bed dorm-€18,

LISBON

D-€68, includes sheets and breakfast, 24-hour access, elevator, Wi-Fi, café and bar, laundry, luggage storage, Rua Andrade Corvo 46 near Avenida da Liberdade, Metro: Picoas, tel. 213-532-696, fax 213-537-541, www.hihostels.com, lisboa@movijovem.pt).

Boutique Hostels in the Baixa

Among hostel aficionados, Lisbon is famous for having the best hostels anywhere. They welcome travelers of any age and come with an artistic flair and plenty of double rooms. Here are four that are conveniently located in the center of town.

$ **Lisbon Destination Hostel** feels designed for backpackers—young and old—who appreciate style, peace, and quiet. Located upstairs in the Rossio train station, it provides a wonderful value and experience (formerly Rossio Patio Hostel, 85 beds, 23 rooms, €20/ bed in 4-10-bed dorms, S-€30, Sb-€35, D-€50, Db-€60, includes breakfast, free Wi-Fi, lockers, movie night in lounge, tel. 213-466-457, www.destinationhostels.com, contact@destinationhostels.com).

$ **Home Lisbon Hostel** is a little more rough and homey, with free laundry, movies, and a friendly management (91 beds, €15/ bed in 4-8-bed dorms, Rua de São Nicolau 13, near corner of Rua dos Fanqueiros, Metro: Baixa-Chiado, tel. 218-885-312, www.my lisbonhome.com, info@mylisbonhome.com).

$ **Living Lounge Hostel** is clean, modern, and in a very central location near the Baixa-Chiado Metro stop. Each room is uniquely decorated (€18-25/bed in 4-8-bed mixed dorms, S-€32-37, D-€27-32; includes breakfast, sheets, and towels; air-con, elevator, lockers, laundry service, bike rentals, free tours and excursions, free Internet and Wi-Fi, Rua Crucifixo 116, second floor, tel. 213-461-078, www.livingloungehostel.com, info@living loungehostel.com).

$ **Lisbon Lounge Hostel,** run by the same folks as the Living Lounge Hostel above, offers the same amenities, style and prices, but no singles. It's in the Baixa, roughly midway between Praça da Figueira and Praça do Comércio (€18-25/bed in 4-8-bed mixed dorms, D-€27-32, Rua de São Nicolau 41, tel. 213-462-061, www. lisbonloungehostel.com, info@lisbonloungehostel.com).

Away from the Center

$$$ **Hotel As Janelas Verdes,** next door to the Museum of Ancient Art, is another of Hotel Lisboa Plaza's sister properties. An 18th-century mansion that's now a boutique hotel, it has 29 cushy rooms and comfortably elegant public spaces. The third-floor library overlooks the river (Sb/Db-€160-300, check website for specials, buffet breakfast, air-con, elevator, free Wi-Fi, Rua das Janeles Verdes 7, bus #714 stops nearby, tel. 213-968-143, fax 213-968-144, www.asjanelasverdes.com, janelas.verdes@heritage.pt).

$$ Ibis Hotels: Three Ibis hotels offer no-stress, no-character rooms for a good price in soulless areas away from the center—but near handy Metro stations. Each has non-smoking floors, air-conditioning, and €5 breakfasts. One child under 12 stays for free and a third adult is €10 (www.ibishotel.com). **Ibis Liberdade** has the best location (70 rooms, Sb/Db-€75, 2 blocks uphill from Avenida da Liberdade's Hotel Tivoli, Metro: Avenida, Barata Salgueiro 53, tel. 213-300-630, fax 213-300-631). The others are **Ibis Saldanha** (116 rooms, Sb/Db-€70, 2-minute walk from Metro: Saldanha, Avenida Casal Ribeiro 23, tel. 213-191-690, fax 213-191-699) and **Ibis José Malhoa** (211 rooms, Sb/Db-€61, next to Metro: Praça de Espanha, Avenida José Malhoa, tel. 217-235-700, fax 217-235-701).

Apartments

Cross-Pollinate is an online booking agency representing B&Bs and apartments in a handful of European cities, including Lisbon. Unlike huge aggregator websites like HomeAway or VRBO, Cross-Pollinate handpicks its listings, selectively presenting each one as if recommending it to a friend. Search their website for a listing you like, then submit your reservation online. If the place is available, you'll be charged a small deposit and emailed the location and check-in details. Policies vary from owner to owner, but in most cases you'll pay the balance on arrival in cash. Lisbon listings range from a Rossio guesthouse room for two for €70 per night to a two-bedroom Alfama apartment sleeping four for €100 per night. Minimum stays vary from one to three nights (US tel. 800-270-1190, www.cross-pollinate.com, info@cross-pollinate.com).

Eating in Lisbon

Each district of the city comes with fun and characteristic restaurants. (Good eateries in Belém are described on page 99.) Ideally, have one dinner with a fado performance—several good options for music with your meal are listed in this section, with more fado options described earlier, under "Entertainment in Lisbon."

Snack Bars

Lisbon seems enthusiastic about serving quick, light meals at characteristic bars. On just about any street, you can belly up to a bar, observe, and order what looks good for a tasty, memorable, and extremely cheap meal. You'll see lots of *pastel de bacalhau* (€1), Lisbon's ubiquitous and delicious cod cake. Strangely, this national dish of Portugal comes from Norway—salted cod. It's never fresh, always salty, and goes well with Portuguese red wine. Another good standby is a *bifana*, a pork sandwich made with a secret sauce to give it character (€2.20).

Restaurants in the Alfama

You'll invariably be sightseeing in the Alfama. While there, make a point to enjoy a good meal. Or come back later in the evening for a dinner with a fado performance: **A Baiuca** is small but full of cheer, with lively fado accompanying its home-style meals (Rua de São Miguel 20). **Clube de Fado** offers expensive dinners with its quality fado (Rua São João da Praça 94); see listings under "Entertainment in Lisbon."

Restaurante Santo Antonio de Alfama, buried scenically in the Alfama, is bohemian yet dressy and intimate. "Actors" (notice the classic cinema theme) serve a global cuisine with creative €9 tapas and €15 main courses. While it's tempting to cobble together a tapas meal, I liked the main dishes better. On a balmy evening, the small courtyard seating overlooking the classic Alfama square must be the best shabby-romantic setting in Lisbon (Wed-Sun 12:00-16:00 & 19:30-23:00, closed Tue, Beco de São Miguel 7, tel. 218-881-328).

Restô do Chapitô is a hip collection of pubs, patios, and BBQ joints connected to a circus school and capped by a bohemian-chic restaurant. It offers good, creative international cuisine to a young and trendy crowd, and has superb views of the river. This is a memorable place for dinner, no matter which venue you choose: You can climb the tight iron spiral staircase to dine upstairs amid the tasteful and woody warm decor with a big view (€20-25 plates); or you can drink and munch tapas (more cheaply) in the pub or on the welcoming, tented bohemian patio (nightly 19:30-24:00, cash only; leaving the castle, head downhill to the right, then take a right on Rua Milagre Santo António; the restaurant is 100 yards ahead on the left at Rua Costa do Castelo 7; tel. 218-867-334).

Farol de Santa Luzia, which offers a nice seafood feast with a delicate and delightful dining area, is a favorite of mine for lunch in the Alfama. A family-run place with a local clientele, they offer the Algarve *cataplana* style of cooking (€6-8 daily specials, €20 big sharable special *cataplana*, €17.50 fixed-price *menu turistico,* indoor seating only, Mon-Sat 12:00-23:00, closed Sun, Largo Santa Luzia 5, across from Santa Luzia viewpoint terrace, tiny sign, tel. 218-863-884).

Lunch on Largo do Contador Mor: Two basic restaurants—**A Tasquinha Restaurante** and **Comidas de Santiago**—feed hungry tourists on this leafy square just below the castle. Both specialize in plates of grilled sardines, called *sardinhas grelhadas*, and are handy for a simple lunch.

Authentic Dining near Largo Rodrigues de Freitas: For more

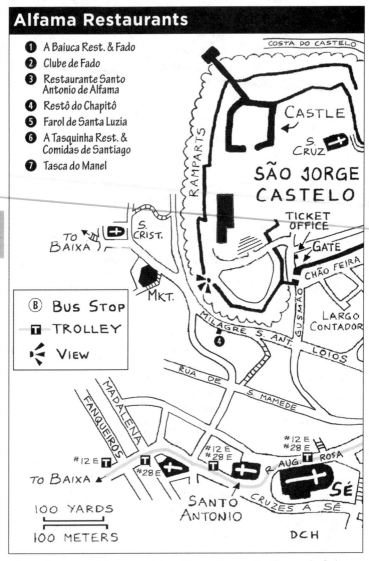

Alfama Restaurants

1. A Baiuca Rest. & Fado
2. Clube de Fado
3. Restaurante Santo Antonio de Alfama
4. Restô do Chapitô
5. Farol de Santa Luzia
6. A Tasquinha Rest. & Comidas de Santiago
7. Tasca do Manel

COSTA DO CASTELO

CASTLE

S. CRUZ

SÃO JORGE CASTELO

RAMPARTS

TICKET OFFICE

GATE

CHÃO FEIRA

S. CRIST.

TO BAIXA

MKT.

MILAGRE S. ANT.

GUSMÃO

LARGO CONTADOR

LOIOS

B BUS STOP
T TROLLEY
◄ VIEW

RUA DE S. MAMEDE

MADALENA

FANQUEIROS

#12 E

#12 E
#28 E

#12 E
#28 E

R. AUG. ROSA

TO BAIXA ◄

#28 E

CRUZES A SÉ

SÉ

SANTO ANTONIO

DCH

100 YARDS

100 METERS

of an adventure with your meal, walk past Largo das Portas do Sol and follow the trolley tracks along Rua de São Tomé to a square called Largo Rodrigues de Freitas—if riding trolley #12E, it's the first stop over the big hill).

Tasca do Manel is run by Manel's English-speaking son, Fernando. This humble neighborhood diner, with black-and-white photos strewn across its walls, serves traditional Portuguese dishes, especially *pastel de bacalhau,* with back-street elegance (€6-10 fish meals, Mon-Sat 12:00-15:30 & 18:30-22:30, closed Sun, Rua de

São Tome 20, tel. 218-862-021). The neighborhood around this restaurant is a gritty chunk of pre-earthquake Lisbon, full of interesting eateries. Brighten a few dark bars. Have an aperitif—taste the *branco seco* (local dry white wine). Make a friend, pet a chicken, contemplate the graffiti, and ponder the humanity ground between the cobbles.

Bairro Alto, Lisbon's "High Town"

For perhaps the most memorable dining experience in the Bairro Alto, consider **Canto do Camões** (Travessa da Espera 38) or **Restaurante Adega do Ribatejo** (Rua Diario de Noticias 23) for good meals and fado music (see listings under "Entertainment in Lisbon").

Near São Roque Church

These first four recommendations are all within a three-minute walk of São Roque Church.

Restaurante Bota Alta ("The Old Boot") is a classic little eatery with a timeless Portuguese ambience and reliably good food. Portions are big, reservations are smart, and Paula offers a fun dessert sampler plate (€10-15 main dishes, Mon-Sat 19:00-23:00, closed Sun, straight up from lottery kiosk in front of São Roque Church, at corner of Travessa da Queimada and Rua da Atalaia, tel. 213-427-959).

Cervejaria da Trindade, a bright, boisterous, Portuguese-style beer hall, is full of historic tiles, seafood, and tourists. While overpriced and in all the guidebooks, people enjoy its atmosphere (€15-20 meals, confirm prices—especially since seafood is charged by weight, daily 12:00-24:00, liveliest 20:00-22:00, closed holidays, air-con, courtyard, a block down from São Roque Church at Rua Nova da Trindade 20-C, tel. 213-423-506). They have five Portuguese beers on tap—Sagres is the standard lager, Sagres Preta is a good dark beer (like a porter), and Bohemia is sweet, with more alcohol. Light meals and cheaper snacks are served at the bar and in the front. The beautifully tiled first room, once a refectory (monks' dining hall), still holds the pulpit from which the Bible was read as the monks ate. The monastery was abolished in 1836—you'll notice that while the oldest tiles have Christian themes, the later ones are all about the beer.

H3 Hamburgology is a modern and trendy joint for fancy hamburgers. Thinking out of the box, they've invented dozens of creative hamburger patties, all displayed with photos on the menu wall. The *menu* price includes a potato, rice, or salad and a drink for €7 (daily 12:00-23:00, 13 Rua da Trindade, tel. 213-803-110).

Aqui Ha Peixe, well-lit and innovative, serves quality fish dishes under antique arches. Owner Miguel Reino insists on serving only the freshest fish (€10 lunch plates, €15-22 dinner plates, Tue-Sun 12:00-15:00 & 19:00-23:00, closed Mon, Rua da Trindade 18A, tel. 213-432-154).

Near the Top of the Elevador da Glória Funicular

Buddha Sushi Buffet has a great formula, fun energy, and handy location. While the Portuguese say *obrigado* and the Japanese say

The Bairro Alto & Chiado Restaurants

LISBON

1. Canto do Camões Rest. & Fado
2. Restaurante Adega do Ribatejo Fado
3. Restaurante Bota Alta
4. Cervejaria da Trindade
5. H3 Hamburgology
6. Aqui Ha Peixe
7. Buddha Sushi Buffet & The Independente Restaurant
8. Lost in Esplanada Bar
9. To Pavilhao Chines Bar
10. Armazéns do Chiado Mall

arigato, sushi doesn't exactly come to mind when you think about Lisbon. Still, this place serves a hearty sushi buffet for a painless price—especially if you get it to go (€8 at lunch, €11 at dinner, €4 to-go box, delightful picnic-friendly park across street, long hours daily, Rua São Pedro de Alcântara 65, mobile 964-396-927).

Lost in Esplanada Bar is understandably popular, with a Zen-like terrace, a mellow teahouse interior, a splash of Pakistan, and a view patio. The hippies who run this place brag they have the third-best view in Lisbon. They offer tasty light meals, soup, salads, and ommmm-my-goodness cocktails (a few blocks uphill from the funicular, at Rua D. Pedro V 56, mobile 917-759-282).

The Independente Restaurant, youthful and classy, serves modern Portuguese dishes from a creative, accessible menu to an in-the-know crowd in one big woody, candlelit ground-floor dining hall. While a bit of a splurge, it's run by a hostel (reservations smart, Rua São Pedro de Alcântara 81, tel. 213-461-381).

Pavilhao Chines Bar has only sandwiches and is no place to come for a real meal, but it's one of the most entertaining pubs in town, with a sexy, museum-like, belle époque interior. With no live music and a long list of cocktails and ports, it's a great place to talk (daily from 18:00, a couple blocks uphill from funicular at Rua D. Pedro V 89, tel. 213-424-729).

Near Rossio

Lisbon's "Eating Lane" (North of Rossio)

Rua das Portas de Santo Antão is Lisbon's "eating lane"—a galaxy of eateries, many specializing in seafood (off the northeast corner of Rossio). While the waiters are pushy and it's all very touristy, the lane—lively with happy eaters—is enjoyable to browse. This is a fine spot to down a beer, snack on some snails, and watch people go by.

The small side street, Travessa de Santo Antão, is famous for its family-friendly diner-style restaurants. They each crank out tasty, roasted chicken (paint on some spicy African *piri-piri* sauce) and fries, for eating inside or out. **Bonjardim** (with two branches on either side of the street) has the best chicken.

Casa do Alentejo Restaurante specializes in Alentejo cuisine and fills an old, second-floor dining hall. The Moorish-looking building is a cultural and social center for people from the traditional southern province of Portugal (see jokes in Évora chapter, page 184) living in Lisbon. While the food is mainly hearty and simple (like the Alentejanos), the ambience is fabulous. It's a good place to try regional specialties such as pork with clams, or the super-sweet, eggy almond dessert called *charcada*. The full-bodied Alentejo red wine is cheap and solid (€10 two-course daily lunch special, €10-15 main dishes at dinner, daily 12:00-15:00 & 19:00-22:30, slip into the closed-looking building at Rua das Portas de

Santo Antão 58 and climb stairs to the right, tel. 213-469-231). On the ground floor, the **Casa do Alentejo Bar** serves cheap bar food and wine (same hours as restaurant, spicy meat plates, hearty cheese, other tapas). They host folk dancing in the grand ballroom (often Sat at 15:00).

Restaurante Solar dos Presuntos keeps the theater crowd happily fed with meat and seafood specialties. Its upstairs is more elegant, while the downstairs—with a colorful, open kitchen—is touristy and rowdy. Photos of Lisbon's celebrities and politicians who eat here enliven the walls of this family-run establishment. Pedro and his hardworking gang offer fine service and reliably wonderful food, making this my favorite fine meal in town. Reservations are smart (€15-25 meals, big splittable portions, great and affordable wine list presented on an iPad, Mon-Sat 12:00-15:30 & 19:00-23:00, closed Sun, at the top end of Rua das Portas de Santo Antão at #150, tel. 213-424-253).

On Avenida da Liberdade (North of Rossio)

Cervejaria Ribadouro is a popular splurge with locals because of its quality meat and shellfish (€15-20 meals, daily 12:00-24:00, Avenida da Liberdade 155, at intersection with Rua do Salitre, Metro: Avenida, tel. 213-549-411). Note that seafood prices are listed by weight; the waiter will help you determine the cost of a portion. To limit the cost, write down the number of grams you want. For a fun, quick €10 per-person meal, order a small beer, 100 grams (about a quarter of a pound) of *percebes* (barnacles), and *pão torrado com manteiga* (toasted bread with butter).

On and South of Rossio

Pastelaria Suíça (SWEE-sah) provides a serviceable, air-conditioned, and comfortable place for a no-stress meal. It's popular with locals despite its surly waitstaff and relatively high prices. Along with pastry, they serve light meals, sandwiches, salads, and fruit cups (daily 7:00-21:00, least expensive at the bar, reasonable at inside tables, pricey at outside tables overlooking Rossio or Praça da Figueira, located between the two squares with entrances and terraces on each—choose sun or shade, tel. 213-214-090).

Confeitaria Nacional has been proudly satisfying sweet-tooths for 180 years, and was once the favorite of Portuguese royalty. Stop in for a tasty pastry downstairs. Or, for a peaceful and inexpensive three-course lunch (Mon-Fri 12:00-16:00 only), go upstairs, where you'll choose between a €7 meal in the cafeteria or a €9 meal with service and Old World sophistication in the elegant dining room (smaller snacks and sandwiches at all hours, Mon-Sat 8:00-20:00, closed Sun, Praça da Figueira 18, tel. 213-424-470 or 213-243-000).

LISBON

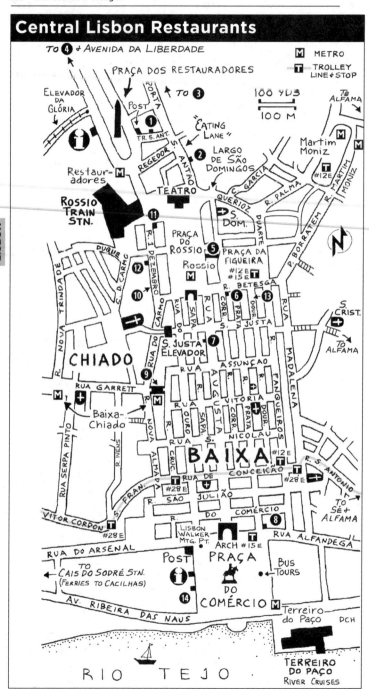

Central Lisbon Restaurants

Central Lisbon Restaurants Key

1. Bonjardim Restaurante
2. Casa do Alentejo Rest.
3. To Rest. Solar dos Presuntos
4. To Cervejaria Ribadouro
5. Pastelaria Suiça
6. Confeitaria Nacional
7. Casa Brasileira
8. Martinho da Arcada
9. Armazéns do Chiado Mall Eateries
10. Rua 1 de Dezembro Eateries
11. Restaurante Beira-Gare
12. Restaurantes Leao d' Ouro
13. Rua dos Douradores Eateries
14. Vini Portugal Wine-Tasting Center

Casa Brasileira is a wonderful, venerable, high-energy eatery with a busy bakery in the basement keeping locals well-fed and watered at great prices. Study the action. The fast lunch deals are served only at the bar (descriptions on the wall). This is a great place to get what is arguably the best *pastel de nata* in town (daily 7:00-24:00, 100 yards from Praça da Figueira at Rua Augusta 265). If nothing else, drop by here just for a coffee or a glass of fresh-squeezed OJ with a *pastel de nata* hot out of the oven, and to hang out at the bar and sample the local scene.

Martinho da Arcada is a fine option under the arcades on Praça do Comércio. Founded in 1782—when the wealthy would come here to savor early ice cream (made with mountain snow, lemon, and spices)—it still enjoys a good reputation, with formal-vested waiters serving tasty, traditional cuisine (daily specials, €20 meals, Mon-Sat 12:00-15:30 & 19:00-22:00, closed Sun, Praça do Comércio 8 at the corner of Rua da Prata, tel. 218-879-259). Enjoy coffee and pastry in the café bar or dine in the fancy dining hall. This place was one of poet Fernando Pessoa's old haunts (they display a few Pessoa artifacts). In the early 20th century, painters, writers, and dreamers shared revolutionary ideas here over coffee.

Armazéns do Chiado Mall: This shopping center, between the Bairro Alto and the Baixa, has a sixth-floor food court with few tourists in sight, offering a selection of fun eateries, from traditional Portuguese to Chinese (daily 12:00-23:00, between Rua Garrett and Rua da Assunção; from the lower town, find the inconspicuous elevator at Rua do Crucifixo 89 or 113, next to the Baixa-Chiado Metro entrance). Some of the mall's eateries are actual restaurants (quiet from about 15:00-18:00); others are smaller fast-food counters that share a common eating area and serve all day.

One of the mall's restaurants, **Chimarrão,** serves Brazilian cuisine and offers an impressive €11 *Rodizio:* an all-you-can-eat buffet of salad, veggies, and endless beef, ham, pork, sausage, and chicken. They also have daily €7 specials, desserts, and tropical

LISBON

juices and fruits. The largely Brazilian staff doesn't speak much English, but it doesn't matter (daily 12:00-16:00 & 19:00-23:00, tel. 213-479-444).

At the opposite end of the mall on the same floor, you'll find **Loja das Sopas,** which offers hearty soups with €5 fixed-price meals (find a table in the food court nearby). A lot of these places have castle views. **Companhia** offers up healthy, big-bowl pasta salads topped with tropical fruits.

Rua 1 de Dezembro: This street, which stretches from Rossio Station to the Elevador de Santa Justa, is lined with cheap restaurants. It's lively for lunch, but dead at dinner. Walk the street and determine the prevailing menu of the day. Most options are self-service, with speed being the priority for the busy office workers who eat here. The **Ca das Sandes** sandwich shop chain has a location here, offering salads and healthy sandwiches that you design Subway-style (daily 9:00-20:00). **Tasquinha do Celeiro** is a self-service vegetarian joint at #53.

Restaurante Beira-Gare is my choice for a quick, cheap meal near Rossio Station. A classic greasy-spoon diner, it dishes out cod and vegetables prepared faster than a Big Mac and served with more energy than a soccer team. The house specialty is a pork sandwich *(bifana no pão).* Consider their soup-and-sandwich special (Mon-Sat 6:00-24:00, closed Sun, stand at the bar or grab a table, in front of Rossio Station at Rua 1 de Dezembro, tel. 213-420-405).

Restaurantes Leao d' Ouro is actually two restaurants set side-by-side. One is your basic place serving decent food at fair prices, and next door is its hardworking cafeteria cousin, offering a cheap-and-hearty buffet all day (€6 at lunch, €8 at dinner, long hours daily, just a block from Rossio Station at Rua 1 de Dezembro 105, tel. 213-342-6195).

Rua dos Douradores: This street, cutting from Praça da Figueira through the Baixa, is lined with very competitive little eateries. It's fun to browse down this lane on an empty stomach. If you're craving Indian food, stop at **Restaurante Gandhi Palace,** which has a friendly staff and nonstop Bollywood movies on TV (Rua dos Douradores 214, tel. 218-873-839).

Lisbon Connections

By Train

If leaving Lisbon by train, check to see if your train requires an advance reservation (look for a boxed "R" in the timetable).

From Lisbon by Train to: Madrid (1/day, "Lusitânia" over-night 22:30-9:00, 9.5 hours; first class seat-€76, second class seat-€60; ticket and bed: €84 in quad, €105 in double, €151 in single; discount with railpass—for example, about €30 for a bed in quad,

€50 in double, €95 in single; cash only; train departs from Santa Apolónia Station, arrives at Madrid's Chamartín Station), **Paris** (1/day, overnight 16:30-13:50, 20 hours, departs Santa Apolónia, change at Hendaye, arrives at Paris' Gare Montparnasse), **Évora** (4/day, 1.5 hours), **Lagos** (6/day, 3.5-4 hours, departs Oriente, transfer in Tunes or Faro, €24), **Tavira** (5/day, 4-5 hours, transfer in Faro, departs Oriente), **Coimbra** (almost hourly, 2 hours, departs Santa Apolónia, see page 38 for details), **Nazaré/Valado** (3-5/day, 3.5-4 hours, involves 2-3 transfers; bus is better—see below), **Óbidos** (3/day, 2.25-3 hours, transfer in Mira Sintra-Melecas or Cacém, departs Oriente), **Porto** (almost hourly, 3 hours, departs Santa Apolónia), **Sintra** (4/hour, 40 minutes, departs Rossio, €4.60 round-trip; for suggested day-trip connections, see page 140). For train info, call tel. 808-208-208, visit www.cp.pt, or check Germany's excellent all-Europe website, www.bahn.com. Note: Any train leaving from Santa Apolónia passes through Oriente Station (which has Metro access from downtown) a few minutes later.

To Salema: To reach Salema, you'll first need to get to **Lagos,** which is about 3.5-4 hours from Lisbon by train (see above) or bus (see below). Trains from Lisbon to the Algarve leave from Oriente Station on the Lisboa-Faro line. At Tunes, there is a transfer to a local train that takes you as far as Lagos. From there, it's a cheap bus ride or a pricier taxi ride to Salema (see page 167 for details).

By Bus

Bus tickets to Spain are sold by InterCentro Lines in Lisbon, but the service is run by Alsa (www.alsa.es). All buses leave from Lisbon's Sete Rios bus station (Metro: Jardim Zoológico, tel. 707-223-344).

From Lisbon by Bus to: Coimbra (hourly, 2.5 hours, €14), **Nazaré** (6/day, 2 hours, €11), **Fátima** (hourly, 1.5-2.5 hours, €11.50), **Batalha** (4/day, 2 hours, €11.50), **Alcobaça** (6/day, 2 hours, some transfer in Caldas da Rainha, €11.20), **Óbidos** (8/day, 1.25 hours, transfer in Caldas da Rainha), **Porto** (almost hourly, 3 hours), **Évora** (almost hourly, 1.5 hours, €13), **Lagos** (10/day, 4 hours, some transfer in Albufeira, €20, easier than train, must book ahead, get details at TI), **Tavira** (9/day direct, 4.25 hours, €19.50), **Madrid** (2/day, 8-9 hours, €47.50, www.avanzabus.com), **Sevilla** (2/day, 7 hours, may be less off-season, €37; you can also get to Sevilla by taking the overnight train to Madrid, then the hourly AVE train, but the bus is your better, faster, and cheaper option).

By Plane

You can generally buy a plane ticket from Lisbon to Madrid on short notice for as little as €30 or as much as €300, depending on the time of the year. Shop around to get the best deal. Vueling (www.vueling.com) and EasyJet (www.easyjet.com) usually have the cheapest flights, but specials by Iberia (www.iberia.com) can sometimes beat their prices. For more information, see "Cheap Flights" on page 347.

LISBON

SINTRA

For centuries, Portugal's aristocracy considered Sintra the perfect place to escape from Lisbon. Now tourists do, too. Sintra (SEEN-trah) is a mix of natural and man-made beauty: fantasy castles set amid exotic tropical plants, lush green valleys, and craggy hilltops with hazy views of the Atlantic and Lisbon. For centuries, Sintra—just 15 miles northwest of Lisbon—was the summer escape of Portugal's kings. Those with money and a desire to be close to royalty built their palaces amid luxuriant gardens in the same neighborhood. Lord Byron called this bundle of royal fancies and aristocratic dreams a "glorious Eden," and even though it's mobbed with tourists today, it's still magnificent. Also consider checking out Europe's westernmost tip (at Cabo da Roca) and nearby resort towns.

Planning Your Time

Sintra makes a great day trip from Lisbon, especially on Monday, when many museums in Lisbon are closed, but all major Sintra sights are open. Here you can climb through the Versailles of Portugal—the Pena Palace—and romp along the ruined ramparts of a deserted Moorish castle on a neighboring hilltop.

Try to arrive in Sintra by 9:15, since most major sights open between 9:00 and 9:45. Pick up a map at the train station's TI, and catch bus #434 up to the Pena Palace. After touring the palace and gardens, walk down to the Moorish Castle ruins, a nice spot for a picnic lunch. From here, you can hike 30 minutes down a steep, wooded path into town (get hiking instructions and map at castle entry; fork in path leads down from within the castle grounds) or catch the bus back to town (bus leaves from either castle). Have

Near Lisbon

Major Train Stations
❶ Santa Apolónia
❷ Oriente
❸ Rossio
❹ Cais do Sodré

lunch (if you didn't already picnic at the Moorish Castle), explore the town, and visit the National Palace, then catch the train back to Lisbon in time for dinner. This general plan also works well for drivers, who ideally should leave their car in Lisbon (or at least park in Sintra) and take advantage of public transportation.

With extra time, explore the rugged and picturesque westernmost tip of Portugal at Cabo da Roca. You can also mix and mingle with the jet set (or at least press your nose against their windows) at the resort towns of Cascais or Estoril (for information on how to reach these destinations, see "Near Sintra," at the end of the chapter).

Getting to Sintra

Catch the **train** to Sintra from Lisbon's central Rossio Station (direct, 4/hour, 40 minutes). Buy your ticket upstairs (at track level) from the ticket window or an automated machine (select English, then "Buy Ticket + Card," then "Titulos CP Lisboa/Bilhete Simple/Inteiro," select "Sintra" from the list of destinations, hit "+" for return ticket, then pop in coins or small bills; €4.60 round-trip, includes €0.50 fee for reusable Viva Viagem card; TV monitor lists departure times). Pass your card over the scanner at the turnstile to enter. Your card will eventually be checked by someone on board, and you'll need to scan it again when you leave the station in Sintra. During your ride, take in the views of the 18th-century aqueduct (on the left) and the workaday Lisbon suburbs. Relax...Sintra is at the end of the line.

Sintra is far easier by train than by **car** from Lisbon. Consider waiting until after you visit Sintra to pick up your rental car. If you do drive to Sintra, see my "Route Tips for Drivers" on page 140.

Orientation to Sintra

Sintra is small. The town it-self sprawls at the foot of a hill, a 10-minute walk (or quick bus ride) from the train station. The National Palace, with its unmis-takable pair of cone-shaped chim-neys, is in the center of the town, a block from the TI. But the other two main sights are a steep, long, uphill walk from town; most prefer to take the bus. If you're trying to decide, look up from the train sta-tion or center of town to see the Moorish Castle wall on top of the hill—it's quite a hike. The Pena Palace is beyond that.

Tourist Information

Sintra has two TIs: a small one in the train station (tel. 219-241-623) and a larger one a block off the main square in the Museu Re-gional building (both open daily June-Sept 9:30-19:00, Oct-May 9:30-18:00, both have WCs, tel. 219-231-157, www.askmelisboa. com). Pick up a free map with information on sights and a sched-ule for bus #434. Culture vultures should also pick up a free copy of *Sintra Cultural,* which lists all the current month's events. The TI can arrange *quartos* (rooms in private homes, Db-€35-80) for overnighters.

Arrival in Sintra

By Train: Upon arrival, stop at the TI in the station. To **bus** to the town center or palace, hop on the #434 (exit station to the right to reach the nearest stop, €5 ticket valid all day, schedules posted at stop; for more bus info, see "Getting Around Sintra," later). The bus stops in town first (across from the main TI) before heading up to the Pena Palace. You can also reach the town center on **foot** (exit station and go left; it's about a 10-minute walk).

Sintra

(Map labels:)

N-247
TO CABO DA ROCA
CASA MIRADOURO HOTEL
SEE CENTRAL SINTRA MAP
TOWN HALL
TO LISBON
#403 & #434
T
ESTRADA CARVALHEIRO
CASA DO VALLE GUESTHOUSE
NATIONAL PALACE
COSTA
TRAIN STATION
TO MONSERRATE & CABO DA ROCA
MAIN SQUARE
RIO DO PORTO
P
i
#434
B
T
VOLTA DO DUCHE
QUINTA DA REGALEIRA
i
RUA
MAR. SALDANHA
MAR. RIBEIRO
LIBERDADE PARK
TO LISBON
N-375
OLD TOWN
MOORISH FOUNTAIN
SANTA MARIA
ESTRADA DA PENA
GREAT VIEW!
RUA TRIN.
TO LISBON
MOORISH CASTLE
TRAIL
MOORISH CASTLE PARKING
P
B
#434
TO TRAIN STN.
ESTRADA DE PENA
#434
B
LOWER PARK GATE
PENA PARK
MAIN ENTRANCE
B
#434
PENA SHUTTLE TOURIST BUS
N
PENA PALACE
DCH
TO HIGH CROSS
100 YARDS
100 METERS

T TAXI STAND
P PARKING
B BUS STOP
→ ONE-WAY

SINTRA

By Car: For tips on driving into Sintra, see my "Route Tips for Drivers" on page 140.

Helpful Hints

LisboaCard: This sightseeing pass covers the National Palace and gets you discounts on the Pena Palace, Moorish Castle, Toy Museum, and the Monserrate gardens. It also covers the train ride from Lisbon to Sintra (buy it at a Lisbon TI before you visit Sintra—see page 37). Be sure to bring the LisboaCard booklet, which contains coupons required for some of the discounts.

Festivals: The Festival de Sintra music and dance festival from late May to early July keeps the town lively and fun (www.festival desintra.pt).

Money: ATMs are rare in Sintra. You'll find one at the train station, another inside the main TI, and one on Rua das Padarias, just up the hill from the recommended Piriquita Café.

Local Guide: Christina Quental works mainly in Lisbon, but lives near Sintra and can meet you at the station (Mon-Fri €115/half-day, €180/day; Sat-Sun €140/half-day, €230/day; mobile 919-922-480, anacristinaquental@hotmail.com).

Bring a Picnic: If saving a few euros is important, consider buying picnic items in Lisbon. Sintra's reputation as a tourist destination means high prices for restaurant meals.

Getting Around Sintra

Bus #434 loops together all the important stops—the train station, the town center/TI/National Palace (stop is at TI), the Moorish Castle ruins, and the Pena Palace—before heading back to town and the train station (June-mid-Sept 4/hour, mid-Sept-May 3/hour; €5 ticket good all day for one loop with stops, buy from driver; first bus departs at 9:15 from train station; last bus leaves station at 19:10, 18:10 in winter; entire circuit takes 30 minutes). On your way to the Pena Palace, the bus will stop at the lower Pena Park entrance and the entrance to the Moorish Castle—but don't get off. Instead, continue to the top of the hill; where the bus drops you off, it's still another 10-minute uphill walk to the Pena Palace (or take the €2 green shuttle bus; described later). You can also take a **taxi** from the town center or the train station to the Moorish Castle or the Pena Palace (but it won't get you any closer to the palace entrance than the bus). From the Pena Palace, it's a 15-minute walk backtracking downhill to the Moorish Castle (return to bus-and-taxi stop, then follow signs down road to *Moorish Castle*).

The clip-clop **horse carriages** cost about €30 for 25 minutes (rates posted). They can take you anywhere; you'll likely see them waiting by the parking lot just in front of the National Palace.

Sights in Sintra

▲▲Pena Palace (Palácio de Pena)

This magical hilltop palace sits high above Sintra, above the Moorish Castle ruins. In the 19th century, Portugal had a very romantic prince, German-born Prince Ferdinand. A contemporary and

SINTRA

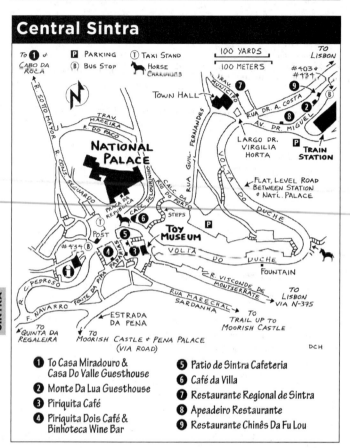

Central Sintra

To ① & CABO DA ROCA · R. SOTTO MAYOR · R. DO PAÇO · TRAV. MACEIRA

Ⓟ PARKING   Ⓑ BUS STOP   Ⓣ TAXI STAND   🐎 HORSE CARRIAGES

100 YARDS   100 METERS

TO LISBON   #403 & #434

TOWN HALL   TRAV. MUNICIPIO   Ⓑ   ⑦   ⑨   Ⓑ

RUA DR. A. COSTA   ②   ⑧   AV. DR. MIGUEL

R. CONS. SEGURADO

NATIONAL PALACE   RUA GUIL. FERNANDES

LARGO DR. VIRGILIA HORTA   **TRAIN STATION**

VOLTA DO DUCHE

PRAÇA DA REPUBLICA   CALÇ. PELOURINHO   CALC. PIGO. PORTO   CALC. PELOURINHO

← FLAT, LEVEL ROAD BETWEEN STATION & NATL. PALACE

Ⓣ   POST   STEPS   Ⓟ

#434   Ⓑ   ⑤   ④   ⑥   **TOY MUSEUM**   ③   FONTE DA PIPA

VOLTA   DO   DUCHE   FOUNTAIN

R. C. PEDROSO   R. VISCONDE DE MONTSERRATE   **TO LISBON VIA N-375**

F. NAVARRO   RUA MARECHAL SARDANHA

TO QUINTA DA REGALEIRA   ESTRADA DA PENA   **TO MOORISH CASTLE & PENA PALACE (VIA ROAD)**   **TO TRAIL UP TO MOORISH CASTLE**

DCH

① To Casa Miradouro & Casa Do Valle Guesthouse
② Monte Da Lua Guesthouse
③ Piriquita Café
④ Piriquita Dois Café & Binhoteca Wine Bar
⑤ Patio de Sintra Cafeteria
⑥ Café da Villa
⑦ Restaurante Regional de Sintra
⑧ Apeadeiro Restaurante
⑨ Restaurante Chinês Da Fu Lou

cousin of Bavaria's "Mad" King Ludwig (of Disneyesque Neuschwanstein Castle fame), Ferdinand was also a cousin of England's Prince Albert (Queen Victoria's husband). Flamboyant Ferdinand hired a German architect to build a fantasy castle, mixing elements of German and Portuguese style. He ended up with a crazy Neo-fortified casserole of

Gothic towers, Renaissance domes, Moorish minarets, Manueline carving, Disney playfulness, and an *azulejo* (tile) toilet for his wife.

Cost and Hours: Palace and gardens-€13.50; combo-ticket with Moorish Castle-€16; daily May-mid-Sept 9:45-19:00, mid-

Sept-April 9:45-17:30, last entry one hour before closing, no photos, tel. 219-105-340, www.parquesdesintra.pt.

Getting In: Purchase your ticket at the small hut opposite the gated main entrance. To avoid the 10-minute uphill climb to the palace (and enjoy a lift back down), catch the green shuttle bus just inside the gate at the *paragem* sign (€2 round-trip, departs every few minutes).

Information: English descriptions throughout the palace give meaning to the rooms. Your ticket also comes with a map showing a circular, 1.5-hour walking route of the park. Be sure to grab the English version of this map if you intend to explore the park after touring the palace.

Eating: The palace has a view café. If you brought your lunch with you, enjoy it in the picnic-perfect gardens either before or after your visit. Wander in, find a spot of shade, and enjoy views fit for a king.

☉ Self-Guided Tour: The palace, built in the mid- to late 1800s, is so well-preserved that it feels as if it's the day after the royal family fled Portugal in 1910 (during a popular revolt that eventually made way for today's modern republic). This gives the place a charming intimacy rarely seen in palaces. Here are the highlights.

SINTRA

Entry: After you hop off the green shuttle bus, walk up through the Moorish archway with alligator decor. Get your ticket torn, cross the drawbridge that doesn't draw, and join an onion-domed world of tourists frozen in deep knee-bends with their cameras cocked. At the base of the stairs, you'll see King Ferdinand, who built this castle from 1840 until 1885, when he died. Though German, he was a romantic proponent of his adopted culture and did much to preserve Portugal's architectural and artistic heritage.

Courtyard: The palace was built on the site of a 16th-century monastery; the courtyard was the former location of the cloister. In spite of its plushness, the palace retains the monkish coziness of several small rooms gathered in two levels around the cloister.

Like its big brother in Belém, the monastery housed followers of St. Jerome, the hermit monk. Like their namesake, the monks wanted to be isolated, and this was about as isolated as you could be around here 500 years ago. The spot was also a popular pilgrimage destination for its statue of "Our Lady of the Feathers" (*pena* means feather—hence the palace's name). In 1498 King Manuel was up here enjoying the view when he spied Vasco da Gama sailing up the river, returning safely from his great voyage. To celebrate and give thanks, the king turned what was a humble wooden monastery into a fine stone palace.

Queen's Bedroom and Dressing Room: Study the melancholy photos of Queen Amelia, King Charles (Carlos I), and their family in this room. The early 1900s were a rocky time for Portugal's royal family. The king and his eldest son were assassinated in 1908. His youngest son, Manuel II, became king until he, his mother the queen, and other members of the royal family fled Portugal during the 1910 revolution. The palm frond on the headboard of the queen's bed was from her last Palm Sunday Mass in Portugal. Poke around. Throughout the palace, you'll see state-of-the-art conveniences (the first flush toilets and hot shower in Portugal). The whole place is lovingly cluttered, typical of the Victorian horror of empty spaces.

King's Bedroom: The king enjoyed cutting-edge comforts, including the shower/tub imported from England, and even a telephone to listen to the opera when he felt that the Lisbon commute was too much (you'll see the switchboard later). The bedroom is decorated in classic Romantic style—dark, heavy, and busy with knickknacks.

Queen's View Balcony: On the upper floor, enjoy a sweeping view from Lisbon to the mouth of the Rio Tejo. Find the Cristo Rei statue and the 25th of April Bridge. The statue on the distant ridge honors the palace's architect.

The New Wing: This spacious addition to the original series of rooms around the cloister includes the apartments of the last king and the fantastically furnished Noble's Room.

End of Palace Tour: Your tour ends at the abundant kitchen; just after, a view café conveniently welcomes us peasants. After touring the palace, you can return directly to the main entrance (walk 10 minutes or catch the green shuttle bus—your ticket covers the round-trip), or you can detour for a self-guided tour of the park.

Pena Palace Park: The lush, captivating, and sprawling palace grounds, rated ▲, are dotted with romantic surprises, including the High Cross (highest point around, with commanding views), chapels, a temple, lakes, giant sequoia trees, and exotic plants. If you want to walk through the park after you tour the palace, take a 30- to 40-minute stroll downhill (following the park map that came with your palace admission) to the lower park gate, where you'll find a bus stop and the Estrada de Pena loop road. From here, it's a five-minute hike uphill to the Moorish Castle, or a 10-minute hike up to Pena Palace's main entrance.

▲Moorish Castle (Castelo dos Mouros)

Sintra's thousand-year-old ruins of a Moorish castle are lost in an enchanted forest and alive with winds of the past. They're a castle lover's dream come true, and a great place for a picnic with a panoramic Atlantic view. Though built by the Moors, the castle was taken by Christian forces in 1147. What you'll climb on today—while dramatic—was significantly restored in the 19th century. The Moorish Castle, with its own bus  #434 stop, is a 15-minute hike down from Pena Palace's main entrance (10 minutes down to the palace bus stop, then a five-minute trek up to the castle), and a 30-minute hike from town.

Cost and Hours: Castle-€7; combo-ticket with Pena Palace and gardens-€16; daily mid-June-mid-Sept 9:00-20:00, May-mid-June and mid-Sept-Oct 9:30-20:00, Nov-April 10:00-18:00, last entry one hour before closing, free flier includes English info and rough map, tel. 219-237-300, www.parquesdesintra.pt.

▲▲National Palace (Palácio Nacional)

While the palace dates back to Moorish times, most of what you'll see is from the 15th-century reign of King John (João) I, with later Manueline architectural ornamentation from the 16th century. This oldest surviving royal palace in Portugal is still used for official receptions. Having housed royalty  for 500 years (until 1910), it's fragrant with history.

Cost and Hours: €7, free Sun until 14:00; open Thu-Tue 9:30-17:30, last entry 17:00, closed Wed; look for white, Madonna-bra building in town center, 10-minute walk from train station, photos allowed, tel. 219-106-840, http://pnsintra.imc-ip.pt.

☉ Self-Guided Tour: The palace is a one-way romp with little information provided. As you tour the place, stop in these notable parts of the palace:

Swan Room: This first room is the palace's banquet room. A king's daughter—who loved swans—married into a royal house in Belgium. The king missed the princess so much that he decorated the ceiling with her favorite animal. These aren't the only creatures in the room, though. Check out the ceramic soup tureens designed in the shape of your favorite barnyard animal.

Courtyard: This was a fortified medieval palace, so rather than having fancy gardens outside, it has a stay awhile courtyard within its protective walls. Notice the unique chimneys. They provide powerful suction that removes the smoke from the kitchen and also create a marvelous open-domed feeling (as you'll see at the end of your tour).

Magpie Room: King John I was caught kissing a lady-in-waiting by his queen. Frustrated by his court—abuzz with gossip—John had this ceiling painted with magpies. But to show what a good-spirited guy he was, around each magpie is the king's slogan—*por bem,* "for good." The 15th-century Moorish tiles are from Spain, brought in before the development of the famous, ubiquitous Portuguese tiles, and are considered some of the finest Moorish-Spanish tiles in all of Iberia.

King's Bedroom: The king portrayed on the wall where you enter the room is King Sebastian (Dom Sebastião), a gung-ho, medieval-type monarch who went to battle in Africa, following the Moors even after they were chased out of Europe. He disappeared in 1578 at age 24 (although he was almost certainly killed in Morocco, "Sebastianists" awaited his mythical return into the 19th century). With the king missing, Portugal was left in unstable times with only Sebastian's great uncle (King Henrique) as heir. The new king died within two years, and the throne passed to his cousin, King Philip II of Spain, leading to 60 years of Spanish rule (1580-1640).

Note the ebony, silver, and painted copper headboard of the Italian Renaissance bed. The tiles in this room are considered the first Portuguese tiles—from the time of Manuel I. The corn-on-the-cob motif topping the tilework is a reminder of American discoveries. Wander through more rooms upstairs, and through more quarters to the blue-and-gold...

Stag Room: The most striking room in the palace honors Portugal's loyal nobility. Study the richly decorated ceiling. The king's coat of arms at the top is surrounded by the coats of arms of his children, and below that, the coats of arms of all but one of Portugal's noble families (the omitted family had schemed a revolt, so received only a blank niche). The Latin phrase circling the room reads, "Honoring all the noble families who've been loyal to the king." The 18th-century tiles hang from the walls like tapestries. Enjoy the view: a garden-like countryside dotted with mansions of nobility who clamored to be near their king, the hill-capping castle, and the wide-open Atlantic. You're in the westernmost room of the westernmost palace on the European continent.

Kitchen: With all the latest in cooking technology, the palace chef could roast an entire cow on the spit, keep the king's plates warm in the iron dish warmer (with drawers below for the charcoal), and get really dizzy by looking up and spinning around three times. OK, you can go now.

More Sights

▲**Quinta da Regaleira**—This Neo-everything (Manueline/Gothic /Renaissance) 1912 mansion and garden has mystical and Masonic twists. It was designed by an Italian opera-set designer for a wealthy but disgruntled monarchist two years after the royal family was deposed. The two-hour English tour is mostly in the garden (as the palace is quite small) and can be longish unless you're into quirky Masonic esoterica. If you like fantastic caves, bring a flashlight and follow the shaded black lines on the provided maps. Ask a local to pronounce "Regaleira" for you, and just try to repeat it.

Cost and Hours: €6 self-guided tour, €10 guided tour by reservation only, frequent tours daily May-Sept, fewer off-season; open daily 10:00-20:00, closes earlier off-season, last entry one hour before closing; 10-minute walk from downtown Sintra, café; book tours online at www.regaleira.pt or by calling 219-106-650.

Toy Museum (Museu do Brinquedo)—Just for giggles, you can wander through a collection of several thousand old-time toys, from small soldiers, planes, cars, trucks, and old tricycles to a dolls' attic upstairs. The 20th-century owner, João Arbués Moreira, started collecting toys when he was 14 and never quit. The collection is displayed in chronological order and comes with no English descriptions. Moreira typically hangs around the museum in his wheelchair, and loves to explain to visitors how he acquired each item.

Cost and Hours: €4, €2 for those under 19, Tue-Sun 10:00-18:00, closed Mon, last entry 30 minutes before closing, kids' play zone, one block in front of National Palace on Rua Visconde de Monserrate, tel. 219-242-171, www.museu-do-brinquedo.pt.

Monserrate—About 2.5 miles outside of Sintra are the wonderful gardens of Monserrate. If you like tropical plants and exotic landscaping, a visit is time well-spent. Many find that the Pena Palace's gardens are just as good as these more famous grounds.

Cost and Hours: €7, €5 extra for guided visit by reservation only, daily mid-June-mid-Sept 9:30-20:00, May-mid-June and mid-Sept-Oct 9:30-19:00, Nov-April 9:30-18:00, last entry one hour before closing, no buses run here—allow about €10 for taxi, tel. 219-237-300, www.parquesdesintra.pt.

Sleep Code

(€1 = about $1.30, country code: 351)
S = Single, **D** = Double/Twin, **T** = Triple, **Q** = Quad, **b** = bathroom, **s** = shower only. Unless otherwise noted, credit cards are accepted, English is spoken, and breakfast is included.

To help you easily sort through these listings, I've divided the accommodations into two categories, based on the price for a standard double room with bath during high season:

$$ **Higher Priced**—Most rooms €80 or more.
$ **Lower Priced**—Most rooms less than €80.

Prices can change without notice; verify the hotel's current rates online or by email.

Sleeping in Sintra

$$ Casa Miradouro is a beautifully restored mansion from 1893. With eight spacious, stylish rooms, an elegant lounge, castle and sea views, and a wonderful garden, it's a worthy splurge (Db-€95-135, less Nov-March, includes buffet breakfast, free Wi-Fi, street parking, Rua Sotto Major 55; from National Palace, go past Hotel Tivoli Sintra and 400 yards downhill, note that it's a stiff uphill hike to return to center; mobile 914-292-203, fax 219-241-836, www.casa-miradouro.com, mail@casa-miradouro.com, Charlotte Lambregts).

$$ Casa Do Valle Guesthouse offers seven comfortable, modern rooms in a peaceful location. They have a lovely garden and large deck with valley and castle views (Db-€70-120, less Nov-March, breakfast-€4-6, free Internet access and Wi-Fi, pool, street parking, behind Casa Miradouro on Rua da Paderna LT-2, tel. 219-244-699, fax 219-244-744, www.casadovalle.com, info@casadovalle.com).

$ Monte Da Lua Guesthouse has seven clean, simple, fine rooms with shiny hardwood floors, facing the train station (one D-€55-60, six Db-€55-70, highest price is for July-Aug, 5 percent discount if you pay cash and mention this book, no breakfast, Wi-Fi, Avenida Dr. Miguel Bombarda 51, tel. & fax 219-241-029, www.montedalua.org, montedalua51@gmail.com, Silvia).

Eating in Sintra

Light Meals

On Rua das Padarias

This touristy little cobbled lane is lined with charming shops and eateries. While there are plenty of appealing options, here are three notable choices:

The venerable **Piriquita Café** bills itself as "the" *antiga fabrica de queijadas*—historic maker of tiny, tasty tarts with a cheesy filling. It's good for a sweet and a coffee or a simple lunch (such as toasted sandwiches). Take a seat to avoid groups who rush in to get pastries to go, or do battle and grab a half-dozen for €4.40 (daily, at the base of the street). Order from the bar (up a few steps).

Piriquita Dois, sister to the Piriquita Café, is a block farther up the lane and may have less commotion. It has a more extensive menu and a view terrace (daily, from Piriquita Café continue uphill and to the right to Rua das Padarias 2).

Binhoteca, a welcoming little *enoteca,* provides wine-lovers with an astonishing array of Portuguese wines and ports available by the glass (€2-6 and way up), along with tasty meat-and-cheese plates and a knowledgeable staff happy to explain what you're enjoying (daily 12:00-22:00, Rua das Padarias 16, tel. 219-240-849).

More Light Choices

Patio de Sintra Cafeteria is a practical lunch stop just a block off Rua das Padarias (Rua Arco do Teixeira 15).

Café da Villa, a favorite of bus drivers and tour guides, is good for a quiet, cheap lunch in a homey pub-like setting (€8 fixed-price meals, open daily, generous portions of homemade-style soups and salads, down the road past horse-drawn carriages at Calçada do Pelourinho 2).

Pizza Hut, at the train station, has a salad bar and to-go boxes for a cheap, healthy meal to munch in the Pena Palace Park, on the grounds of the Moorish Castle, or on the train ride back to Lisbon.

Dining

While there are plenty of tourist eateries in Sintra's old center, I'd head a couple of blocks away to the station area for a serious meal.

Restaurante Regional de Sintra, which feeds locals and tourists very well, is my favorite place for dinner in Sintra. Gentle Paulo speaks English and serves huge, splittable portions (€15 *doses,* daily 12:00-16:00 & 19:00-22:30, 200 yards from train station at Travessa do Municipio 2; exit train station left, go downhill to the first square and to the far right corner; tel. 219-234-444).

Apeadeiro Restaurante, named for the platform along the track at the train station just a block away, is a quality eatery serving good food for a good price. Their daily specials can be split, allowing two to eat for €15 (closed Thu, Avenida Dr. Miguel Bombarda 3, tel. 219-231-804).

Restaurante Chinês Da Fu Lou, across the street from the train station, serves decent Chinese food at a good price, offering an alternative to *bacalhau* and sandwiches (€5-10 entrees, daily 11:00-15:00 & 17:00-23:00, Avenida Dr. Miguel Bombarda 53, tel. 219-242-653).

Sintra Connections

From Sintra by Train and Bus to: Lisbon (4 trains/hour, 40 minutes), **Cascais** (8 buses/day, fewer on weekends, bus #403 also stops at Cabo da Roca, 45-60 minutes, bus stop at the Sintra train station).

Route Tips for Drivers

Sintra Day Trip from Lisbon: If you insist on taking a car to Sintra, take the IC-19 freeway out of Lisbon (allow 30 minutes). When you arrive in Sintra, follow *Centro Histórico* signs. Cars are the curse of Sintra—traffic can be terrible and parking difficult. Park your car and use bus #434 to get around. There's a strip of parking along Volta do Duche, near the town center (€0.50/hour, 4-hour maximum), and a small lot next to the train station. The most central free parking lot is on Rua do Porto in the valley just below and northeast of town (after parking, climb the long set of steps to get up to the main square). If you decide (probably regrettably) to drive to the sights, you'll take a one-way winding loop—park as soon as you can, or you'll risk having to drive the huge loop again (because you can't backtrack).

Loop Trip: It's possible to make a 70-mile circular trip and drive to all the destinations near Lisbon within a day (Lisbon–Belém–Sintra–Cabo da Roca–Cascais–Lisbon), but traffic congestion around Sintra, especially on weekends and during rush hour, can mess up your schedule.

Continuing to the Algarve: Drivers eager for beach time can leave Lisbon, visit Sintra, then head back south to drive directly to the Algarve that evening (4 hours from Lisbon). To get to the Algarve from Sintra/Cascais, get on the freeway heading for Lisbon and exit at the *Sul Ponte A-2* sign, which takes you over the 25th of April Bridge and south on A-2.

Near Sintra

The following sights are worth considering if you have extra time. Though doable by public transportation, they are best reached either with a tour or by car.

If you're bent on seeing everything west of Lisbon (Sintra, Cabo da Roca, Cascais, and Estoril) in a long day, consider a slam-bam swing around the peninsula by **bus tour** with Carris Tours' Sintra tour from Lisbon (€29, €42 option includes entrance to Pena Palace, both options 5 hours, www.carristur.pt; see page 48).

It's possible to make a loop trip around the peninsula using **public transportation,** but it can be frustrating and make for a long day, especially on weekends when fewer buses run. You'll waste 1.5-2 hours at Cabo da Roca waiting for the next bus, with very little to do there. Taking an organized bus tour from Lisbon can be your best bet (as described above). If you do decide to use public transportation, I suggest leaving Lisbon early (around 8:30). In Lisbon, buy a one-way train ticket to Sintra. See the sights in Sintra—but instead of buying a €5 ticket on the #434 bus, buy a €10 day pass. This pass covers both bus #434 up the hill to the Pena Palace as well as bus #403 to Cabo da Roca (catch at the Sintra train station, check schedule posted at bus stop in advance). Hop off at Cabo da Roca, buy a diploma at the TI to prove you were there, then catch the next bus #403 for the jaunt to Cascais and a seafood dinner on the waterfront. From Cascais, returning to Lisbon is a snap—just buy a one-way train ticket to Lisbon at the train station. You'll get off at the last stop on the line (Cais de Sodré Station), a five-minute walk from Praça do Comércio in downtown Lisbon.

Estoril is a short train ride away on the same line to Lisbon, but seeing both Cascais and Estoril is probably redundant, and Cascais is more appealing.

Cabo da Roca

Wind-beaten, tourist-infested Cabo da Roca is the westernmost point in Europe, perhaps the inspiration for the Portuguese poet Luís de Camões' line, *"Onde a terra se acaba e o mar começa"* ("Where land ends and the sea begins"). It has a little shop, a café, and a tiny **TI** that sells a "proof of being here" diploma (daily June-Sept 9:00-20:00, until 19:00 off-season, tel. 219-280-801). Nearby, on the road to Cascais, you'll pass a good

beach for wind, waves, sand, and the chance to be the last person in Europe to see the sun set. For a remote beach, drive to Praia Adraga (north of Cabo da Roca).

Cascais and Estoril

Before the rise of the Algarve, these towns were the haunt of Portugal's rich and beautiful. Today, they are quietly elegant, with noble old buildings, beach-front promenades, a bullring, a casino, and more fame than they deserve. Cascais (see photo) is the more enjoyable of the two; it's not as rich and stuffy, and it  has the cozy touch of a fishing village, great seafood, and a younger, less pretentious atmosphere (**Cascais TI** Mon-Sat 9:00-19:00, Sun 10:00-18:00, Visconde de Luz 14, tel. 214-868-204, www.cascais. net). The **Estoril TI** is at Areada do Parque (same hours as Cascais TI, tel. 214-663-813). Both are a simple day trip from Lisbon (4 trains/hour, 30 minutes from Lisbon's Cais do Sodré Station). Bullfight fans could enjoy a bullfight—if one is scheduled—in either city (ask at the TI).

SINTRA

THE ALGARVE

Salema • Cape Sagres • Lagos • Tavira

The Algarve was once known as Europe's last undiscovered tourist frontier. But it's well-discovered now, and if you go to the places featured in tour brochures, you'll find it much like Spain's Costa del Sol—paved, packed, and pretty stressful. Still, there are a few great beach towns left, mostly on the western tip, and this part of the Algarve, the south coast, is part of any sun-worshipper's dream.

Portugal's warm and dry south coast, stretching for some 100 miles, has beach resorts along the water's edge and rolling green hills dotted with orchards farther inland. The coastline varies from lagoon estuaries in the east (Tavira), to sandy beach resorts in the center (from Faro to Lagos), to rugged cliffs in the west (Sagres).

The Moors (Muslims from North Africa who ruled Portugal for five centuries) chose not to live in the rainy north, but rather along the warm, dry south coast, in the land they dubbed Al-Gharb Al-Andalus ("to the west of Andalucía"—the westernmost edge of the huge Islamic world at the time). Today, the Algarve still holds elements introduced by the Muslims—groves of almond and orange trees, and white-domed buildings with pointy chimneys, blue trim, and traditional *azulejos*.

For some rigorous rest and intensive relaxation, make sunny Salema your Algarve hideaway. Here the tourists and fishermen sport the same stubble. It's just you, a beach full of garishly painted boats, your wrinkled landlady, and a few other globetrotting experts in lethargy. Nearby sights include Cape Sagres (Europe's "Land's End" and home of Henry the Navigator's famous navigation school) and the beach-party/jet-ski resort of Lagos. Or you could just work on a tan and see how slow your pulse can get in sleepy Salema. If not now, when? If not you, who?

Planning Your Time

The Algarve is your vacation from your vacation. How much time does it deserve? It depends upon how much time you have, and how much time you need to recharge your solar batteries. On a two-week trip of Portugal, I'd give it three nights and two days. After a full day of sightseeing in Lisbon (or Sevilla, if you're arriving from Spain), I'd push it by driving four hours around dinnertime to gain an entirely free beach day. With two days, I'd spend one enjoying side trips to Cape Sagres and Lagos, and another just lingering in Salema. The only other Algarve stop to consider is Tavira. (If you're visiting in winter, Tavira—which is lively year-round—makes a better stop than tiny Salema, which slows down.)

Getting Around the Algarve

Trains and buses connect the main towns along the south coast (skimpy service on weekends and off-season). Buses take you west from Lagos, where trains don't go. The freeway crossing the Algarve from Lagos to the Spanish border (and on to Sevilla, Spain) makes driving quick and easy. (See "Route Tips for Drivers in the Algarve," at the end of this chapter.)

Salema

One bit of old Algarve magic still glitters quietly in the sun—Salema. It's at the end of a small road just off the main drag between the big city of Lagos and the rugged southwest tip of Europe, Cape Sagres. Quietly discovered by British and German tourists, this simple fishing village has three beachside streets, many restaurants, a few hotels, time-share condos up the road, a couple of bars, English and German menus, a classic beach with a paved promenade, and endless sun.

Orientation to Salema

Tourist Information

Salema lacks an official TI, but Salema Property and Services (see "Helpful Hints," later) and people in the bars, restaurants, and pensions have heard all the questions and are happy to provide answers. To study ahead, see www.salema.info.

Arrival in Salema

By Train and Bus: To get to Salema, you'll arrive first at Lagos (with the closest train station), the western Algarve's transportation hub. From there, buses go every 1-2 hours between Lagos and Sagres, with Salema about halfway between the two (30-minute ride, 10 miles, last bus departs Lagos at 20:30, fewer buses on weekends, www.algarvebus.info). Catch the bus at either the Lagos bus station (see "Arrival in Lagos," page 163) or at one of the stops along the waterfront of the historic town.

About half the buses go right into the village of Salema (these are usually marked *Salema Village*). You can confirm with the driver by asking: "*Você vai à praia de Salema, por favor?*" (voh-say vy ah pry-ah deh Salema, poor fah-vor).

The rest of the buses—marked with a cross in the schedule—stop at the top of the road, a 20-minute downhill walk into town. (If you're on one of these buses, it's better to stay on the bus and get off at the next stop—Figueira—from there you can backtrack 20 yards, then follow the sign on the right for *Salema*. It's the same distance as the first downhill walk, but there's a sidewalk, so it's safer for pedestrians and easier if you have luggage with wheels.)

By Car: If you're coming from Spain on the A-22 freeway, take the Lagos exit (marked *Lagos/Vila do Bispo/Sagres*) and follow *Sagres/Vila do Bispo* signs. Turn left at the sign for *Salema*. To stop in Lagos before continuing to Salema, take the exit marked *Lagos/Vila do Bispo/Sagres*, but follow signs to *Lagos centro*. Leave Lagos via the street Avenida dos Descobrimentos, and follow signs to *Sagres/Vila do Bispo*.

By Taxi: A cab from Lagos to Salema takes 20 minutes and costs about €25-30 (metered, but ask for an estimate first; see "Helpful Hints," next).

Helpful Hints

Money: Make sure you have plenty of euros before you come to town, because Salema has no ATM. Not all Salema restaurants accept credit cards, and most accommodations require cash. The closest ATMs are at the **Parque da Floresta** golf resort (about two miles inland—the ATM is on the wall outside the reception building), or at the **Intermarche** supermarket in Budens (the town just before Salema when coming from Lagos). A round-trip taxi ride from town to either ATM is about €8.

Internet Access: You can get online at **Salema Property and**

The Algarve

Services (described next) and at **A Aventura Bar** (see "Nightlife in Salema," later).

Handy Services: An agency called **Salema Property and Services** posts bus and train schedules; offers three-day to one-week condo rentals in Salema; arranges excursions; offers Internet access, Wi-Fi, and broadband phone service; and usually has free tourist maps of Lagos and other parts of the Algarve. You can also rent a car (high season: around €110/3 days; low season: around €80/3 days), mopeds, and mountain bikes (€10/day), and even get your laundry done (€3.50/wash-and-dry; usually open Mon-Fri 9:00-13:00 & 15:00-18:00, Sat 9:00-13:00, closed Sun, in tiny strip mall across from Hotel Residencial Salema, tel. 282-695-855, fax 282-695-920, www.salemapropertyandservices.com).

Taxi: Your hotel can arrange a taxi, or call Jose direct. Jose and his wife Isabel (a tour guide who speaks fluent English) have two cars and are happy to answer your questions about the area. It's €25-30 to the Lagos bus station or €60 for a quick 1.25-

hour scenic tour of Cape Sagres/ Cape St. Vincent, with short stops and commentary (can also wait in Sagres for €10/hour). This can be a great value for two couples or a family. You could even taxi to Lisbon, Évora, or Sevilla (€350 and up). You may see Jose at the taxi stall in the center parking lot. Call or email in advance to reserve longer trips (mobile 919-385-139 or 919-422-061, www.vibeltaxis. com, vibeltaxis@vodafone.pt).

Self-Guided Tour

Welcome to Salema

Salema has a split personality: The whitewashed old town is for locals, and the other half was built for tourists—both groups

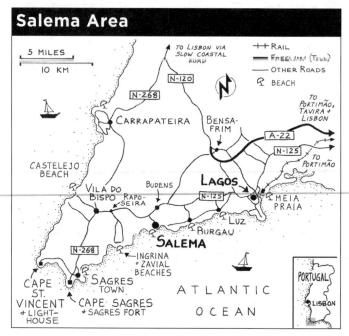

Salema Area

pursue a policy of peaceful coexistence. Tourists laze in the sun, while locals grab the shade.

Town Square Market Action: Salema's recently updated town square sports a parking lot and beachside promenade. The Balneario Municipal building has a WC. A flatbed truck market rolls into the square weekday mornings— one truck each for fish, fruit, and vegetables, and a five-and-dime truck for clothing and other odds and ends. The tooting horn of the fish truck wakes you at 8:00. The bakery trailer sells delightful fresh bread and homemade sweet rolls each morning (about 8:30-11:00). On weekday afternoons around 14:00, the red mobile post office stops by (until either the government cuts its funding or a small office opens in the Balneario Municipal building).

Fishing Scene: Salema is still a fishing village—but just barely. While the fishermen's hut no longer hosts a fish auction, you'll still see the old-timers enjoying its shade, oblivious to the tourists, while mending their nets and reminiscing about the old days when life was "only fish and hunger." To get permission before taking

Salema

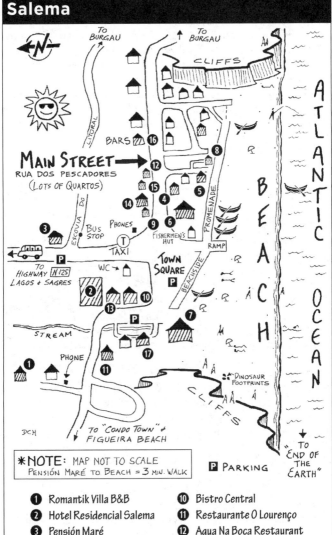

1. Romantik Villa B&B
2. Hotel Residencial Salema
3. Pensión Maré
4. Ribeiro Rooms
5. Acacio Rooms
6. Boia Bar & Rest.
7. Atlântico Restaurant
8. Mira Mar Restaurant
9. Casa Pizza
10. Bistro Central
11. Restaurante O Lourenço
12. Agua Na Boca Restaurant
13. Corsario's Restaurant
14. Salema Market
15. A Tabúa Bar
16. A Aventura Bar
17. Salema Property & Services

THE ALGARVE

their photo, ask *"Posso tirar uma foto, por favor?"* (paw-soo teer-ar oo-mah foh-toh, poor fah-vor).

In the calm of the summer, boats are left out on buoys. In the winter, the community-subsidized tractor earns its keep by hauling the boats ashore. (In pre-tractor days, such boat-hauling was a 10-person chore.)

Octopus is the main catch. The pottery jars stacked everywhere are octopus traps. Unwritten tradition allocates different chunks of undersea territory to each Salema family. The traps are tied about 15 feet apart in long lines and dropped offshore. Octopi, thinking these jars would make a cozy place to set an ambush, climb in and get ambushed themselves. When the fishermen hoist them in, they hang on—unaware they've made their final mistake. The fishermen mace them out of their pot with a squirt of bleach. The octopi flop angrily into the boat bound for the market and, who knows...maybe onto your dinner plate.

Beach Scene: Sunbathers enjoy the beach May through September. (I once got a sunburn in early May.) Knowing their tourist-based economy sits on a foundation of sand, locals hope and pray that the sand returns after being washed away each winter (some winters leave the beach just a pile of rocks). A pre-breakfast stroll eastward is a pristine way to greet the new day.

Locals claim the beach is safe for swimming, and in summer a lifeguard is often on duty, but the water is rarely really warm. You can rent beach items (lounge chair-€5/day, 2 lounge chairs and bamboo sunshade-€12/day) at the Atlântico restaurant, and one- and two-person canoes (€5-7/30 minutes) on the beach in front of the Balneario Municipal. The fountain in front of the building is a reminder of the old days. When water to the village was cut off, this was always running.

At the west end of the beach, look for the dinosaur footprints 200 yards past the Atlântico restaurant in a big, flat, yellowish raised rock (beside the rusty pipe sticking out of the cliff, www.geology.west-algarve.net).

Also on the west end, at low tide, you may be able to climb over the rocks past tiny tide pools to secluded Figueira Beach. (But be aware of when the tide comes in, or your route back will have to be over land.) While the old days of black-clad widows chasing topless Nordic women off the beach are gone, nudism is still risqué today. If you go topless, do so with discretion. Over the rocks and beyond the view of prying eyes, Germans grin and bare it.

THE ALGARVE

Hiking: There are several beautiful hikes from Salema along the beach and through the countryside out to neighboring villages such as Figueira. For routes, ask at your hotel, or see the walks and hikes described at http://salema4u.com/tours.

Community Development: The whole peninsula (west of Lagos) has been declared a natural park, and further development close to the beach is forbidden. But the village of Salema is becoming less and less ramshackle as it's gradually bought up by northern Europeans for vacation or retirement homes. Salema will live with past mistakes, such as the huge hotel in the town center that pulled some mysterious strings to go two stories over code. Up the street is a sprawling community of condos and Club Med-type vacationers who rarely leave their air-conditioned bars and swimming pools.

Across the highway and two miles inland is a big golfing resort, Parque da Floresta, where several well-known European soccer players have recently snapped up holiday homes (main reception open 24 hours, golf reception open daily 8:00-20:00; €21 daily visitor pass for spa, gym, and outdoor pool—spa treatments extra; around €100 to golf, tennis courts available, spa tel. 282-690-007, golf tel. 282-690-054, www.parquedafloresta.com).

Nightlife in Salema

Salema has two late-night bars, each worth a visit to sample the local drinks. *Armarguinha* (ar-mar-GWEEN-yah) is a sweet, likeable almond liqueur. *Licor beirão* (LIK-kor bay-ROW; "row" rhymes with "cow") is Portuguese amaretto, a "double distillation of diverse plants and aromatic seeds in accordance with a secret old formula." *Caipirinha* (kay-peer-EEN-yah), tasty and powerful, is made of fermented Brazilian sugarcane with lime, sugar, and crushed ice. And *moscatel* is the local sweet dessert wine.

Guillerme Duarte's **A Tabúa Bar** is the liveliest by Salema standards, offering patrons its famous sangria. Just up the street, the **A Aventura Bar** offers an intimate atmosphere for sipping drinks and sending email (the *caipirinha* is good, as is the *mojito,* a Cuban specialty with white rum and fresh mint leaves). For a late dessert or a sangria on the beach, drop by the **Mira Mar** restaurant. Or just grab a bench on the promenade and ponder the moon and the waves.

Sleep Code

(€1 = about $1.30, country code: 351)
S = Single, **D** = Double/Twin, **T** = Triple, **Q** = Quad, **b** = bathroom, **s** = shower only. When a price range is given, the lowest is the winter rate and the highest is the peak-season summer rate. Credit cards are accepted only at Pensión Maré and Hotel Residencial Salema. English is spoken unless otherwise noted.

To help you easily sort through these listings, I've divided the accommodations into three categories, based on the price for a standard double room with bath during high season:

$$$ **Higher Priced**—Most rooms €80 or more.
$$ **Moderately Priced**—Most rooms between €45-80.
$ **Lower Priced**—Most rooms €45 or less.

Prices can change without notice; verify the hotel's current rates online or by email.

Sleeping in Salema

Salema is crowded July through mid-September (and August is horribly packed). Prices jump up in July and August, and the place is partially closed down in winter.

For maximum comfort, there's no need to look beyond Pensión Maré. There's also a basic and utilitarian high-rise hotel in the center of town. But for economy, the experience, and an opportunity to practice your Portuguese, stay in a *quarto* (room). *Quartos* are primarily located along the main road that parallels the waterfront. Fisherfolk happily rent out rooms in their homes, most of which have separate private entrances.

Quartos don't serve breakfast, and breakfast at hotels isn't until 8:30 (after the bread guy arrives at Salema). Early birds can enjoy coffee and pastries from 7:30 on at Solmar Café (next to Salema Property and Services, opposite Hotel Residencial Salema) or savor a substantial cooked breakfast at either Corsario's or Bistro Central (both recommended, both on the main square, near Hotel Residencial Salema).

Pensiónes and Hotels

$$$ Romantik Villa B&B, run by Lisa from Brazil, is a chic, artsy house on top of the hill with three rooms, an apartment, a garden, and a swimming pool. It's tastefully decorated and a good spot for people who want quiet—no children or teens are accepted (Db-€80-90, includes breakfast; apartment-€100-120, no breakfast; cash only, extra charge for room cleaning and fresh bedding during your stay, Praia de Salema, tel. 282-695-670, mobile 967-059-806, www.romantikvilla.com, romantikvilla@sapo.pt). The villa is a steep, 10-minute uphill walk—head up from the beach past Restaurante O Lourenço, take a right at the phone booth just after the *Salema Beach Club* sign, go up into Urbanização Beach Villas, and look for the *Romantik Villa* sign on the right. Drivers should take the first left past Restaurante O Lourenço (because of the one-way street, you'll need to go around the block), turn right at the stop sign, head back downhill for a few yards, then take the first left at the phone booth. Go up the steep hill and look for the *Romantik Villa* sign (on your right).

$$$ Hotel Residencial Salema, the large hotel towering above everything else in town, is a good value if you want a basic, comfortable room handy to the beach. Its 32 red-tiled rooms all have air-conditioning, balconies, and partial views (Sb-€81, Db-€94 mid-July-mid-Sept; Sb-€65, Db-€72 June-mid-July and mid-late Sept; Sb-€53, Db-€65 Easter-May and Oct; usually closed Nov-Easter, 10 percent discount with this book, includes breakfast, elevator, bar, tel. 282-695-328, fax 282-695-329, www.hotel-salema.com, info@hotelsalema.com).

$$ Pensión Maré, a blue-and-white building overlooking the village above the main road into town, is the best hotel value in Salema. It's run by friendly Bettina, who offers six comfortable rooms (Sb-€56-64, Db-€70-80, includes wonderful breakfast) and three fully equipped apartments (Db-€70-90) in a tidy paradise (10 percent discount with this book and cash if booked ahead via email, Wi-Fi, next-day laundry service-€3.50/kilo, Praia de Salema, tel. 282-695-165, fax 282-695-846, www.the-mare.com, jorn@algarve.co.uk). Bettina will also hold a room with a phone call and a credit-card number, and her website has good Salema information.

Apartments

Renting an apartment is a popular option that falls comfortably between staying in a hotel and spending the night in someone's home (see information on *quartos*, next). Jorn and Sigrun, a Danish couple, manage a house and apartment near the beach (2-person apartment-€55, 4-person house-€70-150, minimum 2-night stay, cash only, mobile 963-609-205, www.salema4u.com, jorn@salema4u.com).

Quartos and Camping

Quartos provide a great way to connect with locals. Rooms abound along the main street, Rua dos Pescadores ("Fishermen Street"). As you face the beach, the street runs to the left from the village center.

To find a room, ask one of the locals at the waterfront, or check at the Boia Bar or Salema Market. Prices vary with the season, plumbing, and view, but if you're only staying one night in high season, you're bad news. It can be difficult to find a room for less than three nights, especially in July and August. Doubles cost about €25-60 (forget breakfast and credit cards). Many places offer beach-front views, and it's worth paying extra for rooms *com vista* (with a view). Some rooms are bright and sprawling, while others are dark and musty. *Quarto* landladies generally speak only a little English, but they're used to dealing with visitors. Many will do your laundry for about €4 or so. If you're settling

into Salema for a while or are on a tight budget, park your bags and travel partner at a beachside bar and survey several places. Except for August weekends, there are always rooms available for drop-ins. Prices can be soft, especially outside of July and August.

$ Maria Helena and Jorge Ribeiro, a helpful young couple, rent two small, simple doubles (S or D-€35 all year, one has a tiny view) and a charming treehouse-type suite with a kitchen, a view terrace, and a view toilet for Db-€40-50 (Rua dos Pescadores 83, tel. 282-695-289).

$ The Acacio family rents a humble ground-floor double (D-€25-30) and a fine upstairs apartment with a kitchenette, a balcony over the beach, and a great ocean view for up to five people (Db-€50, Tb-€70, Qb-€80, generally €15-20 more July-Aug, Rua dos Pescadores 91, tel. 282-695-473). Silvina doesn't speak English and she pouts if you're staying only one night.

Campers who don't underestimate the high tides sleep free and easy on the **beach** or at a well-run **campground** with bunga-lows a half-mile inland, back toward the main road (ask at Salema Property and Services).

Eating in Salema

Eat fresh seafood here, eternally. The local specialty is *cataplana*—fish, tomatoes, potatoes, onions, and whatever else is available—big enough for two or three, and cooked a long time in a traditional copper pot (somewhere between a pressure cooker and a steamer). Also look for grilled golden bream *(dourada grelhada)* and giant prawns *(camarãos).*

Salema has seven or so places that all serve fine €11 meals. Happily, those that face the beach (the first three listed here) are the most fun and have the best service, food, and atmosphere. For a memorable last course at any of these places, consider taking your *moscatel* (dessert wine), *caipirinha* (Brazilian sugarcane liquor mixed with lime), or coffee to the beach for some stardust on the side.

The **Boia Bar and Restaurant,** at the base of the residential street, has a classy beachfront setting, noteworthy service by a friendly gang, and a knack for doing whitefish just right (always with free seconds on good orange and green vegetables). Their vegetarian lasagna (€10.50) and salads are popular, as are their €8 breakfasts (daily 10:00-24:00, tel. 282-695-382).

The **Atlântico**—noisy, big, busy, and right on the beach—has long dominated the Salema beach scene. It's known for tasty fish (especially swordfish), friendly service, and a wonderful beachside terrace (daily 12:00-24:00, serving until 22:00, also rents lounge chairs and bamboo sunshades, accepts credit cards, tel. 282-695-142).

The intimate **Mira Mar,** farther up the residential street, is a last vestige of old Salema. Florentine and Dieter offer a creative rotating menu for those venturing away from seafood. Their €10 tapas plate—a hearty array of cold meats, veggies, and munchies—can make a meal. Their *caldeirada* is a delightful Portuguese fish-and-veggie stew, but be forewarned—portions are large (Sun-Fri 12:30-16:00 & 18:30-22:30, closed Sat, cash only).

Casa Pizza, across the street from the Boia Bar, isn't on the beach, but its upper deck has a great view. It serves a variety of tasty €7-10 pizzas, salads, and fresh fish, as well as €8-15 meat and pasta dishes (daily 10:00-24:00, Rua dos Pescadores 100, tel. 282-697-968). Get a pizza to go, and eat it on the beach for the best view in town.

Bistro Central—on the town square and open for breakfast, lunch, and dinner—offers a rotating, international menu. Bertrand runs the restaurant while Marc and Natalia cook up a variety of €7-25 fish, meat, pasta, and vegetarian dishes (€8 daily specials, good wine list, homemade desserts, Tue-Sun 9:00-24:00, closed Mon, mobile 934-194-215).

Restaurante O Lourenço, a block up the hill, has no ambience or view but offers good-value meals, has a local clientele, and is *the* place for *cataplana* (€30 for 2 people). Paulo serves, while his mother Aldina cooks (€7.50 fixed-price meal, fresh but expensive "catch-of-the-day" platter around €35—ask price before ordering, Mon-Sat 10:00-23:30, closed Sun, cash only; from Hotel Residencial Salema cross the bridge, restaurant is a half-block uphill on your left; tel. 282-698-622).

Need a break from fish? **Agua Na Boca** ("Mouth Watering"), a sophisticated and atmospheric eatery run by Paulo and his wife-and-chef Irene, serves up-market local cuisine. It's always busy, so reserve ahead (about €60 for three-course meal for 2 people, includes wine; extensive wine list, closed Sun, on Rua dos Pescadores

THE ALGARVE

next to A Aventura Bar, tel. 282-695-651). The pepper steak is excellent, as is everything else Paulo serves.

Corsario's, a simple restaurant next door to Hotel Residencial Salema, provides a hearty cooked English breakfast for €7 that's really a brunch. You'll be served by Pedro Alfonso, a Portuguese motorcycle-racing champion, and his friendly mom, Rosa, who is proud of her homemade desserts. Ask Rosa to show you their collection of signed soccer players' shirts upstairs (daily 8:00 until late, snacks available all day, mobile 918-213-795).

Picnics: Romeu's **Salema Market** has all the fixings for a great picnic to take with you to a secluded beach or Cape Sagres. Look for fresh fruits, veggies, bread, sheep's cheese, sausage, and *vinho verde* (young white wine, a Portuguese specialty with a refreshing taste). Helpful Romeu also changes money and gives travel and *quarto* advice (daily July-Sept 9:00-20:00, Oct-June 9:00-13:00 & 15:00-19:00, on Rua dos Pescadores).

For drivers: Drivers who want a classy meal outside of town should consider the elegant **Vila Velha Restaurante** in Sagres or the more rustic **Castelejo Restaurante** at the surreal Praia do Castelejo (both described later).

Cape Sagres

In the days before Columbus, when the world was presumed to be flat, this rugged southwestern tip of Portugal was the spot closest to the edge of the Earth. Prince Henry the Navigator, determined to broaden Europe's horizons and spread Catholicism, founded his navigators' school here and sent sailors ever farther into the unknown. Shipwrecked and frustrated explorers were carefully debriefed as they washed ashore.

Orientation to Cape Sagres

Portugal's "end of the road" is two distinct capes. Windy **Cape St. Vincent** is actually the most southwestern tip. It has a desolate lighthouse (currently closed for restoration) that marks what was thought of even in prehistoric times as "the end of the world." Outside the lighthouse, salt-of-the-earth merchants sell figs, seaworthy sweaters (€25 average), cotton tea towels (a bargain at €1), and the *"Letzte Bratwurst vor Amerika"* (last hot dog before America). **Cape**

Sagres, with its old fort and Henry the Navigator lore, is the more historic cape of the two. At either cape, look for daredevil windsurfers and fishermen casting from the cliffs.

Lashed tightly to the windswept landscape is the salty **town of Sagres,** above a harbor of fishing boats. Sagres is a popular gathering place for the backpacking crowd, with plenty of private rooms in the center and a barely existent beach and bar scene.

Tourist Information: The TI is on the main street, Avenida Comandante Matoso (Tue-Sat 9:30-13:30 & 14:30-17:30, closed Sun-Mon, tel. 282-624-873).

Sights in Cape Sagres

Sagres Fort and Navigators' School

The former "end of the world" is a craggy, windswept, wedge-shaped point that juts into the Atlantic (short drive or 15-minute walk from Sagres). In 1420, Prince Henry the Navigator used his order's funds to establish a school here for navigators. Today, little remains of Henry's school, except the site of buildings replaced by later (sometimes new) structures. An 18th-century fortress, built on the school's original battlements, dominates the entrance to the point.

Cost and Hours: €3, daily May-Sept 9:30-20:00, Oct-April 9:30-17:30, last entry 30 minutes before closing, tel. 282-620-140.

◉ Self-Guided Tour: After entering through the 18th-century battlements, find the carved **stone plaque** that honors Henry. The ship in the plaque is a caravel, one of the small, light craft that was constantly being reinvented by Sagres' shipbuilding grad students. The astrolabe, a compact instrument that uses the stars for navigation, emphasizes Henry's role in the exploration process.

Sagres' most impressive sight—a circle on the ground, 100 feet across and outlined by round pebbles—is a mystery. Some think it was a large **wind-compass** *(rosa-dos-ventos).* A flag flying from the center could immediately announce the wind's direction. Others speculate it's a large sundial. A pole in the center pointing toward the North Star (at a 37-degree angle, Sagres' latitude) would cast a shadow on the dial showing the time of day.

Prince Henry the Navigator (1394-1460)

No swashbuckling sailor, Henry was a quiet scholar, an organizer, a religious man, and the brains behind Portugal's daring sea voyages. The middle child of King John (João) I of Portugal and Queen Philippa of England, he was one of what was dubbed "The Marvelous Generation" (Ínclita Geração) that drove the Age of Discovery. While his brothers and nephews became Portugal's kings, he worked behind the scenes.

At age 21, he planned the logistics for the large-scale ship invasion of the Muslim city of Ceuta (1415) on the north coast of Morocco, taking the city and winning knightly honors. Awed by the wealth of the city—a terminus of the caravan route— and intrigued by the high-quality maps he found there, Henry decided to organize expeditions to explore the Muslim world. He hoped to spread Christianity, contain Islam, tap Muslim wealth, and find Prester John's legendary Christian kingdom, said to exist somewhere in Africa or Asia.

As head of the Order of Christ—a powerful brotherhood of soldier-monks— Grand Master Henry used their money to found a maritime school at Sagres. While Henry stayed home to update maps, debrief returning sailors, order supplies, and sign paychecks, brave seamen traveled off under Henry's strict orders not to return until they'd explored what was known as the "Sea of Darkness."

The row of buildings beyond the wind-compass is where the **school** once was. The **tower-cistern** (abutting the end of the modern Exhibition Centre) is part of the original dorms. The small, whitewashed, 16th-century **Church of Our Lady of Grace** replaced Henry's church. The former Governor's House is now the restaurant/gift shop complex. Attached to the gift shop is a **windbreak wall** that dates from Henry's time, but is largely rebuilt.

The Sagres school taught mapmaking, shipbuilding, sailing, astronomy, and mathematics (for navigating), plus botany, zoology, anthropology, languages, and salesmanship for mingling with the locals. The school welcomed Italians, Scandinavians, and Germans, and included Christians, Muslims, and Jews. Captured Africans gave guest lectures. (The next 15 generations of Africans were not so lucky, being sold into slavery by the tens of thousands.)

Besides being a school, Sagres was Mission Control for the explorers. Returning sailors brought spices, gold, diamonds, silk, and ivory, plus new animals, plants, peoples, customs, communicable

They discovered the Madeira Islands (1420), which Henry planted with vineyards, and the Azores (1427), which Henry colonized with criminals. But the next expeditions returned empty-handed, having run into a barrier—both a psychological and physical one. Cape Bojador (at the southwest corner of modern Morocco), with its reefs and currents, was seen as the end of the world. Beyond that, sea serpents roamed, while the hot equatorial sun melted ships, made the sea boil, and turned white men black.

Henry ordered scared, superstitious sailors to press on. After 14 unsuccessful voyages, Gil Eanes' crew returned (1437), unharmed and still white, with new knowledge that was added to corporate Portugal's map library.

Henry himself gained a reputation as an intelligent, devout, nonmaterialistic, celibate monk who humbled himself by wearing horsehair underwear. In 1437, Henry faced a personal tragedy. His planned invasion of Tangier failed miserably, and his beloved little brother Fernão was captured. As ransom, the Muslims demanded that Portugal return Ceuta. Henry (and others) refused, Fernão died in captivity, and Henry was devastated.

In later years, he spent less time at court in Lisbon and more in desolate Sagres, where he died in 1460. (He's buried in Batalha; see page 216.) Henry died before finding a sea route to Asia and just before his voyages really started paying off commercially. A generation later, Vasco da Gama would sail to India, capping Henry's explorations and kicking off Portugal's Golden Age.

THE ALGARVE

diseases, and knowledge of the routes that were added to the maps. Henry ordered every sailor to keep a travel journal that could be studied. Ship designs were analyzed and tweaked, resulting in the square-sailed, oceangoing caravels that replaced the earlier coast-hugging versions.

It's said that Ferdinand Magellan (circumnavigator), Vasco da Gama (found sea route to India), Pedro Cabral (discovered Brazil), and Bartolomeu Dias (Africa-rounder) all studied at Sagres (after Henry's time, though). In May 1476, the young Italian Christopher Columbus washed ashore here after being shipwrecked by pirates. He went on to study and sail with the Portuguese (and marry a Portuguese woman) before beginning his American voyage. When Portugal denied Columbus' request to sail west, Spain accepted. The rest is history.

Beyond the buildings, the granite **point** itself is windswept, eroded, and largely barren, except for hardy, coarse vegetation admired by botanists. Walk on level paths around the edge of the bluff (a 40-minute round-trip walk), where locals cast lines and tourists squint into the wind. You'll get great seascape views of Cape St. Vincent, with its modern lighthouse on the site of an old convent. At the far end of the Sagres bluff are a naval radio station, a natural cave, and a promontory called "Prince Henry's Chair."

Sit on the point and gaze across the "Sea of Darkness," where monsters roam. Long before Henry's time, Romans considered it the edge of the world, dubbing it Promontorium Sacrum—Sacred ("Sagres") Promontory. Pilgrims who came to visit this awe-inducing place were prohibited from spending the night here—it was for the gods alone.

In Portugal's seafaring lore, capes, promontories, and land's ends are metaphors for the edge of the old, and the start of the unknown voyage. Sagres is the greatest of these.

Beaches

Many beaches are tucked away on the drive between Salema and Cape Sagres. Most of them require a short walk after you stop along N-125. In some cases, you leave your car on access roads or cross private property to reach the beaches—be considerate. In Salema, ask at Pensión Maré or Salema Property and Services for directions to beaches before you head to Sagres. Furnas beach is fully accessible by car. You can access Ingrina and Zavial beaches by turning south in the village of Raposeira. Many beaches have bars (the one at Ingrina beach is famous for its spicy garlic prawns—*camarão piri-piri*).

The best secluded beach in the region is **Praia do Castelejo,** just north of Cape Sagres (from the town of Vila do Bispo, drive inland and follow the signs for 15 minutes). If you have a car and didn't grow up in Fiji, this really is worth the drive. Overlooking the deserted beach is **Castelejo Restaurante,** which specializes in octopus dishes and *cataplana,* the hearty local seafood stew (daily 12:00-22:00, 7.5 miles from Salema at Praia do Castelejo, tel. 282-639-777). While beaches between Salema and Sagres offer more of a seaside landscape, beaches north of São Vicente are more rugged and wild because they're exposed to ocean wind and weather. If there's no sand in Castelejo when you visit, blame it on nature and enjoy the rock formations instead.

Activities

Cape Cruiser down at Cape Sagres' port takes boat trips out to Cabo São Vincente (around €20/person) and also does fishing trips (cash only, mobile 919-751-175, capecruiser@gmail.com).

Mar Ilimitado offers several daily boat trips, including dolphin watching (€32/person, 1.5 hours, July-Sept tours go every hour 9:30-15:30, March-June and Oct-Nov at 11:30 only); seabird watching (€40/person, 3 hours, by reservation March-Nov at 9:30); and a visit to Cabo São Vincente (€20/person, 1 hour, March-Nov at 16:00; no tours Dec-Feb, mobile 916-832-625, www.marilimitado.com, info@marilimitado.com).

Divers Cape Sagres, located at the port, is a diving school offering dive classes and various excursions (mobile 965-559-073, www.diverscape.com).

Sagres Natura Sport and Adventure Shop gives surf classes and offers canoeing and mountain bike expeditions (just behind Surf Planet on Rua São Vincente, tel. 282-624-072, www.sagresnatura.com, sagresnatura@hotmail.com). They also rent bikes (€15/day with ID).

Sleeping in Cape Sagres

(€1 = about $1.30, country code: 351)

$$$ Pousada do Infante, lavish and on the waterfront, provides a touch of local elegance in Sagres. This classy *pousada* (historic inn) is a reasonable splurge with a magnificent setting. At breakfast, you can sip coffee and enjoy the buffet while gazing out to sea (Sb/Db-€100-200, check website for discounts, tel. 282-620-240, fax 282-624-225, www.pousadas.pt, recepcao.infante@pousadas.pt).

$$$ Memmo Baleeira Hotel, overlooking the port of Sagres, is chic and minimalist, with pure white bedrooms and sea views (July-Aug Sb-€145, Db-€180; off-season Sb-€90, Db-€105; swimming pool, sauna, Turkish bath, tel. 282-624-212, fax 282-624-425, www.memmohotels.com, hotel@memmobaleeira.com). Dinners in the restaurant are reasonably priced.

$$ Casa de Sagres' Guest House, at the bus-stop end of town, will put you up in a perfectly reasonable room for a great price (July-Sept Sb-€50, Db-€75; off-season Sb-€30, Db-€45; Praça da República, tel. 282-624-358).

Eating in Cape Sagres

Vila Velha Restaurante offers wonderfully unforgettable meals, especially their rabbit stew (mid-July-mid-Sept daily 18:30-22:00, closed Mon, reservations smart, Rua Patrão Antonio Faustino, near the *pousada* listed above, tel. 282-624-788).

THE ALGARVE

Raposo (Fox) Restaurante, by the tiny, sandy, and picturesque Mareta Beach (Praia da Mareta), is a fun spot for lunch on a terrace. Have a dip in the sea right after your meal. Sometimes German tour groups descend and swamp this cute little eatery (light snacks, €3-5 creamy milkshakes, €15-20 fish dishes, €45 steaming *cataplana* with seafood for 2, daily 10:00-20:30, tel. 282-624-168).

Bossa Nova Pizzeria, in a converted stable, serves tasty pizzas, pastas, salads, and vegetarian dishes (mid-April-Sept daily 12:00-23:00; Oct-mid-April Tue-Sun 17:00-23:00, closed Mon; eat in or take away, along Avenida Comandante Matoso, tel. 282-624-219). It's behind the Dromadário Bar (daily 10:00-2:00 in the morning, check out the camel mosaics on the wall).

Cape Sagres Connections

From Salema, Sagres is a 20-minute drive or a 30-minute bus trip (runs every 1-2 hours, bus stop is just below Pensión Maré—flag it down). You can check bus times at Salema Property and Services or online at www.algarvebus.info. Some buses continue to Cabo São Vincente, but not all; check schedules beforehand.

A taxi ride from Salema to Sagres costs about €25-30 (€60 for 1.25-hour round-trip, plus €10/hour for waiting time in Sagres; see Salema's "Helpful Hints," earlier in this chapter). Taxi driver Vittorino can take you from Salema to Cabo São Vincente to Sagres and back with short photo stops for €60 (mobile 919-385-139).

Lagos

With a beach-party old town and a jet-ski marina, Lagos (LAH-goosh) is as enjoyable as a big-city resort can be. This major town on the west end of the Algarve was the region's capital in the 13th and 14th centuries. The first great Portuguese maritime expeditions embarked from here, and the first African slave market in Europe was held here. Today this site operates as a small museum on the Praça do Infante.

Orientation to Lagos

The old town, defined by its medieval walls, stretches between Praça Gil Eanes and the fort. It's a whitewashed jumble of pedestrian streets, bars, funky craft shops, outdoor restaurants, mod fountains and sculptures, and sunburned tourists. Search out the sea-creature designs laid in the pavement—some of them will probably be on your plate at dinner. The beaches with the exotic rock formations—of postcard fame—begin just past the fort, with easy access via hiking trails.

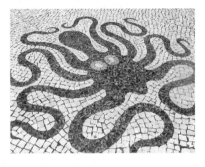

Tourist Information

The Câmara Municipal TI is downtown on Praça Gil Eanes and covers Lagos and the entire Algarve. Stop in for a town map and transportation schedules (June-Sept Mon-Sat 9:30-19:00, Oct-May Mon-Sat 9:30-17:30, closed Sun year-round, tel. 282-763-031).

Arrival in Lagos

By Train or Bus: The train and bus stations are a five-minute walk apart, separated by the marina and a pedestrian bridge over a river. Neither station has baggage storage.

By Car: If you're coming from Spain on the A-22 freeway, exit at Lagos and follow signs to centro. The most convenient free parking lot is just outside the old city wall off Rua Infante de Sagres. There are other pay lots near the marina and a large, long-term, underground parking garage on Avenida dos Descobrimentos, near Praça do Infante.

Helpful Hints

Internet Access: Western Union Exchange, behind the statue on Praça Gil Eanes, multitasks as an Internet café and currency bureau (€1.75/30 minutes, daily 8:30-21:00).

Car Rental: English-speaking Nuno at **Lagorent Rent-a-Car** can set you up with four wheels (Avenida dos Descobrimentos 43, tel. 282-762-467, fax 282-763-967, www.lagorent.com, info@lagorent.com).

Sights in Lagos

Coastal Boat Tours—Along the harborfront, you'll be hustled to take a sightseeing cruise. Old fishermen ("who know the nickname of each rock along the coast") sit at anchor on board, while their salespeople on the promenade hawk 45-minute exotic rock-and-cave tours for €10 (cash only, 2-person minimum).

More serious maritime adventures are sold by a string of established companies with offices in the marina strip mall over the marina bridge (credit cards accepted). There are some pleasant cafés in the mall—sip a *sumo de laranja* (fresh orange juice) while observing the comings-and-goings of the yachts.

Bom Dia offers several different tours by sailboat: a two-hour €25 grotto tour (with a chance to swim), a half-day €53 BBQ cruise that's basically a grotto tour with a meal, and a three-hour €40 family friendly fishing trip (cash only, in marina at Lagos 10, WC on board, smart to reserve at least a day ahead in Aug, tel. 282-087-587, www.bomdia.info, info@bomdia-boattrips.com).

▲**Church of Santo António**—Rebuilt in part after the 1755 earthquake, this is considered one of the best Baroque churches in Portugal, and is dedicated to the patron saint of the military, António. The church, with an incredible gilded altar and paintings of António's life, is only accessible through the adjoining regional archaeological and ethnology museum.

Cost and Hours: €2.60, Tue-Sun 9:30-12:30 & 14:00-17:00, closed Mon, museum entrance just beyond the church.

▲**Mercado de Escravos (Slave Market Museum)**—This small museum, located on the site of the original Lagos slave market, documents the tragic history of slavery in the region, which began at this very spot in 1444. Displays include some 15th-century coins, African ceramics and beads, and a skeleton—one of several found in a nearby rubbish dump.

Cost and Hours: €1.50, Mon-Sat 10:00-17:30, closed Sun.

Sleeping in Lagos

(€1 = about $1.30, country code: 351)

When a price range is given, the lowest is the winter rate and the highest is the August rate. Lagos is enjoyable for a resort its size, but remember that Salema, a village paradise, is a short taxi or bus ride away. If you missed the last bus to Salema (leaves Lagos at 20:30), Albergaria Marina Rio and Pensão Residencial Solar are both within 100 yards of the bus station. Everyone speaks English.

$$$ Albergaria Marina Rio is big, slick, and comfortable, and faces the marina and the busy main street immediately in front

THE ALGARVE

of the bus station. Its 36 modern, air-conditioned rooms come with all the amenities but not-so-smiley service. Pricier marina views come with noise; quieter rooms are in the back. All rooms have twin beds (Sb-€56-108, Db-€66-111, extra bed-€20-36, includes breakfast and tax, elevator, Internet access, pay Wi-Fi, small rooftop pool and terrace, laundry service, Avenida dos Descobrimentos, Apartado 388, tel. 282-780-830, fax 282-780-839, www.marinario.com, marinario@net.vodafone.pt).

$$$ Hotel Riomar is a blocky, 1980s-feeling, tour-group-friendly place providing 42 rooms for a decent price (Db-€30-105, Tb-€40-115, Qb-€50-150, includes breakfast, air-con, elevator, back rooms lack street noise, Rua Candido dos Reis 83, tel. 282-770-130, fax 282-763-927, www.hotelriomarlagos.com, hotel riomar@sapo.pt).

$$ Pensão Residencial Solar rents 29 very basic rooms (Sb-€25-50, Db-€35-65; includes breakfast, a big smile, and a fan; cheaper D-€20-40 rooms in annex up the hill and in *quartos* in the center, elevator, Internet access and Wi-Fi, Rua António Crisogno dos Santos 60, tel. 282-762-477, fax 282-087-692, http://solar guesthouse.blogspot.com, hotelsolarlagos@hotmail.com).

$ The **youth hostel** is a busy, social, hammocks-in-the-courtyard experience (dorm bed in quad-€11-18, five Db-€30-45, includes breakfast, kitchen facilities, Internet access and Wi-Fi, priority given to hostel members, non-members of any age welcome, Rua Lançarote de Freitas 50, tel. 282-761-970, fax 282-769-684, http://microsites.juventude.gov.pt, lagos@movijovem.pt).

Eating in Lagos

You'll find a variety of lively choices for dinner branching out in all directions from Praça Gil Eanes. Most of them offer a similar sampling of grilled fish with plenty of vegetables, but other options range from Italian to Indian. Home-style cooking is better closer to the market.

O Pescador, popular with locals and tourists alike, serves good grilled fish and meat in a simple, bright, paper-napkin atmosphere. Their mouthwatering prawns with rice *(camarãos com arroz)* comes in a big steaming pot, perfect for two with a jug of the house *vinho verde* (daily 12:00-22:00, until 23:00 in summer, Rua Gil Eanes 6-10, tel. 282-767-028). Hardworking João speaks little English but is eager to please. Take note that the "scallops" on the menu are pork, not shellfish.

Meu Limão ("My Lemon") is a handy, citrus-fresh little tapas-and-wine bar right by the Church of São Antonio (€3-4 tapas, €6.50 salads, €5-10 daily specials, Portuguese wines by the glass; Thu-Tue 11:30-23:00, closed Wed; tel. 282-767-946).

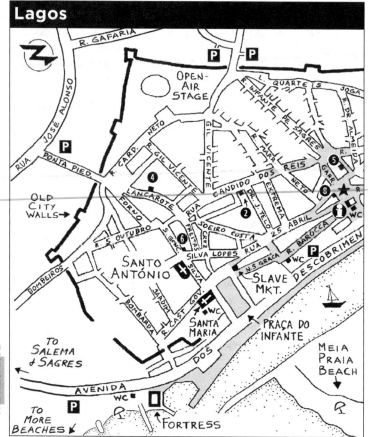

THE ALGARVE

Picnics: **Ecomarche** supermarket has a wide selection of food (daily 8:00-21:00, on the waterfront opposite the marina, look for the blue-and-white canopy). The big market hall two minutes beyond it has an impressive array of local fish downstairs; upstairs are fantastic fresh fruits and vegetables, dried figs, nuts, and spicy homemade *piri-piri* sauce (Mon-Sat until 13:00, closed Sun).

Lagos Connections

From Lagos by Train and Bus to: Lisbon (6 trains/day, 3.5-4 hours, transfer in Tunes or Faro, €24; 10 buses/day, 4 hours, some transfer in Albufeira; €20), **Évora** (3 trains/day, 5-6 hours, transfer in Pinhal Novo and Tunes or Faro; 3 buses/day with transfer in Albufeira or Faro, 1 bus/day direct in summer only, 4.5-5 hours), **Tavira** (8 trains/day, 2.5-4 hours; 6 buses/day, 3.5-4 hours, both transfer in Faro). Confirm times locally. Train info: tel. 808-208-

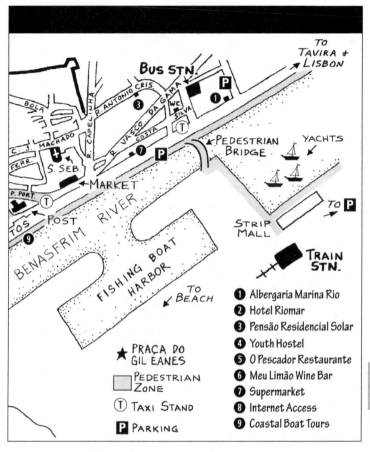

TO TAVIRA & LISBON

BUS STN

R. ANTONIO CRIS

R. VASCO DA GAMA

WC

SILVA

P

1

3

T

BOLA

R. CAPELINHA

MACHADO

C. J.

FERR

S. SEB.

COSTA

7

P

PEDESTRIAN BRIDGE

YACHTS

TO P

STRIP MALL

TRAIN STN.

←MARKET

P. PORT

T

TOS

POST

BENASFRIM RIVER

9

FISHING BOAT HARBOR

TO BEACH

★ PRAÇA DO GIL EANES

PEDESTRIAN ZONE

T TAXI STAND

P PARKING

❶ Albergaria Marina Rio
❷ Hotel Riomar
❸ Pensão Residencial Solar
❹ Youth Hostel
❺ O Pescador Restaurante
❻ Meu Limão Wine Bar
❼ Supermarket
❽ Internet Access
❾ Coastal Boat Tours

THE ALGARVE

208, www.cp.pt. Bus info: tel. 289-899-760 or 282-762-944, www. eva-bus.com or www.algarvebus.info.

Connecting Lagos and Sevilla, Spain, by Bus: There are four buses per day in each direction during summer (€21, about 5.5 hours from Lagos bus station to Sevilla's Plaza de Armas bus station, buy ticket a day or two in advance May-Oct, 2/day in off-season). Ask the TI or a local travel agency for the latest bus schedule, or check www.algarvebus.info or www.eva-bus.com. This is the usual schedule, but confirm it locally: Lagos 6:15 to Sevilla 11:30; Lagos 7:30 to Sevilla 14:00; Lagos 12:30 to Sevilla 17:45; Lagos 14:45 to Sevilla 21:15. From Sevilla 7:30 to Lagos 10:45; Sevilla 8:00 to Lagos 13:00; Sevilla 13:30 to Lagos 16:45; Sevilla 16:15 to Lagos 20:45. Note that Spanish time is one hour ahead of Portuguese time.

From Lagos to Salema: Take a bus (every 1-2 hours, fewer on weekends, 30 minutes) or a taxi (€25-30, 20 minutes); see

"Orientation to Salema" on page 144 for details. In Lagos, to get to the bus station from the train station (ignore the "*quartos* women" who tell you Salema is 40 miles away), walk left out of the train station, go through the pink strip mall, cross the arched pedestrian bridge and then the main boulevard, and angle right over to the white-and-yellow EVA bus station (bus info: tel. 289-899-760 or 282-762-944, www.eva-bus.com). Before heading to Salema, pick up return bus schedules and train schedules for your next destination (though as a fallback, Salema Property and Services in Salema has posted schedules, or check www.algarvebus.info).

Tavira

Straddling a river, with a lively park, chatty locals, and boats that share its waterfront center, Tavira (TAH-vih-rah) is a low-rise, easygoing alternative to the other more aggressive Algarve resorts. It's your best eastern Algarve stop. Because Tavira has good connections by bus and train (it's on the trans-Algarve train line, with frequent departures both east and west), many travelers find the town more accessible than Salema. If you're driving from Sevilla to Salema, it's the perfect midway stop on the four-hour trip (just two miles off the freeway). You can also get to Tavira by bus from Sevilla.

You'll see many churches and fine bits of Renaissance architecture sprinkled throughout the town. These clues are evidence that 500 years ago, Tavira was the largest town on the Algarve (with 1,500 dwellings according to a 1530 census) and an important base for Portuguese adventurers in Africa. The silting up of its harbor, a plague, the 1755 earthquake, and the shifting away of its once-lucrative tuna industry left Tavira in a long decline. Today, the town has a wistful charm and lives off its tourists.

Orientation to Tavira

Tavira straddles the Rio Gilão two miles from the Atlantic. Everything of sightseeing and transportation importance is on the south bank. A clump of historic sights—the ruined castle and main church—fills its tiny fortified hill and tangled Moorish lanes. But today, the action is outside the old fortifications along the riverside Praça da República square and the adjacent shady fountain- and bench-filled park. The old market hall is beyond the park. And beyond that is the boat to the beach island. The old pedestrian-only Roman Bridge leads from Praça da República to the north bank (with two recommended hotels and most of the evening and restaurant action).

Tourist Information

The TI is on the main square, Praça da República, right across from the town hall (May-Oct Tue-Thu 9:30-13:00 & 14:00-19:00, Fri-Mon until 17:30; Nov-April closes some weekends and daily at 17:30, Rua Galeria 9, tel. 281-322-511). The TI's free leaflet describes a dozen churches with enthusiasm. But for most tourists, the town's sights can all be seen quickly (see "Welcome to Tavira" walk, later).

Arrival in Tavira

By Train: The train station is a 20-minute walk from the town center *(centro)*. To get to the center, leave the station in the direction of the blue *Turismo* sign, and follow this road downhill to the river and Praça da República (or take a cab from the station for around €4). The riverside bus station is three blocks from the town center; simply follow the river into town.

By Car: Drivers can park on the street, along Rua da Liberdade, for up to two hours (€0.40/hour, look for *zona pago* signs, pay at green boxes marked *caixa,* change required). Free parking is usually available on the street near the Pingo Doce supermarket.

Helpful Hints

Internet Access: Café Anazu has a gang of computers available (€3/hour, daily 8:30-24:00 but may close on off-season weekends, over the Roman Bridge on the right at Rua Pessoa 11). A few free terminals are at **City Hall**—it's the white building with the flags on Praça da República (Mon-Fri 9:00-22:00, Sat 10:00-13:00, closed Sun, 30-minute free access, check in at the desk). Free Wi-Fi is available in the old market hall and at many cafés in town.

Bike Rental: You can rent bikes at **Sport Nautica** (€6/day, just down from Café Anazu at Rua Pessoa 26, tel. 281-324-943).

Taxi: A taxi stand is across the Roman Bridge on Praça Dr. António Padinha.

Shopping Tip: You can buy your own copper *cataplana* pot for about €35 at the yellow hardware store at the far end of Rua Alexandro Herculano (first street on your left after the City Hall on Praça da República).

THE ALGARVE

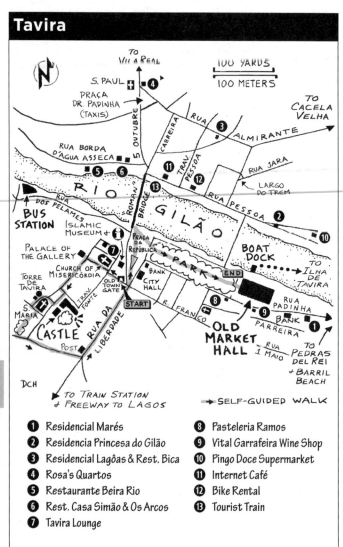

Tavira

100 YARDS
100 METERS

1. Residencial Marés
2. Residencia Princesa do Gilão
3. Residencial Lagôas & Rest. Bica
4. Rosa's Quartos
5. Restaurante Beira Rio
6. Rest. Casa Simão & Os Arcos
7. Tavira Lounge
8. Pasteleria Ramos
9. Vital Garrafeira Wine Shop
10. Pingo Doce Supermarket
11. Internet Café
12. Bike Rental
13. Tourist Train

Self-Guided Walk

Welcome to Tavira

This quick walk starts in front of the TI on Praça da República (the town square) and covers everything of importance.

Old Town Gate

This unimpressive gate (to the left of the TI) is one of the few sections left from Tavira's 16th-century walls (another section is next door, inside the Islamic Center Museum). Check out the gate's crown and spheres—meant to remind visitors that they are in the kingdom of Portugal—and the holes for bars that once locked the door.

• *At the top of the lane, find the church that faces the city gate.*

Church of Misericórdia

Its facade, dating from 1541, is considered the best Renaissance facade in the Algarve. Inside, you'll see a multitude of blue-and-white tile panels that show you how to lead a good Christian life. Meanwhile, a zealous attendant will make sure you don't take any photos inside.

Cost and Hours: Free, Mon-Sat 9:00-12:30 & 14:00-19:00, off-season until 17:30, closed Sun.

• *Across the street from the Church of Misericórdia (above the TI), find the...*

Islamic Center Museum (Núcleo Islamico)

This recently opened museum showcases the Islamic history of the city. Inside you can see a large section of the old town wall, along with various artifacts from the 11th and 12th centuries. Many of the pieces were found at this very location during the construction of a bank. The highlight of the museum is the Vase of Tavira, a large vessel decorated with figures of animals and people carrying weapons and musical instruments.

Cost and Hours: €2, Tue-Sat 10:00-13:00 & 15:00-18:30, off-season until 17:30, closed Sun-Mon year-round.

• *From the museum, hike left up the stepped lane to the...*

Palace of the Gallery

This 17th-century Baroque palace, nearly the town's highest point, is nicknamed "Tavira's Acropolis." It's the biggest private mansion in town, but it also houses a smaller exhibition center, open to the public, with rotating themes: contemporary art or Tavira's maritime history. Even if you don't go into the museum itself, pop inside the door to see some Phoenician ritual pots, visible through glass covers on the foyer floor.

Cost and Hours: €2, Tue-Sat 10:00-12:30 & 15:00-18:30, off-season until 17:30, some summer nights until 23:00 for special exhibits, closed Sun-Mon year-round, free Tavira maps.

• *Climb left to the big Church of Santa Maria (which we'll return to in a minute). On your left is a hunk of castle with a door leading to the...*

Castle Garden

The base of the castle wall is supposedly Neolithic, while later inhabitants—the Phoenicians in the eighth century B.C., the Moors in the eighth century A.D., and the Portuguese in the 13th century—added their own layers to the structure. The castle grounds are now a fragrant garden, offering a fine city view. Overlooking the city, notice Tavira's unique "treasury" rooftops—a little roof for each room of a building, likely inspired by visions brought home from Asia by local explorers. Gaze to the right and see tower-wall remnants sprouting up between houses.

Cost and Hours: Free, Mon-Fri 8:00-17:00, Sat-Sun 10:00-17:00, daily until 19:00 in July-Sept.

• *Return to the...*

Church of Santa Maria

Once a mosque, this church was transformed in the 13th century. It may be closed for repairs when you visit. If it's open, go inside and check out the second chapel on the left—the only part of the church that survived the 1755 earthquake. The third chapel has fine pink columns. The "marble" is actually painted wood, since there was no marble in the Algarve and no money to import it.

There's a small charge to enter the church's museum (crude but beautiful art in three rooms) and bell tower (peer past the bells to enjoy a commanding city view, with surviving bits of town wall and coastline nearby). Japanese-inspired paintings show Portuguese sailors braving the stormy seas off Tavira (WC at base of bell tower).

• *Facing the rear of the church, turn right. Just around the corner is the...*

Torre de Tavira and Câmara Obscura (Tavira Tower and Dark Room)

This 1931 water tower has been converted into a viewpoint, with a dark room designed to act like an early optical device called a camera obscura. Clive, the British owner, gives a 15-minute, 360-degree view of Tavira in real time as he describes the town's history.

Cost and Hours: €3.50, daily May-Sept 10:00-18:00, Oct-April 10:00-17:00, shorter hours and closed weekends in winter, elevator, tel. 281-321-754, www.cdepa.pt.

• *Return to the church. From its front door, walk straight down through a small garden to the street, turn left, and make another left on Rua da Liberdade. Reach the riverfront, and find the pedestrian bridge on your left.*

Roman Bridge

The "Roman Bridge" may not be Roman, but it was here when the Moors came. The current structure is from 1657, with parts rebuilt after a 1989 flood. The more functional bridge on your right was designed to be temporary, until the Roman Bridge was fixed, but

THE ALGARVE

it was better than the Roman Bridge for car traffic—so since 1989, the old bridge has been pedestrian-only.

• *Don't cross it yet, but continue to the...*

Riverside Park and Old Market Hall

This is where old folks gossip and children play. Walk past the bandstand and more "treasury" roofs (on the right) to the old market hall. A few black-and-white photos show how, in the 1990s, this was a noisy, colorful fish and produce market. Today, the hall has cafés, gift shops, and free Wi-Fi.

Beyond the market hall are a few fishing boats. Local fishermen are weathering tough times as the "natural park" classification of the coastal areas makes aggressive netting illegal, and Spanish fishermen are selling their catch for far less.

If you're in the mood for a snack, **Pasteleria Ramos,** near the market end of the park opposite a green kiosk, produces sweet and sticky *tartes de almendoas partidos* (almond cakes-€2*)*, perfect with a *galão* (milky coffee) at their red outside tables (daily 8:00-24:00).

Sights in Tavira

▲**Ilha de Tavira**—Tavira's great beach island is a hit with travelers. Ilha de Tavira is a long, almost treeless sandbar with a campground (open April-Sept, mobile 964-515-075, ask for Isabel), several restaurants, and a sprawling beach. A summer-only boat takes bathers painlessly from downtown Tavira to the island (€1.90 round-trip, July-mid-Sept about hourly 8:00-20:00, timetable at TI, departs from dock next to old market hall). A year-round water taxi provides service in the off-season (5-minute walk beyond the old market hall, opposite Barclays Bank, mobile 966-615-071). It's an enjoyable ride even if you just go round-trip without getting off.

You can also bus, taxi, ride a rental bike, or bake during a shadeless 1.25-mile walk out of town, past the salt pans and fish farms, to Quatro Aguas, where a five-minute ferry shuttles sunbathers to Ilha de Tavira (€1.50 one-way, year-round ferry runs constantly with demand, last trip at 19:00 or near midnight in high season to accommodate diners). A cheesy **tourist train** runs out to Quatro Aguas on its hour-long tour of Tavira's highlights (€3.50, first departure at 10:00, then usually every 30-60 minutes until around 20:00, leaves from across the Roman Bridge).

Near Tavira

▲**Barril Beach**—This fine beach resort is 2.5 miles from Tavira. Walk, rent a bike, or take a city bus to Pedras del Rei, and then catch the little train (usually runs year-round), or walk 10 minutes through Ria Formosa Natural Park to the resort. Get details at the TI.

Cacela Velha—This tiny village lies through the orange groves about eight miles east of Tavira (half mile off the main road and the bus route). It sits happily ignored on a hill with its fort, church, one restaurant, a few *quartos* and apartments (try Maria Antoinetta, mobile 965-858-630), and a beach with the open sea just over the sandbar a short row across its lagoon. The restaurant—Casa De Igreja—serves sausages *(chouricos)* and cheese *(queijo)* specialties fried at your table, along with local oysters (€10/dozen, great with *vinho verde;* daily July-Sept 12:30-14:00 & 19:00-21:30, March-June weekends only, closed Oct-Feb, tel. 281-952-126, Patricio speaks English). If you're driving, swing by, if only to enjoy the coastal view and to imagine how nice the Algarve would be if people like you and me had never discovered it.

Sleeping in Tavira

(€1 = about $1.30, country code: 351)
Everyone speaks English unless otherwise noted. Prices usually shoot up in August. For the best value, head to Rosa's, described below.

$$$ Residencial Marés, on the busy side of the river amid all of the strolling and café ambience, has 24 good rooms, friendly reception, an upscale restaurant, and an inviting rooftop terrace with lounge chairs. Some second-floor rooms have balconies overlooking the river (Sb-€30-65, no singles in Aug; Db-€99 in Aug, €85 in July and Sept, otherwise €55; extra bed-€10, includes breakfast, air-con, Internet access, sauna-€5; Rua José Pires Padinha 134/140, on the TI side of the river just beyond old market hall; tel. 281-325-815, fax 281-325-819, www.residencialmares.com, maresresidencial@mail.telepac.pt). Be careful—the hot water can be very hot.

$$ Residencia Princesa do Gilão, modern and hotelesque, offers 22 clean, bright rooms. Choose between riverfront or quiet rooms on the back with a terrace (prices vary with the month, Sb-€42-52, Db-€48-58, Tb-€58-68, Qb-€78-88, includes breakfast, grumpy management, Wi-Fi, Rua Borda de Agua de Aguiar 10, cross Roman Bridge and turn right along river, tel. & fax 281-325-171, www.residencial-gilao.com, maresa@residencial-gilao.com).

$ Residencial Lagôas is spotless, homey, and a block off the river. Friendly Claudia and Miquel offer a communal refrigerator, laundry washboard privileges, and a rooftop patio with a view made for wine and candles (S-€20, D-€30, Db-€40, Tb-€50, no gouging in July and Aug, cheaper off-season, no breakfast, cash only, Wi-Fi, Rua Almirante Candido dos Reis 24, tel. 281-328-

243, al.lagoas@hotmail.com). Cross the Roman Bridge from Praça da República, follow the middle fork on the other side, and turn right where it ends.

$ Rosa's Quartos offers a quiet, comfortable stay that's worth the communication struggles. Rosa rents 11 big, gleaming, marble-paved rooms on a quiet alley behind her front-door entrance. These bright rooms are comfier and larger than most hotels in town (S-€25-30, D-€30, Db-€40, T-€45, Tb-€50, €5 more in Aug, cash only, tel. 281-321-547, ring bell, friendly Rosa doesn't speak English). To get to Rosa's, go over the bridge and through Jardim da Alagoa square to Rua da Porta Nova 4, immediately across from the St. Paul church courtyard (unmarked door).

Eating in Tavira

Tavira is filled with reasonable restaurants. Lively, top-end places face the riverbank just beyond the old market hall. A few blocks inland, hole-in-the-wall options offer more fish per dollar. After dinner, take a stroll along the fish-filled river, with a pause on the Roman Bridge or in the park (if there's any action in the bandstand).

To find three good riverside eateries, cross the Roman Bridge, turn left, go through the tunnel, and you'll see the tables on the waterfront. **Restaurante Beira Rio,** the farthest of the three, has great fish, an extensive menu, and an attached, lively Irish bar (€15 meals, nightly 18:30-22:30, tel. 281-323-165, mobile 916-822-117). The neighboring **Restaurante Casa Simão** and **Os Arcos** are simpler, with cheap and tasty grilled fish. Os Arcos, a simple paper-tablecloth eatery, offers a basic €7 dish of the day *(prato do dia)* at lunch, such as a huge, splittable plate of *feijoada*—a traditional bean-and-pork stew served with rice (Thu-Tue from 12:00, closed Wed).

For seafood, I enjoy the inexpensive and relaxed **Restaurante Bica,** below the recommended Residencial Lagôas, a favorite of locals and tourists alike (€7-10 fish plates, daily specials under €10, daily 12:00-23:00).

Tavira Lounge serves lunch and dinner in a cozy, modern setting, with a menu including tapas, sandwiches, desserts, coffee, and cocktails (€8 specials, daily 12:00-24:00, closes earlier off-season, just north of Praça da República at Rua Gonçalo Velho 16-18).

Vital Garrafeira houses a small supermarket with picnic supplies, but it's mainly about port. It has an excellent, well-priced selection of port, plus higher-end Portuguese wines that are difficult to find elsewhere (daily 8:00-13:00 & 14:30-19:00, Rua José Padinha 66, tel. 281-322-482). Senhor Vital is a real connoisseur.

Supermarket: Forage for picnic fixings at the popular and

well-stocked **Pingo Doce** supermarket chain (daily 9:00-21:00, across the river, go along Rua Pessoa past the garages, where it's set back behind some trees).

Tavira Connections

From Tavira by Train and Bus to: Lisbon (5 trains/day, 4-5 hours, transfer in Faro, arrive at Oriente; 9 direct buses/day, 4 hours), **Lagos** (8 trains/day, change in Faro, 2.5-3 hours; 6 buses/day, 3.5-4 hours, change in Faro), **Sevilla** (4 buses/day in summer, 2/day in winter, 3-4 hours, via Ayamonte and Huelva; summer bus leaves at 8:10, 10:05, 14:25, and 16:20, check TI or bus station to verify schedules; buy ticket a day or two in advance May-Oct, note that Spain is an hour ahead when calculating arrival times). Luggage storage is not available. Train info: tel. 808-208-208, www.cp.pt. Bus info: tel. 281-322-546, www.eva-bus.com or www.algarve bus.info, bus ticket office open 7:30-19:00, closed 12:00-15:00 on weekends.

Route Tips for Drivers in the Algarve
Lisbon to Salema (185 miles, 3.5 hours): Following the blue *Sul Ponte* signs, drive south over Lisbon's 25th of April Bridge. A short detour just over the bridge takes you to the giant concrete statue of Cristo Rei (Christ in Majesty). Continue south by freeway until you hit the coast, and follow signs west to Lagos. Take the Lagos/Vila do Bispo exit and follow signs to *Vila do Bispo* and *Sagres*. If you pay attention, you'll see the turnoff for Salema before Vila do Bispo. A modern freeway, less traffic, and the glory of waking up on the Algarve make doing this drive in the evening after a full day in Lisbon a reasonable option.

Algarve to Sevilla (175 miles, 3 hours): Drive east along the Algarve. It's a 1.5-hour drive from Salema to Tavira, with some hills crowned by rotting windmills and others by mobile-phone towers. In Lagos, parking is most convenient in the free lot near the old city wall off Rua Infante de Sagres (pay parking at marina and underground parking garage near Praça do Infante). From Lagos, hit the freeway (A-22, direction: Lisboa/Faro, then Espanha) to Tavira. Leaving Tavira, follow the signs to *Espanha*. You'll cross over the bridge into Spain (where it's one hour later) and glide effortlessly (1.5 hours by freeway) into Sevilla. Be aware that there is a new electronic tolling system on the A-22 highway from the Spanish border to Lagos. Your rental car may come with a sensor, or you may need to pay the toll at a gas station or other "pay shop" (for details, see "Tolls" in the driving section of the appendix).

ÉVORA

Deep in the heart of Portugal, in the sizzling, arid plains of the southern province of Alentejo, historic Évora (EH-voh-rah) has been a cultural oasis for 2,000 years. With an untouched provincial atmosphere, a fascinating whitewashed old town, museums, a cathedral, a chapel of bones, and even a Roman temple, Évora (pop. 55,600) stands proudly amid groves of cork and olive trees.

Évora—a traditional, conservative city with a small-town feel—added a university about 35 years ago. You'll see plenty of college-age students here, along with lots of retirees—but comparatively few 30- to 40-year olds. There's not much to keep graduates around, and this generation gap gives the town an intriguing mix of old and new—trendy shops and strong traditions.

Planning Your Time

With easy bus and train connections to Lisbon (buses almost hourly, four trains a day; both take 1.5 hours), Évora makes a decent day trip from Portugal's capital city. You can stop by for an overnight stay en route to or from the Algarve, which is five hours away (3-4 buses a day). Drivers can sandwich Évora between Lisbon and the Algarve, exploring dusty droves of olive groves and scruffy seas of peeled cork trees along the way. Take the freeway from the Algarve to Beja, and the nearly-as-fast highway from Beja to Évora. A super freeway zips you from Évora to Lisbon in 90 minutes.

With a day in Évora, follow the "Welcome to Évora" walk outlined on page 182, have a quick lunch, see the remaining sights, and enjoy a leisurely, top-notch dinner. After dinner, stroll the back streets and ponder life, like the retired men of Évora seem to do so expertly.

Orientation to Évora

Évora's old town, contained within a medieval wall, is surrounded by the sprawling newer part of town. The major sights—the Roman Temple and early Gothic cathedral—crowd together at the old town's highest point. A subtle yet still-powerful charm is contained within the medieval walls. Find it by losing yourself in the quiet lanes of Évora's far corners.

Tourist Information

Pick up a free map at the TI on the main square at Praça do Giraldo 73 (daily 9:00-19:00, Nov-March until 18:00, tel. 266-777-071, www2.cm cvora.pt/guiaturistico, cmevora.dpt@mail.evora.net).

Arrival in Évora

By Bus: The bus station is west of the center, on Avenida São Sebastião. To reach the town center from the station, it's either a short taxi ride (€5) or a 10-minute walk (exit station right, and continue straight all the way into town, passing through the city walls at the halfway point).

By Train: The train station is south of the center, on Avenida Dr. Barahona. To get from the train station to the center, you can take a taxi (€7), or walk a long 25 minutes up Avenida Dr. Barahona, continuing straight on Rua da República after you enter the city walls.

By Car: Drivers will find Évora's old town frustrating because of its tiny one-way streets. Park in one of the big, free parking lots that circle the town just outside the walls. Assuming you choose the right lot, you'll have an easy walk to your hotel. The green-and-white Trevo shuttle bus (see below) serves the parking lots and most hotels.

Helpful Hints

Internet Access: The big place in town is **Cybercenter,** with 16 computers, Wi-Fi, and lots of local kids playing games (€2/ hour; Mon-Sat 9:30-23:00, Sun 12:00-21:00; just downhill from Praça do Giraldo at Rua Serpa Pinto 36). The town hall, on Praça de Sertório, has six free—but often busy—computers (Mon-Fri 9:00-17:00, closed Sat-Sun; this is a stop on my self-guided town walk, page 182). You can also find free Wi-Fi at many cafés and on both Praça do Giraldo and Praça de Sertório.

Taxis: Cabs wait on the main square (€3.90 minimum for 2.5

miles—4 kilometers—likely the farthest you'd go in compact Évora).

Shuttle Bus: The blue line on the streets marks the route of the green-and-white Trevo shuttle bus that circles through the town, offering tired locals a convenient ride and tourists easy transport to and from the parking lots outside the walls. Hop on for a city joyride (€1, they stop for anyone who waves).

Fado Entertainment: Fado is not as popular here as it is in Lisbon or Coimbra. The recommended **Adega Típica Bota Alta** has live fado music on Friday and Saturday evenings. The TI can suggest other places to hear fado.

Fun Ice-Cream Stop: Gelateria Zoka, a local favorite for ice cream, has tables on a charming and quiet square just 100 yards off the main square, Praça do Giraldo (Largo de S. Vicente, Rua Miguel Bombarda 14, tel. 266-703-133).

Tours in Évora

Walking Tour—A group of local guides offer excellent two-hour city walks every morning, departing from the TI at 10:00 (€12, 2-person minimum, call ahead to confirm the tour will run, mobile 963-702-392, info@alentejoguides.com). The tour hits the sights already described in this chapter, but it's a great opportunity to connect with a local and enliven your visit. While the regular tour departs at 10:00, they are also happy to schedule tours at other times (€24, 2-person minimum).

Bus Tours—A bus tour is a good option if you want to see the prehistoric sights near Évora, since getting there by public transport is nearly impossible. **Ebora Megalithica Guided Tours** runs an interesting daily minivan tour, led by archaeologists, to four megalithic sites: Cromeleque dos Almendres, the Zambujeiro burial mound, the standing stone of Menir dos Almendres, and Alto de São Bento (€25/half-day, morning and afternoon departures; reserve a day ahead through the TI, at most hotels, by phone, or via email; tel. 964-808-337, www.eboramegalithica.com, eboramegalithica@gmail.com).

RSI offers several half-day bus and minivan tours into the surrounding countryside. Their "Megalithic Circuit Tour" visits the main prehistoric sights, including Cromeleque dos Almendres (€33/half-day, 2-person minimum, discounts for larger groups, pick up flyer at TI, smart to reserve a day ahead, mobile 917-907-099, www.rsi-viagens.com, info.evora@rsi-viagens.com).

Local Guides—Professor **Libânio Murteira Reis**—who has a passion for his native Alentejo region and loves to share it with others—organizes town and regional tours; he'll even take you around in his car (€80/half-day, €150/day, car tours start at €180/

Évora

1 Pousada dos Loios
2 Albergaria do Calvario
3 Solar Monfalim
4 Residencial Os Manuéis
5 Residencial Policarpo
6 Hotel Santa Clara
7 Hotel Ibis
8 Casa Hóspedes "O Alentejo"
9 Restaurante Cervejaria 1/4 Para As 9
10 Adega do Alentejano Rest.
11 Taberna Típica Quarta-Feira
12 Restaurante O Fialho
13 Tasquinha D'Oliveira
14 Adega Típica Bota Alta
15 BL Lounge
16 Condestável Café Bistro
17 Rota dos Vinhos do Alentejo Wine Tasting Center
18 Gelateria Zoka
19 Internet Café
20 Praça de Sertório & Oficina de Terra Clay Workshop
21 Public Market
22 Carriage Museum
23 Vasco da Gama House
24 Casa do Rua dos Burgos

ÉVORA

AQUEDUCT

CIRCUNVAL

CANDIDO DOS REIS

R. DOS PENEDOS

MANU

GAR

PRAÇA AGUIAR

CITY WALLS

G. VITOR

RUA SERPA

RUA

DOS MERCA

RAIMUN

S. SEB.

CIRCUNVALAÇÃO

RUA DO

R. RAM

TO BUS STATION

CEMETERY

N

TO MEGALITHIC SITES & LISBON ←

AV. T. ESPANCA

AV.

P PARKING

➡ SELF-GUIDED WALK
(STARTS & ENDS AT
PRAÇA DO GIRALDO)

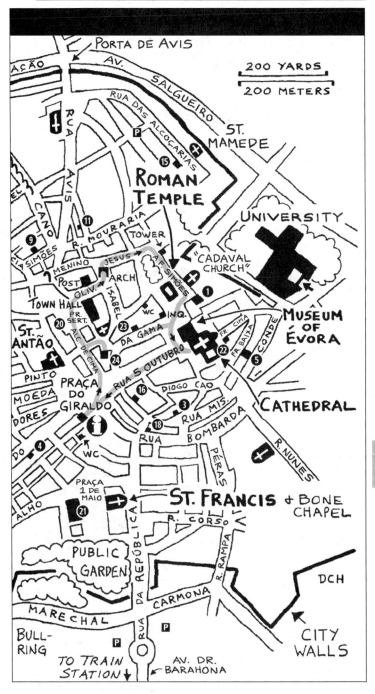

day—price varies with distance, tel. 917-236-025, best to contact via email at m.murteira@mail.telepac.pt).

Maria Pires does walking tours of Évora as well as car tours of the surrounding area (€80/half-day, €180/day, price of car tours varies with distance, tel. 917-232-147, m-jose-pires@hotmail.com).

Self-Guided Walk

Welcome to Évora

Évora's walled city is compact, and these sights are all within a five-minute walk of the main square, Praça do Giraldo (PRA-suh doo zhee-RAHL-doo). The walk takes about an hour, plus time visiting sights. If it's going to be a hot day, try to go early in the morning (the cathedral opens at 9:00).

Background: Named a World Heritage Site in 1986, the city has strictly preserved the old center. It works hard to be people-friendly and inviting. The charming colors you see are traditional in Alentejo: Yellow trim is believed to repel evil spirits, and blue actually does keep away flies. Monster garbage cans hide under elegant smaller ones; at night, trucks lift entire hunks of sidewalk to empty them. Jacaranda trees—imported from Brazil 200 years ago—provide shade through the summer and purple flowers in the spring.

From Romans to Moors to Portuguese kings, this little town has a big history. Évora was once a Roman town (second century B.C. to fourth century A.D.), important because of its wealth of wheat and silver, as well as its location on a trade route to Rome. We'll see Roman sights, though most of Évora's Roman past is buried under the houses and hotels of today (often uncovered by accident when plumbing work needs to be done in basements).

The Moors ruled Évora from the 8th to the 12th centuries. Around the year 1000, Muslim nobles divided the caliphate into small city-states (like Lisbon), with Évora as this region's capital. And during its glory years (15th-16th centuries), Évora was favored by Portuguese kings, even serving as the home of King John III (1502-1557, Manuel I's son who presided over Portugal's peak of power...and its first decline).

• *Start at Évora's main square.*

Praça do Giraldo: This square was the market outside the old city wall during the Moorish period, and remains a center of commerce and conviviality for country folk who come to Alentejo's big city for their weekly shopping visits. It was named for Giraldo the Fearless, the Christian knight who led a surprise attack and retook Évora from the Moors in 1165. As thanks, Giraldo was made governor of the town and the symbol of the city. (Évora's coat of arms is a knight on a horse; see it crowning the lampposts.) On this square, all that's left of several centuries of Moorish rule is their artistry, evidenced by the wrought-iron balconies of the buildings that ring the square (and the occasional, distinctive Mudejar "keyhole" window found throughout the town).

Until the 16th century, the area behind the TI was the Jewish Quarter. At the time, Christians believed that the Bible prohibited them from charging interest for loans. Jews did the moneylending instead, and the streets in the Jewish Quarter still bear names related to finance, such as Rua da Moeda (Money Street) and Rua dos Mercadores (Merchants' Street).

The Roman triumphal arch that once stood on Praça do Giraldo was demolished in the 16th century to make way for the Church of Santo Antão (which overlooks the square today). In front of the church is a 16th-century fountain—once an important water source for the town (fed by the end of the aqueduct) and now a popular hangout for young and old.

King John III lived in Évora for 30 years. The TI is inside the palace where the king's guests used to stay, but others weren't treated as royally. A fervent proponent of the Inquisition, King John sanctioned the deaths of hundreds of people who were burned as heretics on this square.

Until recently, the square was a traditional cattle-and-produce market. While ranchers and farmers no longer gather here to make deals, old-timers still gravitate to this square out of habit. Notice the C.M.E. board (opposite the TI, near the start of Rua 5 de Outubro), where people gather to see a list of who has died recently. You'll see the initials "C.M.E." all over town, from lampposts to manhole covers. It's an abbreviation for Câmara Municipal de Évora—Évora's town hall. The characteristic arcades fit the weather—providing shelter in the winter and shade in the summer.

• *Leave the square on Rua 5 de Outubro (opposite the TI office). On the first corner, Alforge is a good little shop for gifty gourmet goodies from the region. Outside, note how the back of the shop incorporates the old Roman-Arab wall. From here head left (past Mr. Pickwick's Restaurante) on Alcárcova de Cima, which means "the place with water" in Arabic. A few steps farther on, you'll see another portion of a Roman wall built into the buildings on your right.*

Roman Remnants: A series of modern windows shows more of the Roman wall, which used to surround what is now the inner

Alentejo Region

Southeastern Portugal is very sunny and very dry. The rolling plains of the Alentejo (ah-len-TAY-zhoo) are dotted with large orchards and estates, Stone Age monoliths, Roman aqueducts, Moorish-looking whitewashed villages, and thick-walled, medieval Christian castles.

During the Christian reconquest of the country, Alentejo was the war zone. When Christian conquerors were victorious over the Muslims, they turned over huge tracts of recaptured land to the care of soldier-monks. These recipients came from various religious-military orders, including the Knights Templar and the Order of Christ (which Prince Henry the Navigator once headed—see the Prince Henry sidebar on page 158). Évora was governed by the House of Avis, which produced the kings of Portugal's Age of Discovery.

Despite its royal past, the Alentejo (the land "beyond the River Tejo," from the Latin *alem Tejo*) is an unpretentious land of farmers. Having been irrigated since Roman and Moorish times, the region is a major producer of wheat, cattle, wine... and trees. You'll see cork trees (green leaves, knotted trunks, red underbark of recently harvested trunks), oak (native to the country, once used to build explorers' caravels), olive (dusty green-silver leaves, major export crop), and eucalyptus (tall, cough drop-smelling trees imported from Australia, grown for pulp). Today, the Alentejo region is known for being extraordinarily traditional, and is even considered backward by snooty Lisboans.

The people of Alentejo don't mind being the butt of jokes; in fact, they consider it classy to be able to laugh at themselves. It's said you'll see them riding motorcycles in pajamas...so they can better lay into the corners. Many Portuguese call porno flicks "Alentejo karate." A sad old guy from Alentejo told me he had been on the verge of teaching his burro how to live without food...but it died. In traditional Alentejo homes, there's always a chair next to the bed, so people can sit down to rest after they get up. And you can tell when an Alentejo man is finished with work...he takes his hands out of his pockets.

While in other lands "time is money," here "time is time." Alentejanos enjoy living well.

ÉVORA

core of the town. Through the last window, you can see the red paint of a Roman villa built over by the wall. If you look at your town map, you'll notice how the Roman wall, which surrounded the ancient city, left its footprint in the circle of streets defining the city core. The bulk of the wall that currently encircles Évora is from the 14th century, with a more modern stretch from Portugal's 17th-century fight for independence from Spain.

• *Walk straight, sniffing the wonderful scent of pastries coming from the kitchen of Café Arcada (we'll visit the café at the end of this walk), and cross the intersection to find the...*

Aqueduct: This blunt granite-columned end of the town's aqueduct is a relic from the 16th century. The Portuguese have such a fondness for their aqueduct reservoirs that they give them a special name—*Mãe d'Agua* (Mother of Water). As you walk, notice the abnormally high sidewalk to your left. It's the aqueduct channel, supported by stone pillars on the outskirts of town. (Here, it's at street level.)

• *Turn around and take a left onto Rua Nova, walking up the street until you reach the corner. Take a right on Rua dos Burgos to enter #5, the...*

Casa do Rua dos Burgos: This 17th-century house with a Roman foundation contains a small museum, with temporary exhibits on the main floor and a section of Roman wall below (free, Mon-Fri 9:00-18:00, closed Sat-Sun). Walk through the courtyard and beyond the glass door to view a small collection of Roman artifacts and a large section of the original town wall.

• *Exit the museum and retrace your steps, making a right at the aqueduct onto Travessa de Sertório. For a fun distraction, pop into the* **Oficina de Terra** *(clay workshop) where Tiago sculpts and his partner Magda paints fanciful clay creations—religious scenes, children's fairy tales, and caricature portraits (Travessa do Sertório 6). Within a block, you'll reach a square that was once congested with parked cars and is now a good example of how the town has become very pedestrian-friendly.*

Praça de Sertório and the Town Hall: The tallest white building on the square is the town hall. Any up-and-coming project for Évora is displayed inside here, including aerial views and scale models that visualize what the future city will look like (Mon-Fri 8:00-17:30, closed Sat-Sun, six computers with free Internet access).

Inside the town hall, in the corner on the right, is a view of a Roman bath that was uncovered during some building repair. Step through the glass door to the right of this overlook for a peek at the ongoing excavation.

• *Exit the town hall to the right. Look up to see a church and convent built into a Roman tower (once part of the Roman wall you saw earlier). The grilled windows on the top of the tower enabled the cloistered sisters to enjoy looking at the busy town without being seen. Take a right turn and walk under the arcades past the post office* (correios) *and take the first left, on Rua de Dona Isabel. You'll immediately see a...*

Roman Arch: This arch, the Porta de Dona Isabel, was once a main gate in the Roman wall. Below are some of the original Roman pavement stones, which are large and irregular in size and placement.

When you pass under the Roman wall, you're entering a neighborhood called Mouraria (for the Moors). After Giraldo the Fearless retook Évora, the Moors were still allowed to live in the area, but on the other side of this gate, beyond the city walls. They were safe here for centuries...until the Inquisition expelled them in about 1500.

• *Passing under the old arch, turn right, and walk along the road past sod-capped water reservoirs to a patch of grass showing Évora's coat of arms: Giraldo on horseback again. Turn right at the tower, called the Five Corners (Cinco Esquinas) for its five sides, and walk a block up Rua A. F. Simões to...*

Évora's Sight-Packed Square: Here, at the town's high point (1,000 feet above sea level), you'll see the Roman Temple, a public garden, and the dressy Jardim do Paço restaurant, known for its beautiful garden setting (and €13 buffet lunches and dinners). Also on the square is the recommended Pousada dos Loios, once a 15th-century monastery but now a luxurious hotel with small rooms (blame the monks).

• *To the left of the* pousada, *stairs lead down to a church.*

Igreja dos Loios dos Duques de Cadaval: Stop in to see the church's impressive gold altarpiece. This is the lavish mausoleum chapel of the noble Cadavals (still a big-time family, which is why they charge a fee to enter). You'll walk upon Cadaval tombstones throughout your visit; taped chants and liturgical music add to the ambience. Look for the two small trapdoors in the floor that flank the aisle, midway up the church. One opens up to a well (the palace and its church sit upon the remains of a Moorish castle—this was its cistern); the other reveals an ossuary stacked with bones. Above the pews, the noble box is a reminder that the aristocratic family didn't worship with commoners below. The tilework around the altar is from the 17th century—mere decoration with traditional yellow patterns. Along the nave, the tiles are 18th-century, with scenes illuminating Bible stories. The popularity of these tiles (inspired by the blue-and-white tiles of Delft in the Netherlands) coincided with the flourishing of tapestries in France and Belgium that had the same teaching purpose.

The grilled windows were for confessions. The room to the right of the altar contains rare Muslim tilework (the small squares behind glass), ancient weaponry, and religious art, including a cleverly painted Crucifixion (€3, skip the €5 combo-ticket that includes the palace, Tue-Sun 10:00-12:30 & 14:00-17:00, closed Mon, photos allowed, but no flash—strictly enforced).

• *Located across the square is the...*

Roman Temple: With 14 Corinthian columns, this temple was part of the Roman forum and the main square in the first century A.D. Today, the town's open-air concerts and events are staged here against an evocative temple backdrop. It's beautifully floodlit at night. While previously known as the Temple of Diana, it was more likely dedicated to the emperor.

Museum of Évora: This museum stands where the Roman forum once sprawled. An excavated section of the forum is in the museum's courtyard, surrounded by a delightful mix of Roman finds, medieval statuary, and 16th-century Portuguese, Flemish, Italian, and Spanish paintings (€4, free Sun before 14:00, open Tue-Sun 10:00-18:00, closed Mon, English info sheets, Largo Conde de Vila Flor, tel. 266-702-604, http://museudevora.imc-ip.pt). The museum also contains megalithic artifacts, including some found near Évora at the tomb known as the Anta Grande do Zambujeiro (described on page 193).

• *Across the square from the museum is a white building with the top windows trimmed in yellow. This is the...*

Tribunal of the Inquisition: This building may be closed for renovation when you visit. When finished, it will house a new modern art museum. The building itself stands as a reminder of Évora's notorious past. Here, thousands of innocent people, many of them Moors and Jews, were tried and found guilty. After being condemned, the prisoners were taken in procession through the streets to be burned on the main square. In front of this building is a granite sculpture of a coffin with a body inside—a memorial to those who were killed.

• *Go to the left of the Inquisition headquarters to find a little street called...*

Rua de Vasco da Gama: Globetrotting da Gama lived on this street after he discovered the water route to India in 1498. His house is 30 yards down the street—find the smudged #15 on your right. Note the fine circa-1500 horseshoe-arch window above. Plans call for da Gama's home to someday open to the public as a museum.

• *Backtrack and turn right for the...*

Cathedral: Located behind the museum, this cathedral was built after Giraldo's conquest—on the site of the mosque. (For a description of the cathedral, its cloister, and its museum, see "Sights in Évora," below.)

• *Head downhill on the little street opposite the cathedral's entrance You're walking on...*

Rua 5 de Outubro: This shopping street, which has served this same purpose since Roman times, connects Évora's main sights with its main square. The name of the road celebrates October 5, 1910, when Portugal shook off royal rule and became a republic. The street is lined with products of the Alentejo region: cork (even used as postcards), tile, leather, ironwork, and Arraiolos rugs (handmade, with a distinctive weave, in the nearby town of the same name).

On the shopping street, after you pass the intersection with Rua de Burgos, look left to see a blue **shrine** protruding from the wall of a building. The town built it as thanks to God for sparing it from the 1755 earthquake that devastated much of Lisbon. Ahead of you is the main square. The Chapel of Bones and town market are just a few blocks away on your left. But first, stop by the venerable **Café Arcada,** under the arcade near the church. Considered the best pastry shop in town (with the surliest staff), it serves good coffee and the local specialty: fresh, sweet cheese tarts (*queijada,* kay-ZHAH-duh, pre-pay at the bar).

Sights in Évora

▲▲**Cathedral**—Portugal has three archbishops, and one resides here in Évora. This important cathedral of Santa Maria de Évora, built in the late 12th century, is a transitional mix of Romanesque and Gothic. As usual, this was built upon a mosque after the Reconquista succeeded here. That mosque was built upon a Christian Visigothic chapel, proving that religious and military tit for tat is nothing new.

Cost and Hours: Church and cloister—€2.50; museum—€3.50; combo-ticket including church, cloister, tower, and museum—€4.50; July-Sept Tue-Sun 9:00-17:00, Oct-June Tue-Sun 9:00-12:30 & 14:00-16:00, closed Mon (audioguide not very useful, photos OK except in museum, WC under cloister entry).

Visiting the Cathedral: Inside the **cathedral,** midway down the nave on the left, is a 15th-century painted marble statue of a pregnant Mary. It's thought that the first priests, hoping to make converts out of Celtic pagans who worshipped mother goddesses, felt they'd have more success if they kept the focus on fertility.

Throughout Alentejo, there's a deeply felt affinity for this ready-to-produce-a-savior Mary. Loved ones pray here for blessings during difficult deliveries.

Across the aisle, a more realistic Renaissance Gabriel, added a century later, comes to tell Mary her baby won't be just any child. The 16th-century pipe organ still works, and the 18th-century high altar is Neoclassical. Step up close to the high altar to view the ornately decorated chapel filling the apse. The royal box (high on the right) looks down on the space, which is decorated almost entirely by colored marble. Only the muscular Jesus is not marble—it's carved in wood, yet matches the marble all around.

Each corner of the **cloister** bears a carving of one of the four evangelists. In the corner near where you enter, a tight spiral stairway leads to the "roof," providing a close-up view of the cathedral's fine lantern tower, fortress-like crenellations, and grand views of the Alentejo plains. The small but proud relief carved in the wall shows the local Christian hero with two severed Muslim heads. This "fortress of God" design was typical of the Portuguese Romanesque style. Back on ground level, a simple chapel niche (on opposite corner from cloister entry) has a child-sized statue of another pregnant Virgin Mary (midway up wall on left) and the sarcophagi of four recent archbishops.

The **cathedral museum** has several highlights, including an intricate 14th-century, French-made, puzzle-like ivory statue of Mary *(Virgem do Paraiso)*. Her "insides" open up to reveal the major events in her life. A photo below shows Mary folded up and ready to travel. The museum has a good selection of crude 16th-century Alentejo paintings, an extremely dramatic Rococo crucifix, and the sacred treasures of this church. The richest in Alentejo, the treasures feature a sparkling reliquary with pieces of the supposed True Cross (in a cross shape), heavily laden with more than a thousand true gems. The relic rotates within its display case, brightly spotlighted to show off every facet.

Carriage Museum (Museu de Carruagens)—The humble museum behind the cathedral has a handful of old carriages, with a fun collection of paintings showing them in action.

Cost and Hours: May be closed for renovation, otherwise free, Mon-Sat 10:00-12:30 & 14:30-18:00, closed Sun, English info sheets, Largo Doutor Mário Chico 4, tel. 266-743-712.

▲▲**Church of St. Francis and the Chapel of Bones**—This church dedicated to St. Francis and its Chapel of Bones are located on the road to the train station, near the farmers market and public gardens. To get to the church from the main square (Praça do Giraldo), take the road to the left of the imposing Bank of Portugal. At the end of the arcade, turn right on Rua da República. You'll see the church to your right just ahead.

Cost and Hours: Church—free; Bone Chapel—€2 (additional €1 to take photos); June-Aug Mon-Sat 9:00-12:45 & 14:30-17:45, Sept-May Mon-Sat until 17:15, opens at 10:00 Sun and holidays.

Visiting the Church and Chapel: Imagine the **church** in its original, pure style—simple, as St. Francis would have wanted it. It's wide, with just a single nave lined by chapels. In the 18th century, it became popular for wealthy families to buy fancy chapels, resulting in today's gold-leaf hodgepodge. The huge Baroque chapel to the left of the altar is over-the-top, with St. Francis and Claire, his partner in Christ-like simplicity, surrounded by anything but poverty. It's slathered in gold leaf from Brazil. The fine 18th-century tiles tell stories of St. Francis' life.

The entrance to the **bone chapel** (Capela dos Ossos) is outside, to the right of the church entrance. The intentionally thought-provoking message above the chapel reads: "We bones in here wait for yours to join us." Inside the macabre chapel, bones line the walls, and a chorus of skulls stares blankly at you from walls and arches. They were unearthed from various Évora churchyards. This was the work of three monks who were concerned about society's values at the time. They thought this would provide Évora, a town noted for its wealth in the early 1600s, with a helpful place to meditate on the transience of material things in the undeniable presence of death. The bones of the three Franciscan monks who founded the church in the 13th century are in the small white coffin by the altar.

▲**Public Market**—Pop into the modernized yet still charming farmers market, across the square in front of the Church of St. Francis. It's busiest in the morning and on Saturday (closed Mon). Wander around. It's a great slice-of-life look at this community. People are proud of their produce. *"Posso provar?"* (POH-soo proo-VAHR) means "Can I try a little?" *Provar* some cheese and stock up for a picnic (perhaps in the adjacent gardens).

▲**Public Gardens**—Take a refreshing break in the Jardim Publico (main entrance across from market, at the bottom of Praça 1 de Maio). Just inside the gate, Vasco da Gama looks on with excitement as he discovers a little kiosk café nearby selling sandwiches, freshly baked goodies, and drinks. For a quick little lunch, try an *empada de galinha* (tiny chicken pastry—€1.10 each) and perhaps a *queijada* (sweet cheese tart—a local favorite). The gardens, bigger than they look, contain an overly restored hunk of the 16th-century Royal Palace (right of the entry gate). Behind the palace, look over the stone balustrade to see a kids' playground and playfields. Life goes on—make no bones about it.

▲▲**University**—First known as the College of the Holy Spirit, this institution was established as a Jesuit university in 1559 by

Dom Henrique, the cathedral's first archbishop (1512-1580). He later became King Henrique after his great-nephew, the young King Sebastian, presumably died in North Africa in a disastrous attempt to chase the Moors out of Africa. (Not the brightest plan.) Because Henrique was a cardinal—and therefore supposedly chaste—he left no direct descendants when he died only two years later. Portugal's throne passed to his cousin, King Philip II of Spain, beginning 60 years of Spanish rule—and the start of Évora's decline.

Two hundred years after the Jesuit university was established, Marquês de Pombal (see sidebar, page 63), the powerful minister of King José I, decided that the Jesuits had become too rich, too political, and—as the sole teachers of society—too closed to modern thinking. He abolished the Jesuit society in 1759 and confiscated their wealth. The university was closed. In the 19th century it became the local high school. Then, after the revolution in 1976, it reopened as a secular university. Injecting 8,000 students into this town of almost 56,000 people (with 11,000 inside the walls) brought Évora a new vitality...and discos. Unlike an American-style centralized campus, the colleges are scattered throughout the town.

Cost and Hours: Free to enter, usually open long hours daily. Info tel. 266-740-800.

Visiting the University: The university's main entrance is the old courtyard on the ground level (downhill from the original Jesuit chapel). Enter the inner courtyard. While it's fun to visit when classes are in session, on Sunday all the rooms—though empty—are wide open for visitors. Attractive blue-and-white tiles (one of the biggest and best-preserved collections south of Lisbon) ring the walls of the courtyard as well as the classrooms lining the courtyard arcades. Peek into the classrooms; the tiles portray the topic of the class originally taught in each room. Notice the now-ignored pulpits. (Originally, Jesuit priests were the teachers, and information coming from a pulpit was not to be questioned.)

On Sundays, you can enter the room directly across the courtyard from the entrance. Major university events are held here under the watchful eyes of Cardinal Henrique (the painting to the left) and young King Sebastian (to the right).

The university shop to the right of this room gives you a great look at the tiles. In the 16th century, this was a classroom for students of astronomy—note the spheres and navigational instruments mingled with cupids and pastoral scenes. Imagine the class back then. Having few books, if any, the students (males only) took notes as the professor taught in Latin from the lectern in the back.

Eating: The university cafeteria, open only on weekdays, thrives with students and offers anyone super-cheap meals (Mon-Fri 8:30-18:00, closed Sat-Sun, WC). It's located off the second smaller courtyard behind the main one; notice the big marble washbasin just outside.

Rota dos Vinhos do Alentejo Wine Tasting Center—This inviting place offers free tastings of three or four local wines, bottles of which are also available for purchase. They can give you details about the Alentejo wine route and schedule visits to nearby cellars (free, Mon 14:00-19:00, Tue-Fri 11:00-19:00, Sat 10:00-13:00, closed Sun, English information sheets, Praça Joaquim António de Aguiar 20-21, tel. 266-746-498, www.vinhosdoalentejo.pt).

Near Évora

Megalithic Sights—Near Évora, you'll find stony sights, including menhirs (solitary standing stones, near Guadalupe and elsewhere), cromlechs (rocks in an oval formation similar to Stonehenge, at Cromeleque dos Almendres), and dolmens (such as the rock tombs of Anta Grande do Zambujeiro, near Valverde, and Anta Capela de São Brissos, near the town of São Brissos). The two most interesting to visit are Cromeleque dos Almendres and the Anta Grande do Zambujeiro, both described next. Depending on how much you want to see, you can do a 15- to 45-mile loop from Évora by **bus tour** or hire a **guide** with a car (see "Tours in Évora," earlier), or **rent a car** to do the loop on your own (Évora's TI has a list of rental-car agencies and a map of the sites).

▲**Cromeleque dos Almendres**—This Portuguese Stonehenge, dating from about 5500 B.C., stands in the midst of cork trees down a dirt road that's a five-mile (20-minute) drive west of Évora (take the main highway to Lisbon in the direction of Guadalupe, then

Évora & Nearby

■ MEGALITHIC SIGHTS

TO LISBON & ALGARVE VIA A-2

MONTEMOR-O-NOVO

A-6

N-114

N-2

ALENTEJO

TO ELVAS & BADAJOZ (SPAIN)

A-6

SÃO SEBASTIÃO DE GIESTEIRA

N-370

N-18

N-254

SANTIAGO DO ESCOURAL

MENHIR

GUADALUPE

N-114

ÉVORA

❸

SÃO BRISSOS

❶

N-19

TO LISBON

❷

VALVERDE

N-380

RAIL LINE

TO BEJA & ALGARVE

CASA BRANCA

N-2

TO ALGARVE

TO BEJA

3 MILES

5 KM

N

PORTUGAL

LISBON

❶ Anta Grande do Zambujeiro   ❸ Cromeleque dos Almendres

❷ Anta Capela de São Brissos

follow clear signposts to stones). If you're in a rush, skip the first signposted site (a lone 10-foot menhir) and continue to the second—95 rounded granite stones erected in the shape of an oval. It's the largest megalithic monument in Iberia and one of the oldest in Europe, some 2,000 years older than Stonehenge. Look closely at the stones; some have raised carvings, barely visible, of circles and shapes resembling a shepherd's hook.

Some believe that Stone Age sun-worshippers gathered at this pagan sanctuary (similar to the churches, synagogues, and mosques of today) in search of harmony between the "micro" environment on earth and the "macro" environment of the entire cosmos. The stones functioned as a celestial calendar, with the far ends of the ellipse lining up with the rising and setting sun on each solstice. A posted description (in English) at the site tells more. Stop and comfort a peeled cork tree, or pet the sheep that are often grazing nearby.

▲**Anta Grande do Zambujeiro**—This large dolmen (burial tomb) is located about 20 minutes southwest of Évora, near the town of Valverde (take N-380 toward Valverde and follow posted signs). It's one of the tallest of its kind and dates to 4,000-3,000 B.C. The tomb was originally completely covered by a large mound of dirt, which unfortunately was removed when the dolmen was excavated in 1964, leaving the structure exposed to the elements. A roofed enclosure was built to protect the dolmen, but it's believed the tomb will eventually collapse. Walk up behind the structure and look into the bare interior. This once contained one of the largest caches of artifacts ever found in Iberia: weapons, ceramics, gold and ivory jewelry, as well as 30 male skeletons, which had been buried here over several generations. Some of these artifacts are now on display at the Museum of Évora. Off to the side you can see the original capstone, which was blasted off with dynamite during excavation.

Bullfighting—Évora's bullring (just outside the southern city wall) is used only about four times a year for bullfighting, but routinely draws crowds as a concert venue. While bullfights are rare in Évora, nearby towns advertise fights on Saturday and Sunday through the season (roughly Easter-Sept, details from TI). Notice that women are on the program now (perhaps to give a tired sport a little kick).

Sleeping in Évora

$$$ Pousada dos Loios, formerly a 15th-century monastery, is now a luxury hotel renting 30 well-appointed cells. While the rooms are tiny, this hotel sprawls with fine public spaces, courtyards, and a swimming pool in a peaceful garden (Db-€160, less Nov-March, book ahead online for best price, air-con, free parking, Convento dos Loios, across from Roman Temple, tel. 266-730-070, fax 266-707-248, www.pousadas.pt, recepcao.loios@pousadas.pt).

$$ Albergaria do Calvario is a stylish 22-room hotel on the site of a 16th-century olive mill. Friendly Peter and Nina will take very good care of you and offer an upgrade to their best available room—and free fluff-'n'-fold laundry service—with a two-night stay when you reserve direct by email or phone and mention this book (Sb-€72-82, Db-€90-108, suites-€110-150, prices depend on season and room size, extra bed-€30, air-con, Wi-Fi, easy parking, excellent organic breakfast, just inside the old town walls at the Porta da Lagoa entrance, Travessa dos Lagares 3, tel. 266-745-930, fax 266-745-939, www.albergariadocalvario.com, hotel@albergaria docalvario.com).

$$ Solar Monfalim, the labyrinthine house of a 16th-century noble, seems unchanged from when it received its first hotel guests in 1892. This elegant hacienda-type accommodation, with homey lounges and a Valium ambience, rents 26 rooms in a central and quiet location (Sb-€50-60, Db-€60-85, extra bed-€20-25, air-con, pleasant breakfast room with balcony, Largo da Misericordia 1, tel. 266-750-000, fax 266-742-367, www.monfalimtur.pt, reservas@ monfalimtur.pt).

Sleep Code

(€1 = about $1.30, country code: 351)
S = Single, **D** = Double/Twin, **T** = Triple, **Q** = Quad, **b** = bathroom, **s** = shower only. Unless otherwise noted, credit cards are accepted, English is spoken, and breakfast is included. High season is June through September.

To help you easily sort through these listings, I've divided the accommodations into three categories, based on the price for a standard double room with bath:

$$$ **Higher Priced**—Most rooms €100 or more.
$$ **Moderately Priced**—Most rooms between €50-100.
$ **Lower Priced**—Most rooms €50 or less.

Prices can change without notice; verify the hotel's current rates online or by email.

$$ Residencial Os Manuéis rents 14 cozy rooms surrounding an airy central patio. Breakfast can be served on the terrace with views of the sweeping Alentejo plains, while the Church of St. Francis looms in the distance. Eduardo and Vasco make you feel at home and love to share their knowledge of Portugal (Sb-€30-45, Db-€45-60, suite-€60-80, extra bed-€15, 10 percent discount when you book direct and pay cash, air-con, no elevator, free parking, Rua do Raimundo 35, tel. 266-769-160, fax 266-769-161, www.residencialosmanueis.com, res.osmanueis@sapo.pt).

$$ Residencial Policarpo, filling another 16th-century nobleman's mansion, also has a homey feel, with 20 simple rooms—each one unique—tucked around a courtyard. There are fine public spaces and an inviting sun terrace. Joaquim, Michele, and David Policarpo carry on the family tradition of good hospitality (S-€30, Sb-€52, D-€36, Db-€52, Tb-€62, about €10 less in low season, cash only, double-paned windows, air-con in rooms with bathroom, no elevator, terrace, fireplace, free and easy parking, two entrances: Rua da Freiria de Baixo 16 and Rua Conde da Serra, near university, tel. 266-702-424, fax 266-703-474, www.pensaopolicarpo.com, mail@pensaopolicarpo.com). For those on a very tight budget, their doubles without private bathrooms are perhaps the best cheap beds in town.

$$ Hotel Santa Clara, renting 41 comfortable rooms on a quiet side street, is solid, professional, and tour-friendly. Part of the Best Western chain, it lacks character, but comes with a good location and price (Sb-€60-65, Db-€65-75, air-con, free parking, Travessa do Milheira 19; from Praça do Giraldo, take Rua Pinto Serpa downhill, then right on Milheira; coming from the bus

ÉVORA

station, turn left on Milheira after you enter city wall; tel. 266-704-141, fax 266-706-544, www.bestwesternhotelsantaclara.com, hotelsantaclara@mail.telepac.pt).

$$ Hotel Ibis, a cheap chain hotel, has 87 identical Motel 6-type rooms that are a 15-minute walk from the center, just outside the city walls. Simple to find and offering easy parking, it's a cinch for drivers—but staying here is like eating at McDonald's in Paris (Sb/Db-€35-59, check website for deals, breakfast-€6, one child under 12 sleeps free, air-con, elevator, parking, Quinta da Tapada, tel. 266-760-700, fax 266-760-799, www.ibishotel.com).

$ Casa Hóspedes "O Alentejo," an old noble house renting 22 well-worn but thoroughly cared-for rooms, comes with a homey TV salon and endearing attention to quaint detail (Sb-€25-30, Db-€37-48, Tb-€45-59, Qb-€50-75, no breakfast, air-con, Rua Serpa Pinto 74, tel. 266-702-903, residencial.oalentejo@gmail.com, Rosa speaks very little English).

Eating in Évora

The region has its own proud cuisine—rustic and hearty, with lots of game and robust red wines. Don't ask for *vinho verde* here. And don't ask for *porto* either. A good local *vinho licoroso* (sweet dessert wine) is Mouchão.

Restaurante Cervejaria 1/4 Para As 9 ("Quarter to Nine") is a big, square, rustic dining room with an open kitchen that steams up with local families and tourists chowing down on favorites such as *arroz de tamboril,* a rice and seafood stew, and *açorda de marisco,* a spicy soup with clams, shrimp, and bread spiced with Alentejo herbs like cilantro (Thu-Tue 12:00-16:00 & 19:30-22:00, closed Wed, some outdoor seating, Rua Pedro Simões 9, near exposed kink in aqueduct off Rua do Menino Jesus, tel. 266-706-774).

Adega do Alentejano is like an aboveground wine cellar. Locals choose from cheap (€8-12/plate) traditional dishes, including tasty pork options. The menu is scrawled on chalkboards. Ask to watch them pour your *jarro* of house wine from the large earthenware vats at the back. If you didn't try *ginjinha* in Lisbon or Óbidos, finish your meal with a glass of this house-made cherry liqueur (Mon-Sat 12:00-15:00 & 19:00-22:00, closed Sun, cash only, Rua Gabriel Victor do Monte Pereira 21-A; from main square go alongside church on Rua João de Deus, then take third left and keep walking; tel. 266-744-447).

Taberna Típica Quarta-Feira is a rustic 14-table tavern, festooned with patriotic Portuguese decor, where Zé Dias and his family proudly and expertly serve country cooking, including rabbit and partridge in season. Don't expect to be able to order from a menu here—they usually serve just the food that they felt like

Versatile Cork

The cork extracted from the bottle of wine you're having with dinner is probably more local than the wine. The Alentejo region is known for producing cork. From the center of a baseball to a gasket on the space shuttle, from bulletin boards to coasters, cork is a remarkable substance, spongy and pliable, but resistant to water.

Cork—used mainly for bottle stoppers—comes from the bark of the cork oak *(Quercus suber)*, a 30-foot tree with a

sprawling canopy and knotty trunk that grows well in dry heat and sandy soil. After 25 years, a tree is mature enough for harvest. The outer bark is stripped from the trunk, leaving a "wound" of red-colored "blushing" inner bark. It takes nine years for the bark to grow back, and then it can be harvested again—a cork tree keeps producing for more than 100 years. After harvesting, the bark is boiled to soften it up, then flattened. Machines cut the cork into the desired shape, or punch out bottle stoppers. These are then polished, producing tasteless, odorless seals for wine bottles.

Portugal produces more than half the world's supply of cork (with Spain making much of the rest). These days, many wine stoppers are made from plastic, which could become a threat to cork production. So far the business remains strong, thanks to cork's insulating and acoustical applications, but some fear that if cork eventually loses its economic value, the survival of the forests—and the special ecosystem they support—will be at risk.

cooking that day, making this a truly unique experience. Sit down and enjoy the "Trust Zé Special" (€25). He'll bring out the works, offering fun samples of whatever's in season, including his house wine (there's no wine list...just one decent house wine), fine desserts, dessert wine, and coffee (Mon 12:30-15:00, Tue-Sat 12:30-15:00 & 19:30-22:00, closed Sun, hidden on a narrow street just north off Rua da Mouraria at Rua do Inverno 16, tel. 266-707-530). Zé's taverna is no place for vegetarians.

Restaurante O Fialho is a famous place where white-coated waiters feed Alentejo cuisine to Bogart-like locals. With €30 meals, it's expensive but enjoyably pretentious, offering arguably the best food in town (Tue-Sun 12:30-24:00, closed Mon, arrive before 20:00 or make a reservation, air-con, Travessa das Mascarenhas 16; from main square go right alongside church—Rua João de Deus—for a 5-minute walk, take first left after public square with theater;

tel. 266-703-079). Enjoy photos of VIP diners on the wall, and ask Gabriel for a look at the photo book showing O Fialho's great moments since it opened in 1945. For decades, this was virtually the only fine restaurant in town. Go all-local with your waiter's recommendations. For a delightful mix of nun-inspired sweets, ask for the *misto de convento*.

At **Tasquinha D'Oliveira,** Mr. Olive Tree (Manuel, who was a cook for years at O Fialho) and his wife, Carolina, offer a more intimate dining experience with all the quality of his mentor's restaurant, but less pretense. In a tiny, 14-seat abode of cooking love, they work with a respect for Alentejo cuisine and heritage. Note that you will be brought several plates of appetizers—if you nibble, you will pay. Most are €6-8, but the crab appetizer is €18. Just leave them on the table or refuse the dish (€15-25 main dishes are easily splittable, closed Sun, reservations smart, Rua Cândido dos Reis 45, tel. 266-744-841).

Adega Típica Bota Alta is a charming eight-table place, worth checking out on weekends for their live fado music. Esperança runs "her house" with a loving passion for the art of fado (see page 104 for more on fado). You'll find yourself singing along with the locals. Diners should arrive no later than 20:30 and finish their meals before the music starts at 22:00, so they don't interrupt the show. You're welcome to come after dinner; you'll pay €10 for a seat (€25-30 plates, fado music Fri-Sat 22:00-3:00 in the morning, closed in Aug, Rua Serpa Pinto 93, tel. 968-655-166).

At **BL Lounge,** friendly Antonio offers a break from the traditional by serving Alentejo cuisine with a modern and international twist. Try the *risotto com espargos e gambas* (asparagus risotto with prawns), and be sure to save room for the chocolate cake, which is *muito bom* (€10-20 meat and seafood plates, extensive wine list, Mon-Sat 12:30-15:00 & 19:30-22:00, closed Sun, Rua das Alcoçarias 1, near São Mamede Church, tel. 266-771-323).

Condestável Café Bistro, a good choice for a light, inexpensive lunch or dinner, serves soup, salads, grilled chicken, pork, and steak, as well as several vegetarian options—all under €9. Their €12 daily special includes soup, main course, drink, dessert, and coffee (daily 9:00-24:00, just off Rua 5 do Outubro at #3 Rua Diogo Cão, tel. 266-747-314).

Évora Connections

From Évora by Bus to: Lisbon (almost hourly, 1.5 hours, €12.50), **Lagos** (3-4/day, 4.5-5 hours, 1/day direct in summer only, 3/day with transfer in Albufeira or Faro, €18), **Coimbra** (4/day direct, 4 hours, €18.50, more options with transfer in Lisbon), **Madrid** (2/day, 7.5-10 hours, €38, tickets at Eurolines/Intersul office on second floor of bus station; the 10-hour bus is overnight). Portugal bus info (no English spoken): tel. 266-769-410.

From Évora by Train to: Lisbon (4/day, 1.5 hours, arrives at Lisbon's Oriente Station, €12), **Coimbra** (4/day direct, 4 hours, more options with change in Lisbon, €18.50), **Lagos** (3/day, 5-6 hours, change in Pinhal Novo and Tunes or Faro, €28). Check with TI or online at www.cp.pt for schedules.

NAZARÉ and NEARBY

Nazaré • Batalha • Fátima • Alcobaça • Óbidos

Nazaré, an Atlantic-coast fishing town turned resort, is both black-shawl traditional and beach-friendly. Several other worthy sights are within easy day-trip distance of Nazaré (NAH-zah-ray). You can drop by Batalha to see its monastery, the patriotic pride and architectural joy of Portugal. If the spirit moves you, the pilgrimage site at Fátima is nearby. Alcobaça has Portugal's largest church (and saddest romance). And Portugal's incredibly cute walled town of Óbidos is just down the road.

Planning Your Time

While the far north of Portugal has considerable charm, those with limited time can enjoy maximum travel thrills here—in its "Midwest." This area is an ideal stop if you're interested in a small, resort-town side-trip north from Lisbon, or if you're coming in from Salamanca or Madrid, Spain.

On a two-week trip through Portugal, Nazaré merits a day. There's another day's worth of sightseeing in Alcobaça, Batalha, and Fátima (I'd prioritize in that order). See Óbidos on the way between Nazaré and Lisbon.

Nazaré

I got hooked on Nazaré back when colorful fishing boats littered its long, sandy beach. Now, rather than crashing through the surf to reach the beach in the town center, the boats motor comfortably into a new harbor 30 minutes' walk south of town. Today Nazaré's beach is littered with frolicking families, and it seems that most of the town's 10,000 inhabitants are in the tourist trade. But I still like the place.

You'll be greeted by the energetic applause of the surf, widows with rooms to rent, and big plates of *percebes* (barnacles). Relax in the Portuguese sun in a land of cork groves, eucalyptus trees, ladies in petticoats, and men who stow cigarettes and fishhooks in their stocking caps.

Even with its summer crowds, Nazaré is a fun stop that offers a glimpse of old Portugal amid the tourists. Somehow the traditions survive, and the townspeople are able to go about their old-school ways. Wander the back streets for a fine look at Portuguese family-in-the-street life. Laundry flaps in the wind, kids play soccer, and fish sizzle over tiny curbside hibachis. Squadrons of sun-dried and salted fish  are crucified on nets pulled tightly around wooden frames and left under the midday sun. (Locals claim they are delightful...but I don't know.) Off-season Nazaré is almost empty of tourists— inexpensive, colorful, and relaxed, with enough salty fishing-village atmosphere to make you pucker.

Nazaré doesn't have any blockbuster sights. The beach, tasty seafood, and the funicular ride up to Sítio for a great coastal view are the bright lights of my lazy Nazaré memories.

Plan some beach time here. Sharing a bottle of chilled *vinho verde* (young white wine, a specialty of Portugal) on the beach at sundown is a good way to wrap up the day.

Orientation to Nazaré

Nazaré faces its long beach, stretching north from the new harbor to Sítio (SEE-tee-oh), the hill-capping old part of town. Survey the town from Avenida da República, which lines the waterfront. Scan the cliffs. The funicular climbs to Sítio. Also to your right, look at the road kinking toward the sea. The building (on the kink)

Nazaré Fashions: Seven Petticoats and Black Widows

Nazaré is famous for its women who wear skirts with seven petticoats (one for each day, or for the seven colors of the rainbow, or...make up your own legend). While this is partially just a creation for the tourists, there is some element of truth to the tradition. In the old days, women would sit on the beach waiting for their fishermen to sail home. To keep warm in the face of a cold sea wind while staying modestly covered, they'd wear several petticoats in order to fold layers over their heads, backs, and legs. Even today, older and more traditional women wear short skirts made bulky by several—but not seven—petticoats. The ensemble is completed with house slippers, an apron (embroidered by the wearer), a small woolen cape, head scarf, and flamboyant jewelry, including chunky gold earrings (often passed down from generation to generation).

You'll see some women wearing black, a sign of mourning. Traditionally, if your spouse died, you wore black for the rest of your life. While this tradition is still observed, mourning just ain't what it used to be—in the last generation, widows began remarrying.

with the yellow balconies is the recommended Ribamar Hotel. Just beyond the Ribamar, you'll find the main square (Praça Sousa Oliveira, with banks and ATMs) and most of my hotel listings.

Sitting quietly atop its cliff, the Sítio neighborhood feels like a totally separate village. Its people don't fish; they farm. Take the funicular up to the top for a spectacular view.

Tourist Information: The TI faces the beach on Avenida Manuel Remigio, a 10-minute walk south of the main square in the Cultural Center building (look for *Centro Cultural da Nazaré,* daily July-Aug 9:00-21:00, April-June and Sept 9:00-13:00 & 14:30-19:00, Oct-March 9:30-12:30 & 14:30-18:30, tel. 262-561-194, www.cm-nazare.pt). Ask about summer activities and bullfights in Sítio.

Helpful Hints

Markets: The colorful **town market** bustles with fresh fish, produce, and caged rabbits in the morning (daily 8:00-13:00 except closed Mon Oct-May, a few blocks up from the beach on Avenida Vieira Guimarães, in the green building just behind the taxi stand), and a **flea market** pops up near Nazaré's town

Nazaré

— MAIN ROADS
— OTHER ROADS
☐ SQUARES
Ⓣ TAXI STAND
🅿 PARKING

100 YARDS
100 METERS

TO VALADO
TRAIN STN. &
ALCOBAÇA

TO TOWN HALL,
N-242,
ÓBIDOS & LISBON

BARRANCOS

RUA DOS

POST

RUA

ALBUQUERQUE

RUA DR. ROSA

RUA MOZINHO

RUA ADRIÃO

RUA GIL

RUA BATALHA

RUA VICENTE

SUB-VILA

AV. VIEIRA

MARKET

Ⓣ

🅿

❻

❸ GUIMARÃES

R. REDOL

MERCADO

R. DR. JUNIOR

ABEGARIAS

❾

❶❹ R. TRAIN

SÍTIO
FUNICULAR
STATION

RUA LEIRIA

ELEVADOR

❶❷ ❷

❶❶

PRAÇA
ARRIAGA

❼

❶❶⓪

RUA DA REPÚBLICA

TO
DRYING FISH,
BUS STN.
& PORT

❶❸

❶❶

TO
SÍTIO

❽

❹

AVENIDA

❶ ❺

BEACH

ATLANTIC
OCEAN

WC &
SHOWERS

PRAÇA SOUSA
OLIVEIRA
(MAIN SQUARE)

❶ Hotel/Rest. Mar Bravo
& Rest. O Casalinho
❷ Hotel Maré
❸ Hotel Praia
❹ Residencial A Cubata
❺ Ribamar Hotel-Restaurant
❻ Hotel Âncora Mar
❼ Julia Pereira Rooms

❽ To Restaurante O Luis
❾ Taberna D'Adelia
❶⓪ Restaurante A Tasquinha
❶❶ Rest. Conchinha da Nazaré
❶❷ Mr. Pizza
❶❸ To Internet Access (2)
❶❹ Laundry

NAZARÉ

hall every Friday, except in August (9:00-13:00, also on Avenida Vieira Guimarães).

Internet Access: Café.com offers the fastest connection in town (daily 10:00-23:00, four terminals, Wi-Fi, in Edifício Atlântico on Avenida da República toward the new port), but the new **Municipal Library** offers 30 minutes for free (Mon-Fri 9:30-13:00 & 14:00-19:00, Internet center closed Sat-Sun, big black-and-white modern building a few blocks behind the Cultural Center at Rua Grupo Desportivo "Os Nazarenos").

Laundry: At **Lavanderia Nazaré,** Fátima will wash, dry, and fold your laundry for pickup the next day (€3.20/kg—about 2 lbs, Mon-Sat 9:00-13:00 & 15:00-19:00, closed Sun, Rua Branco Martins 17, tel. 262-552-761).

Regional Guide: Manuela Rainho, who works out of Alcobaça and has a car, is a helpful guide for anyone interested in seeing this part of Portugal (€150/day, plus €25 with car, mobile 968-076-302, manuelarainho@gmail.com).

Sights in Nazaré

The Beach—It's the domain of the summertime beach tents, a tradition in Portugal. In Nazaré, the tents are run as a cooperative by the old women you'll see sitting in the shade ready to collect €6 or more a day. The beach is groomed and guarded, and in the evening, piped music is played. Flags indicate danger level: red (no one allowed in the water), yellow (wading is safe), and green (no problem).

If you see a mass of children parading through town down to the beach, they're likely from a huge dorm in town, where poorer kids from inland areas of this part of the country are put up for a summer break.

Boats used to line the beach in summer and fill the squares in winter, but when the harbor was built in 1986, that's where the boats ended up. Today, only re-creations occur (on most Sundays in May), when boats line the main square to show the hands-on fishing process of the past (confirm exact days with the TI).

If you stroll south along the promenade toward the new harbor, you'll come to a few traditional boats in the sand, with prows high to cut through the surf. Try to imagine the beach before 1986, littered with boats like these, with old men mending their nets. Oxen (and later, tractors) hauled the boats out each day. (Across the street is the town's Cultural Center—with interesting exhibits and the TI.) Near the boats is a mackerel crucifixion zone—where ladies still sun-dry their mackerel and sardines. (They may try to sell them to you, but the fish need to be cooked again before eating.) Preparing and selling fish is the lot of Nazaré women married to fishermen. Stroll to people-watch. Traditions survive even among younger women.

The buildings beyond this point are new. While it may seem that in Nazaré most of the people are older than most of the buildings, the town is a Portuguese Coney Island—thriving with young people who flock here for fun-in-the-sun on the beach.

NAZARÉ

Sítio

- 1 Funicular Station
- 2 Main Square
- 3 Vasco da Gama Memorial & Chapel
- 4 Barnacle Ladies
- 5 Sardine Grills
- 6 Rest. O Luis
- 7 To Rest. Arimar

P PARKING
VIEW

NOR-PARQUE WATER PARK

SÍTIO MUSEUM

CHURCH OF OUR LADY OF NAZARÉ

BELVEDERE

CLIFFS

ATLANTIC OCEAN

BEACH

FUNICULAR

BULL RING

TO NAZARÉ

TO NAZARÉ

TO NAZARÉ

TO 7
10 MIN. WALK TO LIGHTHOUSE & FORT

100 YARDS
100 METERS

Head back into town. Just under the bluff (near the funicular to Sítio) is the oldest square in Nazaré, Praça Sousa Oliveira. This square is lined with the oldest buildings in the lower town.

In Sítio

To get to Sítio, take the **funicular.** It was originally built in 1889—the same year as the Eiffel Tower—by the same disciple of Eiffel who built the much-loved Elevador de Santa Justa in Lisbon. The equipment and stations, however, have been modernized. To get to the lift, follow signs to *ascensor;* it goes every 15 minutes (€1.15 each way, first run at 7:15, July-Aug every 5 minutes until 22:30, then every half-hour until 2:00 in the morning; Sept-June on the quarter-hour until 21:30, then every half-hour until midnight; WCs at each station). Upon arrival at the top, walk downhill and turn left to reach the main square and the promontory.

Sítio's Main Square—Historic Sítio seems to gather around its dominant square. Survey the square to see...

The Church of Our Lady of Nazaré: The town's main church, built in the late 16th century and proudly restored by small local donations, is on the pilgrimage trail. The faithful circulate around and then go up to the high altar to venerate the Black Madonna, brought here by two fishermen in the seventh century from Jesus' hometown of Nazareth (hence the name of this town: Nazaré). The Madonna, hidden in nearby rocks throughout the Muslim Moorish rule, was rediscovered during the Christian Reconquista in the 12th century, when interest in the relic led to the establishment of  the town. Today the church, with its gilded Neoclassical interior and 17th-century Delft tiles (from the Netherlands), is popular for weddings and other family religious occasions (which is why it has lots of flowers).

On the left side of the nave, a large blue tile shows the story you'll find all over town: Dom Fuas, a noble from the area, was hunting deer and became so absorbed in the chase that he didn't realize he was about to go over the cliff. The Virgin Mary appeared suddenly and stopped him, saving his life. (The unfortunate deer didn't see Mary in time.) In front of the church, admire the view from...

The Belvedere: From the edge of the bluff you can survey Nazaré and its golden beach stretching all the way to the new harbor. In the distance are the mostly uninhabited Berlenga Islands. The pillar on the belvedere ("beautiful view") is a stone **memorial** for Vasco da Gama, erected in 1497 after he stopped  here before leaving Europe for India. The tiny chapel next to the monument sits on the spot where the Black Madonna hid in the rocks for 400 years, as if waiting for the Moors to leave and for the Christians to return.

Several women (mostly from the same family, but competitive nevertheless) camp out here in their over-the-top traditional fashions, selling munchies and Nazaré knickknacks. This is a fine opportunity to buy *percebes*—boiled, addictively tasty, and ready-to-eat **barnacles.** Two euros will get you 100 grams (that's the size of their tiny wooden box). From here the road dead-ends a 10-minute walk away at the Farol lighthouse, where you can enjoy panoramic views of the north beach *(praia norte).*

The bandstand marking the center of the square is a reminder that this is the main venue for the town's busy festival schedule. In the summer, smoke rises from the many outdoor grills, and the savory fragrance entices you to sit down for a plate of sardines.

Sítio Museum (Museu Etnográfico e Arqueológico)— Dedicated to Dr. Joaquim Manso, this museum is the only place in Nazaré where you can see artifacts of the colorful traditional fishing culture—boats, gear, costumes, historic photos, and so on.

Cost and Hours: €1, June-Aug Tue-Sun 10:00-18:00, Sept-May Tue-Sun 10:00-13:00 & 14:30-18:00, closed Mon year-round, one block inland from Sítio's main square, Rua Dom Fuas Roupinho, tel. 262-562-801, http://mdjm-nazare.blogspot.com.

Activities at Sítio—Sítio stages Portuguese-style **bullfights** on Saturday nights in summer (July-mid-Aug, tickets from €10 at kiosk in Praça Sousa Oliveira). Sítio's NorParque is a family-friendly **water park** with a pool, slides, and Jacuzzi (€12 for adults, €9 for kids ages 6-11, cheaper after 14:00, June-mid-Sept 11:00-19:00, closed mid-Sept-May, opening may be delayed until July depending on weather, confirm hours at TI, watch for free shuttle bus parked on the main drag, tel. 262-562-282).

Restaurante Arimar, on the left along the way to the lighthouse, is a good place to **take in the sunset** with drinks or dinner (avoid windy days). Restaurante O Luis, also in Sítio, is worth finding (see "Eating in Nazaré," later).

Sleeping in Nazaré

You should have no problem finding a room, except in August, when the crowds, temperatures, and prices are all at their highest. I've never arrived in Nazaré without a welcoming committee of eager hustlers inviting me to sleep in their *quartos* (rooms in private homes). They line the street coming into town, hit up tourists on the beachfront promenade, and meet each bus as it pulls into the station (you may enjoy dropping by for the commotion as the grannies fight over the tourists).

Prices vary wildly with the season. I've listed rough prices for the medium-high season (approximately April-mid-July and Sept-Dec). Expect to pay about 50 percent more from mid-July through mid-August. Outside of this highest season, you'll save serious money if you arrive with no reservations and try your hand at bargaining, even at hotels. Most hotels don't have single and triple rooms as such—instead, they generally offer single travelers a double room at about €10 off, and they make a triple by cramming in an extra bed for €10-20 more.

Hotels

$$$ Hotel Mar Bravo is on the main square and the waterfront. Its 16 comfy rooms are great—modern, bright, fresh—and they come with balconies, nearly all of them with views (Db-€60-90, owner Fatima promises a 10 percent discount with cash and two-

Sleep Code

(€1 = about $1.30, country code: 351)
S = Single, **D** = Double/Twin, **T** = Triple, **Q** = Quad, **b** = bath-room, **s** = shower only. Unless otherwise noted, credit cards are accepted; breakfast is included at hotels, but not *quartos;* and English is spoken.

To help you easily sort through these listings, I've divided the accommodations into three categories, based on the price for a standard double room with bath during the medium-high season (April-mid-July and Sept-Dec):

$$$ Higher Priced—Most rooms €50 or more.
$$ Moderately Priced—Most rooms between €30-50.
$ Lower Priced—Most rooms €30 or less.

Prices can change without notice; verify the hotel's cur-rent rates online or by email.

night stay, double-paned windows, view breakfast room, air-con, elevator, Wi-Fi, attached restaurant serves good seafood with a sea view, Praça Sousa Oliveira 71-A, tel. 262-569-160, fax 262-569-169, www.marbravo.com, info@marbravo.com). Parking for the Mar Bravo is several blocks away at the Hotel Praia on Avenida Vieira Guimarães.

$$$ Hotel Maré, just off Praça Sousa Oliveira, is a big, mod-ern, American-style hotel with 46 rooms, some tour groups, and a rooftop terrace (Db-€50, €100 in July, €120 in Aug; extra bed-€15, one kid under 10 stays free, air-con, balconies, double-paned windows, elevator, Wi-Fi, parking-€5/day, Rua Mouzinho de Al-buquerque 8, tel. 262-550-180, fax 262-550-181, www.hotelmare.pt, reservas@hotelmare.pt).

$$$ Hotel Praia, run by the folks who run Hotel Mar Bravo, shares the Bravo's modern look and design, but not its beach loca-tion (instead, it's on the main road into town). It does, however, have a roof-top terrace with a pool, 80 bright rooms with double-paned windows, and parking in an adjacent underground garage for €5 per day (Db-€70 in low season, €140 in Aug; singles-€10 less, extra bed-€20, air-con, Wi-Fi, Avenida Vieira Guimarães 39, tel. 262-569-200, fax 262-569-201, www.hotelpraia.com, geral@hotelpraia.com).

$$$ Residencial A Cubata, a funky place on the water-front on the north end, has 22 small rooms with older bathrooms. Rumor has it the place will be remodeled sometime in 2013 (Db-€40-70, depends on view, noisy bar below, Avenida da República 6, tel. 262-561-706, fax 262-561-700). For a peaceful night, forgo the private balcony, take a back room on the top floor (saving some money), and enjoy the communal beachfront balcony.

$$ Ribamar Hotel-Restaurant has a prime location on the waterfront, a rare Old World atmosphere, and 25 small rooms with dark wood and four-poster beds. To spot the hotel from the waterfront, look for its yellow awnings and balconies (Db-€30-65, a couple of suites cost same as doubles in off-season, four rooms with balconies, good attached restaurant downstairs; parking-€10/day, €15 in Aug; Rua Gomes Freire 9, tel. 262-551-158, fax 262-562-224, www.ribamarnazare.com, geral@ribmarnazare.com). If you don't get a reply to your email, try sending a fax.

$$ Hotel Âncora Mar is a big, modern, almost institutional place, with 26 spacious, bright, and functional rooms and a generous roof terrace with a pool. It's on a quiet street a block from the bus station (Db-€35-45, €60-80 in July, €95 in Aug; free parking, Wi-Fi in lounge, Rua Sub-Vila, tel. 262-569-010, fax 262-569-011, www.ancoramar.com, info@ancoramar.com).

Quartos

I list no dumpy hotels or cheap pensions, because the best budget options are *quartos*. Like nowhere else in Iberia, locals renting spare rooms clamor for your business here. Except perhaps for weekends in August, you can stumble into town any day and find countless women hanging out on the street (especially along the waterfront and near the bus station) with fine modern rooms to rent. I promise. If you need an inexpensive room, they've got it. Their rooms are generally better than cheap hotel rooms—for half the cost. Your room is likely to be large and homey, with old-time-elegant furnishings (with no plumbing, but plenty of facilities down the hall). Many *quartos* are located in a quiet neighborhood, six short blocks off the beachfront action. I'd come into town and have fun looking at several places. Hem and haw, and the price goes down.

$ Julia Pereira rents five nice rooms with private baths in a small building over her daughter's café. Rooms overlook a charming square that faces the beach and comes with night noise (Db-€30, €50 July-Aug, reception desk at ground-floor café run by same family, on Praça Dr. Manuel Arriaga, mobile 967-468-011, or call Julia's daughter Eduarda at mobile 262-189-458, eduardacorreia@gmail.com).

Eating in Nazaré

Nazaré is a fishing town, so don't order *hamburguesas*. Fresh seafood is tasty all over town, more expensive (but plenty affordable) along the waterfront, and cheaper farther inland. Waiters will usually bring you food (such as olives or bread) that you didn't order.

Nibble and you pay—or ask for it to be removed. Double-check your bill to make sure you're not being charged for something you didn't eat.

In this fishing village, even the snacks come from the sea. *Percebes* are boiled barnacles, sold as munchies in bars and on the street. Merchants are happy to demonstrate how to eat them and let you sample one for free (say *"Posso provar?"*). They're great with beer in the bars. Connoisseurs know that they are fresh only April through September (otherwise they're frozen). Sardines are fresh only in July, August, and the first half of September.

Try Portugal's light, young wine, *vinho verde;* with its champagne-like taste, it's perfect with shellfish. *Amêndoa amarga* is the local amaretto. For a tasty pastry, try a *pastel de feijão* (fay-ZHOW) from any café. This small tart with a puff-pastry shell has a filling similar to pecan pie, but it's actually made of white beans.

Restaurante O Luis in Sítio serves excellent seafood and regional cuisine to an enthusiastic crowd in a cheery atmosphere. While few tourists go here, the friendly white-coated waiters make you feel welcome (€10-20 dinners, Fri-Wed 12:00-24:00, closed Thu, reserve on weekends, air-con, Rua Dos Tanques 7, tel. 262-551-826, David speaks English). This place is worth the trouble if you want to eat well: Ride the funicular up to Sítio and exit right; turn right on the main drag and walk to the bullring; it's one block downhill to the left of the bullring (Praça de Touros).

Taberna D'Adelia is a family-run *restaurante típico* popular with Portuguese visitors for its honest service, fresh fish, and unpretentious jovial ambience. You can enjoy the menu and the appetizers without being ripped off here. Marco and his family pride themselves on respecting the customer (open daily, reservations smart in summer, one block off the beach at Rua das Traineiras 12, tel. 262-552-134).

Restaurante A Tasquinha dishes up authentic Portuguese cuisine with a cozy blue-and-white picnic-bench ambience. Friendly, hardworking Carlos and his family serve their fish with a special sauce (Tue-Sun 12:00-15:00 & 19:00-22:30, closed Mon, Rua Adrião Batalha 54, tel. 262-551-945).

Restaurante Conchinha da Nazaré offers home-style seafood dishes—not fancy but hearty—in a small, traditional restaurant a few blocks up from the beach. Try the *caldeirada Nazarena,* the house specialty (€8-15 seafood and meat plates, daily 8:00-13:00 & 15:00-2:00, Rua de Leiria 17, tel. 262-186-156).

Mr. Pizza has decent pizzas, which can be a welcome break from all the seafood. Order to go and eat down on the beach (€6-12 pizzas, daily 12:00-23:00, across the street from Hotel Maré at Rua Mouzinho de Albuquerque 15, tel. 262-560-999).

Eating on the Beachfront: Competitive restaurants line the beach. Two good values are **Mar Bravo,** serving fresh seafood at charming on-square tables, with a prime location overlooking the beach and a friendly staff (10 percent discount for readers of this guidebook, inside hotel of the same name, Praça Sousa Oliveira), and **Restaurante O Casalinho** (good outdoor seating, plain decor, and a solid reputation; on the main square by the sea, Praça Sousa Oliveira 7).

Public Market for a Picnic: To experience the colorful market, buy a picnic there and enjoy it on the beach. The covered market is just up the street from the bus station (daily 8:00-12:00, closed Mon Oct-May, produce and bread sold below, fish above). Other to-go and picnic options can be found in any number of mini-markets along Rua Sub-Vila.

Nazaré Connections

By Bus

Nazaré's bus station was demolished in 2012 to make way for an apartment building. A temporary station is in a small portable building behind the library on Avenida do Municipio, a few blocks inland from the Cultural Center and beach. A new, permanent station will likely be built within the next few years, but it's anyone's guess where. Service drops on Sundays, so verify schedules beforehand at the station. Bus info: Tel. 707-223-344.

If you're heading to Lisbon, buses are faster and more direct than trains. You will arrive at Lisbon's Sete Rios bus station, a Metro (or taxi) ride away from the center.

Nazaré by Bus to: Alcobaça (stopping at Valado, 12/day, 20 minutes), **Batalha** (5/day, 1 hour, some change at São Jorge), **Obidos** (12/day, 40-60 minutes, some direct, most transfer in Caldas da Rainha), **Fátima** (2/day, 1.5 hours), **Coimbra** (5/day, 2 hours), **Lisbon** (6/day, 2 hours, €11). Buses are scarce on Sunday. Bus info: Tel. 707-223-344.

By Train

The nearest train station is at Valado (three miles toward Alcobaça, connected by semi-regular €1.25 buses and reasonable, easy-to-share €8-10 taxis). The train to Lisbon requires a bus or taxi ride from Nazaré to the station in Valado, then several transfers—not worth the hassle. To avoid this train-station headache, consider using intercity buses instead of trains.

From Nazaré/Valado by Train to: Coimbra (3/day, 2.5 hours, transfer in Bifurcação de Lares; bus is faster), **Lisbon** (3-5/day, 3.5-4 hours, involves 2-3 transfers in Caldas da Rainha, Cacém, and possibly Melecas; bus is better). Train info: Tel. 808-208-208.

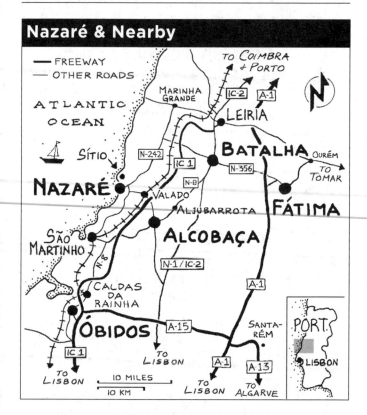

Day-Tripping from Nazaré to Alcobaça, Batalha, Fátima, or Óbidos

Traveling by bus, you can see both Alcobaça and Batalha in one day (but not on Sunday, when bus service is sparse). Alcobaça is easy to visit on the way to or from Batalha (and both are connected by bus with Óbidos). Ask at the bus station or TI for schedule information, and be flexible. Fátima has the fewest connections and is farthest away. Without a car, Fátima is not worth the trouble for most, but if you're heading by bus to Coimbra, you can go via Fátima. A taxi from Nazaré to Alcobaça costs about €15; agree on the price before leaving town.

Batalha

On August 14, 1385, two armies faced off on the rolling plains of Batalha (bah-TAHL-yah) to decide Portugal's future—independence or rule by Spanish kings? King John (João) I of Portugal ordered his 7,000 men to block the road to Lisbon. The Spanish Castilian king, with 32,000 soldiers and 16 modern cannons, ordered his men to hold their fire. But when the Portuguese knights dismounted from their horses to form a defensive line, some hotheaded Spaniards—enraged by such a display of unsportsmanlike conduct by supposedly chivalrous knights—attacked.

Shoop! From the side came 400 arrows from English archers fighting for Portugal. The confused Castilians sounded the retreat, and the Portuguese chased them, literally, all the way back to Castile. A mere half-hour (and several hundred deaths) after it began, the Battle ("Batalha") of Aljubarrota was won. King John I claimed the Portuguese crown, and thanked the Virgin Mary with a new church and monastery.

The only reason to stop in the town of Batalha is to see its great monastery, considered Portugal's finest architectural achievement. Batalha's market day is Monday morning (market is 200 yards behind monastery).

Tourist Information: The TI, behind the monastery, has free maps, information on buses, and free Internet access for up to 15 minutes (daily May-Sept 10:00-13:00 & 15:00-19:00, Oct-April 10:00-13:00 & 14:00-18:00, Praça Mouzinho de Albuquerque, tel. 244-765-180).

Arrival in Batalha: If you take the bus to Batalha, you'll be dropped off a block behind the monastery and TI. If you have difficulty locating the monastery, ask anyone to point you toward the *mosteiro*. There's no official luggage storage, but you can leave luggage at the TI if you ask nicely, or at the monastery's ticket desk while you tour the cloisters. If you're driving, follow the signs to *Batalha* and park free alongside the church.

Sights in Batalha

▲▲▲Monastery of Santa María

This monastery, the symbol of Portugal's national pride, was built by King John I after winning the Battle of Aljubarrota. Unfortunately, the highway runs directly in front of the monastery, but at least there's no missing it from the road.

Batalha's Monastery of Santa María

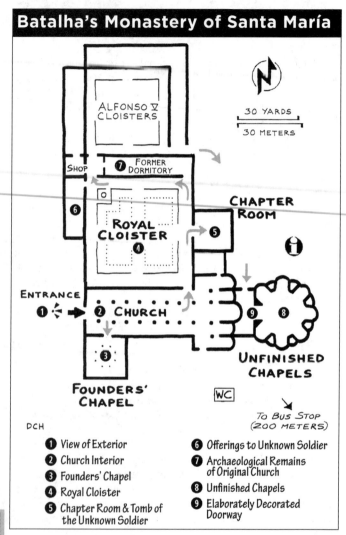

DCH

1 View of Exterior
2 Church Interior
3 Founders' Chapel
4 Royal Cloister
5 Chapter Room & Tomb of
the Unknown Soldier

6 Offerings to Unknown Soldier
7 Archaeological Remains
of Original Church
8 Unfinished Chapels
9 Elaborately Decorated
Doorway

Cost and Hours: Church—free, cloisters—€6 except free Sun until 14:00; open daily April-Sept 9:00-18:30, Oct-March 9:00-17:30, last entry 30 minutes before closing; tel. 244-765-497.

Getting In: On your way in to the church, buy a ticket for the cloisters (at the ticket counter on your immediate left); the staff at the Founders' Chapel will ask to see it.

⊙ **Self-Guided Tour:** Here's a walk through Batalha's most important sight. Start by surveying the...

Exterior (1388-1533): The Church of Our Lady of Victory (c.

1388-1550) is a fancy late Gothic (pointed-arch) structure decorated with lacy Gothic tracery—stained-glass windows, gargoyles, railings, and Flamboyant pinnacles representing the flickering flames of the Holy Spirit. (Inside, we'll see even more elaborate Manueline-style ornamentation, added toward the end of its construction.) The church's limestone has mellowed over time into a warm, rosy, golden color.

The equestrian statue outside the church is of Nuno Alvares Pereira, who commanded the Portuguese in the battle and masterminded the victory over Spain. Before entering the church, study the carvings on the main entrance (much-restored after serious damage in the 1755 earthquake). Notice the six lanes of heavenly traffic in the archway over the entrance: inside track—angels with their modesty wings; second track—the angel band with different instruments, including a hillbilly washboard; third—evangelists (those holding scrolls are from the Old Testament, those holding books are from the New Testament); fourth—Biblical kings and secular kings (those with globes in their hands); fifth—doctors of the Church with symbols of their martyrdom; and the express lane—female saints. Overseeing all this traffic is Jesus with the four evangelists in the tympanum. And the 12 apostles provide a foundation for it all. The statues are 19th-century copies of 14th-century originals. At the top of the pointed arch are two small coats of arms: Portugal's on the right and the House of Lancaster's on the left (a reminder of the marriage of John I and Philippa that cemented centuries of friendship between Portugal and England).

• *Enter the church.*

Church Interior: The tall pillars leading your eye up to the "praying hands" of pointed arches, the warm light from stained-glass windows, the air of sober simplicity—this is classic Gothic, from Europe's Age of Faith. The church's lack of ornamentation reflects the vision of the project's first architect, Afonso Domingues (worked 1388-1402). Compared to Alcobaça's monastery (described later), this interior is dimmer and feels more somber, though the stained glass more dramatically colors the floors and columns (only the glass around the altar is original).

• *The first chapel on the right is the...*

Founders' Chapel (Capela do Fundador): Center-stage is the

NAZARÉ

double sarcophagus (that's English style) of King John I and his English queen, Philippa. The tomb statues lie together on their backs, holding hands for eternity. This husband-and-wife team ushered in Portugal's two centuries of greatness.

John I (born 1357, ruled 1385-1433), the bastard son of Dom Pedro I (King Peter I, see sidebar on page 227), repelled the Spanish invaders, claimed the throne, consolidated his power by confiscating enemies' land to reward his friends, gave Lisbon's craftsmen a voice in government, and launched Portugal's expansion overseas. His five-decade reign greatly benefited Portugal. John's motto, *"Por bem"* ("For good"), is carved on his tomb. He established the House of Avis (see the coat of arms carved in the tomb) that would rule Portugal through the Golden Age (and eventually challenge the House of Hertz in the car-rental business). John's descendants (through both the Avis and Bragança lines) would rule Portugal until the last king, in 1910.

John, indebted to English soldiers for their help in the battle, signed the friendship Treaty of Windsor with England (1386). To seal the deal, he was requested to marry Philippa of Lancaster, the granddaughter of England's king. You can see their respective coats of arms carved at the head of the tomb.

Philippa (c. 1360-1415)—intelligent, educated, and moral—had already been rejected in marriage by two kings. John was also reluctant, reminding the English of his vow of celibacy as Grand Master of the Order of the Cross. He retreated to a monastery (with his mistress) before finally agreeing to marry Philippa (1387). Exceeding expectations, Philippa won John's admiration by overseeing domestic policy, boosting trade with England, reconciling Christians and Jews, and spearheading the invasion of Ceuta (1415) that launched the Age of Discovery.

At home, she used her wide knowledge (she was trained personally by Geoffrey Chaucer and John Wycliffe) to inspire her children to greatness. She banished John's mistress to a distant convent, but raised his bastard children almost as her own, thus sparking the rise of the Bragança line that would compete for the throne.

John and Philippa produced a slew of talented sons, some of whom rest in tombs nearby. These are the golden youth of the Age of Discovery that the Portuguese poet Luís de Camões dubbed "The Marvelous Generation" *(Ínclita Geração)*.

Henrique (wearing a church for a hat and marked by a metal wreath on the floor in front) is Prince Henry the Navigator (1394-1460, see sidebar on page 158). When Philippa was on her deathbed with the plague, she summoned her son Henry to her side and made him swear he would dedicate his life to finding the legendary kingdom of Prester John—sending Henry on his own journey to explore the unknown.

Fernão (tomb on far left), Henry's kid brother, attacked the Muslims at Tangier (1437) and was captured. When his family refused to pay the ransom (which would have meant returning the city of Ceuta), he died in captivity. Son Pedro (tomb on far right), a voracious traveler and student of history, ruled Portugal as regent while his six-year-old nephew Afonso grew to manhood (heir Afonso's father, Duarte—John and Philippa's eldest—died of the plague after ruling for only five years).

The Founders' Chapel is a square room with an octagonal dome. Gaze up (like John and Philippa) at the ceiling, an eight-pointed star of crisscrossing pointed arches—a masterpiece of the Flamboyant Gothic style—that glow with light from stained glass. The central keystone (with John's coat of arms) holds all the arches-within-arches in place. Remember this finished chapel—a lantern roof atop tombs in an octagonal space—when you visit the Unfinished Chapels later. Don't miss out on the original paint job of red-and-green arches.

• *From the church, you enter the adjoining...*

Royal Cloister (Claustro Real): Architecturally, this open courtyard (show your ticket again to enter) exemplifies Batalha's essence: Gothic construction from circa 1400 (the pointed arch-

es surrounding the court-
yard) filled in with Manueline
decoration from circa 1500.
The tracery in the arches features the cross of the Order of
Christ (headed at one time by
Prince Henry the Navigator)
and armillary spheres—skel-
etal "globes" that showed what
was then considered the center

of the universe: planet Earth. The tracery is supported by delicate columns with shells, pearls, and coils of rope, plus artichokes and lotus flowers from the recently explored Orient.

Stop here and picture Dominican monks in white robes, blue capes, and tonsured haircuts (shaved crown) meditating as they slowly circled this garden courtyard. They'd stop to wash their hands at the washbasin (*lavabo*, in the northwest corner, with a great view back at the church) before stepping into the adjoining refectory (dining hall) for a meal.

• *Continue to the...*

Chapter Room: The self-supporting star-vaulted ceiling spans 60 feet, an engineering tour-de-force by Master Huguet, a foreigner who became chief architect in 1402. Huguet brought Flamboyant Gothic decoration to the church's sober style. The ceiling was considered so dangerous to build (it collapsed twice) that only

Portugal's House of Avis and Its Coat of Arms

Seen on monuments at Belém, Batalha, Sagres, and even on the modern Portuguese flag, the Avis coat of arms is a symbol of the glorious Age of Discovery, when Portugal was ruled by kings of the Avis family.

In the center of the shield are five smaller shields arranged in the form of a cross. (One theory says that, after several generations of battle, the family shield—passed down from father to son—got beaten up, and the cross ripped apart into five pieces, held there by nails—the dots on the coat of arms.) Around the border are castles, representing Muslim cities conquered by Portugal's Christian kings. (Some versions have fleurs-de-lis and personal emblems of successive kings.)

Some Important House of Avis Kings

Pedro I (Peter I, r. 1357-1367)—Buried with his beloved Inês de Castro at Alcobaça (see sidebar on page 227).

John I (r. 1385-1433)—Pedro's bastard son, who protected Portugal from a Spanish takeover and launched overseas expansion.

Manuel I (r. 1495-1521)—Ruler when all the overseas expansion began to pay off financially. He built the Monastery of Jeróni-mos at Belém, decorated in the ornamental style that bears his name (see architecture sidebar on page 92).

John III (r. 1521-1557)—Ruler during Portugal's peak of power... and at the beginning of its decline.

Sebastian (r. 1557-1578)—Because he was lost in battle, the nation lost its way, leading to takeover by Spain.

NAZARÉ

prisoners condemned to death were allowed to work on it. (Today, unknowing tourists are allowed to wander under it.) The architect who helped Huguet come up with the strong-enough, interlocking, spider-web design for this vast vault supposedly silenced skeptics by personally spending the night in this room. (It even survived the 1755 earthquake.) He's remembered with a little portrait figurine supporting the column in the far right corner of the room. Besides this ceiling, Huguet designed the Founders' Chapel and the Unfinished Chapels.

Portugal's **Tomb of the Unknown Soldier** sits under a mutilated crucifix called *Christ of the Trenches,* which accompanied Portuguese soldiers into battle on the western front of World War I. The three small soldiers under the flame—which burns Portuguese olive oil—are dressed to represent the three most valiant chapters in Portuguese military history: fighting Moors in the 12th century, Spaniards in the 14th century, and Germans in the 20th century.

In the refectory (through the door near the fountain in the corner) is a collection of all the **offerings** from various countries to the Portuguese unknown soldier. Of particular interest is a photograph taken in the trenches of the WWI crucifix (the crucifix itself is the one displayed in the Chapter Room you just visited). Walk past the ho-hum **archaeological remains** of the original church construction and into the next cloister. It's not nearly as interesting as the Royal Cloister (although you may see art students learning about sculpture on the far side).

• *Follow the exit signs to a square outside the church. Head right, to the...*

Unfinished Chapels (Capelas Imperfeitas): The Unfinished Chapels are called by that name because, well, that's not a Gothic sunroof overhead. This chapel behind the main altar was intended as an octagonal room with seven niches for tombs, topped with a rotunda ceiling (similar to the Founders' Chapel). But only the walls, support pillars for the ceiling, and a double tomb were completed.

King Duarte and his wife, Leonor, lie hand in hand on their backs, watching the clouds pass by, blissfully unaware of the work left undone. Duarte (1391-1438), the oldest of John and Philippa's sons, was the golden boy of the charmed family. He wrote a how-to book on courtly manners. When, at age 42, he became king (1433), he called a *cortes* (parliament) to enact much-needed legal reforms. He financed and encouraged his brother Prince Henry's initial overseas explorations. And he began work on these chapels, hoping to make a glorious family burial place. But Duarte died young of the plague, leaving behind an unfinished chapel, a stunned nation, and his six-year-old son, Afonso, as the new king.

Leonor became the regent while Afonso grew up, but she proved unpopular as a ruler, being both Spanish and female. Duarte's brother Pedro then ruled as regent before being banished by rivals.

In 1509, Duarte's grandson, King Manuel I, added the elaborately decorated **doorway** (by Mateus Fernandes), a masterpiece of the Manueline style. The series of ever larger arches that frame the door are carved in stone so detailed that they look like stucco. See carved coils of rope with knots, some snails along the bottom, artichokes (used to fend off scurvy), corn (from American discoveries),

NAZARÉ

and Indian-inspired motifs (from the land of pepper). Contrast the doorway's Manueline ornamentation with the Renaissance simplicity of the upper-floor balcony, done in 1533.

Manuel abandoned the chapel after Vasco da Gama's triumphant return from India, channeling Portugal's money and energy instead to building a monument to the Age of Discovery launched by the Avis family—the Jerónimos Monastery in Belém (where both Manuel and, some believe, da Gama are buried).

Batalha Connections

From Batalha by Bus to: Nazaré (5/day, 1 hour, some change at São Jorge), **Alcobaça** (8/day, 30 minutes), **Fátima** (3/day, 1 hour), **Coimbra** (3/day, 1 hour), **Porto** (4/day, 3 hours), and **Lisbon** (4/day, 2 hours). Expect fewer buses on weekends. The café across the street from the Batalha bus stop sells bus tickets (not sold by drivers).

By Car: Batalha is an easy 10-mile drive from Fátima. You'll see signs from each site to the other.

Fátima

On May 13, 1917, three children were tending sheep when the sky lit up and a woman—Mary, the mother of Christ, "a lady brighter than the sun"—appeared standing in an oak tree. (It's the tree to the left of the large basilica.) In the midst of bloody World War I, she brought a message that peace was coming. The war raged on, so on the 13th day of each of the next five months, Mary dropped in again to call for peace and to repeat three messages. Word spread, bringing many curious pilgrims. The three kids—Lucia, Francisco, and Jacinta—were grilled mercilessly by authorities trying to debunk their preposterous visions, but the children remained convinced of what they'd seen.

Finally, on October 13, 70,000 people assembled near the oak tree. They were drenched in a rainstorm when suddenly, the sun came out, grew blindingly bright, danced around the sky (writing "God's fiery signature"), then plunged to the earth. When the crowd came to its senses, the sun was shining and the rain had dried.

In 1930, the Vatican recognized the Virgin of Fátima as legit. And today, tens of thousands of believers come to rejoice in this modern miracle. Many walk from as far away as Lisbon. Depending on the time of year you visit, you may see scores of pilgrims with reflective vests walking along the smaller highways. Fátima,

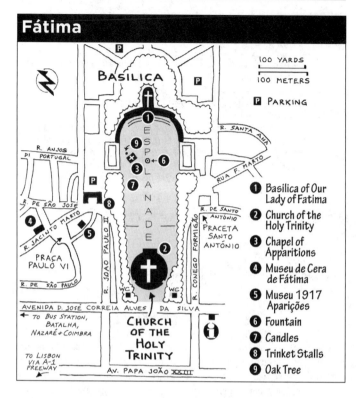

Fátima

BASILICA

P PARKING

100 YARDS
100 METERS

R. SANTA ANA

R. ANJOS
DI PORTUGAL

E S P L A N A D E

RUA F. MARTO

R. DE SANTO ANTÓNIO

PRACETA SANTO ANTÓNIO

R. DE SÃO JOSÉ

R. JACINTO MARTO

R. JOÃO PAULO II

R. CONEGO FORMIGÃO

PRAÇA PAULO VI

R. DE SÃO PAULO

WC WC

AVENIDA D. JOSÉ CORREIA ALVES DA SILVA

← TO BUS STATION, BATALHA, NAZARÉ & COIMBRA

CHURCH OF THE HOLY TRINITY

TO LISBON VIA A-1 FREEWAY

AV. PAPA JOÃO XXIII

❶ Basilica of Our Lady of Fátima
❷ Church of the Holy Trinity
❸ Chapel of Apparitions
❹ Museu de Cera de Fátima
❺ Museu 1917 Aparições
❻ Fountain
❼ Candles
❽ Trinket Stalls
❾ Oak Tree

Lourdes (in France), and Međugorje (in Bosnia-Herzegovina) are the three big Mary sights in Europe.

Orientation to Fátima

The pilgrim-friendly, modern Fátima (FAH-tee-mah) is a huge complex, with two big churches bookending a vast esplanade, adjacent to a practical commercial center. Wandering through the religious and commercial zones, you see the 21st-century equivalent of a medieval pilgrimage center: lots of beds, cheap eateries, fields of picnic tables and parking lots, and countless religious souvenir stands—all ready for the mobs of people who inundate the place each 12th and 13th day of the month from May through October. Any other day, it's just big and empty.

At the start of the commercial zone, browse through the horseshoe-shaped mall of stalls selling religious trinkets—wax body parts, rosaries (which pilgrims get blessed after attending Mass here), and so on.

Those arriving by car can simply follow the *Sanctuario parques* signs to vast lots behind the church.

NAZARÉ

Mary's Three Messages

1. Peace is coming. (World War I is ending. Later, during World War II, Salazar justified keeping Portugal neutral by saying it was in accordance with Mary's wishes for peace.)

2. Russia will reject God and communism will rise, bringing a second great war.

3. Someone will try to kill the pope. (This third message was kept a secret for decades, supposedly lying in a sealed envelope in the Vatican. In 1981, Pope John Paul II was shot. He visited Fátima in 2000, meeting the surviving visionary, beatifying the two who had died, and publicly revealing this long-hidden third secret.)

Tourist Information: The TI is near the church (daily April-Sept 10:00-13:00 & 14:00-19:00, Oct-March 10:00-13:00 & 14:00-18:00, Avenida José Alves Correia da Silva, tel. 249-531-139, www.rt-leiriafatima.pt).

Sights in Fátima

Esplanade—The huge assembly ground facing the basilica is impressive even without the fanfare of a festival day. The fountain in the middle provides holy water for pilgrims to take home. You'll see the information center; the oak tree and Chapel of the Apparitions marking the spot where Mary appeared; a place for lighting and leaving candles (with an inferno below where the wax melts into a trench and flows into a vat to be resurrected as new candles); and a long smooth route on the pavement for pilgrims to approach the chapel on their knees.

Basilica of Our Lady of Fátima—The towering Neoclassical basilica (1928-1953) has a 200-foot spire with a golden crown and crystal cross-shaped beacon on top. Its facade features Mary of the Rosary, flanked by mosaics in the porticoes of the 14 Stations of the Cross (under the statues of the four Portuguese saints). At the top of the steps, an open-air altar, cathedra (bishop's chair), and pulpit await the next 13th of the month, when the masses will enjoy an outdoor Mass.

Dress modestly to enter the church. Inside, huge letters arc across the ceiling above the altar, offering up a request for Mary in Latin, "Queen of the Holy Rosary of Fátima, pray for us." A huge painting depicting the vision is flanked by chapels dedicated to the Stations of the Cross, and the tombs of the children who saw the vision. Two died in the flu epidemic that swept the world shortly after the visions. Francisco's tomb (died 1919) is to the right of the altar. Jacinta (died 1920) and Lucia rest in a chapel to the left of the altar. Lucia (the only one with whom Mary actually conversed) passed away at the age of 97 in 2005. She lived as a Carmelite nun near Coimbra for most of her life. The basilica is busy with many Masses throughout each day.

Cost and Hours: Free, daily 6:00-21:00.

Church of the Holy Trinity (Igreja da Santíssima Trindade)—In 2005, Pope John Paul II began the construction of this grand new church with a stone from St. Peter's actual tomb in the Vatican. Completed in late 2007, it can hold 9,000 devotees, 10 times the capacity of the older basilica. The striking architecture and decoration is intentionally multinational—the architect was Greek; the large orange iron crucifix in front is German; the dazzling mosaic mural inside (on the left, depicting Mary with the three children she visited and all the people who witnessed her in the last apparition in October 1917) is Slovenian; and the crucifix at the altar (with the strikingly different Jesus) is Irish. The church is circular, symbolizing the world. Each of its 12 doors is named for an apostle. Outside, statues of two popes kneel facing the esplanade (Paul VI, who was here on the 50th anniversary in 1967, and John Paul II, who had a special place for Fátima in his heart and visited three times). The long, smooth approach for pilgrims making their way to the Chapel of Apparitions on their knees starts here, with a pilgrims' prayer posted.

Cost and Hours: Free, daily 9:00-19:00, services Sat at 11:00 and Sun at 15:00 and 16:30, www.santuario-fatima.pt.

Chapel of Apparitions—This marks the spot where Mary appeared to the three children (located outside the church, next to the big old oak tree, beneath a canopy). Services take place daily 6:30-21:30 in a variety of languages; check the posted schedule for English.

Pilgrimage—On the 13th of each month from May through October, and on August 19, up to 100,000 pilgrims come to Fátima. Some shuffle on their knees, traversing the mega-huge, park-lined esplanade (which is more than 160,000 square feet) leading to the church. Torch-lit processions occur on two nights (usually the 12th and 13th). In 1967, on the 50th anniversary of the miracle, 1.5 million pilgrims—including the pope—gathered here.

Museums—Unfortunately the Catholic Church hasn't yet put together an exhibition befitting this beautiful sight. Instead, two tacky and overpriced for-profit "museums" compete for your euros—each within a couple of blocks of the esplanade in the modern town. The

Museu de Cera de Fátima is a series of rooms filled with wax figures that tell the story of Fátima's visitation one scene at a time. Its €7.50 tickets—the proceeds from which don't go to a good cause—make it the worst sightseeing value in Portugal (daily April-Oct 9:30-18:30, Nov-March 10:00-17:00, English leaflet describes each vignette). The **Museu 1917 Aparições,** telling the same story with a 15-minute-long low-tech sound-and-light show, is a better value and experience (€3.50, daily April-Oct 9:00-19:00, Nov-March 9:00-18:00, in shopping complex behind enormous Hotel de Fátima, worthless without English soundtrack—ask at the ticket window). Both exhibits are pretty cheesy for those not inclined to take Fátima too seriously.

Fátima Connections

From Fátima by Bus to: Batalha (3/day, 1 hour), **Alcobaça** (3/day, 1 hour, more frequent with transfer in Batalha), **Coimbra** (8/day, 1 hour), **Nazaré** (2/day, 1.5 hours), and **Lisbon** (hourly, 1.5-2.5 hours, depending on route); service drops on Sunday. Note that the stop closest to the basilica is listed on bus schedules as Cova de Iria, *not* Fátima.

Alcobaça

This pleasant little town is famous for its church, one of the most interesting in Portugal. I find Alcobaça (ahl-koh-BAH-sah) a better stop than Batalha.

Tourist Information: The English-speaking TI is across the square from the church (daily May-Sept 10:00-13:00 & 15:00-19:00, Oct-April closes at 18:00, Praça 25 de Abril, tel. 262-582-377).

Arrival in Alcobaça: If you arrive by bus, it's a five-minute walk to the town center and monastery. Exit right from the station (on Avenida Manuel da Silva Carolino), walk a half-block uphill (car parking lot visible in distance), take the first right, and continue straight (on Rua Dom Pedro V). Hang a left just after passing a small plaza, and you are in the main square.

If you're arriving by car, follow the *Mosteiro* or *estação rodoviário* (bus station) signs at the roundabout. A parking lot just uphill from the bus station is currently free, and streets in front of the monastery have plenty of pay-and-display parking.

Sights in Alcobaça

▲▲Cistercian Monastery of Santa Maria—This abbey church, despite its fully Baroque facade, represents the best Gothic building-ing in Portugal. It's also the country's largest church, and a clean and bright break from the heavier Iberian norm. Afonso Henriques began construction in 1178 after taking the nearby town of Santarém from the Moors.

The first Cistercian monks arrived in 1228 and proceeded to make this one of the most powerful abbeys of the Cistercian Order and a cultural center of 13th-century Portugal. This simple abbey was designed to be filled with hard work, prayer, and total silence.

Cost and Hours: €6, daily April-Sept 9:00-19:00, Oct-March 9:00-17:00, last entry 30 minutes before closing, tel. 262-505-128.

❷ Self-Guided Tour: As you view the church from the expansive square facing it, you can sense its former importance. The wings stretching to the right and left from the facade housed monks and pilgrims. As was generally the case with monasteries, the monastery was an industrial engine (making ceramics and other products), and by the 16th century a town had grown around the abbey. When the abbey was dissolved in 1834, the town declined, too.

Stepping inside, you find a suitably grand yet austere house of prayer—just straight Gothic lines. The only decor is organic (such as leafy capitals).

Nave and Tombs of Dom Pedro and Inês: A long, narrow nave leads to a pair of finely carved Gothic tombs (from 1360). These are of Portugal's most tragic romantic couple, Dom Pedro (King Peter I, 1320-1367, on the right) and Dona Inês de Castro (c. 1323-1355, on the left). They rest feet-to-feet in each transept, so that on Judgment Day they'll rise and immediately see each other again. Pedro, heir to the Portuguese throne, was hopelessly in love with the Spanish aristocrat Inês (see sidebar).

NAZARÉ

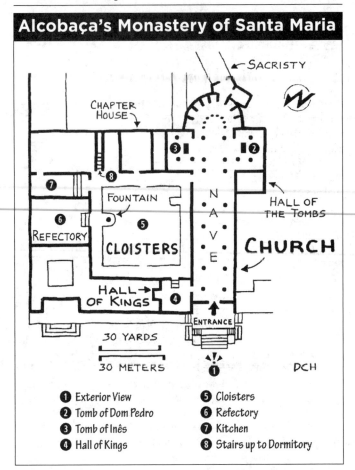

Alcobaça's Monastery of Santa Maria

- SACRISTY
- CHAPTER HOUSE
- FOUNTAIN
- REFECTORY
- CLOISTERS
- NAVE
- HALL OF THE TOMBS
- CHURCH
- HALL OF KINGS
- ENTRANCE
- 30 YARDS
- 30 METERS
- DCH

1 Exterior View
2 Tomb of Dom Pedro
3 Tomb of Inês
4 Hall of Kings
5 Cloisters
6 Refectory
7 Kitchen
8 Stairs up to Dormitory

NAZARÉ

Notice the carvings on the tombs. Like religious alarm clocks, the attending angels are poised to wake the couple on Judgment Day. Pedro will lie here (as inscribed on the tomb) *"Até ao fim do mundo"*—until the end of the world, when he and Inês are reunited. The "Wheel of Life" below Pedro's finely combed head features the king on the throne at the top and the king in his tomb at the bottom, with the good things in life on the left and the bad things (including Inês' beheading) on the right.

Scenes from the life of St. Bartholomew—famous for being skinned alive (Pedro's patron saint, reflecting his life of sacrifice)—circle the tomb. Pedro's tomb is supported by lions, a symbol of royalty. Opposite, Inês' tomb is supported by the lowly scum who murdered her...one holding a monkey, a symbol of evil. Inês' tomb features vivid scenes from the life of Christ, and the relief at her feet features Heaven, the dragon mouth of Hell, and jack-in-the-

Pedro and Inês

Twenty-year-old Prince Pedro met 17-year-old Inês, a Galician noblewoman, at his wedding to Inês' cousin Constance. The  politically motivated marriage was arranged by Pedro's father, the king. Pedro dutifully fathered his son, the future king Fernando, with Constance in Lisbon, while seeing Inês on the side in Coimbra. When Constance died, Pedro settled in with Inês. Concerned about Spanish influence, Pedro's father, Afonso IV, forbade their marriage. You guessed it—they were married secretly, and the couple had four children. When King Afonso, fearing rivals to his ("legitimate") grandson's kingship, had Inês murdered, Prince Pedro went ballistic. He staged an armed uprising (1355) against his father, only settled after much bloodshed.

Once he was crowned King Pedro I the Just (1357), the much-embellished legend begins. Pedro summoned his enemies, exhumed Inês' body, dressed it in a bridal gown, and put it on the throne, making the murderers kneel and kiss its putrid rotting hand. (The legend continues...) Pedro then executed Inês' two murderers—personally—by ripping out their hearts, eating them, and washing them down, it is said, with a fine *vinho verde*. Now that's *amore*.

box coffins on Judgment Day. Although Napoleon's troops vandalized the tombs, the story of Pedro and Inês endures *até ao fim do mundo*. Return toward the entrance and find the doorway on the right to the...

Hall of Kings: This hall features terra-cotta ceramic statues of most of Portugal's kings. The last king portrayed is Joseph, who ruled when the earthquake hit in 1755. Since then there has been no money for fancy statues. The next empty pedestal (to the left of Joseph) is wider than the rest—in anticipation of the reign of Portugal's first queen, Mary I, and her big fancy dress. The walls feature 18th-century tiles telling the story of the 12th-century conquest of the Moors and the building of the monastery (each with Latin supertitles and Portuguese subtitles). In the last scene, the first king lays the monastery's first stone.

The sculpture facing the entrance features a fantastical image of Afonso Henriques, first king of Portugal and founder of this monastery, being crowned by Pope Innocent III and St. Bernard. From here, steps lead to the...

NAZARÉ

Cloisters: Cistercian monks built the abbey in 40 years, starting in 1178. They inhabited it until 1834 (when the Portuguese king disbanded all monasteries). The monks spent most of their lives in silence, and were allowed to speak only when given permission by the abbot. To enjoy this cloister like the monks did: Meditate, pray, exercise, and connect

with nature. As you multitask, circle counterclockwise until you reach the fountain—where the monks washed up before eating. Traditionally, in any cloister, the fountain marks the entry to the...

Refectory (Dining Hall): Imagine the hall filled with monks eating in silence as one reads from the Bible atop the "Readers' Pulpit." Food was prepared next door.

Kitchen: The 18th-century kitchen's giant three-part oven could roast seven oxen simultaneously. The industrious monks rerouted part of the River Alcoa to bring in running water. This kitchen fed huge numbers: The population of monks here maxed out at 999 (triple the Trinity), and peasants who worked the church-owned land were rewarded with meals here.

Dormitory: Take the stairs up to the bare dormitory, from which you can peer down on the transept of the church where Inês and Pedro lie buried. On this floor, there is also a terrace onto the adjacent cloister and a stairway to the upper cloister with views to the abbey.

▲Mercado Municipal—An Old World version of Safeway is housed happily here under huge steel-and-fiberglass arches. Inside the covered market, black-clad dried-apple-faced women choose fish, uncaged and feisty chickens, ducks, and rabbits from their respective death rows. Wander among figs, melons, bush-

els of grain, and nuts (Mon-Sat 9:00-13:00, closed Sun, best on Mon). Imagine having a lifelong relationship with the person who grows your produce. Women from Nazaré—with their distinctive dress—sell fish in a separate room. The market is a five-minute walk from the TI (just down the block from the bus station); ask a local, *"Mercado municipal?"* There's also a flea market in town on Mondays by the Alcoa River.

NAZARÉ

Alcobaça Connections

From Alcobaça by Bus to: Lisbon (6/day, 2 hours, some transfer in Caldas da Rainha), **Nazaré** (12/day, 20 minutes, stops at Valado), **Batalha** (8/day, 30 minutes), **Fátima** (3/day, 1 hour, more frequent with transfer in Batalha), **Óbidos** (3/day, 1.5 hours). Bus frequency drops on Sunday. A taxi to the Nazaré/Valado train station costs about €7; to Nazaré, up to €10. Bus info: tel. 808-200-370.

Óbidos

Postcard-perfect Óbidos (OH-bee-doosh) sits atop a hill, its 14th-century wall (45 feet tall) corralling a bouquet of narrow lanes and flower-bedecked whitewashed houses. Its name, dating from ancient Roman times, means "walled town." The 16th-century aqueduct connect-

ing it like an umbilical cord to a nearby spring is a reminder of the town's importance during Portugal's boom century. Óbidos—now protected by the government from modern development—is ideal for photographers who want to make Portugal look as pretty as it can be.

Founded by Celts (c. 300 B.C.), then ruled by Romans, Visigoths, and Moors, Óbidos was known as Portugal's "wedding city." In 1282, when King Dinis brought his bride Isabel here, she liked the town so much he gave it to her. (Whatta guy.) Later kings carried on the tradition—the perfect gift for a king to give to a queen who has everything. (Beats a toaster.) Today, this medieval walled town is popular for lowly commoners' weddings. Preserved in its entirety as a national monument, it survives on tourism. Every summer morning at 9:30, the tour groups flush into town. Óbidos is especially crowded in August, but it's worth a quick visit anyway. Ideally, arrive late one day and leave early the next, enjoying the town as you would a beautiful painted tile. Or arrive midday and encounter the crush of tour groups.

Tourist Information: The TI is at Óbidos' main pay parking lot (€0.60/hour, TI open daily May-Sept 9:30-19:30, shorter hours off-season, tel. 262-959-231). The TI rents bikes for €10 a day (€5/half-day).

NAZARÉ

Internet Access: Net, across from the pillar on the main street at Rua Direita 107, has 14 terminals and offers free Internet access (daily in summer 10:00-22:00, shorter hours off-season).

Arrival in Óbidos: Ideally, take a bus to Óbidos and leave by either bus or train. Because there's no bus station and the train station is unstaffed, there's no official place to store luggage in town.

If you arrive at the train station, you're faced with a 20-minute uphill hike into town. The bus drops you off much closer, right outside the main gate (upon arrival, go up the steps and through the archway on the right). If leaving by train, you can catch a taxi to the station in the lot outside the main gate (about €10).

If you arrive by car, don't drive into tiny, cobbled Óbidos. Ample tourist parking is provided just outside the main gate. The closest lot (by the TI and a public WC) is pay-and-display (€0.60/hour). The huge lot across the street (lined by the 16th-century aqueduct) is a bit cheaper (€0.50/hour), but first check for a space in the perfectly good free lot just south of here, or in the small free lot near the *pousada*. If you're staying inside the town walls and want to park near your hotel, be sure to get details beforehand. Some hotels inside the walls have one or two spots, but it's generally easier to park outside the walls.

Self-Guided Walk

Welcome to Óbidos

Main Gate: Enter through the main gate in Óbidos' 14th-century wall. Stop to gaze up at the scenes related to the town's history—depicting centuries of battles and religion in blue-and-white tiles. Tiles like these covered the entire face of the walls here until the 1755 quake shook them down.

Step into the town, and like Dorothy entering a medieval Oz, you're confronted by two wonderful cobbled lanes. The top lane is the town's main drag, littered with tourists shopping and leading straight through Óbidos to its castle (ahead, you can see its square tower, where this walk finishes).

Town Wall: After entering the old town through the main gate, notice the steep stairs (to your left) accessing the scenic if treacherous sentry path along the wall (other access points are near the castle/*pousada*, and uphill from the main church). You'll get views of the city and surrounding countryside from the 45-foot-high walls. The west (uphill) wall is best, letting you look over the town's white buildings with red roofs and blue or yellow trim. You can almost gaze at the Atlantic, six miles away. Until the 1100s, when the bay silted up, the ocean was half as far away, making this a hilltop citadel guarding a natural port. The aqueduct is from the 16th century.

Rua Josefa d'Óbidos: Continue straight along this less-traveled, lower brick lane and notice the whitewash that keeps things cool; the bright blue-and-yellow trims, traditionally designed to define property lines; and the potted geraniums, which bloom most of the year, survive the summer sun well, and keep mosquitoes away. The **Church of St. Peter** has a fine, newly restored Baroque altar covered with Brazilian gold leaf, which contrasts with the otherwise Gothic interior built before the 1755 earthquake. The Maltese-type crosses carved into the rock throughout the church are a constant reminder that this fine building was "brought to you by your friends in the Order of Christ" (daily 9:30-12:30 & 14:30-19:00, until 17:00 Oct-March). After peeking in, exit the church and climb uphill to the main tourist drag.

• *Then turn right on...*

Rua Direita: Walking toward the castle on this main shopping drag, you'll pass typical shops and a public WC before reaching the...

• *Bypass the wall walk for now and head into town. Follow...*

Town Square: The lone column at the side of the road is the 16th-century **pillory.** Bad boys were tied to this to endure whatever punishment was deemed appropriate. Studying it closely, you'll notice it's capped by Queen Leonor's crown. On the side facing the castle, the carved hanging shrimp net represents how fishermen found the body of 16-year-old Afonso, son of Manuel I and Leonor, in the Rio Tejo after a tragic and mysterious death. The net eventually became part of the queen's coat of arms. The huge pots you see beneath the awning overlooking the square on the left were once in the central market and held olive oil instead of flowers. The small **Municipal Museum,** opposite the flowerpots, is not worth the €1.50 unless you enjoy stairs, religious art, and Portuguese inscriptions. But at the bottom of the square, do enter the...

Church of St. Mary of Óbidos: Grab a seat on a front pew, surrounded by classic 17th-century tiles (church open daily). Notice the fine painted-wood ceiling over each of the three naves. To the left of the altar is a niche with a delicate Portuguese Renaissance tomb, featuring a pietà carved out of local limestone. On the right are three paintings, including *The Mystical Marriage of St.*

Óbidos

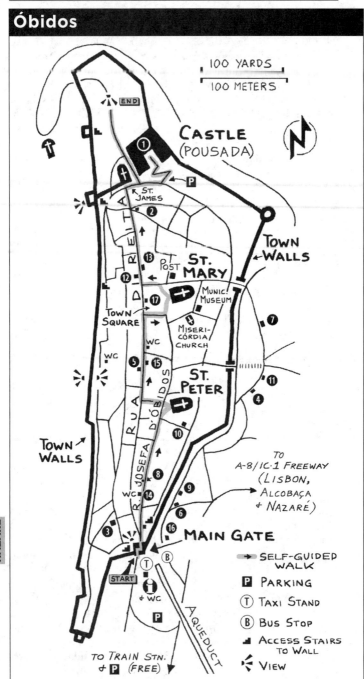

100 YARDS
100 METERS

END

① CASTLE (POUSADA)

N

P

ST. JAMES
②

TOWN WALLS

⑬
POST
⑫
ST. MARY

⑰
Munic! Museum

TOWN SQUARE

Miseri-córdia Church

⑦

WC

WC
⑤
⑮

ST. PETER

TOWN WALLS

④

⑪

⑩

TO A-8/IC-1 FREEWAY (LISBON, ALCOBAÇA & NAZARÉ)

⑧
WC ⑭

⑨

③

⑥
⑯ MAIN GATE

START
T
WC

B

P

→ SELF-GUIDED WALK
P PARKING
T TAXI STAND
B BUS STOP
▰ ACCESS STAIRS TO WALL
❮ VIEW

AQUEDUCT

TO TRAIN STN. & P (FREE) ▼

NAZARÉ

Óbidos Key

❶ Pousada (Castle)
❷ Casa de S. Thiago do Castelo
❸ Casa de S. Thiago do Castelo Annex
❹ Estalagem do Convento
❺ Hotel Rainha Santa Isabel
❻ Albergaria Josefa d'Óbidos
❼ Casa do Relogio
❽ Restaurante Burgo
❾ Rest./Pizzaria Muralhas
❿ 1st de Dezembro Café & Restaurante
⓫ Troca-Tintos Wine Bar
⓬ Pasteleria Dom Afonso
⓭ Bar Ibn Errik Rex
⓮ Small Grocery
⓯ Large Grocery
⓰ Tiny Market
⓱ Pillory & Internet Access

Catherine, by Óbidos' most famous artist, the nun Josefa d'Óbidos (1634-1684).

To peek into another church, head a few steps below and to the right of the Church of St. Mary. The **Misericórdia church** was built as part of the queen's charity institution. It's lined with 16th-century "carpet tiles." To the right of the altar you can see one of the "religious floats" and a cross that's carried through town during Holy Week festivities.

• *Return to the main shopping drag and turn right for the...*

Final Stretch to the Castle: On the left, pop into the **Pasteleria Dom Afonso** (#113). This welcoming little coffee bar, dominated by a big old grape press, serves good pastries and sandwiches. Try the local version of *pastel de nata* with chocolate (open daily 8:30-20:00, on the main drag). Across the street, **Bar Ibn Errik Rex** (#100) is the most characteristic—and touristy—of several Óbidos *ginjinha* bars—the town is famous for its much-loved Portuguese cherry liqueur. Bruno will take good care of you, with a backdrop of his dad's 30-year-old collection of mini liquor bottles (but you'll pay €2.50 a glass here, as opposed to only €1 a shot in several other small shops along the main street).

• *The main drag dead-ends at the top of town and the...*

Pousada: This former castle is now a fancy hotel with nine rooms (Db-€170-265, tel. 262-955-080, fax 262-959-148, www.pousadas.pt, recepcao.castelo@pousadas.pt). Visitors are welcome to drop in for a fancy cup of coffee.

On January 11, 1148, Afonso Henriques (Portugal's first king) led a two-pronged attack to liberate the town from the Moors. Afonso attacked the main gate at the other end of town (where tourists enter), while the Moorish ruler huddled here in his castle. Meanwhile, a band of Afonso's men, disguised as cherry trees, snuck up the steep hillside behind the castle. The doomed Moor ignored his daughter when she turned from the window and asked him, "Daddy, do trees walk?"

NAZARÉ

A lane to the left leads to the stairs accessing the town wall. But go uphill to the right, following the *pousada* signs to the terrace with the telescope for a look at the city. After savoring the view, go back to the top of Rua Direita and enter the archway to your right. Walk uphill for a minute until you see the town wall. Turn around for a spectacular view of the castle—it's yours for the taking.

• *You can return to your starting point three ways: hiking along the upper town wall, exploring photogenic side lanes, or shopping and drinking your way back down the main drag.*

Sights in Óbidos

The main sight in Óbidos is the town itself. Wander the postcard-perfect streets, climb the town walls, and sample some *ginjinha* (cherry liqueur) in a chocolate cup. You will find several shops selling chocolates and *ginjinha* along the main street, Rua Direita. Then explore the side streets, away from the throngs of tourists.

Near Óbidos

Caldas da Rainha—A 10-minute drive or taxi ride from Óbidos, Caldas da Rainha is famous for its therapeutic springs, which have attracted royalty looking for rheumatism cures and aristocrats wanting to make the scene. A venerable hospital now sits on the source of those curative waters. The charming old center is more workaday than Óbidos, as mono-block development has swamped the outskirts. But the town is still filled with unexpected surprises. Stroll the lovely public gardens near the hospital, uncover the hidden meanings of the various stenciled graffiti, and gaze at a multitude of Art Deco buildings. Caldas da Rainha provides a good glimpse of everyday Portugal, with the charm punched up just a notch. Ideally, drop by any morning (except Mon), when its farmers' market fills Praça da República with fruits, veggies, nuts, flowers, and lots of busy locals.

Sleeping in Óbidos

(€1 = about $1.30, country code: 351)

To enjoy Óbidos without tourists, spend the night. Here are reasonable values in this overpriced toy of a town. In the first three weeks in August, prices spike up beyond those listed here.

$$$ Casa de S. Thiago do Castelo, a fancy and characteristic little guesthouse at the base of the *pousada*/castle, rents eight elegantly appointed rooms around a chirpy *Better Homes and Tiles* patio. Lower levels offer three different, welcoming salons to relax in, including one with a classy billiards table (Sb-€65, Db-€80, free parking, Largo de S. Thiago, tel. 262-959-587, fax 262-959-

NAZARÉ

557, www.casas-sthiago.com, reservas@casas-sthiago.com, Alice speaks English). They also have an annex near the main gate, where they book overflow guests at busy times.

$$$ Estalagem do Convento was built to house nuns—but they never showed up. Now it welcomes guests to its 28 rooms with solemn charm (Sb-€85, Db-€100, suites-€116-150, extra bed-€40, located outside wall with easy parking, Rua Dom João de Ornelas, tel. 262-959-216, fax 262-959-159, www.estalagemdoconvento. com, estconventhotel@mail.telepac.pt).

$$$ Hotel Rainha Santa Isabel is a forgettable, hotelesque place marked by flags on the main drag in the center of the old town. If you're driving, call first to let them know you're approaching, stop long enough to drop your bags and get a parking permit, and drive on to the town square to park (Sb-€40-65, Db-€65-90, Tb-75-95, price depends on room, prices soar in Aug, air-con, elevator, on the main one-lane drag, Rua Direita, tel. 262-959-323, fax 262-959-115, www.obidoshotel.com, arsio@mail.telepac.pt).

$$$ Albergaria Josefa d'Óbidos, located just outside the town walls, is a fine value. Its 34 rooms are clean and well-appointed. Half the rooms have been recently updated with modern bathrooms and new furnishings; the older rooms are somewhat dated, but have nice *azulejo*-tiled bathrooms (Sb-€45-65, Db-€60-80, Tb-€70-90, suites-€110-115, air-con, Wi-Fi in reception and bar, free parking, Rua Dom João de Ornelas, tel. 262-959-296, fax 262-959-770, www.josefadobidos.com, josefadobidos@iol.pt). The attached restaurant serves nice fish and meat dishes starting at €13, and also offers vegetarian options.

$$ Casa do Relogio is a rustic eight-room place at the downhill end of town, just outside the wall. It's friendly and easygoing, providing no-stress parking and great comfort for the price. English-speaking Sarah offers a big sun terrace and happily does her guests' laundry for no extra charge (Sb-€35-45, Db-€45-60, Tb-€60-80, same prices in peak of summer, ask for Rick Steves discount, cash only, Rua da Graça 12, tel. & fax 262-959-282, casa. relogio@clix.pt).

Eating in Óbidos

Óbidos is tough on the average tourist's budget. Consider a picnic or one of the many cafés that offer cheap, basic meals.

Restaurante Burgo, just inside the main gate on the lower road, is a lively place with good seating inside and out on the cobbled street (€10-15 meat and fish dishes, open long hours daily, good ice cream, Rua Josefa d'Óbidos 11).

Restaurante/Pizzaria Muralhas serves traditional Portuguese and Italian cuisine. Dine indoors or on the back patio (€6-8 pizzas, €13-16 meat and fish dishes, Thu-Tue 12:00-15:00 & 19:00-22:30, closed Wed, Rua Dom João de Ornelas 6, tel. 262-958-550).

1st de Dezembro Café & Restaurante serves inexpensive pizza, salads, and omelets. Daily specials start at €11 (€7 meat and fish plates, Mon-Sat 8:00-24:00, closed Sun, next door to the Church of St. Peter on Largo de San Pedro, tel. 262-959-298).

Troca-Tintos is a good spot for a glass of wine and light meal of *petiscos* (Portuguese tapas) in an intimate atmosphere. The only downside is that smoking is allowed. Sit at one of the outdoor tables if possible (€4-14, Mon-Sat 18:00 until late, closed Sun, Rua Dom João de Ornelas, next to Hotel Real, tel. 966-928-689). They have fado every Monday, 20:30-23:30, €4 cover, €3 with food.

Picnics: Pick up your picnic at the small grocery store just inside the main gate (on the lower brick road), the larger grocery in the center on Rua Direita, or the tiny market just outside the town wall.

Óbidos Connections

From Óbidos to: Nazaré (12 buses/day, 40-60 minutes, some direct, most transfer in Caldas da Rainha), **Lisbon** (8 buses/day, 1.25 hours; 3 trains/day, 2.25-3 hours, transfer in Cacém or Mira Sintra-Melecas), **Alcobaça** (3 buses/day, 1.5 hours). Far fewer buses run on weekends, be sure to check schedules at the TI.

By Car to Lisbon: From Óbidos, the tollway zips you directly into Lisbon in about an hour (€6).

COIMBRA

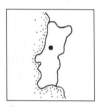

The college town of Coimbra—just two to three hours north of Lisbon by train, bus, or car—is Portugal's Oxford, and the country's easiest-to-enjoy city.

Don't be fooled by the drab suburbs. Portugal's center for 200 years, Coimbra (koh-EEM-brah) remains second only to Lisbon culturally and historically. It served as Portugal's leading city while the Moors controlled Lisbon. The ports of Lisbon and Porto only surpassed landlocked Coimbra when Portugal's maritime fortunes rose. Today, Coimbra is Portugal's third-largest city (pop. 168,000) and home to its oldest and most prestigious university (founded 1290). When school is in session, Coimbra bustles. During school holidays, it's sleepy. But any time of year, you can explore the great Arab-flavored old town—a maze of people, narrow streets, and tiny *tascas* (restaurants with just a few tables).

Planning Your Time

On a two-week swing through Portugal, give Coimbra a day. Browse through its historic university, fortress-like cathedral, and lively old town. If you're driving from central Spain, Coimbra makes a good first stop in Portugal.

Orientation to Coimbra

Coimbra is a mini-Lisbon, with everything good about urban Portugal without the intensity of a big metropolis. I couldn't design a more delightful city for a visit. Skip Coimbra's modern center (with the shopping malls) and stick to the charming old town.

From Largo da Portagem, the main square by the river, everything is within an easy walk. The TI and plenty of good budget rooms are within several blocks of the train station. The best views are from its low and high points: looking up from the far end of Santa Clara Bridge (Ponte Santa Clara) and looking down from the observation deck of the old university.

Coimbra's old town—a maze of timeworn shops, houses, and stairways—has two parts: the lower (Baixa) and the upper (Alta). The dividing line between these two sections is the main pedestrian street, which is named Visconde da Luz at one end and Rua de Ferreira Borges at the other. It runs from the Praça 8 de Maio to the Mondego River.

To get to the university from this main pedestrian thoroughfare, follow the streets that wind their way up the side of the hill. These little lanes, which give the area a village-like feel, meander like a Moroccan medina up to the city's highest point, the old university. To save yourself some uphill climbing, use Coimbra's elevator and/or little electric minibus (see "Getting Around Coimbra," later).

Tourist Information

Pick up a free info-packed map and the monthly cultural calendar at the helpful English-speaking TI at Largo da Portagem (June-Sept Mon-Fri 9:00-20:00, Sat-Sun 10:00-18:00; Oct-May Mon-Fri 9:00-18:00, Sat-Sun 9:30-12:30 & 13:30-17:30; entrance on Avenida Emídio Navarro, tel. 239-488-120, www.turismodocentro.pt, info.coimbra@turismodocentro.pt). You can get bus schedules printed out for you here and find information on sights in central Portugal.

Arrival in Coimbra

By Train

There are two main Coimbra train stations, Station B and Station A. Both stations provide train information and schedules, and have windows selling train tickets and reservations (daily 6:15-23:00, tel. 808-208-208), including an international window for trips to Spain (Station A—daily 10:00-12:00 & 14:00-18:00, Station B—daily 15:00-20:30). There's a car-rental office at each station. Neither has baggage storage.

Some local trains (e.g., from Valado—near Nazaré—and other nearby towns) stop at both stations, but major trains (e.g., from

Lisbon and Salamanca) stop only at **Station B** (think Big). From there, you can take a five-minute shuttle train to the very central Station A (free with the ticket that got you to Station B). To find out exactly which train to take to get from B to A, ask any station employee, *"Para Coimbra A* (ah)*?"* Taxis wait across the tracks from Station B (figure about €4 to Station A or your hotel).

From **Station A,** train connections to other destinations may be efficient—or they may not (in which case, taking a quick taxi ride or the shuttle train to Station B is smarter). Most of my recommended hotels are within a three-minute walk of Station A.

By Bus

The bus station, on Avenida Fernão de Magalhães (tel. 239-855-270), has two ATMs (one inside, one outside). A baggage storage facility—which looks like a mailroom—is across from the *informações* office and to the right (€1/bag, Mon-Fri 8:00-18:30, closed Sat-Sun). The station is an easy 15-minute walk from the center; exit the bus station to the right, and follow the busy street into town.

There's no need to make a special trip to the bus station just to get bus schedules (the TIs print timetables upon request) or to buy tickets (travel agencies sell them; see "Helpful Hints," later). If you're walking to the bus station to catch a bus to leave Coimbra, take Avenida Fernão de Magalhães almost to its intersection with Cabral, and look to the left—the Neptuno café is by the station's subtle entrance.

By Car

From Lisbon, it's an easy two-hour straight shot on the slick Auto-Estrada A-1 (€13 toll). You'll pass convenient exits for Fátima and the Roman ruins of Conímbriga along the way. Leave the freeway on the easy-to-miss first Coimbra exit (Coimbra Sul), then follow the *Centro* signs. Two and a half miles after leaving the freeway, you'll cross the Mondego River. Take Avenida Fernão de Magalhães directly into town. Most recommended hotels are near Station A and the Santa Clara Bridge. If you arrive from north Portugal or central Spain, follow signs for *Centro/Largo da Portagem.*

The large lot immediately across the river offers free parking (but it's dangerous overnight). You can also look for free parking along the streets over the river. In town, you'll find big, convenient, clearly marked pay garages. The largest in-town parking lot is centrally located under the government office, called Loja da Cidadão (on Avenida Fernão de Magalhães, 800 spots, €1/hour 7:00-20:00, €0.70/hour overnight). Most hotels can provide advice on the best parking options.

Coimbra

TO
BUS STN.
– A BORING
15 MIN WALK

TO
COIMBRA'S B
TRAIN STN.

CAMARA
MUNICIPAL

JARDIM
DE MANGA

RUA SOFIA

RUA DIREITA

FERNÃO DA

PRAÇA
8 DE MAIO

MOEDA

LARGO
OLARIAS

LOUÇA

P

MAGALHÃES

PAD.

6

7 MARTINS

5

CORPO DEUS

COUTIN.

18

R. VEIGA

END

15

TRAIN
STN. A

RUA

AZEIT.

3

WC

14

WC

MONDEGO
RIVER

NAVARRO

SOTA

WC

4

13

RUA
QUEBRA
COSTAS

VISCONDE DA LUZ

RUA F. BORGES

2

LARGO
DA
PORTAGEM

i

COUR.

100 YARDS

100 METERS

P

16

P

PONTE S. CLARA

AV.

FREE
P

1

START

PARQUE
DR. M. BRAGA

TO
LITTLE PORTUGAL,
SANTA CLARA CONVENT
& CONÍMBRIGA

TO E-3

NAZARÉ &
LISBON

DCH

Self-Guided Walk

❶ Santa Clara Bridge
❷ Largo da Portagem
❸ Praça do Comércio
❹ Edifício Chiado Museum
❺ À Capella Fado
❻ Church of Santa Cruz

❼ Café Santa Cruz
❽ Mercado Municipal
❾ Elevador do Mercado
❿ Machado de Castro Museum
⓫ Iron Gate to Old University

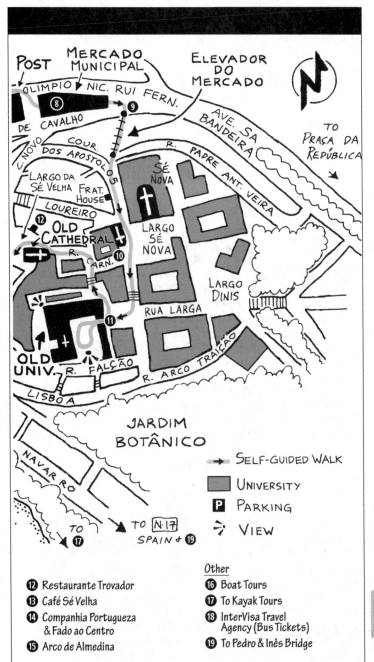

Legend:
- ➡ Self-Guided Walk
- ▢ University
- 🅿 Parking
- ⇗ View

12 Restaurante Trovador
13 Café Sé Velha
14 Companhia Portugueza & Fado ao Centro
15 Arco de Almedina

Other
16 Boat Tours
17 To Kayak Tours
18 InterVisa Travel Agency (Bus Tickets)
19 To Pedro & Inês Bridge

Helpful Hints

Money: ATMs and banks (Mon-Fri 8:30-15:00, closed Sat-Sun) are plentiful.

Internet Access. I**nternet Coimbra Câmara Municipal** has free Wi-Fi, plus six computers offering free Internet access (must reserve 30-minute time slot with passport to use computers, no reservation needed for Wi-Fi, open Mon-Fri 10:00-20:00, Sat-Sun 10:00-22:00; coming from the pedestrian street, it's past Praça 8 de Maio on your left at #38). **Centro de Copias do Quebra,** on the steps below the cathedral at Rua Quebra Costas 50, has several computers (€1.20/30 minutes, Mon-Fri 9:30-20:00, Sat-Sun 10:30-19:00, public pay WCs just up the steps).

Car Rental: **Avis** has a tiny office in Station A (Mon-Fri 8:30-12:30 & 15:00-19:00, closed Sat-Sun, tel. 229-436-900, toll-free tel. 800-201-002), **InterRent Car** has one in Station B (Mon-Fri 9:00-13:00 & 15:00-18:00, Sat 10:00 13:00, closed Sun, tel. 239-496-559), and **Hertz** is near the bus station at Rua Padre Estevão Cabral (tel. 239-834-750).

Bus Tickets: The **InterVisa travel agency** sells Intercentro company international tickets to Salamanca, Spain (€36), and beyond. They charge a small commission, but it's worth it (Mon-Fri 9:00-12:30 & 14:30-18:30, closed Sat-Sun; Avenida Fernão da Magalhães 11—leaving Station A, walk 100 yards to your left, then take the first left; tel. 239-823-873).

Local Guides: While the city doesn't offer walking tours, the TI has a list of private guides, such as **Cristina Bessa** (mobile 917-200-180, ccfb64@hotmail.com), **Maria Jose Fernandes** (mobile 934-093-542, mariajf@portugalmail.pt), and **Rosa Lopez** (mobile 966-103-277, mrosastoscano@gmail.com). Local guides charge €100 for a half-day tour.

Getting Around Coimbra

If you're arriving by train at Station B, you'll need to take the free shuttle train to Station A (see "Arrival in Coimbra," earlier), which is within about a 10-minute walk of everything I've listed.

While most visitors do the entire city on foot, **taxis** are cheap (around €4-5 for a short ride) and a good option if you've been up and down too many hills.

The cute little electric **minibus** (nicknamed *pantufinhas,* or "grandma's slipper") is silent and easy; it's designed to get grandmas—and anyone else—up and down the steep hills of the old town. It makes a continuous 20-minute loop through the lower old town (Baixa) and around the upper old town (Alta), passing through Largo da Portagem, down the pedestrian shopping lane to Praça 8 de Maio, and by the old cathedral. There are no regular

COIMBRA

stops—you just wave it down to get on, and tell the driver when you want off (pay driver €1.50, or use a multiple-ride pass—described next).

Local **buses** are expensive (€1.50, better-value 3-ride pass-€2, 11-ride pass-€6.10, no time limit, sharable, also a €3.20 one-day pass, all are sold at kiosks). These passes are also valid for Coimbra's Elevador do Mercado from Mercado Municipal to the top of town (described on page 247).

Metro Mondego, a new light-rail system starting at Station B and mostly serving the suburbs, is scheduled to begin running sometime in the next few years.

Self-Guided Walk

Welcome to Coimbra's Old Town

Coimbra is fun on foot, especially along its straight (formerly Roman) pedestrian-only main drag. This tour takes about two hours, including a visit to the university.

• *Start your walk at the...*

Santa Clara Bridge: This bridge, Ponte Santa Clara, has been an important link across the Mondego River since Roman times. For centuries, it had a tollgate *(portagem)*. The non-Coimbra end of the bridge offers a fine Coimbra view.

Coimbra is redeveloping its long-neglected riverside. A park stretches past several recommended restaurants to the romantic pedestrian bridge, linking the town with the far riverbank, where an improved, people-friendly zone is envisioned. The bridge is named for Dom Pedro and Dona Inês (Portugal's Romeo and Juliet—see page 227).

• *At the end of the bridge on the Coimbra side is...*

Largo da Portagem: Much of the old center is ornamented with Art Nouveau architecture (circa 1900) from a boom period; notice the fancy bank building and Hotel Astória behind it. This square is a great place for coffee or a pastry. Try Pastelaria Briosa (best pastries) or Café Montanha (with a big brass palm tree inside). The town's two special treats are *pastel de Santa Clara* (pastry made with almonds and marmalade) and *pastel de Tentúgal* (rolls of puff pastry stuffed with eggs and cream, and dusted with powdered sugar, €1 each). In the center of the square is a statue of the prime minister who, in 1834, shut down the city's convents and monasteries, and earned the nickname "friar killer."

• *Stroll down Rua de Ferreira Borges—pedestrianized and a delight*

Coimbra in History

1064 Coimbra is liberated from the Moors.

1139 Portugal's first king, Afonso Henriques, makes Coimbra his capital.

1211 Portugal's first parliament of nobles *(cortes)* convenes at Coimbra.

1256 Lisbon replaces Coimbra as Portugal's capital.

1290 The university is founded under "the poet king," Dinis (r. 1279-1325). Originally in Lisbon, it moved to Coimbra in 1308.

1537 The university, after moving back to Lisbon, finally settles permanently in Coimbra under Jesuit administration.

1810 Napoleon's French troops sack Coimbra, then England's Duke of Wellington drives them out.

1928 António Salazar, a professor of political economy at Coimbra, becomes Minister of Finance and eventually dictator of Portugal.

since the 1990s. After a 200-yard-long gauntlet of clothing stores, take the stairs (to your left) leading to a terrace overlooking the square below (pay public WC, sanitários, in the stairwell).

Praça do Comércio: This pleasant square is shaped like a Roman chariot racecourse—and some speculate that it used to be one 2,000 years ago. In the Middle Ages, they used this place for bullfights. Beyond Praça do Comércio stretches the heart of the old town. Look at your map. The circular street pattern outlines the wall used by Romans,

Visigoths, Moors, and Christians to protect Coimbra. Historically, only the rich could afford to live within the protective city walls (the Alta, or high town). Even today, the Baixa, or low town, remains a poorer section, with haggard women rolling wheeled shopping carts, children running barefoot, and men lounging on the square like it's their life's calling. But it's a fine area for wandering around during the day to explore small shops and eateries, and to get thoroughly disoriented.

• *Return to the pedestrian street.*

At the top of the stairs, you'll see the **Edifício Chiado** (part of the Museu Municipal, with a small but interesting permanent collection, described on page 255). Next door is a lottery shop—these are much loved in Portugal. At the corner (on your right), steps lead up through an ancient arched gateway—Arco de Almedina—into the old city and to the old cathedral and university. Later, after visiting the university, we'll finish this walk by going downhill through this arch.

A block farther along the pedestrian drag, stop at the picturesque corner (where the building comes to a triangular corner). The steep road climbs into Coimbra's historic ghetto (no Jewish community remains) and the wonderful and recommended **À Capella** fado nightclub (see "Fado" sidebar, page 104).

As you stroll along, you'll know it's graduation time if students' photos are displayed in photographers' windows. Check out the graduates decked out in their traditional university capes (displaying rips on the hem—left side for family, right side for friends, backside for girl- or boyfriends) and color-coded sashes indicating their field of study.

• *The pedestrian street ends at Praça 8 de Maio with the...*

Church of Santa Cruz: Enjoy this church's impressive facade. Notice the low-key white wires on the statuary—they're electrified to keep pigeons from dumping their corrosive loads on the tender limestone. Go inside; it's the most active religious spot in town. The musty church is lavishly decorated with 18th-century tiles that tell the stories of the discovery of the Holy Cross (on left) and the life of St. Augustine (on right; the church is of the Augustinian order). The pulpit is considered one of the finest pieces of Renaissance work in Portugal. St. Anthony of Padua is known as St. Anthony of Lisbon around here. He studied in Coimbra as a young monk in the 13th century. A statue of him dressed as an Augustinian monk is the centerpiece of a side altar on the left.

Step behind the altar for a close-up look at two fine 16th-century tombs. On the left lies the first Portuguese king, Afonso Henriques (1095-1185). Afonso "The Conqueror" reclaimed most of Portugal from the Moors, declared himself king, got the pope to approve the title, and settled down in his chosen capital—Coimbra. There, his wife gave birth to young Sancho, who later became king. Sancho I (1154-1211, tomb on right) was known as "The Populator." He saw the destruction that war had brought to the country, and set about rebuilding and repopulating, inviting northern European Crusaders (such as the Knights Templar) to occupy southern Portugal and giving trade privileges to border towns to strengthen his country's economy.

Notice that these tombs are carved in the richly ornamented Manueline style. In the 16th century, while on a pilgrimage to Santiago de Compostela, the great King Manuel I dropped by this church and was underwhelmed by the two kings' original tombs. He commissioned these beautifully carved replacements—much more fit for kings. Study the intimate faces. Notice how the kings seem only to be resting. (To make themselves more comfortable, they've "hung" their helmets and arm-guards just behind them.)

Church of Santa Cruz Sacristy: For €2.50, you can explore the sacristy (entrance to right of main altar), see the treasures of the church, and pass through the impressive chapter room into a Manueline Cloister of Silence (Mon-Fri 9:00-17:00, Sat 9:00-12:00 & 14:00-17:00, Sun 16:00-17:30). The first room is the actual sacristy (with "carpet tiles" blanketing the walls and huge banks of drawers for priests' vestments). The next room has relics, including the skull of St. Teotonio, the first Portuguese saint. The chapter room (with St. Teotonio's tomb) opens into the Cloister of Silence, where monks used to meditate, inspired by the tiled scenes of Christ teaching the beatitudes.

• *Exit the church into the main square. People (and pigeons) survey the Praça 8 de Maio scene from the terrace of the recommended...*

Café Santa Cruz: Located to the right of church, this recommended coffeehouse was itself built as a church. It was abandoned with the dissolution of the monasteries in 1834, when the government took possession of many grand buildings and rich public spaces. As a café, this was the 19th-century haunt of the town's intellectuals. The altar is now used for lectures, poetry readings, small concerts, and art exhibits (the women's restroom is in a confessional).

• *Continue past the church and the city hall (Câmara Municipal, pop in quickly for a glance at a hilly 3-D model of Coimbra, or make an appointment across the street for free Internet access—see "Helpful Hints," earlier). At the noisy street, turn right, and go a block to find a park with a fountain (once a monastery cloister and Renaissance garden) and the cheap, handy, and recommended self-service restaurant **Jardim da Manga**. Keep going uphill along the busy Rua Olímpio Nicolau di Fernandes past the big post office to the...*

Mercado Municipal: This modern covered market is fun to explore and great for gathering picnic supplies (Mon-Sat 8:00-14:00 but some stalls open later, closed Sun). It's clean and hygienic, but maintains the colorful appeal of an old farmers' market. See the "salt of the earth" in the faces of the women selling produce (their men are off in the fields...or the bars). These ladies aren't shy about trying to sell their goods, even to tourists. For a sandwich and glass of wine for less than €4, head to the Bar do Mercado Requinte at the end of the ground floor. Check out the photos of the old market on the wall, and then go upstairs for bread, more meat, and veggies. Follow your nose to the glass doors at the far end, with all the fresh fish and

dried cod. The Portuguese are the world's biggest cod eaters, but because cod is no longer found in nearby waters, the local favorite is imported from Norway. To the Portuguese, cod *(bacalhau)* tastes much better dried and salted than fresh. This section housed the original market—you can recognize the wrought-iron work from the photos you've just seen on the ground floor at the bar.

• *From the fish hall, swim outside and find the sleek city elevator.*

Elevador do Mercado: Take the elevator/funicular to the top of the hill (€1.60/trip if you pay elevator operator; covered by bus passes described on page 243; elevator runs Mon-Sat 7:00-22:00, Sun 10:00-22:00). Don't insert your ticket in the machine until the elevator operator is there.

The lift whisks you up the long, steep hill (stop midway to transfer to funicular, no need to validate ticket again), offering commanding views of Coimbra en route. At the top, exit to the right and head uphill, following signs to *Universidade.* Fifty yards up the cobbled lane, at the first intersection and crest of the hill, you'll find a fraternity house called Real República Corsários das Ilhas ("Royal Commune of the Island Pirates"). Notice the prominent skull-and-crossbones graffiti on the wall, linking McDonald's and the G8 (group of the eight most powerful countries). Look around for other examples of graffiti. These small university frat houses, called *repúblicas,* are communes that traditionally house about a dozen students from the same region or provincial town. While some are highly cultured, the rowdier ones are often decorated with plunder from their pranks—stolen traffic signs and so on—giving rise to the local saying, "At night, many things happen in Coimbra."

• *Walk three blocks on past the **Machado de Castro Museum** (on right, described on page 253) to the big, fascist-designed university square (Praça da Porta Férrea). The **Iron Gate** entry to the old university is on your right.*

University: Explore the university (described later, under "Sights in Coimbra"), then continue this town walk.

• *Leave the university—pass back out through the Iron Gate, turn left immediately and take the steps down into the old town (following the steep lanes toward the old cathedral).*

As you wander, notice the white-paper diamonds in the windows—they indicate that there's a student room available for rent. Continuing on, you'll come to the **old cathedral** (Sé Velha, described later, under "Sights in Coimbra"). Facing the cathedral is the recommended **Restaurante Trovador,** offering fado performances every night in summer (reservations essential for fado). The colorful little **Café Sé Velha** (great for a quick and tasty €9 lunch), on the corner immediately below the cathedral, is tiled with fine, traditional scenes from Coimbra. From there, a blue line on the cobbles marks the route of the electric minibus. Take the steep stairway leading down (past the public WCs) to the Rua Quebra Costas, the "Street of Broken Ribs." At one time, this lane had no steps, and literally *was* the street of broken ribs. During a strong rain, this becomes a river. The lane's many shops show off the fine local blue-and-white ceramic work called *faiança*.

• *Half-way down the steps on your right, take a peek into the...*

Companhia Portugueza: Located at #35, this store sells only traditional and nostalgic Portuguese products that are still used today. Check out the children's primers from the Salazar era, which some parents still prefer to use.

• *Farther down on the same side of the street is the recommended **Fado ao Centro**—if you're here at noon or around 15:00, this would be a good time to see a show. Or drop in to make a reservation for the 18:00 performance (see page 255 for details). Rua Quebra Costas ends at...*

Arco de Almedina: This is the double set of arches (named "Gate to the Medina") we saw earlier from the pedestrian street Rua de Ferreira Borges. Part of the old town wall, the arches act as a double gate with a 90-degree kink in the middle for easier defense. Looking back and up, notice the two square holes in the ceiling, through which soldiers would pour boiling oil, turning attacking Moors into fritters. The holes are rudely nicknamed *matacães* (dog killers). The second arch was added later (likely for Reconquista defense). Pass through and you'll end up unscathed back on the pedestrian street.

Sights in Coimbra

▲▲▲Coimbra's Old University

This venerable 700-year-old university, founded in 1290, was modeled after Bologna's university (Europe's first, founded in 1139). It's a stately three-winged former royal palace (from when Coimbra was the capital), beautifully situated overlooking the city. At first, law, medicine, grammar, and logic were taught. Then, with the rise of seafaring in Portugal, astronomy and geometry were added.

Coimbra's Old University

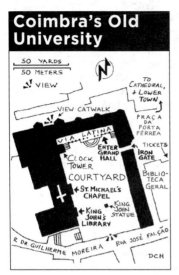

While Lisbon's university is much larger, Coimbra's university (with 25,000 students) is still the country's most respected. For visitors, the university marks the top of the old town. While most of it is fascist-era sprawl, the old core of the university (the palace section, with its iron gate, courtyard, fancy ceremonial halls, chapel, and library) makes for an interesting visit.

Cost and Hours: A combo-ticket for the two university sights that charge admission—the Grand Hall and King John's Library—is €7, daily April-Oct 8:30-19:30, Nov-March 10:00-16:00, ticket office closes 30 minutes before sights, www.uc.pt/en/informacaopara. Buy your ticket at the counter located inside the Biblioteca Geral (the large building to the left and outside of the Iron Gate). Your library entry time will be printed on the receipt that comes with your ticket; you'll need to show the receipt later to enter either sight.

Getting There: To get to the university, consider taking the "Welcome to Coimbra's Old Town" walk (earlier), and using the elevator from the Mercado Municipal to get to the top of the hill. Or take a taxi to the Iron Gate, then sightsee Coimbra downhill.

Iron Gate (Porta Férrea)—Find the gate to the old university (on Praça da Porta Férrea). Before entering, stand with your back to the gate (and the old university) and look across the stark, modern square at the fascist architecture of the new university. In what's considered one of the worst cultural crimes in Portuguese history, the dictator António Salazar tore down half of Coimbra's old town to build these university halls. Salazar, proud that Portugal was the last European power to hang onto its colonial empire, wanted a fittingly monumental university here. After all, Salazar—along with virtually everyone of political influence in Portugal—had been educated at Coimbra, where he studied law and then became an economics professor. If these bold buildings are reminiscent of Mussolini's E.U.R. in Rome, perhaps it's because they were built in part by Italian architects hired by Portugal's little Mussolini.

OK, now turn and walk through the Iron Gate. Traditionally, freshmen—proudly wearing their black capes for the first time—pass through the Iron Gate to enroll. Also traditionally, they had to pass through an Iron Gate gauntlet of butt kicks from upperclassmen to get out.

Walk into the...

Old University Courtyard—The university's most important sights all face this square: the Grand Hall (up the grand stairway on the right between you and the clock tower), St. Michael's Chapel (straight ahead, through the door, then to the left), and King John's Library (across the square, farthest door on left, flanked by columns).

The statue in the square is of King John III. While the university was established in 1290, it went back and forth between Lisbon and Coimbra (back then, university students were adults, privileged, and a pain to have in your town). In 1537, John III finally established the school permanently in Coimbra (away from Lisbon). Standing like a good humanist (posing much like his contemporary, England's King Henry VIII), John modernized Portugal's education system in the Renaissance style. But he also made the university the center of Portugal's Inquisition.

Survey the square with your back to the gate. The dreaded sound of the clock tower's bell—named the "baby goat" for its nagging—calls students to class. On several occasions, the clapper has been stolen. (No bell...no class. No class...big party.) A larger bell (the "big goat") rings only on grand and formal occasions.

The arcaded passageway (upstairs) between the Iron Gate and the clock tower is called Via Latina, from the days when only Latin was allowed in this part of the university.

See the following sights in any order you like. If you want to visit the Grand Hall and/or King John's Library, remember that you need to purchase your ticket at the Biblioteca Geral (to the left and outside of the Iron Gate). It doesn't hurt to show up before the time printed on your ticket—regardless of the admission time you're given to see the library, they may let you in early.

The Grand Hall (Sala dos Capelos)—Enter from the middle of Via Latina, climb the tiled stairway, and show your ticket. The Grand Hall is the site of the university's major academic ceremonies, such as exams and graduations. Tourists look down from balconies above the room. This was originally the throne room of the royal palace. Today, the rector's light-green chair sits like a throne in front. During ceremonies, students in their formal attire fill the benches, and teachers sit along the perimeter as gloomy portraits of Portuguese kings watch from above. The fine, old, painted ceiling features "Indo-Portuguese" themes, reminding Portugal's next generation of leaders of the global reach of their nation. There is no clapping during these formal rituals, but a brass band (on the wooden platform in the back) punctuates the ceremonies with solemn music.

View Catwalk *(Varanda):* Continue around the Grand Hall, past an ornately decorated former royal stateroom (now a place where students take their oral exams as portraits of past university rectors look on with interest). Go out onto the narrow observation deck for the best possible views of Coimbra (the viewpoint may be closed in bad weather). The "only 10 people on the balcony at a time" rule is enforced by an on-duty guard who has the door key.

From the viewpoint, scan the old town from right to left. Remember, before Salazar's extension of the university, this old town surrounded the university. The Baroque facade breaking the horizon is the "new" cathedral—from the 16th century. Below that, with the fine arcade, is the Machado de Castro Museum, housed in the former bishop's palace and located atop a Roman site (described later). And below that, like an armadillo, sits the old cathedral with its tiled cupola.

Gaily painted yellow-and-blue windows mark *república* frat houses. If you visit during late October, November, or May, you might see a student festival: Parades of rowdy students in funny costumes, draped in signs, dragging tin cans—these are all part of the traditional initiation rites marking the beginning and end of the school year. May provides the biggest spectacle, when new students receive—and graduating students burn—the small colored ribbons of their chosen major (see sidebar, next page). Look beyond the houses to the Mondego River, the longest river that flows entirely in Portugal. Over the bridge is the 17th-century Santa Clara Convent—at 590 feet, the longest building in Coimbra.

St. Michael's Chapel—This chapel is behind the 16th-century facade (enter through door to the right of facade—once inside, push the door on the left marked *capela*, free admission). The architecture of the church interior is Manueline—notice the golden "rope" trimming the arch before the altar. The decor is from a later time. The altar is 17th-century Mannerist, with steps unique to Portugal (and her South American colonies), symbolizing the steps the faithful take on their journey to heaven. The 2,100-pipe, 18th-century German-built organ is notable for its horizontal "trumpet" pipes. Found only in Iberia, these help the organist perform the

COIMBRA

The Burning of Ribbons

Europe's third-oldest university has long-standing traditions to match. If you're lucky enough to be in Coimbra at the end of the academic year (sometime in May, depending on the academic calendar), you'll witness a big party that's not to be missed.

The "Burning of Ribbons" *(Queima das Fitas)* began in the 1850s, when a group of students who passed their final fourth-year exams gathered outside the Iron Gate and marched together to the lower town. They burned their ribbons (which were used to bind and carry their books) in a small fire, representing their passage from student to professional. Fifty years later, that simple event had become enormously popular and was added to the other academic celebrations. Floats and parades came later, and the ribbon-burning was done at night. The following day was made an academic holiday—the official time when all students move up one level.

Students who will enter their last year of studies as well as recent graduates *(finalistas)* participate in the party these days, but of course the graduates get the most attention. Women wear simple white shirts with black skirts and black stockings. Men dress more formally in black suits—some with tails—as well as their university cape, a wide sash with various badges, a top hat, and a cane. Different accent colors, proudly displayed on the top hats and canes, represent the different departments and indicate which degree the student earned (yellow for medicine, red for law, light blue for computer science, etc.). For good luck after graduation, men take their canes and tap other students' top hats three times. (Of course, the taps get out of control, and lots of students end up losing the tops of their hats.)

Much drinking accompanies this rite of passage, but it's the one time of year when folks in Coimbra don't seem to mind. Ribbon-burning parties are also celebrated in Porto, and to a lesser extent in Lisbon. Join the fun, and offer an appropriately colored flower to a new graduate. You may be invited to the party.

allegorical fight between good and evil—with the horizontal pipes trumpeting the arrival of the good guys. The box seats for the royal family are above the loft in the rear. Students and alums enjoy the privilege of having their weddings here.

The **Museum of Sacred Art,** farther down the corridor, may still be closed for renovation. When it reopens, a painting of John the Baptist will again point the way to art that nuns and priests find fascinating. The museum was created in 1910 to keep the art in Coimbra when the new republic wanted to move it all to Lisbon. (Also in the corridor, you'll find WCs—free with entry ticket—

and a cheap student-filled café with a lovely view of the river from the terrace.)

▲**King John's Library**—One of Europe's best surviving Baroque libraries, this grand building displays 30,000 books in 18th-century splendor. The zealous doorkeeper locks the door at every opportunity to keep out humidity. Buzz (on left) to get into this temple of thought. While ticket-sellers are quick to issue entry times requiring a long wait, you're likely to get in early if you humbly ask the attendant

if you can enter now. Once you've received permission to enter, you might still have to wait outside a while, as other groups finish their 10-minute visits (followed by a 10-minute closure to control humidity level). Inside, at the "high altar," stands the library's founder, the absolute monarch King John V (1698-1750), who considered France's King Louis XIV an inspiration.

The reading tables, inlaid with exotic South American woods (and ornamented with silver ink wells), and the precious wood shelves (with clever hideaway staircases) are reminders that Portugal's wealth was great—and imported. Built Baroque, the interior is all wood. Even the "marble" on the arches of triumph that divide the library into rooms is just painted wood. (Real marble would add to the humidity.) The resident bats—which live in the building, but not the library itself—are well cared for and appreciated. They eat insects, providing a chemical-free way of protecting the books, and alert the guard to changing weather with their "eee-eee" cry. Look for the trompe l'oeil Baroque tricks on the painted ceiling. Gold leaf (from Brazil) is everywhere, and the Chinese themes are pleasantly reminiscent of Portugal's once vast empire. The books, each dating from before 1755, are in Latin, Greek, and Hebrew. Imagine being a student in Coimbra centuries ago, when this temple of learning stored the world's knowledge like a vast filing cabinet. As you leave, watch how the doorman uses the giant key as a hefty doorknob.

More Sights in Coimbra

Machado de Castro Museum—Housed in the old bishop's palace, the Machado de Castro contains a Roman excavation site, ceramics, and 14th- to 16th-century religious sculpture (mostly taken from dissolved monasteries). Though it's long been closed for extensive restoration, you can still visit its Roman section, with the rest of the museum scheduled to finally reopen sometime in 2013.

Cost and Hours: €2 during renovation but likely around €5 once fully reopened, Tue-Sun 10:00-12:30 & 14:00-18:00, closed Mon, http://mnmachadodecastro.imc-ip.pt. Visit this before or after the old university, since both are at roughly the same altitude.

Visiting the Museum: If you're here after the renovation is complete, first go upstairs and look for the impressive 14th-century *Cristo Negro* carved in wood. Until a decade ago, when this statue was cleaned (and the black—from candle soot—came off), it was considered to be a portrait of a black Christ. Before you return downstairs, enjoy the views from the top-floor arcade.

If you're visiting while the museum's mostly closed, it's still worth popping in to see the excavations downstairs. The Roman building, with a basement crisscrossed with empty tunnels, provided a level foundation for an ancient Roman forum that stood where the museum does today. At the entrance, read the Latin-inscribed Roman stone: bottom line—"Aeminiens," referring to the people who lived in Roman Coimbra, then called Aeminium; fifth line—the fourth-century emperor of the day, "Constantio"; and the second line—a reference perhaps to an early alliance of barbarian tribes from the North Atlantic. Notice the few economical "plug-on" Roman busts—from the days when they'd keep the bodies, but change the heads each time a new emperor took power. The museum sometimes houses art exhibitions here in the Roman tunnels or on the ground floor.

Old Cathedral (Sé Velha)—Same old story: Christians build a church on a pre-Christian holy spot (Visigoths in sixth century), Moors destroy the church and build a mosque (eighth century), then Christians push out the Moors (1064), tear down their mosque, and build another church. Notice the crenellations along the roof of this fortress-like Romanesque church; the Moors, though booted out, were still considered a risk. If this reminds you of Lisbon's cathedral, it should—it was designed by the same French architect.

Cost and Hours: Church—€2, no-photos policy rarely enforced; cloisters—€1; open Mon-Sat 10:00-18:00, closed Sun.

Visiting the Cathedral: The giant holy-water font shells are a 19th-century gift from Ceylon (now Sri Lanka), and the walls are lined with 16th-century tiles from Sevilla, Spain. The three front altars are each worth a look. The main altar is a fine example of Gothic styling. The 16th-century chapel to the right contains one of the best Renaissance altars in the country. The apostles all look to Jesus as he talks, while musical angels flank the holy host. To the left of the High Altar, the Chapel of St. Peter shows Peter being crucified upside down. Note that the local limestone is soft and therefore quite weathered.

On the right, just before the transept, is a murky painting of Queen Isabel (St. Elizabeth) with a skirt full of roses. This 13th-century Hungarian princess—with family ties to Portugal—is a local favorite with a sweet legend. Against the wishes of the king, she always gave bread to the poor. One day, when he came home early from a trip, she was busy doling out bread from her skirt. She pulled the material up to hide the bread. When the king asked her what was inside (suspecting bread for the poor), the queen—unable to lie—lowered the material and, miraculously, the bread had turned to roses. For this astonishing act, she was canonized as a saint in 1625.

The peaceful cloister (entrance near back of church) is the oldest Gothic cloister in Portugal. Well-maintained, though its walls are decaying, the courtyard offers a fine, framed view of the cathedral's dome. A tomb from 1064 in the cloister belongs to Coimbra's first Christian, post-Reconquista governor.

Edifício Chiado Museum—Originally the site of Coimbra's first Chiado department store, this refurbished building is notable for its construction—it was one of the first buildings in Portugal to be built around an iron framework (like the then-revolutionary American skyscrapers). It now houses an eclectic assortment of artworks and textiles donated by local collector José Telo de Morais.

Cost and Hours: €1.70, Tue-Sat 10:00-13:00 & 14:00-18:00, no mid-day break April-Sept, closed Sun-Mon year-round, Rue Ferreira Borges 85, tel. 239-840-754, www.cm-coimbra.pt.

Visiting the Museum: Take the elevator up to the top floor and walk your way down, noticing the exposed iron beams. The third floor has ceramics, drawings, and a collection of silverware. The second floor has 17th- and 18th-century furniture as well as religious paintings and objects. The first floor holds oil and pastel paintings from the 19th and early 20th centuries. The ground floor houses temporary exhibits.

▲▲Fado Music—Portugal's unique, mournful traditional music, fado, is generally performed by women. But in Coimbra, men sing the fado. Roving bands of male students—similar to the *tuna* bands in Spain's Salamanca—serenade around town for tips and the hearts of women.

Fado ao Centro is reputed to have the best fado singers in Coimbra. This all-male ensemble of current and former Coimbra university students sings fado in the unique local style. They offer three shows daily—two short, half-hour shows at 12:30 and 15:00 (€5), and a 50-minute show at 18:00, which includes a glass of port wine (€10). This is a nice alternative to late-night shows, but can be popular with tour groups; reservations are smart in summer for the evening show (just past the Arco de Almedina on Rua Quebra Costas #7, tel. 913-236-725).

À Capella, on the hill above the Church of Santa Cruz, offers an intimate fado experience. The tiny chapel has been turned into a temple for Coimbra-style traditional music, and it's fado every night all year long (three musicians perform from 22:30 to about 24:00, but they often start late). Come for the music, the cool scene, and the snacks and drinks (€10 cover, reservations smart in summer, at the triangular corner midway down the main drag, climb the steep Rua do Corpo de Deus 100 yards until you see the old chapel on your left, tel. 239-833-985). If you're coming to eat, note that the chapel opens nightly at 21:00 and serves snack-like meals at a fair price.

Fado Diligência is a bar famous for its informal music schedule—locals love to come here and just jam (guitar and voice). It's a good spot for a folk or fado sing-along in a warm, relaxed atmosphere. They even know a few Beatles tunes, so request your favorite and take center stage if you're feeling bold. I'd eat elsewhere and come here for drinks. There's a reasonable €5 minimum (shows daily 22:30-2:00 in the morning; from Praça 8 de Maio, take Rua Sofia to your second left, Diligência is 2 blocks up on your right at Rua Nova 30; tel. 239-827-667).

More Fado: During the tourist season, you'll find sit-down fado nightly at the recommended **Restaurante Trovador.** The mayor organizes Thursday street concerts that feature fado music through the summer. The **Galeria Almedina,** under the Arco de Almedina, also puts on free fado shows (Sat in June-Aug, ask at TI for details). The recommended **Café Santa Cruz,** next to the Church of Santa Cruz, hosts live fado several nights a week.

Parque Dr. Manuel Braga—Coimbra's inviting riverside park sprawls upstream from the Santa Clara Bridge to the Pedro and Inês Bridge. You'll find boat tours, some recommended restaurants, a strip of trendy evening spots, and the Portuguese Pavilion from the Hannover Expo (2000 World's Fair in Hannover, Germany).

Little Portugal (Portugal dos Pequenitos)—Across the Santa Clara Bridge is a children's (or tourists') look at the great buildings and monuments of Portugal and its former empire in miniature, scattered through a park a couple of blocks south of town, straight across the Santa Clara Bridge. Wanting to boost national pride, Salazar commissioned architect Cassiano Branco to build these mini-replicas in 1940. If you've been through some of Portugal already, it's fun to try and identify the buildings you've already seen and look at what's to come.

Cost and Hours: €9, kids ages 3-13-€5.50, kids under 2 free, daily March-May 10:00-19:00, June-mid-Sept 9:00-20:00, mid-Sept-Feb 10:00-17:00, last entry 30 minutes before closing, Rossio de Santa Clara, tel. 239-801-170, www.portugaldospequenitos.pt.

Kayaks, Cruises, and Adventure Sports—To enjoy the region's natural beauty, consider these activities.

Kayaking: The company called **O Pioneiro do Mondego**

buses you from Coimbra to Penacova (15 miles away), where you can kayak down the Mondego River for about four hours back into Coimbra (€22.50, 10 percent discount with this book, daily June-Sept, one- and two-person kayaks available, book by phone or email, meet at park near TI, tel. 239-478-385, www.opioneiro domondego.com, info@opioneirodomondego.com, Kristien and Jonas speak English). Most people stop to swim or picnic on the way back, so it often turns into an all-day journey. For the first 12.5 miles, you'll go easily with the flow, but you'll get your exercise paddling the remaining stretch. To avoid the workout (and the more boring part of the Mondego River), ask to be picked up 2.5 miles before Coimbra, at Portela do Mondego, where the river's current slows down.

Cruises: If you'd rather let someone else do the work, **Basófias** boats float up and down the river on a 55-minute joyride that runs daily except Monday (€6.50; departures from dock across from TI at 15:00, 16:00, and 17:00; in summer also at 18:00 and 19:00; schedule posted at dock, no narration, tel. 969-830-664, www.basofias.com).

Adventure Sports: Located in the nearby town of Foz da Figueira, **Capitão Dureza** specializes in at-your-own-risk activities: rappelling, rafting, mountain biking, hiking, and canyoning (pickup and drop-off in Coimbra, tel. 918-315-337, www.capitao dureza.com).

Near Coimbra

▲**Conímbriga Roman Ruins**—Portugal's best Roman sight is impressive...unless you've been to Rome. What remains of the Roman city is divided in two, in part because its inhabitants tore down buildings to erect a quick defensive wall against an expected barbarian attack. Today, this wall cuts crudely through the site.

Cost and Hours: €4, daily June-Sept 10:00-19:00, Oct-May 10:00-18:00, museum closed Mon but ruins are open, www .conimbriga.pt.

Getting There: The ruins are nine miles southwest of Coimbra, on the road to Lisbon. On weekdays, two **buses** leave for the ruins each morning across from Coimbra's Station A (€2.15; Mon-Fri at 9:00, 9:30, 12:30, and 15:30; Sat-Sun at 9:30, 12:30, and 15:30; bus stop is on the riverside opposite the station, 30-minute trip). The return bus leaves from Conímbriga's parking lot (Mon-Fri at 12:55, 16:25, and 17:55; Sat-Sun at 13:25 and 18:25). Confirm the destination by asking, *"Vai para Conímbriga?"* Otherwise, you could end up on one of the frequent buses to Condeixa (runs twice hourly) that stops a mile short of the ruins.

Drivers should consider going to Conímbriga on the way to or from Coimbra; the Conímbriga freeway exit is clearly marked from the A-1. To get there from the town center, cross the Santa Clara Bridge and go uphill, following signs to *Condeixa*. Continue straight through town, and you will see brown signs guiding you to the ruins.

◐ Self-Guided Tour: Purchase your tickets inside the main building, then enter the ruins before visiting the museum. Helpful arrows guide you through the sight. Explore the remnants of the old town first, and save the mansion—under the protective modern roofing—for the grand finale. You'll first see remains of different houses and shopping arcades, most with wonderful mosaics intact. Note how the columns are made of preformed wedges. After you see the public baths, walk around the wall.

The Wall: Locals hastily built this immense structure for their own protection, and it shows. Once the Roman Empire retreated from this area, invaders from the north went on the offensive (beginning around A.D. 465). A Christian Germanic tribe conquered the city and built a basilica at the end of this wall.

Continuing along the wall, you'll see parts of a house belonging to a local landowner. Walk through the fields to the rest of the ruins. Other houses and public baths are out there, even though they're poorly signposted. As you explore, you'll see the sparse ruins of the old forum. Backtrack to pass under the aqueduct and go around it. Look for the fallen stones, which once supported the structure, until you reach the most important find (under a protective roof). The **House of the Fountains** is an entire dwelling, with most of its rooms and mosaics intact. Don't spend €0.50 on the lazy fountain show (wait for one of the school groups to do it for you), but enjoy the stories told in the mosaics. Simple portraits, horses, and numerous hunting scenes illustrate the daily routine in this town during Roman times.

The Museum: Return to the delightful museum that shows the discoveries from decades of excavation. The room to the right of the ticket counter describes daily life in Conímbriga. You'll see coins, dinnerware, and even grooming utensils (find the spoon-shaped ear cleaners)—all with good English descriptions. The opposite room contains a miniature replica of the forum, along with fine mosaics and a few tombstones. The best mosaic is of the mythological, bull-headed Minotaur—follow the maze from the center until you are safely out. The museum's café is an excellent spot to have lunch before catching the return bus to Coimbra (€7 meals, same hours as museum). Or bring a picnic lunch, and eat in the gardens.

Sleep Code

(1 = about $1.30, country code: 351)
S = Single, **D** = Double/Twin, **T** = Triple, **Q** = Quad, **b** = bathroom, **s** = shower only. Unless indicated otherwise, credit cards are accepted and English is spoken.

To help you easily sort through these listings, I've divided the accommodations into three categories, based on the price for a standard double room with bath during high season (April-Sept). The rest of the year, it's 10-20 percent less.

$$$ **Higher Priced**—Most rooms €80 or more.
 $$ **Moderately Priced**—Most rooms between €50-80.`
  $ **Lower Priced**—Most rooms €50 or less.

Prices can change without notice; verify the hotel's current rates online or by email.

Sleeping in Coimbra

These listings are an easy walk from the central Station A and Santa Clara Bridge. For the cheapest rooms, simply walk a block from Station A into the old town, and choose one of countless *dormidas* (cheap pensions). River views come with traffic noise.

Traditional Hotels and Pensions

$$$ Hotel Astória gives you the thrill of staying in the city's finest old hotel with Coimbra's first Art Deco lounges. Their 62 rooms are rated among the most characteristic in Portugal. Though it's a bit worn around the edges, this venerable place retains its charm (Sb-€92, Db-€112, superior Db at curved end of the building-€137, extra bed-€35, 10 percent discount if you mention this book when you reserve direct by email or phone—show it at check-in, includes breakfast, air-con, Wi-Fi, elevator, public parking opposite hotel-€0.50/hour but free overnight, central as can be at Avenida Emídio Navarro 21, tel. 239-853-020, fax 239-822-057, www.almeida hotels.com, astoria@almeidahotels.com). Rooms with river views don't cost extra, but come with some street noise. I prefer the quieter city-view rooms at the back.

$$ Hotel Bragança's dark lobby leads to 83 clean and comfortable but sometimes smoky rooms with modern bathrooms. The wood paneling and furniture transport you back to Portugal in the 1950s (Sb with shower-€35, Sb with tub-€48, smaller Db with shower-€55, larger Db with tub-€60, Tb with tub-€75, Qb-€85, 10 percent discount with this book, includes breakfast, air-con, elevator, Wi-Fi, free parking in small lot at entrance if space available, Largo das Ameias 10 next to Station A, tel. 239-822-171, fax 239-836-135, www.hotel-braganca.com, geral@hotel-braganca.com).

$ Residência Coimbra provides hotel quality in a 10-year-old building for pension prices. Its 15 fine air-conditioned rooms are buried in the old town on a quiet pedestrian lane, yet it's only 250 yards from Station A (Db-€40-50, 5 percent discount with this book when you reserve direct via email, includes breakfast, Wi-Fi, all rooms have double beds, Rua das Azeiteiras 55, tel. 239-837-996, www.residenciacoimbra.com, residenciacoimbra@gmail.com, Maria and Jose).

$ Residencial Vitória is a clean, well-located hotel renting 18 rooms over a restaurant, which is its main business. About half of the rooms were recently renovated (Db-€45-50, Tb-€60, breakfast-€5, air-con, elevator, a block from Station A at Rua da Sota 9, tel. 239-824-049, fax 239-842-897, www.residencialvitoria.net, rrvitoria@gmail.com).

$ Residência Lusa Atenas, which rents 20 rooms and has a fine TV room, is on a big noisy street but is reasonably quiet (Sb-€20-25, Db-€30-40, third person-€10, cash only, cheaper rooms in annex, breakfast extra, air-con, two blocks from Station A at Avenida Fernão de Magalhães 68, tel. 239-826-412, fax 239-820-133, www.residencialusatenas.com, mail@residencialusatenas.com, no English spoken).

$ Hotel Domus, tucked away in a corner, rents 20 decent rooms in a cozy atmosphere (Sb-€28, Ds-€30, Db with air-con-€40-45, double beds €5 cheaper than twins, Tb-€45, 10 percent discount with this book, includes breakfast, Wi-Fi, Rua Adelino Veiga 62, tel. 239-828-584, fax 239-838-818, www.hoteldomus.com.pt, hoteldomus@sapo.pt, Sra. and Sr. Santos). They rent five small, basic, cheaper rooms in the simpler **Annex Manuela** across the street (Ds-€28-35, twin beds-€3 extra, WC on floor, 10 percent discount with book).

$ Hotel Larbelo, with Old World character, mixes frumpiness and former elegance in its 17 rooms. The old-fashioned staircase, classic breakfast room, and gentle non-English-speaking management take you to another age (Sb-€25-30, Db-€35-45, Tb-€50, cheaper Oct-March, breakfast-€2.50, air-con, Wi-Fi, in front of the Santa Clara Bridge at Largo da Portagem 33, tel. 239-829-092, fax 239-829-094, www.larbelo.net, residencial.larbelo@sapo.pt).

Modern High-Rise Hotels

$$$ Hotel Tivoli Coimbra, a classy, Houston-esque skyscraper, is the handiest place offering contemporary luxury, such as flat-screen TVs and a swimming pool. It rents 80 big rooms with all the modern amenities, but it's a 10-minute walk from Station A and any Coimbra charm (Db-€85-160 depending on season and Web specials, book on their website for best deal, Rua João Machado, tel. 239-858-300, fax 239-858-345, www.tivolicoimbra.com, reservas. htc@tivolihotels.com).

$ Ibis Hotel, a modern high-rise, has 110 orderly little rooms that come with all the comforts. Well-located near the riverside Parque Dr. Manuel Braga, this impersonal but reliable chain hotel is three blocks past the Santa Clara Bridge and the old town (Sb/Db-€35-55, breakfast-€6, two smoke-free floors, elevator, easy €6/day parking in basement, Avenida Emídio Navarro 70, tel. 239-852-130, fax 239-852-140, www.ibishotel.com, h1672@accor.com).

Hostel
$ Pousada de Juventude, the youth hostel, offers 71 rooms on the other side of town in the student area past Praça da República. It's friendly, clean, and well-run, but is no cheaper than a simple *pensão* (€12/bed in 4- to 6-bed rooms, S-€28, Db-€30, Rua António Henriques Seco 14, tel. 239-822-955, coimbra@movijovem.pt).

Eating in Coimbra

Specialties of this hilly Beira region include *leitão* (suckling pig), *cabrito* (baby male goat), *chanfana* (goat cooked in wine), *Serra* cheese, and rich, red *Bairrada* and *Dão* wines. For a sweet and herby *digestivo*, try Licor Beirão. The local pastries are *pastel de Santa Clara* (made with almonds and marmalade) and *pastel de Tentúgal* (flaky puff pastry with a sweet egg filling and a dusting of powdered sugar). Be aware that many of these restaurants—as well as most of Coimbra—shut down on Sunday.

Dining with Fado
Restaurante Trovador, while fairly touristy, serves good food in a classic, romantic setting, with entertaining dinner fado performances nearly nightly in summer from 21:30 (Fri-Sat only off-season). It's *the* place for an old-town splurge (€15-20 daily fixed-price meals, Mon-Sat 12:30-15:00 & 19:30-22:30, closed Sun, facing the old cathedral on Largo de Sé Velha 15, reservations essential to eat with the music—ask for a seat with a music view, tel. 239-825-475).

Eating Cheap in the Old Town
Adega Paço do Conde knows how to grill, and Coimbra's students know it. Choose your seafood or meat selection from the display case as you enter. They'll pop it on the grill, serve it up, and then you can grab your table. The goat stew is a specialty. Students, solo

Coimbra Hotels & Restaurants

1 Hotel Astória
2 Hotel Bragança
3 Residência Coimbra
4 Residencial Vitória
5 Residência Lusa Atenas
6 Hotel Domus
7 Hotel Larbelo
8 To Hotel Tivoli Coimbra
9 Ibis Hotel
10 Restaurante Trovador
11 Adega Paço do Conde
12 Self-Service Rest. Jardim da Manga
13 Café Santa Cruz

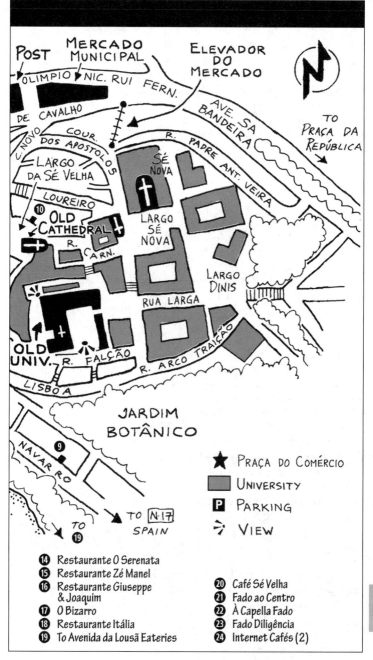

POST

MERCADO MUNICIPAL

ELEVADOR DO MERCADO

OLIMPIO NIC. RUI FERN.

DE CAVALHO

C. NOVO

COUR. DOS APOSTOLOS

AVE. SA BANDEIRA

TO PRAÇA DA REPÚBLICA

LARGO DA SÉ VELHA

LOUREIRO

SÉ NOVA

R. PADRE ANT. VEIRA

⑩ OLD CATHEDRAL

R. CARN.

LARGO SÉ NOVA

LARGO DINIS

RUA LARGA

OLD UNIV.

R. FALÇÃO

R. ARCO TRAIÇÃO

LISBOA

JARDIM BOTÂNICO

NAVARRO

⑨

TO N·17 SPAIN

TO ⑲

★ PRAÇA DO COMÉRCIO

▮ UNIVERSITY

🅿 PARKING

⇗ VIEW

⑭ Restaurante O Serenata
⑮ Restaurante Zé Manel
⑯ Restaurante Giuseppe & Joaquim
⑰ O Bizarro
⑱ Restaurante Itália
⑲ To Avenida da Lousã Eateries

⑳ Café Sé Velha
㉑ Fado ao Centro
㉒ À Capella Fado
㉓ Fado Diligência
㉔ Internet Cafés (2)

travelers, families, and pigeons like this homey place (€5-12 meals, Mon-Sat 11:00-22:00, closed Sun, Rua Paço do Conde 1; from Praça do Comércio, take the last left—Rua Adelino Veiga, opposite the church, and walk 2 blocks to small square—Largo Paço do Conde; tel. 239-825-605, Alfredo).

Self-Service Restaurant Jardim da Manga is handy for a quick, easy, and cheap meal with locals. Sit indoors or outdoors next to a cool and peaceful fountain. Just slide a tray down the counter and pick what you like (€7-10 meals, Sun-Fri 12:00-15:00 & 19:00-22:00, closed Sat, in Jardim da Manga, behind Church of Santa Cruz, tel. 239-829-156).

Café Santa Cruz, next to the Church of Santa Cruz, is Old World elegant, with great coffee, simple toasted sandwiches, and outdoor tables offering great people-watching over Praça 8 de Maio. Coffee costs €0.60 at the bar and just €0.80 outside at a table (Mon-Sat 8:00-24:00, Sun 8:00-20:00). The café hosts live fado several nights a week—check with the TI or café for performance times.

Restaurante O Serenata is country-kitchen cozy and fun, with about 20 tables and a fresh, bright atmosphere. They serve simple €10-15 meals (Mon-Sat 12:00-15:00 & 19:00-23:00, closed Sun, between Station A and Largo da Portagem at Largo da Sota 6, tel. 239-826-729).

Restaurante Zé Manel is tiny, rustic, and authentic. Judging from the walls—caked with notes from happy eaters—and the line of people waiting for a table, this place is a popular favorite. They serve a dozen good typical Coimbra dishes. To order, I'd trust Mario, who speaks a lee-tle English. The *ossos* (bones) are the hot dish here (€8 for one person, €14 for two, Mon-Sat 12:00-15:00 & 19:30-22:00, closed Sun and off-season, no reservations taken, arrive early or wait; sign is high above on lamppost, 20 yards directly behind Hotel Astória at Beco do Forno 12, tel. 239-823-790).

Restaurante Giuseppe & Joaquim serves good Portuguese and Italian meals in a large, elegant dining area (€6 salads, €5-10 pizzas, €10 pastas, €16-20 meat and fish plates, good €8 lunch buffet available Mon-Fri 12:00-14:30, open daily 12:00-24:00, behind Hotel Astória at Rua da Sota 12, tel. 239-098-990).

O Bizarro is a small, family-run, white-tablecloth hole-in-the-wall that serves up tasty Portuguese food at a good price (one €7 *dose* is designed to serve—and fill—two, goat stew is the house specialty, daily 12:00-15:00 & 18:00-22:00, 30 yards behind Hotel Astória at Rua Sargento Mor 44, Rafael speaks English).

Trendy Dining on the River

Restaurante Itália—at Parque Dr. Manuel Braga, opposite the TI—literally hangs over the river. It serves good Italian food indoors and out. Dinner reservations are smart (€8-12 pizza and pastas, €12-23 fish and meat plates, pizza available to go, daily 12:00-24:00, riverside tables limited to parties of four when busy, tel. 239-838-863).

Avenida da Lousã Eateries: A modern building on Avenida da Lousã houses a strip of trendy restaurants, each with an enthusiastic crowd; modern, air-conditioned seating indoors; and breezy riverside tables set on a common patio. The restaurants (most open daily from 12:00 until late) include:

Rock Café, a burgers-and-Budweiser joint, is understandably popular with the town's students. It's busy on Thursday night, the big party night in Coimbra—the kids go home on Friday (Tue-Sun 12:00-late, closed Mon, tel. 239-836-038).

A Portuguesa Restaurante, the most expensive and contemporary choice, is romantic, serving traditional dishes with a modern twist (prices range widely—from €9 garlic shrimp to €75 lobster, €15-20 beef dishes, reservations smart, tel. 239-842-140).

The Mondego Irish Pub is fun, noisy, and youthful, with live music most nights (generally Irish). It serves burgers, steaks, Guinness on tap, and all you'd expect from an Irish bar, plus a traditional favorite—*francesinha* (€7). Locals love these egg, cheese, and sausage sandwiches made with a spicy sauce (tel. 239-837-092).

Picnics: Shop at the colorful covered market called Mercado Municipal, behind the Church of Santa Cruz (Mon-Sat 8:00-14:00, closed Sun) or at tiny *mini-mercados* in the side streets. The well-maintained gardens along the river across from the TI are picnic-pleasant.

Coimbra Connections

From Coimbra by Bus to: Alcobaça (2/day, 1.5 hours), **Batalha** (3/day, 1 hour), **Fátima** (8/day, 1 hour), **Nazaré** (5/day, 2 hours), **Lisbon** (hourly, 2.5 hours, €14), **Évora** (4/day direct, 4 hours, €18.50, more options with transfer in Lisbon), **Porto** (11/day, 1.5 hours, €12.50). Bus info: tel. 239-855-270. Frequency drops on weekends, especially Sunday.

By Train to: Nazaré/Valado (3/day, 2.5 hours, transfer in Bifurcação de Lares; the bus is a better option—see above—because Nazaré/Valado train station is 3 miles away from Nazaré), **Porto** (nearly hourly, 1 hour on Alfa Pendular line or Intercidades service, 2 hours on slower regional line—confirm before buying; most long-distance trains end at Porto's non-central Campanhã Station), **Lisbon** (almost hourly on Alfa Pendular or Intercidades service, 2

COIMBRA

hours; regional service equally frequent but takes 4 hours; for Lisbon center, get off at Santa Apolónia Station; for Lisbon airport, hop off at Oriente Station and take the bus to airport; all Coimbra/Porto trains stop at both stations 7 minutes apart). Train info: tel. 808-208-208, www.cp.pt.

To Salamanca, Spain: The best option is the direct **bus** (€36, departs daily at 10:30, arrives at 17:30 in Salamanca, then continues on to Madrid). To guarantee a place, book a couple of days in advance. You can confirm schedules and buy your bus ticket by phone or in person at the friendly InterVisa travel agency in Coimbra (see "Helpful Hints," page 242) more easily than at Coimbra's bus station (Intercentro office, tel. 239-827-588, no English spoken).

I'd avoid taking the **train** to Salamanca because of its inconvenient arrival time: One train per day on the Sud-Expresso line departs Coimbra at 18:51 and drops you in Salamanca at 24:32 (4.5 hours, note that Spanish time is one hour later). The Salamanca train station is not centrally located, so it's best to reserve your accommodations in advance, as you won't be tucking into bed until two in the morning, Portuguese time.

PORTO

To get a complete picture of Portugal, visit Porto—the capital of the north and the country's second city (with 238,000 residents and a sprawling metropolitan area that includes 1.7 million people). Porto, proud of the things that make it different, fiercely clings to its long-standing rivalry with Lisbon...especially where soccer is concerned.

Porto (POR-toh) is less polished than Lisbon, but it's also full of Old World charm. Houses with red-tiled roofs tumble down the hills to the riverbank, prickly church towers dot the skyline, mosaic-patterned stones line streets, and flat-bottomed boats called *rabelos* ply the lazy river. The old town was spared the devastation of the great 1755 earthquake, and today is preserved as a World Heritage Site.

The city's name comes from the Romans, who dubbed the port town Portus Cale. When Porto's Christians conquered the Moors in the southern half of the country, the city's name became the name of the whole country. The many British people who have shaped Porto have also dubbed it "Oporto" ("the port"), a corruption of the town's true name. While various guidebooks and postcards call it this, locals never do.

Porto has a gritty warts-and-all character. The people of Porto claim they're working too hard to worry about being pretty. As an oft-repeated saying goes, "Coimbra studies, Braga prays, Lisbon parties...and Porto works."

Straight-laced, nose-to-the-grindstone Porto has enjoyed something of a cultural renaissance in the last decade. In 2001, it was designated as a European Capital of Culture. Two exciting showpieces of contemporary architecture have been built: the

PORTO

Porto

200 YDS.
200 M.

TO AIRPORT

TO HOUSE OF MUSIC, SERRALVES PARK & MUSEUM

CRISTOVÃO

Trindade Ⓜ

CITY

CITY HALL

ALMADA

SÉ BANO R.

CATARINA

BOLHÃO MARKET

DINIS

CARMO CHURCH

Aliados Ⓜ

CENTER

FORMOSA

RENEX BUS STN.

RESTAUR.

TRAM # 18

PRAÇA LIB.

ALIADOS

SÃO BENTO STN.

AV. RODRIGUES

PRAÇA BATALHA FREITAS

TO TRAMWAY MUSEUM, FOZ & ATLANTIC OCEAN

CLÉRIGOS TOWER

FLORES

MOUZ. SILV.

OLD CITY WALL

R. ALC.

REDE EXPRESSOS BUS STN.

HERC.

TO CAMPANHÃ STATION

R. NOVA ALF

STOCK EXCHANGE PALACE

CATHEDRAL

DUQUE

FUNICULAR

G. EIFFEL

SÃO FRAN.

PONTE LUÍS I.

RIVER

DOURO

PRAÇA DO INFANTE

RIBEIRA

R. CABO SIMÃO

TO PONTE MARIA PIA & DOURO VALLEY

CAIS DE GAIA

DCM

LEITE

SERRA DO PILAR MONASTERY

DIOGO

VILA NOVA DE GAIA

Ⓜ METRO STATION   ☊ CABLE CAR   ⚐ VIEW   ☐ SEE DETAIL MAPS

Serralves Museum and the House of Music. European Union money has poured in, funding a revamping of the public transportation system and more. With this ongoing construction, Porto is ever-changing, often chaotic, and worth a visit now more than ever. As a bonus, Porto serves as a handy gateway to the stunning Douro Valley.

Porto offers two high-impact sightseeing thrills: the postcard-perfect ambience of the riverfront Ribeira district and the opportunity to learn more about (and taste) the port wine that ages here. Porto also features other unexpected treats, including sumptuous Baroque churches and civic buildings, a bustling real-world market hall, and quirky but worthwhile museums.

Though the weather is always changing, it's usually marginal. You're likely to get sun and rain at the same time—causing the locals to exclaim, "A widow's going to remarry."

Planning Your Time

Porto offers one very busy day's worth of sightseeing (or better yet, two relaxed days). Begin your day by exploring the city center above the town (poke around the market hall and climb Clérigos Tower for a visual orientation). Wander past the cathedral and clamber down one of the steep lanes to the Ribeira district for lunch. Enjoy touring the breathtaking interiors of the Stock Exchange Palace and São Francisco Church. Then head across the river to tour a couple of port-wine lodges before returning to the Ribeira for dinner. With a second day, slow down, taste more port, cruise the river, and add a visit to the Serralves Museum, its Art Deco mansion, and its plush park.

Ideally, combine your visit to Porto with a trip up the Douro Valley (about two hours away—see next chapter).

Orientation to Porto

Porto sprawls on the hilly north bank of the Douro River, near where the river meets the Atlantic Ocean. The tourist's Porto is compact, but confusing and steep. Get a good map and wear comfortable walking shoes (or just grab a taxi whenever you need a quick connection). It helps to  think of the tourist's Porto in three parts.

Ribeira (ree-BAY-rah): Right on the river, the Ribeira neighborhood has a twisty street plan and oodles of atmosphere. Praça Infante Dom Henrique (Henry the Navigator Square), near the top of the Ribeira, hosts two intriguing sights: the Stock Exchange Palace and São Francisco Church.

City Center: Ramshackle old homes scramble steeply uphill toward the second part of town, the modern city center, which hovers above the Ribeira and surrounds the broad boulevard called Avenue of the Allies (Avenida dos Aliados). This area is the urban business center of Porto, packed with office buildings and shoppers, and peppered with hotels. You'll also find a smattering of squares, monuments, and sights (including the market hall and cathedral). Clérigos Tower stands as the city's most recognizable landmark.

Vila Nova de Gaia: Across the river shine the neon signs of Porto's main tourist attraction, the port-wine cellars *(caves do vinho do porto)* in Vila Nova de Gaia, the third part of Porto, although it's technically another town.

The Douro is spanned by six bridges (two steel, four concrete). The only one you're likely to cross is the monstrous steel **Ponte Dom Luís I** (cars use lower level, Metro trains run along upper level; pedestrians can use either level).

Visitors venturing farther out find Porto to be a city of contrasts. Its outskirts boast bright, spacious, prim residential neighborhoods, such as the areas surrounding the Boavista Rotunda and the Serralves Museum and park.

Tourist Information

Porto has three TIs: in the **city center** across from City Hall (at the top of Avenida dos Aliados, Rua Clube dos Fenianos 25, tel. 223-393-472); at the top of the **Ribeira,** a block above the river, kitty-corner from the Stock Exchange Palace (Rua Infante Dom Henrique 63, tel. 222-060-412); and on the **cathedral square** (all are open daily 9:00-18:00; city hall location open until 20:00 in summer and 19:00 off-season). You'll also find TIs at the **airport** (daily 8:00-23:30, on the arrivals level near Vodafone store and Café Aeroporto), and in **Vila Nova de Gaia,** officially outside the city limits. The TIs share a website: www.visitporto.travel.

At any TI, pick up the free one-page city map (with sights and hotels) and the *Useful Information* pamphlet (€0.50). The city-walk guide (€1) lays out four themed walks. The free quarterly *Agenda Cultural* guide lists cultural events in the city in Portuguese. The monthly *Casa da Musica* guide lists events at the House of Music (www.casadamusica.com). The TI also sells the Porto Card (for sightseeing—described next) and the Andante Card (for transit—described later).

Porto Card: This card offers free entry to some sights and discounts for others, plus discounts on bus tours and some restaurants. It generally pays for itself if you visit four or more sights. The card comes in several versions, but the best choice for most visitors is either the one-day Walker card (€5, covers sights) or the one-day Standard card (€10.50, covers sights and includes a 24-hour AndanteTour Card, which covers all public transit—except trams; described later, under "Getting Around Porto"). If you plan to get around mostly on foot or by taxi, the Walker card is your best bet. If using public transit, the Standard card is a pretty good deal. Either card is good for 24 hours—you choose the start date and time, which are written on the card. Don't get the card for Monday, when many sights are closed; skip it if you're under 26 or a senior (you can get into most sights free or half-price). The card is sold at Porto's TIs, travel agencies, and some hotels, but not at participating sights. A handy guidebook is included. See www.visitporto.travel for details.

Arrival in Porto

By Train: Porto has two train stations. Regional trains, including those serving the Douro Valley, use the very central **São Bento Station** (a sight in itself for its magnificent tiles; see page 283). Facing the exit in the left corner is the helpful Loja da Mobilidade **transport office** (daily 7:30-20:00, international ticket window daily 8:00-12:30 & 13:30-16:30). Here you can purchase train tickets as well as the hassle-free Andante Card (described later, under "Getting Around Porto"), and get answers to your questions about transportation within or out of Porto. The helpful staff can help you understand the bus-station mess and get a handle on the ever-changing local transit picture (tel. 808-208-208, www.stcp.pt).

Trains coming from farther away, including Lisbon and Coimbra, arrive at **Campanhã Station,** on the east edge of town. If your train stops at both stations, get off at São Bento (closer to central hotels). If you have to get off at Campanhã, you have three options for getting into the center: Take a taxi directly to your hotel (€7 with luggage to most city-center accommodations); catch another train to São Bento Station (6/hour, free on any ticket to Porto); or use the Metro across the street (take it to the Trindade stop, then transfer to the yellow line for either Aliados or São Bento stations; €2.30 to load Andante Card with one Zone 4 trip plus €0.50 one-time card fee, buy at TI or from machines at Metro entrance). Note that the Metro is not practical for those staying near the Ribeira.

By Bus: As each of Porto's many bus companies operates its own garage, there's no central bus station. All of the bus garages are more or less in the city center. The main ones are: **Rede Expressos** (to Lisbon and Coimbra; Rua Alexandre Herculano, tel. 222-006-954, www.rede-expressos.pt); **RENEX** (to Lisbon; Campo Mártires da Pátria 37, tel. 222-003-395, www.renex.pt); **Rodonorte** (to points north; Rua Ateneu Comercial do Porto, tel. 222-004-398, www.rodonorte.pt); and **Internorte** (to Spain, including Santiago de Compostela and Madrid; Praça da Galiza 96, tel. 226-052-420, www.internorte.pt). You can also buy bus tickets to Spain from the Abreu Travel Agency on Avenida dos Aliados (at #207, tel. 222-043-500).

By Car: Central Porto is a headache by car. Stow it at your hotel or a nearby parking garage. Approaching from Lisbon and Coimbra on the A-1 expressway, pay a toll and then follow signs for *Ponte da Arrábida*. After crossing the bridge, take the first right and follow *centro* signs (or the little bull's-eyes) into downtown.

By Plane: Porto's Francisco Sá Carneiro Airport (airport code: OPO) is 11 miles north of the city center. Since it's an international

Porto at a Glance

▲▲**Strolling the Cais da Ribeira** Porto's picturesque riverfront, with arcades and colorful traditional homes. **Hours:** Always open. See page 277.

▲▲**Stock Exchange Palace** Astonishing monument to civic pride, with room after sumptuous room. **Hours:** By tour only, daily April-Oct 9:00-18:30, Nov-March 9:00-12:30 & 14:00-17:30. See page 280.

▲▲**Port-Wine Lodges in Vila Nova de Gaia** Porto's most popular tourist activity: touring the cellars where its most famous product ages...and tasting some, too. **Hours:** Vary, but generally daily, last tours at 18:00. See page 287.

▲**Cruising the Douro** Lazy one-hour cruises up and down the river, offering the city's top views. **Hours:** Generally daily 10:00-18:30 in summer (until 17:00 off-season). See page 277.

▲**São Francisco Church** Gothic church dripping with Baroque gold. **Hours:** Daily March-June 9:00-19:00, July-Sept 9:00-20:00, Oct-Feb 9:00-17:30. See page 279.

▲**Avenue of the Allies** Porto's top urban street, where the city goes to work in elaborate buildings. **Hours:** Always open; quiet at night. See page 281.

▲**Clérigos Church and Tower** Porto's towering landmark, with a 225-step climb to sweeping views over the urban sprawl. **Hours:** Daily 9:00-19:00. See page 282.

▲**São Bento Train Station** Entry hall decorated with impressive *azulejo* (tile) murals. **Hours:** Always open. See page 283.

---

airport (with connections beyond Iberia), it's used by people throughout northern Portugal and Spain. The Metro connects the airport to the center (3/hour, 30 minutes to the Trindade stop), or catch a taxi (figure €25). Airport info: tel. 229-432-400.

Helpful Hints

Closed Day: Most Porto museums are closed on Monday.

Festivals: Porto's big holiday is St. João Day (for St. John the Baptist, the city's patron saint) on June 24. Festivities start the

▲**Cathedral (Sé)** Huge church overlooking the town, with fine *azulejo*-decorated cloister and otherwise dull interior. **Hours:** Church—daily in summer 9:00-12:30 & 14:30-19:00, until 18:00 in winter; cloister and sacristy—daily in summer 9:00-12:30 & 14:30-19:00, until 17:30 in winter, closed Sun morning. See page 284.

▲**Rua de Santa Catarina** The main shopping drag, with Art Nouveau and Art Deco landmarks. **Hours:** Traffic-free during the day; quiet at night. See page 286.

▲**Market** Lively old-fashioned produce and meat market...with old-fashioned sanitary conditions. **Hours:** Mon-Fri 8:30-17:00, Sat 8:30-13:00, closed Sun. See page 287.

▲**Serralves Foundation Contemporary Art Museum and Park** Sprawling park with impressive museum, Art Deco mansion, and relaxing grounds. **Hours:** April-Sept Tue-Fri 10:00-17:00, park open until 19:00, Sat-Sun 10:00-19:00; Oct-March Tue-Sun 10:00-17:00; closed Mon year-round. See page 292.

Porto Wine Shop Classy one-stop spot for port tasting. **Hours:** Mon-Fri 11:00-19:00, closed Sat-Sun. See page 281.

Tramway Museum Collection tracing the history of electrical transport. **Hours:** Mon 14:00-18:00, Tue-Fri 10:00-19:00, Sat-Sun 14:00-19:00. See page 278.

House of Henry the Navigator Birthplace of the explorer, with history exhibits. **Hours:** Tue-Sun 10:00-12:30 & 14:00-17:30, closed Mon. See page 281.

House of Music New Modernist concert hall with performances of jazz, fado, and more. **Hours:** Tours daily, concerts nearly nightly. See page 293.

night of June 23 with partying and fireworks, and continue on the 24th with a *rabelo* regatta.

Internet Access: OnWeb Cyber Bar is a handy Internet café with fast access and a youthful, musical ambience (€2/2 hours, Mon-Sat 10:00-2:00 in the morning, Sun 15:00-2:00 in the morning, a block below TI at the top of Avenida dos Aliados across from City Hall at #289).

Laundry: A small self-service laundry hides almost underground at the west end of the Ribeira district (between São Francisco

Church and the river at the top of Rua da Reboleira). Look for the silver *Câmara Municipal* sign (€6, Mon 9:00-14:00, Tue-Sat 8:30-19:00, closed Sun, tel. 222-084-621).

Best Views: There are fine views all along the Ribeira riverfront embankment, but they're even better from across the river in Vila Nova de Gaia (looking back toward Porto, especially from the cable car). You can also enjoy the views from the top of Clérigos Tower, from the terrace next to the cathedral, from the old town wall, or from Mosteiro da Serra do Pilar (the monastery across the river, just above the big steel Ponte Dom Luís I bridge). But the best vantage point of all is from a boat on the river itself (see "Cruising the Douro," page 277).

Getting Around Porto

The city is currently engaged in one of Europe's biggest construction projects—extending its tramlines and gradually building a new, mostly aboveground Metro. (Smug Lisboners love to tease that only Porto would build an aboveground "underground.")

As a result, Porto's public transportation system is often changing and a bit confusing. The network includes buses, trams, the Metro, a funicular, and some trains.

Andante Card: This card is required to ride the Metro, and also covers all other forms of public transit (including the train linking Campanhã and São Bento stations) except trams. Your fare depends on which "zone" you travel in. Zone 2 covers all the recommended sights in this book (€1.15/trip, allows transfers); the airport is in Zone 4 (€2.30/trip). The regular **Andante Card** is reloadable—you can buy as many trips, or *titulos,* as you want (one-time €0.50 card fee, discounted 10-trip card-€12, versions with more trips also available). Unless you're taking just a few rides, it's a better value and simpler to buy the €4.45 one-day **AndanteTour Card,** which is good for 24 hours after its first use. To use any Andante Card, pass it over the scanner on the Metro, bus, or train.

The cards are sold at TIs, the Loja da Mobilidade transport office in the São Bento Station, Andante stores (one at the airport), and some bus, Metro, and train ticket offices (www.linhandante.com).

By Bus

Several local **buses** are useful for tourists, such as the routes that go to the port-wine lodges in Vila Nova de Gaia across the river (#900, #901, and #906). Buses also run from the Ribeira to Foz (#500), and from the beach in Foz to the Serralves Museum (#203). Service is generally speedy, but avoid buses during rush hour, when traffic slows to a crawl.

Individual bus tickets cost €1.85 if purchased from driver; if riding public transportation more than once, it's cheaper to buy an Andante Card (described earlier).

By Tram

Three interconnecting **tram** lines of interest to a tourist are #1, #18, and #22. Tram #1 (Infante/Passeio Alegre) uses a historic car that shudders along the river from the Ribeira, past several museums to the Jardim do Passeio Alegre, a 10-minute walk to the Foz district and the Atlantic Ocean. Tram #18 (Restauração/Cordoaria) begins at Carmo Church and wobbles to the recommended Tramway Museum. Tram #22 makes a loop through the city center, from shopping street Rua de Santa Catarina, down Rua Passos Manuel, cutting through Avenida dos Aliados, and turning near Carmo Church to return along Rua 31 de Janeiro, with a jog across Praça da Batalha to the funicular.

Trams are not covered by the Andante Card. Individual tickets cost €2.50 per ride (purchase from driver). You can also buy a combo-ticket that includes entrance to the Tramway Museum (€4), or an €8 pass that covers unlimited rides on all three lines for a 24-hour period as well as entrance to the Tramway Museum (purchase from driver, or at the Tramway Museum, travel agencies, and some hotels).

By Metro

Metro lines include blue, red, green, purple, and orange (all connecting Campanhã Station to the center). All Metro lines converge at the Trindade stop, two blocks behind City Hall and Avenida dos Aliados. The purple line connects the airport to the center and Campanhã Station; the yellow line includes São Bento Station and Vila Nova de Gaia, across the river. To ride the Metro you must have an Andante Card, described earlier (www.metrodoporto.pt).

By Funicular

A handy funicular (Elevador dos Guindais) connects the Ribeira district (at the base of the Ponte Dom Luís I bridge) to the top of the steep hill above (at the remains of the city wall, down the Rua de Augusto Rosa from Praça da Batalha). Note that the funicular stops running earlier in the off-season (€1.65, covered by Andante Card, every 10 minutes, daily May-Oct 8:00-22:00, Nov-April 8:00-20:00).

By Cable Car

The overpriced Teleférico de Gaia cable car soars above Vila Nova da Gaia, connecting the riverfront with the Jardim do Morro, just under the Mosteiro da Serra do Pilar monastery and the upper part of the Ponte Dom Luís I bridge. The five-minute ride gives a unique view over the port wine lodges and across the river to the city, and can be handy for connecting the upper and lower parts of Vila Nova da Gaia (€5 one-way, €8 round-trip, daily 10:00-20:00 in summer, 10:00-18:00 off-season, www.gaiacablecar.com).

By Taxi

Taxis are a good option in this hilly city. Most rides are fairly short and cost only around €5. For rides within the city limits, the meter should be on "T1" during the day (€2 drop charge) and "T2" at night (21:00-6:00 in the morning, €2.50 drop charge). Each kilometer costs about €0.40. A luggage surcharge of €1.60 is legit. It's easy to find taxi stands, and you'll pay €0.80 more to call one (try Invicta, tel. 225-076-400).

Tours in Porto

ATC/Porto Tours—The city of Porto operates an ingenious, extremely useful tour co-op, allowing all the small tour companies to share one office in an old medieval watchtower next to the cathedral (daily April-Sept 10:00-19:00, shorter hours off-season, Calçada Dom Pedro Pitões 15, tel. 222-000-073, www.portotours.com, reservas@portotours.mail.pt). This organization, which takes no commission and is not biased toward any particular company, will help you sort through all of the walking, bus, boat, bike, Segway, taxi, and even helicopter tour options in Porto and up the Douro. They'll confirm times, answer questions, and sell tickets for the tours. Walking tours on different topics can be reserved online through their website (tours start at €13/person).

ATC/Porto Tours can also help you arrange a private **local guide** (around €130/half-day, higher rates on weekends). Maria Jose Aleixo is good; you can contact her directly (€110/half-day, mobile 969-468-347, aleixo19@sapo.pt).

In this steep, tiring city, a **bus tour** is worth considering. You have two options: a typical stay-mainly-on-the-bus tour (€32, half-day, live guide in 4 languages) and two hop-on, hop-off versions—Red City Sightseeing and Yellow Bus (€13, 2-hour circuit with 9 stops, can hop off and catch a later bus, ticket good for 48 hours, 10 buses/day, daily 9:30-18:30).

A silly **tourist train** includes a stop at a port-wine lodge across the river (€7, 1.25 hours, 2/hour, leaves from in front of cathedral daily on the hour, 10:00-17:00 in high season, less frequently off-season, tel. 800-203-983).

Taxi tours of the town and side-trips to the Douro Valley and even Santiago are also available (details at ATC/Porto Tours, www.rentacab.pt).

Sights in Porto

Along the Riverfront

The riverfront Ribeira (ree-BAY-rah, meaning "riverbank") district is where it's at in Porto. It's the city's most scenic and touristy quarter, with the highest concentration of good restaurants (and postcard racks). I've listed these sights beginning in the Ribeira, then stretching west (toward the Foz district).

▲▲Strolling the Cais da Ribeira (Embankment) and Praça da Ribeira (Square)—This is Porto's best lazy-afternoon activity. As you stroll, imagine the busy port scene before the promenade was reclaimed from the river—riverboats laden with cargo lashed to the embankment, off-loading their wine and produce into 14th-century cellars (still visible). The old arcades lining the Ribeira promenade are jammed with hole-in-the-wall restaurants (made to look more "local" than they actually are) and souvenir shops. Behind the arcades are skinny, colorful houses draped with drying laundry fluttering like flags, while the locals who fly them stand on their little balconies, gossiping.

Riverfront property taxes were based on frontage—promoting the construction of these narrow, deep, and undeniably picturesque buildings.

The Ribeira neighborhood looks up at the Ponte Dom Luís I bridge, rising 150 feet above the river. In the 1880s, Teofilo Seyfrig, a protégé of Gustave Eiffel, stretched this Eiffel Tower-sized wrought-iron contraption across the 500-foot-wide Douro. Eiffel himself designed a bridge in Porto, the Ponte Dona Maria Pia, a bit upstream.

While it offers few individual sights, the Ribeira is Porto's most enjoyable neighborhood for killing time and basking in Old World atmosphere. Shoppers eventually find **O Cântaro,** run by the English-speaking Oliveira family (Mon-Sat 9:00-19:00, closed Sun, a block back from embankment near the east end—toward the bridge—at Rua da Lada 50-56, tel. 223-320-670). Among the trinkets for sale are ceramics, hand-painted tiles, embroidery, and filigree. Ask them for a filigree-making demonstration to see tiny gold and silver wires twisted and soldered into intricate patterns.

▲Cruising the Douro—"Six Bridges" cruises, operated by several different companies, leave continually from the Ribeira riverfront. These relaxing 50-minute excursions float up and down the river, offering a fine orientation and glimpses of all of Porto's bridges (including the majestic steel Ponte Dona Maria Pia, right next to

the new concrete Ponte de São João). The boat trips, which generally run daily 10:00-18:30 in summer (until 17:00 off-season), are all essentially the same—offering a scenic joyride in traditional *rabelos* with no real commentary (€10, boats described below). To avoid being overcharged, shop around a bit before committing to a boat.

Moored in Porto and all along the Douro River are the old-fashioned boats called *rabelos*. These were once the only way to transport wine downriver to Porto. These boats, which look Asian, have flat bottoms, a big square sail, and a very large rudder to help them navigate the rough, twisty course of the river (for more info, see page 313). The region's famous port wine is produced about 60 miles up the river and aged in lodges here.

Fado—If you need to satisfy your fado fix, the **Restaurante Mal Cozinhado**—a couple of blocks up from the Douro—is touristy with forgettable food, but a great place for a late drink and live fado (open for dinner nightly at 20:30 except Sun; if not dining, there's a €10 cover fee; music starts at 21:00 and ends at 1:00 in the morning; Rua do Outeirinho 11, tel. 222-081-319). The recommended Restaurante Guarany (in the city center) also offers live fado, as does the House of Music (northwest of the center; see page 293).

Tramway Museum (Museu do Carro Eléctrico)—Porto is proud of its tram tradition and is committed to bringing them back as an integral part of the public transit system. In 1872 (40 years after being invented in the US), the first trams in Iberia began operating in Porto, pulled by horses and oxen. Dubbed *americanos* based on their origin, the tram network was electrified in 1904. Essential for connecting suburbs with the city center, there were more than 100 tram lines still in use by the 1970s. However, buses and cars—by-products of modern prosperity—almost eliminated this important part of the city's heritage.

This clever museum-in-a-warehouse displays beautifully restored examples of trams from different eras, including 1950s buses and a brand-new hydrogen-powered city bus. You can climb aboard many for a fun, Rice-A-Roni-style experience...just ding the bell.

Cost and Hours: €4, Mon 14:00-18:00, Tue-Fri 10:00-19:00, Sat-Sun 14:00-19:00, Alameda Basílio Teles 51, tel. 226-158-185, www.museudocarroelectrico.pt.

Getting There: The most atmospheric way to arrive at the museum is via tram #1 or #18. Sit on restored wicker seats and see a little of workaday Porto, plus some river views from up above.

Foz—Foz do Douro (or simply "Foz") is one of Porto's trendiest, greenest, wealthiest, and most relaxing quarters, situated where the river meets the Atlantic. There's no real destination in Foz; simply wander through the park (Jardim do Passeio Alegre, with miniature golf, a fancy old WC pavilion, and a nondescript café), hike up to the lighthouse, ponder the sea, watch fishermen mending their nets, and smell the seaweed. If you have the time and good weather, take a boardwalk stroll to the beach, Praia dos Ingleses. It's a relaxing break from the busy downtown area.

Getting There: An antique tram car (line #1) scenically rattles its way from the Ribeira district, along the Douro River, to the Jardim do Passeio Alegre, a 10-minute walk to the center of the Foz district. From the tram stop, you can walk or catch bus #500 to Foz's center. Or bypass the tram by taking bus #500 from the Ribeira directly to Foz (catch tram or bus in front of São Francisco Church, departures roughly every 20 minutes 9:00-19:00, 20-minute trip). Tram #1 used to go all the way to Foz; it's possible this route will be reinstated, so check with the TI or transit office.

Nearby: You can combine a trip to Foz with a visit to the Serralves Museum. From Foz, either catch bus #203—it runs near the beach on Rua de Dui—or take a taxi; it's easy to hail a cab or find a taxi stop *(praça de taxis)*.

Near Praça Infante Dom Henrique

These sights are on or near Praça Infante Dom Henrique (Henry the Navigator Square), a long block uphill from the Ribeira district.

▲**São Francisco Church**—This is Porto's only church in the Gothic style—complete with a rose window, stair-step buttresses, and a statue of St. Francis of Assisi on the front. Today, it's a museum with three parts: a one-room collection of art from the church and monastery; the strange catacombs *(ossário)* under the church, tightly packed with the bones of former parishioners (the bodies were left under the wooden floor boards to rot and then transferred to the neat little niches in the walls—the trapdoor near #32 leads to the bones' final refuge); and, the unquestionable highlight, an extravagant Baroque church interior from the 17th and 18th centuries.

Cost and Hours: €3.50, daily March-June 9:00-19:00, July-Sept 9:00-20:00, Oct-Feb 9:00-17:30, no photos in church, Rua Infante Dom Henrique, tel. 222-062-100.

Visiting the Church: Although the church was ravaged by Napoleon and by the Portuguese during their 19th-century civil war, the interior remains stunning, with lavish chestnut carvings slathered in gold leaf—900 pounds of gold. Wander down the main aisle like a bewildered 18th-century peasant. On the right, find the ornate altar showing how Franciscans weren't always warmly received—at the top they are being cruelly tortured and crucified by Japanese (portrayed with Muslim features), and at the bottom they are being beheaded by Moors. Still, in the center, St. Francis encourages his followers on. On the left, find the over-the-top Jesse's Tree (1718), which is a very literal interpretation of the family tree of Jesus, resting upon Mary. She sits in a boat as Our Lady of Good Voyage, a patron saint of navigators.

▲▲Stock Exchange Palace (Palácio da Bolsa)—This unassuming building is neither a stock exchange nor a palace, but a breathtaking monument to civic and commercial pride, with some of the most lavishly decorated rooms in Portugal.

The people of Porto have always taken pride in being hard workers. Commerce came to define Porto, as royalty or religion would define other cities (like Lisbon and Braga, respectively). The Commercial Association of Porto (Associação Comercial do Porto) even had its own system of courts and a representative to the king. In 1832, the monastery of the São Francisco Church burned down, and the queen offered the property to the Commercial Association. They seized the opportunity to show off, crafting a building that would demonstrate the considerable skill of Porto's tradesmen.

Cost and Tours: The "Palace" can only be visited on a 30-minute guided tour (€7). Tours leave every 30 minutes in whatever language is necessary (often English plus another language). You may have to wait up to 30 minutes for an English tour; it's easy to call ahead to set up an appointment.

Hours: Daily April-Oct 9:00-18:30, Nov-March 9:00-12:30 & 14:00-17:30, last visit 30 minutes before closing, no photos inside, in big building marked *Associação Comercial do Porto* on Rua Ferreira Borges, tel. 223-399-013, www.palaciodabolsa.com. Note that the building still houses the offices of the Chamber of Commerce, and is often rented out for events.

Visiting the Stock Exchange: You'll tour eight rooms. The place is rife with symbolism and intricate, time-consuming craftsmanship intended only to impress: the complex patterned floors, carefully pieced together with Brazilian and African wood (from Portugal's colonies); an incredibly detailed inlaid table, created over three years using wood scraps from those same floors; and a room that looks like it's made of finely carved woodwork and bronze—until you realize it's all painted plaster and gold leaf. Almost everything is original, and little refurbishment has been needed.

The knock-your-socks-off finale is the sumptuous Arabian Room. This grand hall—inspired by Granada's Alhambra—was painstakingly decorated in the Moorish style over 18 years with wood, plaster, and gold leaf.

Porto Wine Shop—This port wine-tasting facility, operated by the Port and Douro Wines Institute (which runs a similar place in Lisbon—see page 53), is Porto's finest spot for sampling an array of ports. The price per taste or per bottle depends on the quality of the port and ranges from €1 to a small fortune. If they call it "port," you'll find it here. While it's more fun to tour the cellars across the river, this is a handy one-stop opportunity to try several ports.

Cost and Hours: Mon-Fri 11:00-19:00, closed Sat-Sun, Rua Ferreira Borges 27, near Stock Exchange Palace, tel. 222-071-669, www.ivdp.pt.

House of Henry the Navigator (Casa do Infante)—Six hundred years ago, Porto's favorite son was supposedly born in this mansion (once the largest house in town and later the main customs house). This scant museum has few artifacts, but fans of ancient history enjoy the Roman mosaics found on-site and the reconstruction of the building when it was the customs house. A free revolving exhibit of town history drawn from the city archives is located in the same building.

Cost and Hours: €2.10, free on weekends, Tue-Sun 10:00-12:30 & 14:00-17:30, closed Mon, last entry 30 minutes before closing, Rua da Alfândega 10, tel. 222-060-400. For more on Hank, see page 158.

In the City Center

The modern urban sector of Porto has few museums, but there are a handful of interesting squares, churches, and monuments here. I've listed these sights in walking order—roughly from north to south, beginning at City Hall (at the top of Avenida dos Aliados, near the TI) and working downhill toward the cathedral and then back around through the shopping district.

▲**Avenue of the Allies (Avenida dos Aliados)**—This is the main urban drag of Porto—named for the alliance created in 1387 when the Portuguese King John (João) I married the English princess Philippa, establishing a long and happy trading partnership between the two nations. Lined with elaborate examples of various architectural eras (mostly Art Nouveau and Art Deco), it reminds me of Prague's Wenceslas Square. This strip is where the city goes to work, watched over by the huge **City Hall** (Câmara Municipal). Behind that is the Trindade Church, and nearby you'll find

Nicolau Nasoni
(1691-1773)

In the 1720s—a boom time in Porto—the Italian Nasoni found work as a painter in Porto. His swirling, colorful paintings wowed Porto, and Nasoni got plenty of work. He married a Portuguese woman, had five kids, and made Porto his home. Soon, he was employed as an architect, hiring skilled local artisans to turn his trademark cherubs, garlands, and cumulus clouds into granite, wood, and poured plaster. Even stark medieval churches had their facades topped with Baroque towers and their interiors paneled and spackled in billowy gilded designs. Prolific to the max, Nasoni redid Porto in the Baroque style (much as Bernini did in Rome), creating palaces and churches throughout the area. His tour de force was the hilltopping Clérigos Church, where he was later buried.

the station (also called Trindade) where all of Porto's Metro lines converge.

The bottom of the avenue is known as **Praça da Liberdade** (Liberty Square). A few steps in front of you is an equestrian statue of King Pedro IV—a hero in the 1832 Civil War who advocated for a limited constitutional monarchy in Portugal (while maintaining his title as Emperor of Brazil). King Pedro prevailed...and he's holding the constitution to prove it.

Orient yourself using an imaginary clock for a compass. Start by facing the horse. The City Hall is at the top of the square. At about 2 o'clock (behind the trees) is the **"Imperial McDonald's,"** perhaps the fanciest in Europe (formerly the Imperial Café). Check it out, and ponder the battle of cultural elegance against global economic efficiency. At 3 o'clock is the way to the blue-tiled church of St. Ildefonso (up the hill, in the shopping district). At 4 o'clock (50 yards away) is the corner of São Bento Station. And at 9 o'clock is Clérigos Church, with its famous view tower.

▲**Clérigos Church and Tower (Igreja e Torre dos Clérigos)**— This oval-shaped church with a disproportionately tall tower is the masterwork of Nicolau Nasoni, a man who chose to go for Baroque (see sidebar).

Cost and Hours: €2, daily 9:00-19:00, Rua São Filipe de Nery, tel. 222-001-729.

Visiting the Church and Tower: This church, which consumed three decades of Nicolau Nasoni's life (1731-1763), shows his flair for theatrics. He fit the structure into its hilltop location, putting the tower at the back on the highest ground, dramatically reinforcing its height. Nasoni worked in stages: first the church, then the Chapter House (residence for priests and monks). He topped it all off with the outsized tower.

The church facade displays Nasoni's characteristic frills, garlands, and zig-zags. Inside is an oval-shaped nave built out of granite and marble, but covered with ornate carvings. See the high altar—a wedding-cake structure with Mary on top—and the tomb of Nasoni, who asked to be buried here.

The real attraction is going up the tower—one of Porto's icons. After climbing 225 steps and 250 feet up to the top, you're greeted by a jumble of tightly packed red roofs and commanding views over the city. Nasoni built the tower in six sections, each one more elaborate than the last, topped with a round dome and spiked with pinnacles.

Nearby: A fancy bookstore a few blocks away is worth a peek. Built in 1906, the **Lello & Irmão bookstore** boasts a lacy exterior and a fancy Art Nouveau interior. It looks like wood, but it's mostly made of painted plaster with gold leaf. Follow the quaint tracks to the book trolley. Climb the sagging staircase to a cute tearoom (Mon-Fri 10:00-19:30, Sat 10:00-19:00, closed Sun, Rua das Carmelitas 144).

• *Backtrack, crossing Avenida dos Aliados, and continue on to the...*

▲**São Bento Train Station (Estação São Bento)**—The main entry hall of this otherwise dull station features some of Portugal's finest *azulejos*. These vivid, decorative hand-painted tiles show historical and folk scenes from the Douro region. Upper tiles on the left (when facing the tracks) show local forces preparing to reconquer the north of Portugal and add it to the kingdom. Tiles on the opposite wall (far right when looking at the tracks) show the 1387 wedding of

Portugal's King John I and the English princess Philippa, which established the Portuguese-English alliance. (Notice the fine portrait of Philippa and the depiction of the cathedral as it looked in

the 14th century.) Below is the immediate result of the marriage—their son, Prince Henry the Navigator, shown conquering Ceuta for Portugal in 1415. While humble Ceuta was just a small chip of Morocco (across from Gibraltar), it marked an important first step in the creation of a soon-to-be vast Portuguese empire. The trackside tiles celebrate the traditional economy, such as the transport of port wine. The multicolored tiles near the top show different modes of transportation, including Roman chariots (left above *Saída* exit sign), and progressing to the arrival of the first train (left corner above Philippa). Notice the words *Douro* and *Minho* near the ceiling. These are the major rivers in this part of Portugal, and the key regions linked by these trains. Porto's favorite meeting point is right here, "under the clock."

To orient yourself from the station, stand outside with your back to the main entrance. Over your right shoulder (two blocks up the hill) is Praça da Batalha (Battle Square), the gateway to Porto's shopping district and old-fashioned market hall (described later). At 2 o'clock is the bottom of Avenida dos Aliados. On the hill to your left is the cathedral. And the streets in front of you lead down to the left to the Ribeira.

▲**Cathedral (Sé)**—This hulking, fortress-like, 12th-century Romanesque cathedral, while graced with fine granite stonework and lavish 18th-century Baroque altars, feels gloomy and stark inside. But the history is palpable. Henry the Navigator was baptized here, and it was the scene of many royal marriages (including John I and Philippa).

Cost and Hours: Cathedral—free, open daily in summer 9:00-12:30 & 14:30-19:00, until 18:00 in winter; cloister and sacristy—€3, daily in summer 9:00-12:30 & 14:30-19:00, until 17:30 in winter, closed Sun morning; Terreiro da Sé, tel. 222-059-028.

Visiting the Cathedral: The **main altarpiece** sums up the exuberance of Porto in the 1720s, when the city was booming, the local bishop was temporarily away in Lisbon, and Italian Baroque was sweeping through town. On the side walls flanking the altar are faded faux-architecture paintings by Nicolau Nasoni (see sidebar on page 282), the Italian who came to Porto to paint the cathedral's sacristy and soon became the city's most influential architect.

Look at the chapel just left of the high altar. Inside is a dreamy, carved-and-painted limestone statue of the Lady of Vendôme, brought to Porto in the 14th century by monks from France. It originally stood at the fortified gate of the city and remains close to the hearts of the townsfolk. Just left of the Lady of Vendôme is the Silver Altar of the Holy Sacrament (circa 1700)—1,500 pounds of silver. When French troops under Napoleon pillaged Porto, the townspeople plastered over the altar to hide it.

The **cloister** and its adjacent rooms are worth the time and entrance fee. The cloister's walls are decorated with elaborate *azulejo* tiles illustrating the amorous poetry of the Bible's "Song of Songs." (The €0.50 pamphlet is skimpy, but the €5 English guidebook explains it all, including the text that inspired the *azulejos*.) The adjacent **Chapel of St. Vincent,** with 17th-century painted carvings of Bible scenes, has a trapdoor into a crypt, where centuries of bishops' bones were ultimately tossed. Upstairs, the richly ornamented chapter room is where the bishop and his gang met in the 17th century to wield their religious and secular power. Note the holy figures depicted on the ceiling and the fine city views from the windows.

Near the Cathedral—In the cathedral's small square, you'll find a fine **view** of the old town, the Baroque spiral pillory (20th-century copy) where harsh justice was once doled out, and the massive **Bishop's Palace,** still the home of the bishop and his offices. The immensity of this 18th-century building reflects the bishop's past power. It dominates the skyline of Porto. A surviving gate from Porto's two-mile-long wall, which protected the city in the 14th century, currently houses the **ATC/Porto Tours** office (see page 276).

Facing the cathedral, walk around to the left to the **statue** of Vímara Peres, a Christian warrior who reconquered this region from the Moors in 868. (It was lost again within two generations, and remained under Muslim control until the final reconquest in about 1100.) From here, survey the city and find the church with the blue facade in the distance. São Bento Station is just to its right, and the tarnished copper dome of the City Hall breaks the skyline above it. Below you spreads the seedy district called **Sé** (meaning "cathedral," it refers to the *Se*at of the Catholic Church). This neighborhood, the oldest in town, is run-down and depopulating; the government is encouraging people to move in by luring them with economic incentives. The streets beyond the medieval gate—once a ratatouille of drug users and prostitutes—twist their way down into the Ribeira district.

Walk 300 yards up the street behind the cathedral on Rua de Saraiva de Carvalho to a leafy square (Primeiro Dezembro) and through the arched doorway to the **Santa Clara church.** Step inside to view its Baroque interior, decorated with carved wood and lots of gold leaf. Exit the church and go right, through another gate (Instituta Nacional Saude), walking straight ahead toward the concrete wall. On your left, you will see the impressive last remains of the **town wall.** Climb the steps to the tower for fine views of the river and Ribeira district (careful, steps are steep and there are no handrails). Go back through the square to the bottom of Rua da Augusto Rosa and the top of the **funicular** (Elevador dos Guindais), which zips down to the Ribeira riverfront. Hike two blocks up Rua da Augusto Rosa to Praça da Batalha (described below) and the start of the shopping district.

Porto's Shopping Neighborhood

Porto's bustling, local-feeling shopping district is a wonderful place to people-watch. Most of the action is along Rua de Santa Catarina, which runs roughly parallel to Avenida dos Aliados a few blocks east. Begin at Praça da Batalha (just up Rua 31 de Janeiro from São Bento Station), and follow this route to the Old World market hall.

Praça da Batalha (Battle Square)—This square has a fine tiled church, the Igreja de Santo Ildefonso (its *azulejo* tiles, reminiscent of Ming dynasty blue-and-white ceramics, were all the rage in Baroque Portugal, depicting scenes from the life of the church's patron saint), the 19th-century National Theater (originally the Opera House), and the impressive Art Deco Cinema Batalha, now closed. This square, with its inviting benches, is where the old guys hang out.

• *At the north end of the square, branching off to the left of the blue-tiled church, is...*

▲**Rua de Santa Catarina**—Porto's main shopping street is busy and (mostly) traffic-free by day, quiet by night. A stroll along here gives you a sense of today's Porto— as well as yesterday's, including the venerable Art Nouveau Café Majestic, the circa-1900 hangout for the local intelligentsia, a block down on your right. Step in. Porto's pet name for a little coffee is *cimbalino*—named for the traditional Italian espresso-making machines. Outside Café Majestic

(on the nearby corner), the FNAC department store has an Art Deco glockenspiel performance (daily at 9:00, 12:00, 15:00, and 18:00) in which Henry the Navigator, St. John the Baptist—Porto's patron saint—and two poets (who look like Lincoln and Einstein) parade around.

The Rua de Santa Catarina sidewalk is a good example of *calçada á portuguesa*, Portugal's unique limestone and basalt mosaic work. It's handmade and high-maintenance...but apparently worth the effort and expense to locals. Notice all of the shoe stores. Along with wine, textile and shoe factories power northern Portugal's industry.

• *If you head up the street two blocks and turn left on Rua Formosa (note the Pearl of the Market shop at #279, filled with traditional and edible souvenirs), you'll run into the...*

▲**Market (Bolhão)**—Porto's vibrant traditional market still thrives, despite competition from newer shopping malls. This is a great place to wander—especially in the morning—and take in the sights, sounds, and smells of real-world Porto (Mon-Fri 8:30-17:00, Sat 8:30-13:00, closed Sun).

As you enter, the butchers and fishermen are on the left and right; produce and flowers (along with cheap eateries serving €3 sardine lunches) are dead ahead. Check out the butcher section, with half-pigs hanging from the ceiling, and display cases full of unusual specialties...such as *sangue cozido* (coagulated cow blood). Then wander through the seafood section. If it's springtime, you may see a favorite local delicacy pulled from the river: *lampreia* (eel). They say eels are so tasty because they dine on the flavorful garbage in the Douro. The market's old-fashioned sanitary conditions aren't quite up to European Union snuff, but the EU seems to look the other way.

Around the market are lively shops. At one corner is Casa Horticula, with a wide variety of seeds. In bakery windows, the big, round, dark *broa* breads, made with corn and rye, are moist inside and hard outside. The breads with bits of sausage baked in are called *folar*. The cheeses on display are either *ovelha* (sheep) or *cabra* (goat). *Bom-apetite!*

Port-Wine Lodges in Vila Nova de Gaia

Just across the river from Porto, the town of Vila Nova de Gaia, or just Gaia (GUY-yuh), is where much of the world's port wine comes to mature. Port-wine grapes are grown, and a young port is produced, about 60 miles upstream in the Douro Valley. Then,

after sitting for a winter in silos, the wine is shipped downstream to Vila Nova de Gaia, to age for years in lodges on this cool, north-facing bank of the Douro. Eighteen companies run these lodges, holding down the port fort and offering tours and tastings. For wine connoisseurs, touring a port-wine lodge *(cave do vinho do porto)* and sampling the product is a ▲▲ attraction. Like so many miniature Hollywood signs climbing the riverbank, you'll see the 18 different company names proudly marking their lodges here.

Vila Nova de Gaia

100 YARDS
100 METERS

TO PORTO CENTER

RIBEIRA
DISTRICT

DOURO
RIVER

PONTE
LUÍS I
UPPER
LEVEL
LOWER
LEVEL

SERRA DO
PILAR
MONASTERY

LARGO
MIGUEL
BOMBARDA

BOAT
TRIPS

Jardim
do
Morro

LARGO
CRUZ

EATERIES

1 Sandeman
2 Cálem
3 Taylor & Restaurante
   Barão de Fladgate
4 Croft
5 Ferreira

6 Kopke Shop
7 Adega E Presuntaria
   Transmontana Rest.
8 Ar de Rio Rest.
9 Real Indiana Rest.

🚡 CABLE CAR
Ⓜ METRO STATION
↗ VIEW

Gaia is technically a separate town from Porto, even though it's just across the river and feels like part of the city. Venturing here is well worth the trip. To taste port from all the different lodges under one roof, visit the Porto Wine Shop (see page 281).

Getting There: From the Ribeira district, walk (or catch a cab) across the Ponte Dom Luís I bridge. From the city center, take bus #900, #901, or #906 (every 30 minutes, stop across from São Bento Station). After crossing the bridge, the bus stops first at the Cálem lodge, then near Sandeman and the TI, then climbs the hill.

Services: Vila Nova de Gaia operates its own handy **TI** with information about the lodges (daily 10:00-18:00, closed Sun off-season, on the riverbank near Sandeman lodge at Avenida Diogo Leite 242, tel. 223-703-735, www.cm-gaia.pt). A string of fine **eateries** line the main drag, Rua Guilherme Gomes Fernandes, just past the Ramos Pinto lodge. Drinks-with-a-view options are available all along the waterfront. A pricey **cable car** links the riverfront with the Jardim do Morro (see page 275).

▲▲Tours and Tastings—Port tasting is a subjective business, and no single lodge is necessarily the best. If you're a port enthusiast, you probably already have a favorite (or can quickly decide on one, with a little enjoyable research).  Though more serious European visitors choose one lodge to visit, American tourists are known to hop between three or four in a single day...before stumbling back to their hotels.

At any lodge, the procedure is about the same. Individual travelers simply show up and ask for a tour. Pass any wait time by learning about the port (via posted information or a video), or simply get started on the tasting. Sometimes the tours and tastings are free; at other lodges, there's a modest entry fee (which may be refunded if you buy a more-expensive bottle). Before you go (or while you're waiting for your tour), read the "Port-Wine Crash Course" sidebar, "Brits on the Douro" (page 311), and "Growing—and Stomping—Grapes in the Douro Valley" (page 312).

Allow 30 minutes per visit. Tours in English depart three or four times per hour. Occasionally, if the lodge is busy, you'll be given a tour time and can come back. Tours generally come with a walk through the warehouse, perhaps a tiny museum tour, a 5- to 10-minute video produced by that label giving you a quick peek at their process and the scenic Douro River Valley, and, finally, two to four tastings. Serious students may opt for more involved tours (generally €12-15, with smaller groups, 5 tastings, book in advance if possible).

Sandeman, the most high-profile company, is sort of the Budweiser of port—a good first stop for novices. They were the first port producer to create a logo for their product, which you'll see everywhere: a mysterious man wearing a black cloak (representing a Portuguese student's cape) and a rakish *Shadow* hat (worn by Spanish horse-riders, symbolizing the sherry that Sandeman makes in Jerez). Sandeman provides the most corporate, mainstream, accessible experience for first-timers—with a short walk led by a caped guide, a 10-minute video, and two tastings. It's also the most crowded, often giving times for you to return or sending you to their sister manufacturers (€4.50, also more extensive €15 tour, daily March-Oct 10:00-12:30 & 14:00-18:00, Nov-Feb 9:30-12:30 & 14:00-17:30, right on the riverfront at Largo Miguel Bombarda 3, tel. 223-740-533, www.sandeman.com). It's exciting to think that the entire Portuguese production of Sandeman Port ages right in this building.

Port-Wine Crash Course

Port is a medium sweet wine (20 percent alcohol), usually taken as a *digestif* after dinner, sometimes with strong cheese to balance its powerful flavor. The wine is fortified with *aguardente* (grape brandy, more like grappa, sometimes called "grape essence") at a ratio of about 4:1. This brandy is also distilled from wine, so it blends nicely with the port. The introduction of brandy halts fermentation early, killing the yeast and leaving more sugar in the port (standard wines ferment for 10-12 days; port for only 2-3 days). Vintners constantly monitor sugar levels to attain the precise sweetness they want. After the brandy is added, the wine ages in wood or in bottles, anywhere from two years to (for big spenders) longer than a century.

For most people, "port" means a tawny port aged 10-20 years—the most common type. But there are multiple varieties of port; the two general categories are wood ports (aged in wooden vats or barrels) and vintage ports (aged in bottles). More than 40 varieties of grapes, both red and white, can be used for port production.

The basics: Inexpensive **ruby** is young (aged three years), red, and has a strong, fiery taste of grape and pepper. Note that some ports are **white**—young and robust, but with white grapes. (Some white "ports" sold today are an attempt to approximate Spain's dry *fino* sherries, but sweet versions exist—look for *lágrima* on the label for these.)

Tawny, the wood port with a leathery color, is the most typical version—the one most Americans imagine when they think of port. It's older, lighter, mellower, and more complex than L.B.V. (described later). It's aged in smaller barrels, maximizing exposure to wood (and, therefore, oxygen)—which gives it a nuttier flavor than the more fruity, younger ports. Tawny port is aged 10, 20, 30, or 40 years, but it's not all the same vintage; to enhance

Cálem, the first place you see after crossing the bridge, offers a fine tour wandering among its huge oak casks (€4.50 includes 2-4 samples—often more samples if the group is small, 20-minute tours depart 4/hour and include 6-minute video in a cask theater, daily 10:00-19:00, last tour at 19:00, off-season closes at 18:00 and fewer tours offered, tel. 223-746-660, www.calem.pt). They also offer 45-minute fado shows that include a port tasting (€16.50, Tue-Sun at 18:30, none on Mon).

the complexity of the flavor, any tawny is a combination of several different ages. So a "30-year-old tawny" is predominantly 30 years old, but also has minor components that are 10 or 20 years old. Once blended, it takes about eight months for the various ports to "marry," though no producer would release an immature tawny. It's ready to consume when you buy it.

Vintage port (if you can afford it) is a ruby. Rather than being a blend from many different years, it comes from a single harvest. Only wine from the very best years is selected by lodges to become vintage. After port ages for two years in wooden casks, it's tasted by the Port Wine Institute to determine whether it's worthy of the vintage label. (If not, it may be kept in wooden casks longer to become L.B.V.) There are usually only two or three vintage years per decade, and the year 2000 was deemed as one of the best ever. If the port is good enough to be classified as vintage, it's bottled and aged another 10-30 years or more. Using glass, rather than wood, makes the difference in the aging process. Sediment is common, so bottles must be decanted. And if a bottle is really old, the cork may deteriorate—so the top of the bottle is heated up with a pair of red-hot tongs, then cold water is poured over it to break it off cleanly. Bottles of port can be stored upright, rather than on their side like regular wines.

Late Bottle Vintage (L.B.V.) was invented after World War II, when British wine-lovers couldn't afford true vintage port. L.B.V. is a blend of wines from a single year, which age together in huge wooden vats for four to six years. The size of the vats means less exposure to wood, which makes it age more quickly, but without losing its fruitiness and color. After five years, it's bottled (later than a vintage port, which ages for only two years—hence the name) and sold. This more-affordable alternative saved the port-wine industry.

Port's stodgy image makes it unpopular among young Portuguese. Lodges have not escaped the multinational conglomerate game, but new owners often retain the brand name to keep loyal customers and invent marketing techniques to attract new ones. Many Americans consider port an acquired taste; for this reason, many port producers along the Douro also make a more straightforward red wine. But as I always say, "Any port in a storm…"

Taylor, for more discriminating tastes, is a growing label that bought one competitor, Croft (described next) in 2001. I toured the classy Taylor lodge—near the top of the hill, with stunning views back on Porto—and enjoyed it. After watching an informative video, I learned a little about the history of the company (which, like many port producers, began in the sheep business) and about the unique microclimates of the Douro Valley. Then I saw the various sizes of wooden vats in which different kinds of ports are aged (free, Mon-Fri 10:00-18:00, also Sat in July-Aug, always closed Sun, high up but worth the hike at Rua do Choupelo 250, tel. 223-742-800, www.taylor.pt). Their restaurant, **Barão de Fladgate**, offers fancy lunchtime views along with an opportunity to recharge for more tastings. Many consider it among the best dining spots in Porto (daily 12:30-15:00 & 19:30-22:00, no dinner served Sun).

Croft offers a similar tour, but you also get to see vintage port being aged in bottles, as well as a fun "library" of dusty old ports (the oldest is from 1834). While the views are not as good as the lodges described earlier, you'll learn how to properly open and present an old bottle of port (free, daily 10:00-18:00, Rua Barão de Forrester 412, tel. 223-756-433, www.croftport.com).

Ferreira's lodge comes with classical music "to help age the wine" (interesting tour, some fine museum artifacts, €4.50 includes two port tastings, daily 10:00-12:30 & 14:00-18:00, look for big sign at the end of the riverfront promenade at Avenida Ramos Pinto 70, tel. 223-746-107).

Kopke is recognized as one of the best in the business because they were the first. Unfortunately, their lodge doesn't receive visitors, but they've opened a shop along the waterfront to allow people to experience—one delightful sip at a time—what they've been doing well since 1638. The staff offers concise explanations and some fine ports by the glass (around €2, daily May-Oct 10:00-19:00, Nov-April 10:00-18:00, Avenida Diogo Leite 312, tel. 220-126-431, www.kopkeports.com).

Away from the Center

▲**Serralves Foundation Contemporary Art Museum and Park (Fundação de Serralves)**—Porto's contemporary art museum, surrounding park, and unique Art Deco mansion are a half-day excursion worth ▲▲▲ for art-lovers...and worthwhile for anyone looking to relax in a lush green space.

The complex is managed by the Serralves Foundation. The Foundation was formed in 1989 with two goals: the advancement of contemporary art and the appreciation of landscape and environment as an artistic concept. These goals, symbolized by the giant red hand shovel near the front gate, drive the layout of the complex: a gigantic contemporary art facility on the edge of a carefully planned park. The whole thing is based around the Art Deco mansion of a count who lived here in the 1930s. When the Foundation was formed, the government bought them the house and surrounding land to encourage them to pursue their goals. A decade later, in 1999, the museum opened.

Cost and Hours: €3 for park/mansion only, €7 for museum, park, and mansion; April-Sept Tue-Fri 10:00-17:00, park open until 19:00, Sat-Sun 10:00-19:00; Oct-March Tue-Sun 10:00-17:00; closed Mon year-round; tel. 808-200-543, www.serralves. pt.

Eating: The museum's restaurant serves a lunch buffet from 12:00-15:00 (€13 Tue-Fri, €16 Sat-Sun, closed Mon). Coffee and snacks are available until 19:00 (17:00 in winter).

Getting There: The complex is about 1.5 miles west of the city center in a wealthy residential neighborhood at Rua Dom João de Castro 210, just south of the busy Avenida da Boavista. From the center, you can reach it most easily via taxi or on a hop-on, hop-off bus tour. Public bus service isn't great, but you can take bus #203 to the Serralves stop (less convenient from downtown—the most central place to catch it is at the big Boavista Rotunda near Casa da Música).

Visiting the Museum and Park: The **museum** presents temporary exhibits by Portuguese and global artists. The enormous, blocky U-shaped building was designed by prominent Portuguese architect Álvaro Siza, who was greatly inspired by the existing mansion. As in most important contemporary-art museums, its vast white exhibition spaces are modified to suit the art displayed (windows and walls continually disappear and reappear).

The **park** around the museum has been designed very carefully to compartmentalize each section; when you're in one part of the grounds, you can't see the rest. This is a very peaceful, romantic place to wander. Hiding in here somewhere are a pleasant rose garden, a tea house overlooking a former tennis court, a lake, a small farm with animals, a gardening school, and Casa de Serralves itself.

The **house (Casa de Serralves)** is, for many, the most interesting part of the whole experience: a huge pink Art Deco mansion that looks like the home of an Old Hollywood star. On two sides, long manicured hedges and fountains stretch to the horizon. Look for the private chapel in back—also pink Art Deco. You can usually go inside the house to check out the cavernous interior. As you step through the fancy gate inside the living room, remember that in the last century, someone actually lived here. Ponder how the design of this place is reflected in the museum. The best part is upstairs: the mirrored, pink-marbled bathroom, dramatically overlooking the grounds.

House of Music (Casa da Música)—This landmark 1,200-seat concert hall opened in 2005. The angular, white concrete building with rippling glass windows was designed by the firm of Dutch architect Rem Koolhaas, called OMA, which also built Seattle's Central Library. Contemporary-architecture fans will find it at the big Boavista Rotunda northwest of the city center (Metro: Casa da

---

Sleep Code

(€1 = about $1.30, country code: 351)
S = Single, **D** = Double/Twin, **T** = Triple, **Q** = Quad, **b** = bathroom, **s** = shower only. Unless otherwise noted, breakfast and taxes are included, credit cards are accepted, and English is spoken.

To help you easily sort through these listings, I've divided the accommodations into three categories, based on the price for a standard double room with bath during high season:

$$$ **Higher Priced**—Most rooms €80 or more.

$$ **Moderately Priced**—Most rooms between €40-80.

$ **Lower Priced**—Most rooms €40 or less.

Prices can change without notice; verify the hotel's current rates online or by email.

Música). Guided tours take you through the interior, or you can attend a concert of anything from world music to classical to jazz to fado. The building is operated by a non-profit foundation established to promote musical culture—tickets are subsidized.

Cost and Hours: €4 tours, 1-2/day in English, 1 hour, focus is on concert hall's unique architecture; concert tickets run €5-25—generally about €15, info/reservation tel. 220-120-220, www.casa damusica.com. For a schedule of upcoming, nearly daily events, pick up the free monthly *Casa da Musica* brochure at any TI.

Sleeping in Porto

There are lots of cheap sleeps in Porto—but none in the desirable Ribeira district (where prices are higher). I've listed two options right in the Ribeira, two just above (near the Stock Exchange Palace), and several better value places in the city center. The cheaper the place, the greater the chance that English isn't spoken (and the grottier the bathroom). You'll almost always have to climb a few stairs to get to the elevator, if they have one.

In the Ribeira

Neither of these two places is a particularly good value. But...location, location, location.

$$$ Pestana Porto Hotel is a stylish splurge, with Porto's best location, right on the Douro in the heart of the Ribeira action. Its 48 rooms occupy two old Ribeira buildings, now converted to plush accommodations and connected by glass walkways (standard Db-€220, river view Db-€210-250, extra bed-€72, air-con, elevator, discounts often available on its website, Praça de Ribeira 1, tel. 223-402-300, fax 223-402-400, www.pestana.com, pestana. porto@pestana.com).

$$$ Guest House Douro is a nice splurge on the river in the center of the Ribeira. It has eight small but tastefully decorated rooms with all the modern comforts. Owners Carmen and João make you feel right at home (Sb/Db-€130-185, higher prices are for river views, air-con, elevator, Wi-Fi, curfew-1:00 in the morning, closed Jan, near House of Henry the Navigator at Rua Fonte Taurina 99-101, tel. 222-015-135, fax 222-015-136, www.guest housedouro.com, guesthousedouro@sapo.pt).

Near the Stock Exchange Palace

$$ Hotel da Bolsa, a few blocks above the Ribeira scene, is swank and modern, with more comfort than character. It has a great location and 36 decent rooms (Sb-€60-80, Db-€74-95, Sb/Db with view-€112, extra bed-€18-21, higher rates are for April-Oct, air-con, elevator, Wi-Fi, Rua Ferreira Borges 101, tel. 222-026-768, fax 222-058-888, www.hoteldabolsa.com, reservas@hoteldabolsa. com).

$ Dixo's Hostel, just a few blocks down the hill from the São Bento Station and up from the Ribeira, is as central as can be. It's run by the friendly brother-and-sister team of Pedro and Joanna, who take pride in their hostel and treat their guests well (bed in 4-,6- or 8-bed mixed dorms-€16-21, D-€44-50, higher rates are for April-Oct, one all-female dorm, free linens, includes breakfast, Wi-Fi, lounge, small rooftop deck, free walking tours and organized evening excursions, Rua Mouzinho da Silveira 72, tel. 222-716-573, www.dixosoportohostel.com, info@dixosoportohostel.com).

In the City Center

$$$ Quality Inn Praça da Batalha offers 113 predictable, big, business-class rooms near São Bento Station. It shares a square with a beautiful *azulejo* church and the beginning of Porto's pedestrian shopping drag (Sb-€65-85, Db-€70-90, third bed-€20, air-con, elevator, Wi-Fi, Praça da Batalha 127, tel. 223-392-300, fax 222-006-009, www.choicehotelseurope.com, quality.batalha@ grupo-continental.com).

$$ B&B Hotel Porto Centro has 125 slick-and-modern, economic-chic rooms occupying a remodeled movie theater. Black-and-white photos of movie stars decorate the walls in tribute to its former life. It's on Praça da Batalha, near the Igreja de Santo Ildefonso *azulejo* church (Sb/Db-€42-46, Qb-€63-69, breakfast buffet-€6, air-con, elevator, Wi-Fi, parking, quiet back patio, Praça da Batalha 32-34, tel. 220-407-000, fax 222-407-010, www.bbhotels. pt, porto-centro@hotelbb.com).

$$ Hotel Internacional fits 35 super-modern rooms into the heavy granite-and-tile shell of an old monastery just two blocks off the Avenida dos Aliados. It offers hotel formality, typical amenities, and a good location at a reasonable price (Sb-€50-65, Db-€60-75, third bed-€20, prices depend on day and season, air-con, elevator, Wi-Fi, Rua do Almada 131, tel. 222-005-032, fax 222-009-063, www.hi-porto.com, info@hi-porto.com).

$$ Grande Hotel de Paris Residencial brags it was the first hotel in Porto with running water in its rooms. Its 45 faded but fine rooms—all with antique furniture—are spread out over three interconnected buildings, each with a grand atrium and sloping floors. This proudly run place has big, classy public spaces strewn across its treehouse-style floor plan (Sb-€65, Db-€70, higher prices in Aug, extra bed-€20, free glass of port with this book, elevator, Internet access, relaxing garden, one block up from Avenida dos Aliados at Rua da Fábrica 27-29, tel. 222-073-140, fax 222-073-149, www.hotelparis.pt, info@hotelparis.pt, David).

$$ Pensão Avenida is stark but functional, renting 16 simple rooms on the fourth and fifth floors above a grand boulevard (Sb-€25-30, Db-€40-45, Tb-€55-65, higher rates are for May-Sept, Avenida dos Aliados 141, tel. 222-009-551, fax 222-052-932, http://pensaoavenida.planetaclix.pt, pensaoavenida@clix.pt).

$ Duas Nações Guest House is a well-run backpacker place with 19 dumpy rooms—as comfy as such a cheap place can be. It overlooks a square straight up Rua da Fábrica, a few blocks from Avenida dos Aliados. The "two nations" are Portugal and Brazil, still friends after all these years (bed in dorm-€10-13, S-€15, Sb-€25, D-€26, Db-€37, T-€40, Tb-€42, Q-€50, Qb-€52, cash only, Wi-Fi, no breakfast but adjacent to handy café, Praça Guilherme Gomes Fernandes 59, tel. 222-081-616, www.duasnacoes.com.pt, duasnacoes@sapo.pt, Paolo). Paolo also rents several apartments—all recently remodeled with small kitchens, washing machines, air-con, double-pane windows, and Wi-Fi (2-person studio-€55-65/night, apartment for up to 8-€110-115).

$ Pensão Residencial Belo Sonho is well-maintained and family-run (no English spoken), and just up the street from Café Majestic and the main shopping drag, Rua de Santa Catarina. Its 15 rooms are a good value (Sb-€20-30, Db-€30-40, Tb-€40-45, higher prices June-Sept, noisy on Fri and Sat nights, Rua Passos Manuel 186, tel. 222-003-389, fax 222-012-850).

$ Pensão Grande Oceano, a good value in a central location, has 15 clean, basic rooms on four floors. All but two of the rooms have private baths and air-con (S/D-€20-30, Sb-€25-30, Db-€35-40, Tb-€45-50, Qb-€65-75, no breakfast, no elevator, free Wi-Fi, Rua da Fábrica 45, just a few doors up the hill from Hotel Paris, tel. 222-038-770, fax 222-038-810, www.pensaograndeoceano. com, geral@pensaograndeoceano.com).

Eating in Porto

Porto is famous for its tripe. Legend has it that when Porto's favorite son, Prince Henry the Navigator, set out for his explorations, the city slaughtered all of its mature livestock to send along with his crew—keeping only the guts for themselves. Porto's cooks then devised many ingenious ways of preparing innards. The tradition stuck, and to this day, people from Porto are known as *tripeiros.* These days, tripe plays a subtler role. You'll most typically see it prepared Porto-style *(tripas a moda do Porto):* barely present in a thick stew, with beans, sausage, chicken, and scant vegetables. The tripe itself doesn't have much taste—though I couldn't keep myself from thinking about digestive processes while I chewed.

For something easier to stomach, try *caldo verde*—a tasty soup made with potatoes and thinly chopped cabbage. For a quick meal, locals like a sandwich called a *francesinha* ("little French girl"), which usually comes with various meats dripping with a spicy tomato- or seafood-based sauce, though some restaurants and different regions have variations (egg, cheese, even vegetarian).

Remember, if the menu has two price columns, in general the cheaper list is for smaller portions *(meia dose,* or "1/2," plenty for one person), and the higher-priced list is for splittable dishes that will easily feed two (listed as *dose,* or "1").

In the Ribeira

There's a wide range of dining options in the Ribeira, and they're all touristy. Strolling along the waterfront and following your nose is a good option. You can also try wandering the back lanes to find a spot that feels right—you'll be trading river views for lower prices and local color. The seafood's fresh, except on Mondays (since fishermen don't go out on Sundays).

D' Tonho, atop the arcade near the bridge, is owned by a popular Porto singer and is everyone's top recommendation for a Ribeira splurge. The place is white-tablecloth classy, at once Old World and mod, with friendly and unpretentious service. The menu is small and seasonal. The dishes—traditional Portuguese cuisine, with an emphasis on fresh fish—are only slightly more expensive than nearby tour-group alternatives. Be warned that the appetizers, while tempting, are even more expensive than the main dishes (you touch, you pay). Baby goat chops and cod dishes, the house specialties with huge and tasty portions, are a great value at €15. While most wines on the list are pricey, the Curva Douro (€16) is very

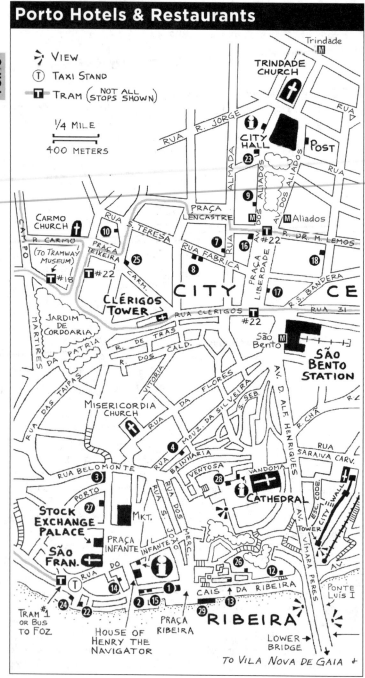

Porto Hotels & Restaurants

↗ VIEW

Ⓣ TAXI STAND

🚃 TRAM (NOT ALL STOPS SHOWN)

¼ MILE

400 METERS

PORTO

TRINDADE CHURCH

Trindade Ⓜ

RUA

CITY HALL
23

Post

RUA DOS ALIADOS

9

RUA JORGE

R. JORGE

RUA

ALMADA

Ⓜ

Ⓜ Aliados

CARMO CHURCH

R. CARMO

(TO TRAMWAY MUSEUM)

Ⓣ #18

CAMPO

10

RUA S. TERESA

PRAÇA TEIXEIRA

Ⓣ #22

25

PRAÇA LENCASTRE

RUA FABRICA

7

16

CARM.

CITY

8

AV. DOS ALIADOS

R. DR. M. LEMOS

#22

18

CE

PRAÇA LIBERDADE

17

R. S. BANDERA

CLÉRIGOS TOWER

JARDIM DE CORDOARIA

MARTIRES DA PATRIA

RUA CLÉRIGOS

Ⓣ #22

RUA 31

São Bento Ⓜ

SÃO BENTO STATION

R. DE TRAS

CALD.

R. DOS

VITORIA

DA FLORES

S. SEB.

RUA DAS TAIPAS

RUA

MISERICORDIA CHURCH

RUA

MOUZ. DA SILVEIRA

AV. D. ALF. HENRIQUES

R. CHA

RUA SARAIVA CARV.

4

BAINHARIA

RUA BELOMONTE

3

PORTO

27

STOCK EXCHANGE PALACE

MKT.

RUA DOS

VENTOSA

28

VANDOMA

CATHEDRAL

Tower

CITY WALL

ESC. CODE

AV. VIMARA PERES

SÃO FRAN.

RUA S. JOÃO

PRAÇA INFANTE

RUA INFANTE

14

1

Ⓣ Ⓣ

24

22

TRAM #1 OR BUS TO FOZ

HOUSE OF HENRY THE NAVIGATOR

2 15

PRAÇA RIBEIRA

MERC.

26

CAIS DA RIBEIRA

13

29

RIBEIRA

12

PONTE LUÍS I

LOWER BRIDGE

TO VILA NOVA DE GAIA

1 Pestana Porto Hotel
2 Guest House Douro
3 Hotel da Bolsa
4 Dixo's Hostel
5 Quality Inn Praça da Batalha
6 B&B Hotel Porto Centro
7 Hotel Internacional
8 Grande Hotel de Paris Res. & Pensão Grande Oceano
9 Pensão Avenida
10 Duas Nações Guest House
11 Pensão Residencial Belo Sonho
12 D' Tonho Restaurant
13 Filha da Mãe Preta Rest.
14 Restaurante A Grade
15 Ora Viva Restaurante
16 Restaurante Guarany (Fado)
17 "Imperial McDonald's"
18 Restaurante Regaleira
19 Restaurante Abadia
20 Confeitaria-Restaurante do Bolhão
21 Café Majestic
22 Restaurante Mal Cozinhado (Fado)
23 Internet Café
24 Laundry
25 Lello & Irmão Bookstore
26 O Cântaro Shop
27 Porto Wine Shop
28 ATC/Porto Tours
29 River Cruises

good. Reservations are a must (daily 12:30-15:00 & 19:30-23:00, indoor and outdoor seating, Cais da Ribeira 13-15, tel. 222-004-307). They also have a portable harborfront location set up directly across the river in Vila Nova de Gaia with wonderful outdoor seating (daily 12:30-15:30 & 19:30-23:00).

Filha da Mãe Preta is a cut above the several interchangeable midrange places along the embankment. Sit outside with Douro views or in the tiled interior (most dishes €9-18, full courses splittable for two people, Mon-Sat 12:00-22:30, closed Sun, check out gigantic mural of Porto upstairs, Cais da Ribeira 40, tel. 222-055-515).

Restaurante A Grade is a small mom-and-pop restaurant one block up from the river. Ferreria serves while wife Elena cooks good, home-style Portuguese food, just like *mãe* used to make. The baked octopus is a favorite among regulars (€15 seafood and meat plates; big, splittable portions; Mon-Sat 12:00-16:00 & 18:30-22:30, closed Sun, Rua de São Nicolau 9, tel. 223-321-130, reservations smart for dinner).

Ora Viva Restaurante is a humble but exuberantly decorated, long-and-skinny dining hall a block off the waterfront. The hardworking Pinto family specializes in traditional grilled meat and fish dishes—especially *cataplana,* a seafood stew. It's a little less touristy than the Ribeira norm, with locals, decent food, and good prices (€8-10 meals, Rua Fonte Taurina 83, tel. 222-052-033). Antonio promises a free glass of port wine (before or after your dinner) if you show him this book.

In Vila Nova de Gaia

Adega E Presuntaria Transmontana serves up quality Portuguese fish and meat plates (€13-17) as well as *petiscos*—Portuguese tapas—for €4-11 (daily 12:00-midnight, near the port lodges, facing the river at Avenida Diogo Leite 80, tel. 223-758-380).

At **Ar de Rio Restaurante,** modern design meets traditional Portuguese cuisine. It's located on the river with great views over the city. You can eat inside, or out on the deck (€11-20 meat and fish plates, €6 daily lunch specials, daily 12:00-1:00 in the morning, modern steel-and-glass "box" at Avenida Diogo Leite 5, tel. 223-701-797).

Real Indiana, right on the riverfront, serves up all the usual tasty Indian dishes. Eat inside or out on the large deck overlooking the river (€12-26 splittable plates, daily 12:00-15:00 & 19:00-23:00, big glass building facing the river at Loja 360, tel. 223-744-422).

In the City Center

Good, cheap restaurants are scattered all around the city center, but since this is a business district, many are lunch-only. Menus are often handwritten (posted on paper tablecloths outside) with €1 soups and €5 plates. Remember that most coffee and pastry shops do double-duty as lunch spots, so wander around and see what people are having. Good locations abound on the pedestrian Rua do Sampaio Bruno and on the side streets of Rua do Almada (one block west of Avenida dos Aliados). The dining's more atmospheric in Ribeira, but these are convenient if you're staying in the center.

Restaurante Guarany, established in 1933, has been the musicians' coffee shop for generations. You'll enjoy Art Deco elegance with a Brazilian flair (read brochure for the charming story of the murals) and crisp yet friendly service. I'd skip the salads and zero in on the fine €14-18 meat and fish plates and daily specials (daily 9:00-24:00, Avenida dos Aliados 85, tel. 223-321-272). There's no extra charge for live music (fado, Cuban, Brazilian, Thu-Sat from 9:30, schedule at www.cafeguarany.com).

Imperial McDonald's, famously inhabiting the former Imperial Café at the bottom of Avenida dos Aliados, is the most elegant fast-food spot you'll ever munch fries in.

Restaurante Regaleira (just around the corner) is a venerable local bistro with no tourists and a great scene (cheaper lunches at bar, open daily except Sat, Rua do Bonjardim 87, tel. 220-006-465).

Restaurante Abadia gives customers a warm welcome and has two floors of happy eaters—locals and tourists—dining on large portions of straightforward Portuguese cuisine. This 300-seat place is a no-brainer for a fine, central meal. Split a huge half-portion of their Porto-style tripe with your travel partner, balanced with something a little more predictable, such as a sizzling mini-hibachi of roasted chicken and potatoes (€11.50 *meia dose*s and tasty omelets, €20 splittable *dose*s, specialty is grilled cod, Mon-Sat 12:00-15:00 & 18:30-23:00, closed Sun, head one block east of Sá da Bandeira near Bolhão market to side street Rua do Ateneu Comercial do Porto 22-24, tel. 222-008-757).

Confeitaria-Restaurante do Bolhão, which faces the market-hall entrance, has been pleasing local shoppers since 1896. This bustling bakery/brasserie offers enticing take-out items in front and an inviting old-time dining hall in the rear (the more elegant basement is less lively and soulful). You'll find fresh baked goods, omelets, and fish, along with €5 soup-and-sandwich specials (daily 6:00-21:00, Rua Formosa 339, tel. 223-395-220).

Café Majestic isn't just a coffee house—it's an institution. This elegant Art Nouveau café has been Porto's neighborhood living room for over a century. Today, it's a fine place for a coffee or a light but expensive lunch (€10-18, Mon-Sat 9:30-24:00, closed Sun, Rua de Santa Catarina 112, tel. 222-003-887). They serve a big breakfast (€15, all day) and fancy tea (€12, 15:00-19:00).

Porto Connections

Trains

Regional trains use the more central São Bento Station; long-distance trains use Campanhã Station on the east edge of town. The two stations are connected by frequent trains (see "Arrival in Porto," page 271). All trains leaving São Bento also stop at Campanhã (the next station). Some trains only depart from Campanhã Station, so check the schedule carefully.

From Porto's São Bento Train Station to: Peso da Régua (3/day direct, 2 hours; more with change in Caide or Penafiel, 2-2.5 hours), **Pinhão** (5/day, 2.5-3 hours, transfer in Peso da Régua).

From Campanhã Train Station: Fast Alfa Pendular and Intercidades trains (both require reservation, buy at station) go to **Coimbra** (almost hourly, 1 hour on Alfa Pendular line or Intercidades service but 2 hours on slower regional line—confirm before buying) and **Lisbon** (almost hourly, 3 hours). Note that Alfa Pendular and Intercidades trains are similarly speedy, but Alfa trains cost more.

To reach **Santiago de Compostela, Spain,** take a train bound for the Spanish port city of Vigo (€11, 2/day, departures at 7:55 and 18:10, 5 hours, ticket only purchased as far as Vigo, must buy another ticket in Spain to continue to Santiago; en route to Vigo, you may change at the border town of Valença). Once in Spain, you can change to the Santiago-bound train in Vigo, but most conductors will encourage you instead to change trains before that, in the town of Redondela. This works fine, since Vigo is on a dead-end track and any train going to Vigo also goes through Redondela on the way. (In other words, if you change in Vigo instead of Redondela, you'll simply spend more time on the train and less time at the station.) Frustratingly, rail-information people in Porto generally can't tell you much about parts of the journey beyond the Spanish border. Consider instead a bus tour if you have extra cash and less time (see next page).

Buses

Remember, each bus company has its own mini-station; there's no central bus terminus (for addresses and telephone numbers, see "Arrival in Porto," page 271). Various companies compete on the same route (for example, four companies go to Lisbon). Ask the transport office at the TI about the handiest bus for your itinerary (see "Tourist Information," page 270; toll-free tel. 800-220-905). Don't bother trying to get to the Douro Valley (Peso da Régua or Pinhão) by bus; it takes twice as long as the train.

From Porto by Bus to: Coimbra (operated by Rede Expressos, Rodonorte, and others; best is Rede Expressos—11/day, 1.5 hours, more frequent early and late, sparse midafternoon), **Lisbon** (best via RENEX or Rede Expressos, at least hourly, 3 hours), **Santiago de Compostela, Spain** (run by Internorte; 6/week in summer, 4/week in winter, 5.25 hours, €26).

Santiago Bus Tour: To get to Santiago de Compostela, Spain, consider taking an expensive but convenient all-day guided bus tour from Porto. It leaves daily at 8:00 and takes two to three hours via the expressway. (You can skip out on the return to Porto.) But this is a pricey alternative—the fares are €98-120. For information on these tours, ask at the ATC/Porto Tours office (see page 276; www.portotours.com).

PORTO

DOURO VALLEY

Vale do Douro

The best single activity in northern Portugal is exploring the scenic Douro (DOH-roh) Valley—the birthplace of port wine—with its otherworldly, ever-changing terrain sculpted by centuries of hardy farmers. The Douro River's steep, craggy, twisting canyons have been laboriously terraced to make a horizontal home for grape vines and olive and almond trees. Unlike the Rhine, the Loire, and other great European rivers, the Douro was never a strategic military location. So, rather than fortresses and palaces, you'll see farms, villages...and endless tidy rows of rock terraces, which took no less work—and are no less impressive—than those castles and châteaux. Locals brag, "God made the earth, but man made the Douro."

The Douro River begins as a trickle in Spain (where it's called Duero), runs west for 550 miles (350 miles of which are in Portugal), and spills into the Atlantic at Porto. The name likely means "river of gold" (though some trace it to a Celtic word for water), perhaps because of the way the sun shines on the water, or the golden-brown silt it carries after a heavy rain.

In the 17th century, British traders developed a taste for the wines from the Douro region. "Op-port-unity" knocked in 1756, when the Marquês de Pombal demarcated the region—establishing it as the only place that port wine could be produced. To this day, port remains the top industry, as well as the top tourist draw, of the Douro Valley. The 50-mile stretch on either side of Pinhão is home to some 4,000 vintners and scores of *quintas*—vineyards that produce port (and often table wine and olive oil). While many *quintas* are private, others offer tours and tastings, and some have accommodations as well.

The Douro hillsides change colors throughout the year, from dusty brown in winter, scrubby green in summer, and glowing gold in fall. The 5,000-foot-high Serra do Marão mountain range guards the region, protecting it from the ocean air and creating a microclimate perfect for growing grapes. The temperature varies from snowy in the winter to arid and 100°F in the summer. Much of the Douro's dramatic ambience changed in the 1970s, when a series of dams were built for hydroelectric power, taming the formerly raging river into the meandering stream seen today.

But while the scenery and the port are sublime, the towns along the Douro (Peso da Régua and Pinhão) are fairly dull. If you've got wheels, consider staying at one of the many *quintas* that offer accommodations—ranging from simple rooms on family farms to one of the most breathtaking *pousadas* in Portugal. To many, the Douro Valley will feel low-energy and underwhelming (especially outside of September's harvest time), but it does have the world's best port and a unique—if subtle—charm.

Planning Your Time

This area merits two days (including travel time to and from Porto, with an overnight along the river). Port-wine enthusiasts may well want more time. If you want only a glimpse, you can see the Douro as a day trip from Porto, either on your own (about 2 hours by car or 2 hours by train each way) or with a package tour (see "*Quintas* Tours and Tasting," later). I find the city of Porto more interesting and would favor it over the Douro Valley when allocating limited vacation time.

Note that since Porto is a business-oriented city, its hotels are often cheaper on weekends. In contrast, the Douro Valley—since it's primarily a tourist zone—is more crowded (and often more expensive) on weekends. Ideally, visit Porto on the weekend and the Douro during the week.

Drivers should make a beeline for this best part of the Douro Valley (see next section), and explore at will. Without a car, you're limited as to where you can stay and which *quintas* you can tour, but you still have enough options to make the trip worthwhile. To maximize sightseeing thrills, take the slow boat cruise from Porto to Peso da Régua. Visit the sights in Régua, then settle in for the night (or, if you're staying in Pinhão, take the train or boat there). In the morning, hike to Quinta de la Rosa (near Pinhão) for the

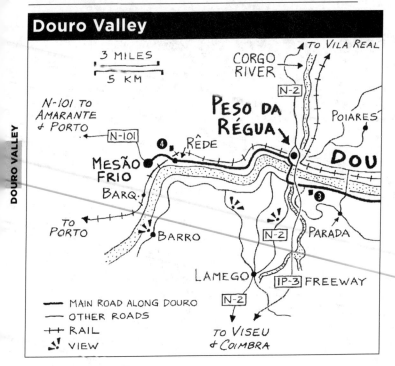

Douro Valley

11:00 tour and tasting. When you've had enough of the wine and rugged scenery, head back to Porto via train.

Orientation to the Douro Valley

The Douro runs for 350 miles through the northern Portuguese heartland. The most interesting segment—and the heart of the port-wine-growing region—is easily the 17-mile stretch between Peso da Régua and Pinhão.

Coming from Porto, you'll see that the first 55 miles of the Douro are pretty and lush. When you reach the town of **Mesão Frio,** the terrain becomes far more arid and dramatic. The prized, demarcated port-wine-growing region of the Douro technically begins here, and stretches all the way to the Spanish border.

Peso da Régua, about seven miles beyond Mesão Frio, is the biggest town of the region and a handy home base. Seventeen miles beyond Peso da Régua is smaller **Pinhão.** Each town has a big, fancy hotel and one or two cheap *residencials,* with a *quinta* nearby. Peso da Régua benefits from more striking scenery, but feels urban and functional; Pinhão enjoys more of a small-town ambience and has better accommodations. Neither is worth going out of your way to visit.

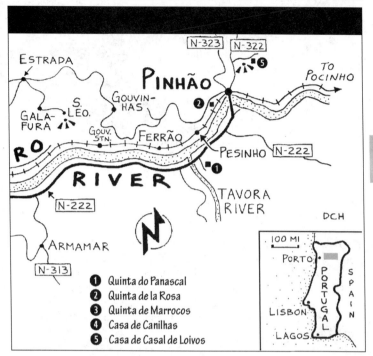

ESTRADA

PINHÃO

N-323 N-322

GOUVIN-HAS

TO POCINHO

GALA-FURA

S. LEO.

GOUV. STN.

FERRÃO

PESINHO N-222

RO

RIVER

TAVORA RIVER

N-222

N

DCH

ARMAMAR

N-313

1. Quinta do Panascal
2. Quinta de la Rosa
3. Quinta de Marrocos
4. Casa de Canilhas
5. Casa de Casal de Loivos

100 MI

PORTO

SPAIN

LISBON

PORTUGAL

LAGOS

DOURO VALLEY

The Douro Azul company has something of a monopoly in the region, operating the biggest tour boats and running several of the accommodations (including Vintage House Hotel in Pinhão).

I've described the most enjoyable and accessible stretch of the Douro, but there's much more—vineyards stretch all the way to Spain. The train goes as far as Pocinho. Just south of Pocinho, Vila Nova de Foz Côa sits between the Douro and a fine "archaeological park" with cave paintings.

A big part of your Douro experience will be determined by where you choose to sleep. The most memorable place is the classic Vintage House Hotel in Pinhão. Both the Quinta de la Rosa and Quinta de Marrocos offer you a homey farm experience. All are described later in this chapter.

Getting Around the Douro Valley

By Boat: Lazy cruise boats float up and down the Douro between Porto, Peso da Régua, and Pinhão. (The feisty Douro was tamed in the 1970s by a series of five dams with locks, including the highest one in Europe, the Barragem do Carrapatelo—which inches boats up and down, like a giant elevator, over 140 feet.)

The boat trip takes about seven hours from Porto to the heart of the Douro, and it comes with lunch and passage through two locks (longer trips include a third lock between Peso da Régua and Pinhão). If you've got the time and don't have a car, this is a slow but scenic way to enjoy the Douro Valley.

Various companies do the trip; generally, several different boats run daily from March through November (no boats Dec-Feb, seniors should ask about discounts, especially on weekdays). Most travelers take a train or bus back to Porto from Régua on the same day as part of a package deal. But if you want to spend the night on the Douro, it's easy to catch a train back on your own (or buy a two-day package, which includes lodging).

The largest company, **Douro Azul,** has big boats that are popular with tour groups. It's often a bit more expensive, but the service is professional and the food is good. The trip includes a boat cruise on one leg of the journey and a return train or bus trip on the other—which leg is which depends on the day (Porto to Régua—€59-82, Porto to Pinhão—€69-92, other routes offered, tel. 223-402-500, www.douroazul.com). They also offer various package itineraries that include overnights at fancy hotels and *pousadas* (see their website for details).

Some travelers prefer smaller companies, which can cost a little less and offer a more personal experience. Your best bet is to comparison-shop the options for the day you want to cruise, with help from the excellent **Porto Tours** office in Porto. Since it's run by the city, this agency offers unbiased advice and charges no commission (daily April-Sept 10:00-19:00, telephone answered daily 9:00-19:00, shorter hours off-season, in medieval watchtower next to cathedral at Calçada Dom Pedro Pitões 15, tel. 222-000-073, www.portotours.com, reservas@porto tours.mail.pt).

By Train: A regional train connects Porto's São Bento Station with Peso da Régua (3/day direct, 2 hours; more with a change in Caide or Penafeil, 2-2.5 hours); some of these trains continue another 30 minutes to Pinhão (5/day). There's also a historic steam train that choo-choos you between Douro towns on Saturdays (late July-early Oct; 3.25-hour round-trip from Régua to Pinhão and back-€77; 6-hour round-trip from Régua to Pinhão, Tua, and back-€125; Douro cruises and train/cruise combos available, tel. 259-338-135, www.cenarios.pt, vilareal@cenarios.pt).

By Car: The region is easy by car. From Porto, zip on the A-4 expressway to Amarante, then N-101 through the mountains to Mesão Frio (total trip to Régua around two hours). Once in the heart of the Douro, the riverside road follows the north bank from Mesão Frio to Régua. From there, you'll cross to the south bank (on the middle of the three bridges) to continue on N-222 into the valley to Pinhão (where you'll cross back to reach the town). The 17-mile stretch of river covered in this chapter is about a 30-minute drive. Everything I've mentioned is no more than a few minutes' side-trip from the river.

When passing through Amarante, it's an easy and logical pit stop to detour into the town center to check out the old Roman bridge and impressive church and convent of São Gonçalo.

If you're driving from Coimbra to the Douro Valley, you'll save time and mileage by coming directly through the mountains (via Viseu and Lamego), rather than taking the expressway up the coast to Porto and then over.

Tours in the Douro Valley

Quintas Tours and Tastings

The main attraction of the Douro Valley is touring the *quintas,* the farms that produce port and table wines. It's an informal scene and easy for drivers; simply pull into any *quinta* listed here (or any marked *rota do vinho do Porto*), and ask for a quick tour and a taste. Even if they have a specific time for tours (listed below where applicable), you can often get a shorter, less formal tour at other times. Ideally, call ahead and ask when you should show up.

Each *quinta* (KEEN-tah) works differently; most tours and tastings are free. The tours of big companies' *quintas* are slick, but feel like stripped-down versions of the tours you'll do in the port-wine lodges back in Porto (with the happy exception of Quinta do Panascal). The smaller, independent *quintas* are more intimate, and offer a chance to meet the people who have devoted their lives to making the best wine they can. At *quintas* operated by big companies, it's fine not to buy. But if a family-run place gives you an

in-depth tour, it's polite to buy at least a token bottle.

These are the best *quinta* experiences on this stretch of the Douro. I've noted the best options for non-drivers.

▲▲**Quinta do Panascal**— This wonderful *quinta* produces Fonseca—a name familiar to port-lovers for its high quality.

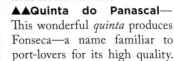

The affordable, tasty Bin No. 27 is their best-known ruby. It's the only *quinta* that allows you to roam on your own through the terraced vineyards. From the riverside road you'll side-trip up the valley of the Távora River. Venturing up the rough gravel road, you'll feel like you are discovering a special, hidden gem. Yet upon arrival, you'll enjoy the slick efficiency of a corporate producer (Fonseca also owns Taylor, and is a port-wine giant). Because of its delightfully remote location, and because it gets you out among the grapes, it's the best *quinta* tour on the Douro.

The tour is self-guided, so there's no wait once you arrive. You'll be given a 30-minute audioguide and set free to wander through the vineyards and take in the sweeping views (while listening to dry, humorless commentary about the history of port and of the company). Then you'll return to the lodge to watch a 10-minute video (which brings the otherwise still fields to life) while tasting two ports.

Cost and Hours: €3, April-Oct daily 10:00-18:00; Nov-March Mon-Fri 10:00-18:00, Sat-Sun by reservation only; tel. 254-732-321, www.quintadopanascalvisitorscentre.wordpress.com.

Getting There: This place is only accessible by car; it's well-marked off the Régua-Pinhão road (N-222), up a thrilling little side road that follows the Távora River as it branches off from the Douro (closer to Pinhão).

▲**Quinta de la Rosa**—This family-run *quinta* is serious about its wine and eager to show it off on an in-depth, friendly one-hour tour of the facility with a generous finale of four tastings. Three-course meals paired with their wines cost €27.50 per person; reserve in advance.

Cost and Hours: €3, but credited toward purchase; tours April-Oct Mon-Fri at 11:00, call to arrange weekends and off-season; tastings available April-Oct Mon-Fri 9:00-18:00 and Sat mornings, none Sun; one mile downstream from Pinhão, tel. 254-732-254, fax 254-732-346, www.quintadelarosa.com.

Getting There: This is perhaps the only family *quinta* that is close enough to a town that you can do it without a car (20-minute hike from Pinhão). For directions and information on their accommodations, see page 319.

Other Tours and Tastings—Many of the accommodations listed in this chapter also offer tours and tastings.

The finest ports—for serious wine-lovers—are at **Vintage House Hotel**'s Academia do Vinho in Pinhão. The tastings are generally in the afternoon; call to check the schedule and reserve

Brits on the Douro: The History of Port

Port is actually a British phenomenon. Because Britain isn't suitable for growing grapes, its citizens traditionally imported wine from France. But during wars with France (17th and 18th centuries), Britain boycotted French wine and looked elsewhere. They considered Portugal—but since it was farther away, wine often didn't survive the long sea journey to England.

The port-making process was supposedly invented accidentally by a pair of brothers who fortified the wine with grape brandy to maintain its quality during the long trip to England. The wine picked up the flavor of the oak, and the English grew to like the fortified taste and oaky flavor. The British perfected port production in the succeeding centuries, hence many ports carry British-sounding names (Taylor, Croft, Graham).

In 1703, the Methuen Treaty reduced taxation on Portuguese wines, making port even more popular. In 1756, Portugal's Marquês de Pombal demarcated the Douro region—the first such designation in Europe. From that point on, only true "port wine" came from this region, following specific regulations of production, just as "Champagne" technically refers to wines from a specific region of France. Traditionally, farmers and landowners were Portuguese, while the British bought the wine from them, aged it in Porto, and handled the export business. But that arrangement changed in the late 19th century, when an infestation of an American insect called phylloxera (which smuggled itself to the Old World in the humid climate of speedy steamboats) devastated the Portuguese—and European—wine industry.

In the Douro Valley, you'll see lasting evidence of the phylloxera infestations in the "dead" terraces, overgrown with weeds and a smattering of olive trees. During the infestations, these particular terraces were treated with harsh chemicals that contaminated the soil, rendering it suitable only for growing olives, but not grapes. Other terraces were left untouched, as Portuguese vintners simply gave up. Unable to produce usable grapes for over a decade, they sold their land to British companies who were willing to wait until a solution could be found. It was, as phylloxera-resistant American rootstock began to be used throughout Europe. Port production resumed, this time on British-owned land.

Today, Porto and the Douro Valley see many British tourists. Though it's largely undiscovered by Americans, this region is a real hot spot among wine-loving Brits.

a spot (€14.50-52 tastings, shop open daily 10:00-19:00, tel. 254-730-230, www.cs-vintagehouse.com, see page 319). The region's red wines are some of Portugal's fruity finest. Since it's right in the center of Pinhão, this place is an easy choice for non-drivers.

At the other end of the spectrum is the loose, informal, family-run **Quinta de Marrocos** (see page 317), a great place to sample simple ports while chatting with the family that made them (€4-10 tastings, daily 10:00-12:00 & 15:00-18:00, www.quintademarrocos.com). You could hoof it here from Peso da Régua (across the river and about 1.5 miles upstream), but it's not as easy by foot as Quinta de la Rosa.

The refined **Solar do Vinho do Porto** (see page 315), in downtown Peso da Régua, is another fine tasting option, especially for those without a car.

Growing—and Stomping—Grapes in the Douro Valley

Port wine can technically only be grown in the Douro Valley, which is unique among European river valleys. One glance at those endless neat rows of terraces—and the harsh, arid terrain that somehow produces something so flavorful—and visitors can't help but wonder: How do they do it?

The heart of the Douro is characterized by microclimates. A few miles can make a tremendous difference in terms of temperature, precipitation, humidity, and farming conditions. Even within the same vineyard, each parcel of land has its own characteristics. These subtle changes infuse the grapes with completely different aromas and flavors. Over the years, vintners have learned to micromanage their grapes, fine-tuning specific qualities to get the very best port for their conditions.

Near Porto, the Douro has moderate temperatures and a fair amount of precipitation. The vineyards you see north of Porto produce not port, but "green wine" (*vinho verde*—Portugal's refreshing and sprightly light white wine). About 55 miles inland, around Mesão Frio, chains of mountains stretch to the north and south. East of here, the climate changes dramatically, becoming very hot and dry in summer, with heavy rainfall and extreme cold in winter.

The terrain around the Douro is dominated by sedimentary rocks

Rabelo **Boats**

Up until the 1970s, when the Douro was tamed by dams, boats called *rabelos* navigated the treacherous waters, carrying port from the hillsides to the cellars of Porto. It was a three-day trip to cover the 50-100 miles. A crew of four loaded the barrels onto the 20-foot boats. For the downstream trip, the captain stood on a platform to spy rocks and shallows ahead, using the long rudder to guide the flat-bottomed boat through whitewater and hairpin turns. It was dangerous work, and the river was once lined with shrines where superstitious sailors prayed.

At Vila Nova de Gaia, they unloaded their cargo—a mere eight barrels, typically—and headed back. For the slow trip upstream, the tall, square sail helped them ride the prevailing westerly winds. Otherwise, they were pulled by ropes up the worst stretches by men or oxen on towpaths that used to line the riverbank.

Nowadays, the Douro is quiet, port is shipped via tanker trucks, and the few remaining *rabelos* are docked by *quintas* for ambience and advertising.

that have been buried, heated, and deformed into a metamorphic rock called schist *(xisto)*. Thanks to geological processes, the easily fractured layers of schist are tilted beneath the soil at an angle, allowing winter rainfall to easily penetrate the earth and build up in underground reserves. The grapevines' roots plunge deep into the ground—up to 30 feet—in order to reach this water through the long, dry summer.

Douro vineyards are terraced, giving the valley an unusually dramatic look. Building and maintaining these terraces *(geios)* is expensive, and grapes planted there must be cultivated by hand. More recently, some of the bigger companies have attempted different methods: using bulldozers to create larger terraces (called *patamares)* that can be worked by machines; or smoothing out the hillside and planting the vines in vertical rows.

(Purists don't like these new methods, which also have their disadvantages—including fewer plants per parcel.) Within the demarcated region, farmers are not allowed to irrigate, except with special permission.

Because the crops here are worked mostly by hand, it can be hard to find good workers (especially for pruning, a delicate task requiring certain skills). Most young people from the Douro move to the cities on the coast. To encourage them to stay, the government offers subsidies and other incentives.

To make the finest port, many *quintas* along the Douro still stomp grapes by foot—not because of quaint tradition, but because it's the best way. Machines would break the grapes' seeds and stems, releasing a bitter flavor—but soft soles don't. During harvest time (late Sept-early Oct), the grapes are poured into big granite tubs called *lagares*. A team of two dozen stompers line up across from each other, put their arms on each other's shoulders, and march, military-style, to crush the grapes. The stomping can last three or four days, and generally devolves into a party atmosphere—with tourists sometimes paying to join in.

Port traditionally stays in the Douro Valley for one winter after it's made, as the cold temperatures encourage the wine and brandy to marry. Then it's taken to Porto, where the more humid, mild climate is ideal for aging. For centuries, port could technically only be aged, marketed, and sold in Porto. But this was deregulated in 1987, and now any Douro *quinta* that offers tours sells its port directly to visitors.

The vineyards along the Douro are traditionally separated by olive trees, many of which produce fine olive oil. The farming demands of olives fit efficiently with those of grapes. There are also almond, orange, apple, and cherry trees, which locals use to make jam.

Peso da Régua

Peso da Régua (PAY-soh dah RAY-gwah)—or simply Régua, as it's called by locals—is the administrative capital of the Douro Valley. With 22,000 people, Régua feels urban, with modern five- and six-story apartment blocks and hotels that somehow seem out of place in these starkly beautiful surroundings. While the town itself isn't worth the trip, the views and access into the surrounding countryside make it worth considering as a home base—or at least a transportation hub.

Orientation to Peso da Régua

Peso da Régua consists of basically two bustling streets that run parallel to the Douro. There are three bridges at the east (upriver) end of town.

Tourist Information: The town's TI is right next door to the train station (daily 9:30-12:30 & 14:00-18:00; Largo da Estacão, tel. 254-312-846).

Arrival in Peso da Régua: The train station, TI, and two recommended hotels are at the edge of the center near the bridges. The boat dock is more or less in the middle of town (disembark to the right, walk up the hill for train station and hotels).

Tours: A cheesy **tourist train** meets arriving boats in summer and does a one-hour circuit (€10, two stops: mountaintop viewpoint and wine cellar for tasting). There are also various informal **boat** trips to villages up and down the Douro (ask TI for details).

Sights in Peso da Régua

Peso da Régua's sights are few, and most worthwhile for people without cars (who can't get into the countryside, where time is better spent). Downtown, you'll find **Casa do Douro,** the grand headquarters of the local port-wine industry (with pretty stained-glass windows inside).

▲**Douro Museum (Museu do Douro)**—This fine little museum—just a block uphill from Casa do Douro—traces the industry and culture of the Douro Valley, with a 3-D relief map of the region, stuffed specimens of local wildlife, models showing the construction of *rabelo* boats, and traditional costumes and musical instruments. You'll also see items relating to port production: tools, casks, barrels, decanters, port-wine bottles and labels, and advertising posters.

Cost and Hours: €5, Tue-Sun 10:00-18:00, closed Mon, tel. 254-310-190, www.museudodouro.pt. The museum shares the old warehouse with the Solar do Vinho do Porto (at Rua Marquês de Pombal in downtown Régua, described next).

▲**Solar do Vinho do Porto**—This facility, run by the Port and Douro Wines Institute, offers tastings and information about the region's products. Atmospherically situated in a renovated old warehouse with comfy chairs, it's a handy place to sample a variety of ports (Tue-Sat 11:00-13:00 & 14:00-18:00, closed Sun-Mon, right downtown at Rua da Ferreirinha, Armazém 43, tel. 254-320-960, www.ivdp.pt). You'll pay €1-20 per glass; the menu has meats, cheeses, and other delicious, traditional port-tasting snacks.

Quinta de São Domingos—This *quinta,* on a hill just above Peso da Régua, produces port for the big company Castelinho. This is the region's giant, impersonal *quinta*—a standard stop for large tour groups. The corporate experience reminds me of some of the port-wine lodges in Vila Nova de Gaia near Porto—not what you came all the way to the rustic Douro Valley for. The only thing good about it is its convenience for those without a car (free 10-minute tour with short movie and two tastes, Fri-Wed 9:00-13:00 & 14:00-18:00, closed Thu, restaurant, tel. 254-320-100, www.quinta desaodomingos.com). It's just above Régua at the train-station end of town (near the bridges); by foot, walk east (upriver) along the tracks, then cross the tracks through the hard-to-find gate (by the small pink building), and continue uphill to the *quinta* (about 15 minutes total).

Sleeping and Eating in Peso da Régua

You have two basic options for sleeping in the Douro Valley: Stay in a boring hotel or *residencial* in one of the towns (most likely Peso da Régua or Pinhão), or sleep at a picturesque *quinta* or *pousada* in the countryside. The in-town hotels are handy for those using public transportation, but if you've got a car, the *quintas* offer a better value and a more memorable Douro experience. The fancier places serve meals and have half-board options.

The Douro is extremely crowded during the grape harvest in late September and early October, and good rooms are in short supply to begin with; if visiting during this time, book as far ahead as possible. Simpler places charge the same rates year-round; more expensive hotels charge more for weekends and during the busy season (roughly April-Oct).

In the city of Peso da Régua, you have two choices, neither of which is traditional or charming: a tasteful, well-located hotel, or a cheap, basic hotel. If you have a car, get out of town!

$$ Hotel Régua Douro is the only classy option in town. With a top-floor panoramic breakfast room and 77 comfortable rooms—many of them with sweeping river views—it's a fine splurge (Sb-€52-68, Db-€67-86, higher prices are for July-Oct, add about €15-25 for weekends, riverview rooms are a good value at only €2-5 more than cityview rooms, suites available, air-con, elevator, expensive Internet in lobby, pool, Largo da Estação da C.P., tel. 254-320-700, fax 254-320-709, www.hotelreguadouro.pt, geral@hotelreguadouro.pt).

$ Império Hotel has a convenient, central location in a stark tower a block from the station and across the street from Hotel Régua Douro. Its 33 recently renovated rooms are basic and surrounded by busy streets, but the price is right (Sb-€35-40, Db-€45-50, Tb-€65-75, includes breakfast, air-con, Wi-Fi, Rua Vasques

Sleep Code

(€1 = about $1.30, country code: 351)
S = Single, **D** = Double/Twin, **T** = Triple, **Q** = Quad, **b** = bathroom, **s** = shower only. Unless otherwise noted, credit cards are accepted, and English is spoken.

To help you easily sort through these listings, I've divided the accommodations into three categories, based on the price for a standard double room with bath during high season.

$$$ Higher Priced—Most rooms €100 or more.
$$ Moderately Priced—Most rooms between €50-100.
$ Lower Priced—Most rooms €50 or less.

Prices can change without notice; verify the hotel's current rates online or by email.

Osório 8, tel. 254-320-120, fax 254-321-457, www.imperiohotel.com, info@imperiohotel.com).

Near Peso da Régua

$$ Quinta de Marrocos is a wonderful option if you want to stay at a real-life family farm. The Sequeira family farmhouse operates a simple shop and a family vineyard making good ports and table wines. The four rooms include a rustic yet deluxe living room, where the port's always out. Staying here, with the four dogs and farmhands, is a fun, authentic experience. It's a rare opportunity to spend time with locals who really love what they do (Sb-€50, Db-€70, 10 percent discount with this book, €20-25 meals with advance notice, on N-222 across the river and about 1.5 miles upstream from Peso da Régua, tel. 254-313-012, fax 254-322-680, www.quintademarrocos.com, info@quintademarrocos.com, Rita and her mother, Maria Elisa). They also rent a private two-bedroom family-friendly house on their property (€120).

Between Rêde and Mesão Frio

$$ Casa de Canilhas, located in the countryside about 15 minutes downriver from Peso da Régua, is an old traditional house set among the vines overlooking the river valley (Db-€60-120, Estrada Municipal de Banduja, Mesão Frio, tel. 254-891-181, mobile 917-558-006, fax 254-893-005, www.canilhas.com, info@canilhas.com).

Pinhão

Pinhão (PEEN-yow)—known locally as the "heart of the Douro"—feels like a real workaday small town, where locals go on with their "im-*port*-ant" business, oblivious to the tourists streaming through their streets. The big white silos are where the wine spends its first winter awaiting shipment downstream to Porto.

Orientation to Pinhão

Pinhão has virtually no sights, but it makes for a handy home base. Even if you don't arrive by train, be sure to check out the **train station**—adorned with tiles illustrating the people and traditions of the countryside. A few accommodations in and near Pinhão don't take credit cards; the lone **ATM** is in the BPI bank, on the left near the west end of town (toward Casal de Loivos).

Arrival in Pinhão: The town has a train station along the main road, and a boat landing down below on the river. The two *residencials* are across the street from the station, and the Vintage House Hotel is just upriver, next to the bridge. If you're arriving by **boat,** disembark to the right for the Vintage House; to reach the *residencials* or the station, leave the boat to the left, then loop up and to the right, around the big concrete wine-storage vats.

Tours: Vintage House Hotel organizes river trips on traditional *rabelo* boats for guests and non-guests (€10-20 for 1- to 2-hour trips, daily April-Oct at 10:30 and 14:30, schedule depends on demand and availability, call to reserve, tel. 254-730-230).

Sleeping in Pinhão

Your in-town options are a plush splurge hotel or two humble *residencials*. The *residencials* are next door to each other, across from the train station. Both operate fine restaurants, and both have riverview rooms that don't cost extra but come with some street noise;

neither has owners who speak English, but each sometimes has an English-speaking son available.

$$$ Vintage House Hotel is *the* place if you want to splurge on a fancy, formal hotel on the Douro (as opposed to a hillside *pousada* or manor house). It's all class, with a wonderfully atmospheric bar (under tree-trunk rafters), a good restaurant with an over-the-top formal interior and riverside terrace outdoor seating, and a wine shop featuring expensive tastings for aficionados (see "*Quintas* Tours and Tastings" on page 309). Each of its 43 rooms has a river view and a terrace or balcony, and elegant tile in the bathroom. The halls are lined with baskets of free local oranges and apples, as well as 19th-century photos of the Douro (Sb-€117-200, Db-€133-220, suites-€175-420, extra bed-€40-60, extra child's bed-€25-30, includes breakfast, air-con, elevator, pool, between train station and bridge at Lugar da Ponte, tel. 254-730-230, fax 254-730-238, www.cs-vintagehouse.com, bookings@cshotel sandresorts.com).

$ Hotel Douro offers 14 basic, clean, and bright rooms, many with cute riverview balconies (Sb-€37-40, Db-€45-60, breakfast-€5, cash only, air-con, Wi-Fi, Largo da Estação 39, tel. & fax 254-732-404, www.hotel-douro.com, geral@hotel-douro.com, Oliveira family).

$ Residencial Ponto Grande has 17 comparable rooms with lower prices and older furnishings (Sb-€25, Db-€40, cash only, air-con, Rua António Manuel Saraiva 41A at Largo da Estação, tel. 254-732-456, Vieira family).

Near Pinhão

$$$ Quinta de la Rosa, a mile downstream of Pinhão, is a riverside winery offering seven comfortable rooms with traditional country furnishings; all but one overlook the river (Sb/Db-€85-120, a bit less for 3 nights, extra child's bed-€20, includes breakfast, ask in advance for the €27.50 three-course dinner including wine and port; tel. 254-732-254, fax 254-732-346, www.quintadelarosa.com, holidays@quintadelarosa.com). They also offer in-depth tours and wine tastings (described earlier), and rent two houses by the week.

Getting There: Drivers leave Pinhão to the west (downriver), cross the concrete bridge, turn left and look for the *quinta* on the left side, up the hill. If walking: From the boat landing, cross the blue pedestrian bridge and continue 20 minutes (or take a €6 taxi from Pinhão station).

Above Pinhão, in Casal de Loivos

$$$ Casa de Casal de Loivos hovers on a lofty perch above Pinhão, with perhaps the most dramatic views in all of the Douro

Valley. The warm Sampayo family converted this 17th-century manor house into a six-room hotel with quaintly rustic furnishings and commanding Douro vistas. The family brags that when the BBC filmed a show about the best views in the world, they set up their camera right here (Sb-€80, Db-€100, discounts for longer stays, includes breakfast, dinner-€25/person without wine, cash only, swimming pool, closed Jan-mid-Feb, tel. & fax 254-732-149, www.casadecasaldeloivos.com, casadecasaldeloivos@ip.pt).

Getting There: The house is in the village of Casal de Loivos, atop the mountain over Pinhão. Leaving Pinhão to the west (downriver), first follow signs for *Alijó,* then for *Casal de Loivos,* and wind your way up the mountain roads. Once in town, look for the poorly marked villa on your right; if you reach the overlook with the white railing, you've gone a block too far. If you don't have wheels, catch a taxi from Pinhão's train station (about €6).

PORTUGAL: PAST and PRESENT

Portuguese Capsule History

2000 B.C.-A.D. 500: Prehistory to Rome

Portugal's indigenous race, the Lusiads, was a mix of peoples from many migrations and invasions—Neolithic stone builders (2000 B.C.), Phoenician traders (1200 B.C.), northern Celts (700 B.C.), Greek colonists (700 B.C.), and Carthaginian conquerors (500 B.C.).

By the time of Julius Caesar (50 B.C.), rebellious Lusitania (Portugal) was finally under Roman rule, with major cities at Olissipo (Lisbon), Portus Cale (Porto), and Ebora (Évora). The Romans brought laws, wine, the Latin language, and Christianity. When Rome's empire fell (A.D. 476), Portugal was saved from barbarian attacks by Christian Germanic Visigoths ruling distantly from their capital in Toledo.

A.D. 711-1400: Muslims vs. Christians, and Nationhood

North African Muslims invaded the Iberian Peninsula, settling in southern Portugal. Christians retreated to the cold, mountainous north, with central Portugal as a buffer zone. For the next five centuries, the Moors made Iberia a beacon of enlightenment in Dark Age Europe, while Christians slowly drove them out, one territory at a time. (Faro was the last Portuguese town to fall, in 1249.) Afonso Henriques, a popular Christian noble who conquered much Muslim land, was proclaimed king of Portugal (1139), creating one of Europe's first modern nation-states. John I solidified Portugal's nationhood by repelling a Spanish invasion (1385) and establishing his family (the House of Avis) as kings.

Eight Dates That Shaped Portugal

1128 "Portucale" separates from Castile.

1498 Vasco da Gama sails Portugal into a century of wealth.

1640 The Spanish are ousted; Portuguese gain their independence.

1755 A massive earthquake rocks Lisbon into poverty.

1822 Portugal loses Brazil as a colony.

1910 The monarchy is deposed, and repressive military regimes rule.

1974 A left-wing revolution brings democracy.

1986 Portugal joins the European Community (the forerunner of the European Union), boosting the economy.

1400-1600: The Age of Discovery

With royal backing, Portugal built a navy and began exploring the seas—using technology the Arabs had left behind—motivated by spice-trade profit and a desire to Christianize Muslim lands in North Africa. When Vasco da Gama finally inched around the southern tip of Africa and found a sea route to India (1498), suddenly the wealth of all Asia opened up. Through trade and conquest, tiny Portugal became one of Europe's wealthiest and most powerful nations, with colonies stretching from Brazil to Africa to India to China. Unfortunately, the easy money destroyed the traditional economy. When King Sebastian died, heirless, in a disastrous and draining defeat in Morocco, Portugal was quickly invaded by Spain (1580).

1600-1900: Slow Fade

The "Spanish Captivity" (1580-1640) drained Portugal. With a false economy, a rigid class system, and the gradual loss of their profitable colonies, Portugal was no match for the rising powers of Spain, England, Holland, and France. The earthquake of 1755 and Napoleon's invasions (1801-1810) were devastating. While the rest of Europe industrialized and democratized, Portugal lingered as an isolated, rural monarchy living off meager wealth from Brazilian gold and sugar.

1900s: The Military and Democracy

Republican rebels assassinated the king, but democracy was slow to establish itself in Portugal's near-medieval class system. A series

Portuguese Notables

Viriato (d. A.D. 139)—Legendary warrior who (unsuccessfully) resisted the Roman invasion.

Afonso Henriques (1095-1185)—Renowned Muslim-slayer and first king of a united, Christian nation.

Pedro I, the Just (1320-1367)—King and Father of John I, famous for his devotion to his murdered mistress, Inês de Castro.

John I (1358-1433)—King who preserved independence from Spain, launched an overseas expansion, fathered Prince Henry the Navigator, and established the House of Avis as the ruling family.

Henry the Navigator (1394-1460)—Devout, intellectual sponsor of naval expeditions during the Age of Discovery.

Bartolomeu Dias (1450-1500)—Navigator who rounded the tip of Africa in 1488, paving the way for Vasco da Gama.

Vasco da Gama (1460-1524)—Explorer who discovered the sea route to India, opening up Asia's wealth.

Pedro Cabral (1467-1520)—Explorer who found the sea route to Brazil (1500).

Ferdinand Magellan (1480-1521)—Voyager who, sailing for Spain, led the first circumnavigation of the globe (1520).

Manuel I, the Fortunate (r. 1495-1521)—Promoter of Vasco da Gama's explorations that made Portugal wealthy. Manueline, the decorative art style of that time, is named for him.

Luís de Camões (1524-1580)—Swashbuckling adventurer and poet who captured the heroism of Vasco da Gama in his epic poem, "The Lusiads."

Marquês de Pombal (1699-1782)—Controversial prime minister who tried to modernize backward Portugal and who rebuilt Lisbon after the 1755 quake.

José I, the Reformer (r. 1750-1777)—Disinterested king who effectively turned over control of Portugal to the Marquês de Pombal.

Fernando Pessoa (1888-1935)—Foremost Portuguese Modernist poet, immortalized in sculpture outside his favorite Lisbon café.

António Salazar (1889-1970)—"Portugal's Franco," a dictator who led for four decades, slowly modernizing while preserving rule by the traditional upper classes.

PAST & PRESENT

Typical Church Architecture

History comes to life when you visit a centuries-old church. Even if you wouldn't know your apse from a hole in the ground, learning a few simple terms will enrich your experience. Note that not every church has every feature, and a "cathedral" isn't a type of church architecture, but rather a designation for a church that's a governing center for a local bishop.

Aisles: The long, generally low-ceilinged arcades that flank the nave.

Altar: The raised area with a ceremonial table (often adorned with candles or a crucifix), where the priest prepares and serves the bread and wine for Communion.

Apse: The space beyond the altar, generally bordered with small chapels.

Barrel Vault: A continuous round-arched ceiling that resembles an extended upside-down U.

Choir: A cozy area, often screened off, located within the church nave and near the high altar, where services are sung in a more intimate setting.

Cloister: An open-air, usually square courtyard surrounded by covered walkways, traditionally where monks and nuns got fresh air.

Facade: The exterior surface of the church's main (west) entrance, generally highly decorated.

Groin Vault: An arched ceiling formed where two equal barrel

---

of military-backed democracies culminated in four decades of António Salazar's "New State," a right-wing regime benefiting the traditional upper classes. Salazar's repressive tactics and unpopular wars abroad (trying to hang onto Portugal's colonial empire) sparked the Carnation Revolution of 1974. After some initial political and economic chaos, Portugal finally mastered democracy.

Portugal Today

The early years of the 21st century were heady days for Portugal. The former backwater was suddenly booming—building super-freeways, planning a bullet train to Madrid, giving out lavish bonuses to workers, and buying fancy consumer goods from the rest of Europe. Scaffolding was everywhere, as the Portuguese scampered to finish a number of projects, which were funded in part by the European Union. The buzz was, "This easy money won't be here for long...it's use it or lose it. Quickly!"

The EU has worked to bring relatively poor regions (like much of Portugal) up to par with more-developed parts of Europe

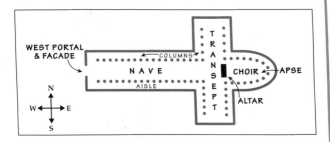

vaults meet at right angles. Less common usage: term for a medieval jock strap.

Narthex: The area (portico or foyer) between the main entry and the nave.

Nave: The long, central section of the church (running west to east, from the entrance to the altar) where the congregation sits or stands through the service.

Transept: In a traditional cross-shaped floor plan, the transept is one of the two parts forming the "arms" of the cross. The transepts run north-south, perpendicularly crossing the east-west nave.

West Portal: The main entry to the church (on the west end, opposite the main altar).

through matching grants and cheap construction loans. Since 1986 this development aid has amounted to about three percent of Portugal's GDP. Until very recently, interest rates for these loans were very low. As part of the EU, Portugal was considered a low-risk bet for lenders. But when the banking crisis shook the US in 2008, things got real. Money became tight worldwide, and lenders began assessing countries on their own merits rather than rolled in with the EU. The risk of lending to Portugal shot up—and so did interest rates.

Today, a hard reality is hitting Portugal: Much of the money it had spent wildly was not in fact a gift but, rather, a loan. And that loan needs to be paid back with interest at rates that have gone way up since 2008. The interest that Portugal owes on EU loans is crushing the local workforce. Unemployment is up to 15 percent. The country produces $230 billion annually—slightly more than the gross domestic product of Louisiana. And that economy is struggling.

In 2012, Portugal's major infrastructure projects have not just stalled—they've come to a full stop. The TGV bullet train from

Portugal's "Law 30"

Portugal has one of the more progressive drug policies today. In 2000, the government passed "Law 30," which decriminalized the consumption of all drugs. The law recently underwent a 10-year review. Although a conservative government has since replaced the more progressive government that established "Law 30," even former opponents agree that its benefits have far outweighed its harms. "Law 30" will continue to be the law of the land.

Portugal was repressed by a dictatorship until 1974. With freedom, people embraced their liberty, and formerly suppressed activities such as drug use temporarily spiked. In 1999, a group of experts came together to find a solution to the drug-use problem. They realized that the "war on drugs" was actually a "war on people." Similar to in the US, only about one percent of Portugal's population (100,000 out of 11 million people) was actually using hard drugs.

The goal of "Law 30" was to establish a legal framework for harm reduction. Drug addicts are considered to be sick, not criminals. Drug use and possession are still illegal, but no longer punishable with jail time. Instead offenders are given treatment, community service, or fines.

The review studied drug consumption trends from 2001 to 2009. Researchers summed up Portugal's experience this way: "Nothing bad happened." The big negatives some had predicted, including the expected advent of "drug tourism," didn't materialize (young backpackers didn't start converging on Portugal as the new drug mecca).

Statistically, the number of Portuguese people who have tried various drugs did increase a little (possibly because the new law made it more comfortable to admit drug use). But there was no change in actual usage rates. Drug use by young people (ages 15-24) actually fell in the long run; after going up in 2003—immediately after the new law went into effect—rates dropped back down by 2005. The slight increase of consumption in Portugal after "Law 30" was similar to increases in Italy and Spain during the same period—likely a regional trend unrelated to the change.

Other outcomes of "Law 30" are that Portugal now has fewer people with HIV and more people in treatment. The police like the law because it frees up resources to focus on violent crime. The burden on Portugal's prisons and criminal system has been reduced. And the Portuguese government went from being the enemy of its drug-using population to being its advocate.

Madrid to Lisbon, Lisbon's new airport, planned freeway expansion—all nice ideas, all put on indefinite hold.

A local friend told me, "In pre-euro days—with the *escudo* as our currency rather than the Deutsch Mark in disguise—when there was no money for chocolate milk, we just made do with white milk. Until 1974, when we won our freedom from Salazar, we were on the donkey system. Everything was slow. Then, with freedom we got the fever. And that accelerated with our membership in the European Union. Dazzled by German standards, we were encouraged to have faith in debt. Portugal got drunk on cheap European loans. And most of what we purchased with those loans was from Germany and France—feeding those economies—now, it seems, at the expense of our own."

In 2011, the EU approved a €78 billion bailout package, but with it came the requirement for strict austerity measures. To enforce these measures, the EU headquarters in Brussels has sent in "The Troika," a trio of managers tasked with helping Portugal get its economy back on a sustainable track. Austerity measures include more tolls on highways, higher deductibles for hospital visits, cutbacks in healthcare, and new taxes, including a 23 percent tax on all restaurant income. Utilities such as electricity are being privatized. The era of protecting traditional and inefficient industries is over. The retirement age has been raised from 65 to 67. And a worker-friendly scheme from the Carnation Revolution, which took a year's wage and broke it into 14 "months" rather than 12 (to give workers a "bonus" each summer and Christmas), has been rescinded. Now workers making more than €650 a month (about $850) get only 12 months' pay. Because this scheme was never really a "bonus" but rather a forced savings account, the change amounts to about a 15 percent pay cut.

The EU's "Troika" consider the Portuguese to be good, receptive workers willing to take their medicine responsibly (especially when compared with Greece). But Portugal's politicians have few resources and no easy solutions, while workers face a future where, it's feared, the only certainty is austerity.

APPENDIX

Contents

Tourist Information

Portugal's **national tourist office** will fill brochure requests and answer your general travel questions by email (info@visitportugal.com). Scan their website (www.visitportugal.com) for practical information and route ideas; you can download many brochures here free of charge.

In Portugal, your best first stop in any new city is the tourist information office—abbreviated **TI** in this book. A TI is a great place to get a city map and information on public transit (including bus and train schedules), walking tours, special events, and nightlife. Many TIs have information on the entire country or at least the region, so try to pick up maps for towns you'll be visiting later in your trip. If you're arriving in town after the TI closes, call ahead or pick up a map in a neighboring town.

For all the help TIs offer, steer clear of their room-finding services (bloated prices, booking fees, no opinions, and they take

Pronunciation of Portuguese Place Names

Lisboa leezh-BOH-ah
Sintra SEEN-trah
Cabo da Roca KAH-boh dah ROH-kah
Cascais kighsh-kighsh (igh = long i)
Salema sah-LAY-mah
Cape Sagres KAH-peh SAH-gresh
Lagos LAH-goosh
Tavira TAH-vih-rah
Évora EH-voh-rah

Nazaré NAH-zah-ray
Sítio SEE-tee-oh
Batalha hah-TAHL-yah
Fátima FAH-tee-mah
Alcobaça ahl-koh-BAH-sah
Óbidos OH-bee-doosh
Coimbra koh-EEM-brah
Porto POR-toh
Douro DOH-roh
Peso da Régua PAY-soh dah RAY-gwah
Pinhão PEEN-yow

a cut from your host). You'll save yourself and your host money by going direct with the listings in this book.

Communicating

Hurdling the Language Barrier

Although many Portuguese people—especially those in the tourist trade, and in big cities—speak English, Portugal can surprise English-speaking travelers with one of the biggest language barriers in Western Europe. Locals visibly brighten when you know and use some key Portuguese words (see "Portuguese Survival Phrases" on page 359). Travel with a phrase book, particularly if you want to interact with local people. You'll find that doors open quicker and with more smiles when you can speak a few words of the language.

If you speak intermediate Spanish, you'll be able to stumble through newspapers and read road signs, even if you can't pronounce the words. (Accent marks are keys to pronunciation, but nothing more.)

Surprisingly, English speakers do much better speaking Portuguese than the Spanish do, because we have roughly the same amount of vowel sounds. Spoken Portuguese sounds like a mix of a Slavic language and Spanish. If you want to take a Portuguese language course before your trip here, make sure your professor is Portuguese, not Brazilian—the accents are very distinct.

If you're having trouble communicating in Portuguese, try English, French, and Spanish, in that order (because some locals give Spanish speakers the cold shoulder). The Portuguese do, however, speak more English than their Spanish neighbors, since English is required in school. (Their American movies are also subtitled, while the Spanish get their Hollywood flicks dubbed.)

Considering how fun it is to eat local dishes, the food phrase list in this book is particularly helpful (see "Typical Portuguese Foods" on page 25). Use it, and you'll eat much better than the average tourist.

Telephones

Smart travelers use the telephone to book or reconfirm rooms, get tourist information, reserve restaurants, confirm tour times, or phone home. This section covers dialing instructions, phone cards, and types of phones (for more in-depth information, see www.rick steves.com/phoning).

How to Dial

Calling from the US to Europe, or vice versa, is simple—once you break the code. The European calling chart later in this chapter will walk you through it.

Dialing Domestically Within Portugal

Portugal has a direct-dial phone system (no area codes). All phone numbers in Portugal are nine digits that can be dialed direct throughout the country. For example, the number of one of my recommended Lisbon hotels is 213-219-030. That's the number you dial whether you're calling it from the Algarve or from across the street.

These instructions apply to dialing from a landline (such as a pay phone or your hotel-room phone) or a Portuguese mobile phone.

If you're dialing within Portugal using your US mobile phone, you may need to dial as if it's a domestic call, or you may need to dial as if you're calling from the US (see "Dialing Internationally," next). Try it one way, and if it doesn't work, try it the other way.

Dialing Internationally to or from Portugal

If you want to make an international call, follow these steps:

• Dial the international access code (00 if you're calling from Portugal, 011 from the US or Canada). If you're dialing from a mobile phone, you can replace the international access code with +, which works regardless of where you're calling from. (On many mobile phones, you can insert a + by pressing and holding the 0 key.)

• Dial the country code of the country you're calling (351 for Portugal, or 1 for the US or Canada).

• Dial the local number. (The European calling chart lists specifics per country.)

Calling from the US to Portugal: To call a Lisbon hotel from the US, dial 011 (US access code), 351 (Portugal's country code), then the hotel's nine-digit number (e.g., 213-219-030).

Calling from any European country to the US: To call my office in Edmonds, Washington, from anywhere in Europe, I dial 00 (Europe's access code), 1 (US country code), 425 (Edmonds' area code), and 771-8303.

Mobile Phones

Traveling with a mobile phone is handy and practical. Whether you're using a smartphone or a conventional cell phone, the basics for how to make calls and send texts are the same. For specifics on using your smartphone to get online, see the sidebar.

Roaming with Your Mobile Phone: Your US mobile phone works in Europe if it's GSM-enabled, tri-band or quad-band, and on a calling plan that includes international calls. Phones from AT&T and T-Mobile, which use the same GSM technology that Europe does, are more likely to work overseas than Verizon or Sprint phones (if you're not sure, ask your service provider). Most US providers will charge you $1.29-1.99 per minute to make or receive calls while roaming internationally, and 20-50 cents to send or receive text messages. If you bother to sign up for an international calling plan with your provider, you'll save a few dimes per minute. Though pricey, roaming on your own phone is easy and can be a cost-effective way to keep in touch—especially on a short trip or if you won't be making many calls.

Buying and Using SIM Cards in Europe: You'll pay much cheaper rates if you put a European SIM card in your mobile phone; to do this, your phone must be electronically "unlocked" (ask your provider about this, buy an unlocked phone before you leave, or get one in Europe—see "Other Mobile-Phone Options," next). Then, in Europe, you can simply buy a fingernail-size **SIM card,** which gives you a European phone number. SIM cards are available at mobile-phone stores and some newsstand kiosks for $5-10, and often include at least that much prepaid domestic calling time (making the card itself almost free). When you buy a SIM card, you may need to show ID, such as your passport.

Insert the SIM card in your phone (usually in a slot behind the battery or on the side), and it'll work like a European mobile phone. Before purchasing a SIM card, always ask about fees for domestic and international calls, roaming charges, and how to check your credit balance and buy more time. When you're in the SIM card's home country, domestic calls average 10-20 cents per minute, and incoming calls are free. Rates are higher if you're roaming in another country, and you may pay more to call a toll number than you would if you were dialing from a landline.

Other Mobile-Phone Options: Some travelers like to carry two phones—both their own US mobile phone (allowing them to stay reachable on their own phone number) and a second, unlocked European phone (which lets them do all their local calling at far cheaper rates). You could either bring two phones from home, or get one in Europe. If you have an old mobile phone sitting around, ask your provider for the "unlock code" so it can be used with European SIM cards. Or buy a cheap, basic phone before you go (search your favorite online shopping site for "unlocked quad-band GSM phone").

In Europe, basic phones are sold at hole-in-the-wall vendors at many airports and train stations, and at phone desks within larger department stores. Phones that are "locked" to work with a single provider start around $40; "unlocked" phones (which work with any SIM card) start around $60. Regardless of how you get your phone, remember that you'll need a SIM card to make it work.

Car-rental companies and mobile-phone companies offer the option to rent a mobile phone with a European number. While this seems convenient, hidden fees (such as high per-minute charges or expensive shipping costs) can really add up—which usually makes it a bad value. One exception is Verizon's Global Travel Program, available only to Verizon customers.

Calling over the Internet

Some things that seem too good to be true...actually are true. If you're traveling with a laptop, tablet, or smartphone, you can make free calls over the Internet to another wireless device, anywhere in the world, for free. (Or you can pay a few cents to call from your computer to a telephone.) The major providers are Skype, Google Talk, and (on Apple devices) FaceTime. You can get online at a Wi-Fi hotspot and use these apps to make calls without ringing up expensive roaming charges (though call quality can be spotty on slow connections). You can make Internet calls even if you're traveling without your own mobile device: Many European Internet cafés have Skype, as well as microphones and webcams, on their terminals—just log on and chat away.

Landline Telephones

As in the US, these days most Europeans do the majority of their phoning on mobile phones. But you'll still encounter landlines in hotel rooms and at pay phones.

Hotel-Room Phones: Calling from the phone in your room can be great for local calls and for international calls if you have an international phone card (described later). Otherwise, hotel-room

Smartphones and Data Roaming

I take my smartphone to Europe, using it to make phone calls (sparingly) and send texts, but also to check email, listen to audio tours, and browse the Internet. If you're clever, you can do all this without incurring huge data-roaming fees. Here's how.

Many smartphones, such as the iPhone, Android, and BlackBerry, work in Europe (though some older Verizon iPhones don't). For voice calls and text messaging, smartphones work like any mobile phone (as described under "Roaming with Your Mobile Phone," earlier)—unless you're connected to free Wi-Fi, in which case you can use Skype, Google Talk, or FaceTime to call for free (or at least very cheaply; see "Calling over the Internet," earlier).

The (potentially) *really* expensive aspect of using smartphones in Europe is not voice calls or text messages, but sky-high rates for data: checking email, browsing the Internet, streaming videos, using certain apps, and so on. If you don't proactively adjust your settings, these charges can mount up even if you're not actually using your phone—because the phone is constantly "roaming" to update your email and such. (One tip is to switch your email settings from "push" to "fetch," so you can choose when to download your emails rather than having them automatically "pushed" over the Internet to your device.)

The best solution: Disable data roaming entirely, and use your device to access the Internet only when you find free Wi-Fi (at your hotel, for example). Then you can surf the net to your heart's content, or make free (or extremely cheap) phone calls via Skype. You can manually turn off data roaming on your phone's menu (check under the "Network" settings). For added security, you can call and ask your service provider to temporarily suspend your data account entirely for the length of your trip.

Some travelers enjoy the flexibility of getting online even when they're not on free Wi-Fi. But be careful. If you simply switch on data roaming, you'll pay exorbitant rates of about $20 per megabyte (figure around 40 cents per email downloaded, or about $3 to view a typical web page)—much more expensive than it is back home. If you know you'll be doing some data roaming, it's far more affordable to sign up for a limited international data-roaming plan through your carrier (but be very clear on your megabyte limit to avoid inflated overage charges). In general, ask your provider in advance how to avoid unwittingly roaming your way to a huge bill.

phones can be an almost criminal rip-off for long-distance or international calls. Many hotels charge a fee for local and sometimes even "toll-free" numbers—always ask for the rates before you dial. Incoming calls are free, making this a cheap way for friends and family to stay in touch (provided they have a good long-distance plan with good international rates—and a list of your hotels' phone numbers).

Public Pay Phones: Coin-op phones are virtually extinct in Portugal. To make calls from public phones, you'll need a prepaid phone card, described next.

Metered Phones: In Portugal, some phone centers and bigger post offices have phones with meters. You can talk all you want, then pay the bill when you leave—but be sure you know the rates before you have a lengthy conversation. Note that charges can be "per unit" rather than per minute; find out the length of a unit.

Types of Telephone Cards

There are two types of phone cards: insertable (for pay phones) and international (cheap for overseas calls and usable from any type of phone). All insertable phone cards and most international phone cards work only in the country in which you purchase them. If you have a live card at the end of your trip, give it to another traveler to use—most cards expire three to six months after the first use.

Insertable Phone Cards: These cards, called *cartãos telefónicos,* can only be used at pay phones in Portugal. They're handy and affordable for local and domestic calls, but more expensive than international phone cards (covered next) for international calls. Insertable cards are sold at post offices and many newsstand kiosks. To use the card, physically insert it into a slot in the pay phone. While you can use these cards to call anywhere in the world, they're only a good deal for making quick local calls from a phone booth.

International Phone Cards: With these cards (called *cartão telefónico com código pessoal*), phone calls from Portugal to the US can cost less than a nickel a minute. The cards can also be used to make local calls, and they work from any type of phone, including your hotel-room phone or a mobile phone with a European SIM card. To use the card, dial a toll-free access number, then enter your scratch-to-reveal PIN code.

The cards are popular and easy to buy—look for them at Internet cafés, newsstands, souvenir shops, youth hostels, and post offices. Ask the clerk which of the various brands has the best rates for calls to America. Buy a lower denomination in case the card is a dud. Before buying a card, make sure the access number you dial is toll-free, not a local number (or else you'll be paying for a local call *and* deducting time from your calling card).

Since you don't need the actual card or receipt to use the account,

European Calling Chart

Just smile and dial, using this key:
AC = Area Code, LN = Local Number.

European Country	Calling long distance within ...	Calling from the US or Canada to ...	Calling from a European country to ...
Austria	AC + LN	011 + 43 + AC (without the initial zero) + LN	00 + 43 + AC (without the initial zero) + LN
Belgium	LN	011 + 32 + LN (without initial zero)	00 + 32 + LN (without initial zero)
Bosnia-Herzegovina	AC + LN	011 + 387 + AC (without initial zero) + LN	00 + 387 + AC (without initial zero) + LN
Britain	AC + LN	011 + 44 + AC (without initial zero) + LN	00 + 44 + AC (without initial zero) + LN
Croatia	AC + LN	011 + 385 + AC (without initial zero) + LN	00 + 385 + AC (without initial zero) + LN
Czech Republic	LN	011 + 420 + LN	00 + 420 + LN
Denmark	LN	011 + 45 + LN	00 + 45 + LN
Estonia	LN	011 + 372 + LN	00 + 372 + LN
Finland	AC + LN	011 + 358 + AC (without initial zero) + LN	999 (or other 900 number) + 358 + AC (without initial zero) + LN
France	LN	011 + 33 + LN (without initial zero)	00 + 33 + LN (without initial zero)
Germany	AC + LN	011 + 49 + AC (without initial zero) + LN	00 + 49 + AC (without initial zero) + LN
Gibraltar	LN	011 + 350 + LN	00 + 350 + LN
Greece	LN	011 + 30 + LN	00 + 30 + LN
Hungary	06 + AC + LN	011 + 36 + AC + LN	00 + 36 + AC + LN
Ireland	AC + LN	011 + 353 + AC (without initial zero) + LN	00 + 353 + AC (without initial zero) + LN

European Country	Calling long distance within ...	Calling from the US or Canada to ...	Calling from a European country to ...
Italy	LN	011 + 39 + LN	00 + 39 + LN
Montenegro	AC + LN	011 + 382 + AC (without initial zero) + LN	00 + 382 + AC (without initial zero) + LN
Morocco	LN	011 + 212 + LN (without initial zero)	00 + 212 + LN (without initial zero)
Netherlands	AC + LN	011 + 31 + AC (without initial zero) + LN	00 + 31 + AC (without initial zero) + LN
Norway	LN	011 + 47 + LN	00 + 47 + LN
Poland	LN	011 + 48 + LN	00 + 48 + LN
Portugal	LN	011 + 351 + LN	00 + 351 + LN
Slovakia	AC + LN	011 + 421 + AC (without initial zero) + LN	00 + 421 + AC (without initial zero) + LN
Slovenia	AC + LN	011 + 386 + AC (without initial zero) + LN	00 + 386 + AC (without initial zero) + LN
Spain	LN	011 + 34 + LN	00 + 34 + LN
Sweden	AC + LN	011 + 46 + AC (without initial zero) + LN	00 + 46 + AC (without initial zero) + LN
Switzerland	LN	011 + 41 + LN (without initial zero)	00 + 41 + LN (without initial zero)
Turkey	AC (if there's no initial zero, add one) + LN	011 + 90 + AC (without initial zero) + LN	00 + 90 + AC (without initial zero) + LN

- The instructions above apply whether you're calling to or from a European landline or mobile phone.

- If calling from any mobile phone, you can replace the international access code with "+" (press and hold 0 to insert it).

- The international access code is 011 if you're calling from the US or Canada.

- To call the US or Canada from Europe, dial 00, then 1 (country code for US and Canada), then the area code and number. In short, 00 + 1 + AC + LN = Hi, Mom!

you can write down the access number and code and share it with friends.

US Calling Cards: These cards, such as the ones offered by AT&T, Verizon, and Sprint, are a rotten value, and are being phased out. Try any of the options outlined earlier.

Useful Phone Numbers

Emergencies and Directory Assistance
Emergency: Tel. 112
Directory Assistance: Tel. 118 for local numbers; tel. 177 for international numbers.

Embassies
US Embassy: Tel. 217-273-300, passport services available Mon-Fri 8:00-17:00 (Avenida das Forças Armadas, Lisbon, http://portugal.usembassy.gov)
Canadian Embassy: Tel. 213-164-600, passport services available Mon-Fri 8:30-12:30 & 13:30-17:00 (Avenida da Liberdade 198-200, third floor, Lisbon, www.canadainternational.gc.ca/portugal)

Travel Advisories
US Department of State: US tel. 202/647-5225 (www.travel.state.gov)
Canadian Department of Foreign Affairs: Canadian tel. 800-267-6788 (www.dfait-maeci.gc.ca)
US Centers for Disease Control and Prevention: US tel. 800-CDC-INFO (800-232-4636, www.cdc.gov/travel)

Trains
Reservations and Information: Tel. 808-208-208, international tel. 351-213-185-990 (www.cp.pt).

Buses
Various regions are served by different bus lines; please see individual chapters for specific bus information.

Airports
The following airports share a website at www.ana.pt.
Lisbon (airport code: LIS): Portela Airport—tel. 218-413-500
Porto (airport code: OPO): Francisco Sá Carneiro Airport—tel. 229-432-400

Internet Access

It's useful to get online periodically as you travel—to confirm trip plans, check train or bus schedules, get weather forecasts, catch up on email, blog or post photos from your trip, or call folks back home (explained earlier, in "Calling over the Internet").

Your Mobile Device: Most hotels and some *pensãos* in Portugal offer Wi-Fi, as do many cafés, making it easy for you to get online with your laptop, tablet, or smartphone. Access is often free, but sometimes there's a fee.

Some hotel rooms and Internet cafés have high-speed Internet jacks that you can plug into with an Ethernet cable. A cellular modem—which lets your device access the Internet over a mobile network—provides more extensive coverage, but is much more expensive than Wi-Fi.

Public Internet Terminals: Most accommodations offer a computer in the lobby with Internet access for guests. If you ask politely, smaller places may sometimes let you sit at their desk for a few minutes just to check your email. If your hotel doesn't have access, ask to be directed to the nearest place to get online. Internet cafés are easy to find in big cities.

Security: Whether you're accessing the Internet with your own device or at a public terminal, using a shared network or computer comes with the potential for increased security risks. Be careful about storing personal information online, such as passport and credit-card numbers. If you're not convinced a connection is secure, avoid accessing any sites that could be vulnerable to fraud (e.g., online banking).

Mail

You can mail one package per day to yourself worth up to $200 duty-free from Europe to the US (mark it "personal purchases"). If you're sending a gift to someone, mark it "unsolicited gift." For details, visit www.cbp.gov and search for "Know Before You Go."

Get stamps at the neighborhood post office, newsstands within fancy hotels, and some mini-marts and card shops. The Portuguese postal service works fine, but for quick transatlantic delivery (in either direction), consider services such as DHL (www.dhl.com).

Transportation

By Car or Public Transportation?

If you're debating between public transportation and car rental, consider these factors: Cars are best for three or more traveling together (especially families with small kids), those packing heavy, and those scouring the countryside. Trains and buses are best for solo travelers, blitz tourists, city-to-city travelers, and those who don't want to drive in Europe.

Portugal's Public Transportation

SANTIAGO
LUGO
OURENSE → TO SAN SEBASTIÁN
VIGO
TUI
VALENÇA
BRAGA
PINHÃO
PORTO
REGUA
POCINHO
GUARDA
→ TO SALAMANCA
PAMPILHOSA
VILAR FORMOSO
→ TO SALAMANCA
FIG. DO FOZ
COIMBRA
NAZARÉ
VALADO
TO MADRID
ÓBIDOS
CÁCERES
SINTRA
ENTRON-CAMENTO
MARVÃO
BAD.
ELVAS
MÉRIDA
CASCAIS
LISBON
ÉVORA
FUNCHEIRA
BEJA
TO MADRID
SALEMA
TUNES
AVE
SAGRES
AYA.
SEVILLA
HUELVA
LAGOS
FARO
TAVIRA
VILA REAL.

S P A I N

—— RAIL LINES
‾AVE‾ AVE HIGH SPEED RAIL - SPAIN
- - - BUS
· · · · BOAT
○ BORDER TOWNS

Overview of Trains and Buses

Portugal straggles behind the rest of Europe in train service, but offers excellent bus transportation. Off the main Lisbon-Porto-Coimbra train lines, buses are usually a better bet. In cases where buses and trains serve the same destination, the bus is often more efficient, offering more frequent connections and sometimes a more central station. If schedules are similar, use the maps in this book to determine which station is closest to your hotel.

The best public transportation option is to mix bus and train travel. Always verify bus and train schedules before your departure, and never leave a station without the next day's schedule options in hand. To ask for a schedule at an information window, say, *"Horario para* (fill in names of cities), *faz favor."* (The local TI will sometimes have schedules available for you to take or copy.) To study train schedules in advance, see www.cp.pt for all domestic and Spain/France routes (schedules are downloadable PDFs). Another good resource, which also has schedules for trains throughout Europe, is German Rail's timetable (www.bahn.com).

Departures and arrivals are *partidas* and *chegadas*, respectively. These key Portuguese "fine print" words may also come in handy in your travels: Both *as* and *aos* mean "on"; *de* means "from," as in "from this date to that date"; *só* means "only," as in "only effective on..."; *não* means "not"; and *feriado* means "holiday." On schedules, exceptions are noted, as in this typical qualifier: *"Não se efectua aos sábados, domingos, e feriados oficiais"* ("Not effective on Saturdays, Sundays, and official holidays").

Trains *(Comboios)*

The fastest Alfa Pendular and Intercidades trains serve the main Lisboa-Porto line with an occasional extension to Faro or Braga and require seat reservations. Regional and Interregional "milk-run" trains serve most other routes, making lots of stops. On Portuguese train schedules, *diario* means "daily" and *mudança de comboio* means "change trains."

Railpasses: Because you'll use a mix of trains and buses on your trip, a Portugal Pass is generally not a good value. If you're traveling beyond Portugal, the Spain-Portugal Pass or Select Eurail Pass can make sense, but use the pass wisely, just for your long train trips. These passes are sold only outside of Europe. For specifics, see www.ricksteves.com/rail. Even if you have a railpass, use buses when they're more convenient and direct than the trains.

Overnight Trains: If you'll be going to Madrid, book ahead for the overnight train to ensure you get a berth and/or seat. It's a pricey Hotel Train called the "Lusitânia" (prices listed on page 124; railpass accepted if you pay extra sleeper fee). No cheaper rail option exists between these two capital cities. You can save money by taking a bus (€47, Intercentro Lines service using an Alsa bus), or save time by taking a plane (see "Cheap Flights," later in this chapter).

Buses *(Camionetas)*

Portugal has a number of different bus companies, sometimes running buses to the same destinations and using the same transfer points. If you have to transfer, make sure to look for a bus with the same name/logo as the company you bought the ticket from. The largest national company is Rede Expressos (covers buses both north and south of Lisbon, www.rede-expressos.pt, Portuguese only); EVA Transportes also covers some areas south of Lisbon (www.eva-bus.com). You can pre-plan bus trips between cities online, but you should always confirm the schedule in person.

If the bus station is not central, ask at the TI about travel agencies near your hotel that sell bus tickets. Don't leave a bus station to explore a city without checking your departure options and buying a ticket in advance if necessary (and possible). Bus service on holidays, Saturdays, and especially Sundays can be dismal.

You can (and most likely will be required to) stow your luggage under the bus. For longer rides, give some thought to which side of the bus will get the most sun, and sit on the opposite side. Even if a bus is air-conditioned and has curtains, direct sunlight can still heat up your seat. Long-distance (and most short-distance) buses are officially non-smoking. Your ride will likely come with a soundtrack: recorded music (usually American pop), a radio, or sometimes videos. If you prefer silence, bring earplugs.

Drivers and station personnel rarely speak English. Buses usually lack WCs but stop every two hours or so for a break (usually 15 minutes, but can be up to 30). Ask the driver, "How many minutes here?" *("Quántos minutos aqui?")* so you know if you have time to get out. Bus stations have WCs (rarely with toilet paper) and cafés offering quick and cheap food.

Bus schedules in Portugal are clearly posted at each major station. *Directo* is "direct." *Ruta* buses are slower because they make many stops en route. Posted schedules list most, but not all, destinations. If your intended destination isn't listed, check at the ticket/information window for the most complete schedule information. For long trips, your ticket might include an assigned seat.

Taxis *(Táxis)*

Most taxis are reliable and cheap. Drivers generally respond kindly to the request, "How much is it to (destination), more or less?" *("Quanto é para* (destination), *mais ou menos?")* Rounding the fare up to the nearest large coin (maximum of 10 percent) is adequate for a tip. City rides cost about $4-8. Keep a map in your hand so the cabbie knows (or thinks) you know where you're going. Big cities have plenty of taxis. In many cases, couples can travel by cab for little more than two bus or subway tickets.

Renting a Car

If you're renting a car in Portugal, bring your driver's license. It's recommended, but not required, that you also have an International Driving Permit (sold at your local AAA office for $15 plus the cost of two passport-type photos; see www.aaa.com); however, I've frequently rented cars in Portugal and traveled problem-free with just my US license.

Rental companies require you to be at least 21 years old and have held your license for one year. Drivers under the age of 25 may incur a young-driver surcharge, and some rental companies do not rent to anyone 75 or older. If you're considered too young or old, look into leasing, which has less-stringent age restrictions (see "Leasing," later).

Research car rentals before you go. It's cheaper to arrange most car rentals from the US. Call several companies and look online to compare rates, or arrange a rental through your hometown travel agent.

Most of the major US rental agencies (including National, Avis, Budget, Hertz, and Thrifty) have offices throughout Europe. The two major Europe-based agencies are Europcar and Sixt. It can be cheaper to use a consolidator, such as Auto Europe (www.autoeurope.com) or Europe by Car (www.ebctravel.com), which compares rates at several companies to get you the best deal. However, my readers have reported problems with consolidators, ranging from misinformation to unexpected fees; because you're going through a middleman, it can be more challenging to resolve disputes that arise with the rental agency.

Regardless of the car-rental company you choose, always read the contract carefully. The fine print can conceal a host of common add-on charges—such as one-way drop-off fees, airport surcharges, or mandatory insurance policies—that aren't included in the "total price," but can be tacked on when you pick up your car. You may need to query rental agents pointedly to find out your actual cost.

For the best rental deal, rent by the week with unlimited mileage. To save money on fuel, ask for a diesel car. I normally rent the smallest, least-expensive model with a stick-shift (cheaper than an automatic). An automatic transmission adds about 50 percent to the car-rental cost over a manual transmission. Almost all rentals are manual by default, so if you need an automatic, you must request one in advance; be aware that these cars are usually larger models (not as maneuverable on narrow, winding roads).

For a two-week rental, allow roughly $675 per person (based on two people sharing a car) for a small economy car with unlimited mileage, including gas, parking, and insurance. For a longer trip, look into leasing; you'll save money on insurance and taxes.

You can sometimes get a GPS unit with your rental car or leased vehicle for an additional fee (around $15/day; be sure it's set to English and has all the maps you need before you drive off). Or, if you have a portable GPS device at home, consider taking it with you to Europe (buy and upload European maps before your trip). GPS apps are also available for smartphones, but downloading maps on one of these apps in Europe could lead to an exorbitant data-roaming bill (for more details, see the sidebar on page 334).

Big companies have offices in most cities; ask whether they can pick you up at your hotel. Small local rental companies can be cheaper but aren't as flexible.

Compare pickup costs (downtown can be less expensive than the airport) and explore drop-off options. When selecting a location, don't trust the agency's description of "downtown" or "city center." In some cases, a "downtown" branch can be on the outskirts of the city—a long, costly taxi ride from the center. Before choosing, plug the addresses into a mapping website. You may find that the "train station" location is more central. Returning a car at a big-city train station or downtown agency can be tricky; get precise details on the car drop-off location and hours, and allow ample time to follow it. Note that rental offices may close from midday Saturday until Monday morning.

When you pick up the car, check it thoroughly and make sure any damage is noted on your rental agreement. Find out how your car's lights, turn signals, wipers, and fuel cap function, and know what kind of fuel the car takes. When you return the car, make sure the agent verifies its condition with you.

Car Insurance Options

When you rent a car, you are liable for a very high deductible, sometimes equal to the entire value of the car. Limit your financial risk by choosing one of these three options: Buy Collision Damage Waiver (CDW) coverage from the car-rental company, get coverage through your credit card (free, if your card automatically includes zero-deductible coverage), or buy coverage through Travel Guard.

CDW includes a very high deductible (typically $1,000-1,500). Though each rental company has its own variation, basic CDW costs $15-35 a day (figure roughly 30 percent extra) and reduces your liability, but does not eliminate it. When you pick up the car, you'll be offered the chance to "buy down" the deductible to zero (for an additional $10-30/day; this is sometimes called "super CDW").

If you opt for **credit-card coverage,** there's a catch. You'll technically have to decline all coverage offered by the car-rental company, which means they can place a hold on your card (which can be up to the full value of the car). In case of damage, it can be time-consuming to resolve the charges with your credit-card company. Before you decide on this option, quiz your credit-card company about how it works.

Portugal by Car: Mileage & Time

100 Kilometers

50 Miles

To Santiago de Compostela

Atlantic Ocean

145m • 3.5h →

60m • 1.5h

Porto • Peso da Régua

Pinhão

15m .5h

75m • 1.5h

100m • 2h

165m • 3h

190m • 4h

Salamanca

60m • 1h

Coimbra

135m • 2.75h

Ciudad Rodrigo

55m • 1h

PORTUGAL

40m • 1h

Nazaré

25m • .5h

Fátima

Óbidos

60m • 1.25h

240m • 4h

SPAIN

60m • 1.25h →

80m • 1.5h

1.25h

60m • 1.25h

Sintra

20m • .5h

90m • 2.5h

3.5h

315m • 5.5h (via Badajoz) →

To Madrid

Lisbon

Évora

185m • 3h

155m • 3h

265m • 5h

185m • 3h

155m • 3h

(via Beja)

13m • .5h

Lagos

Sagres •

70m • 1h

100m • 1.5h

Salema

13m • .5h

Tavira

Sevilla

**m = miles
h = hours**

Note: Your times may vary based on traffic, construction & road conditions.

APPENDIX

Finally, you can buy CDW insurance from **Travel Guard** ($9/ day plus a one-time $3 service fee covers you up to $35,000, $250 deductible, tel. 800-826-4919, www.travelguard.com). It's valid everywhere in Europe except the Republic of Ireland, and some Italian car-rental companies refuse to honor it. Note that various US states differ on which products and policies are available to their residents.

For more on car-rental insurance, see www.ricksteves.com/ cdw.

Leasing

For trips of three weeks or more, consider leasing (which automatically includes zero-deductible collision and theft insurance). By technically buying and then selling back the car, you save lots of money on tax and insurance. Leasing provides you a brand-new car with unlimited mileage and a 24-hour emergency assistance program. You can lease for as little as 21 days to as long as six months. Car leases must be arranged from the US. One of many reliable companies offering affordable lease packages is Europe by Car (US tel. 800-223-1516, www.ebctravel.com).

Driving

Drivers in Portugal encounter sparse traffic and very good roads connecting larger cities.

Road Rules: Be aware of typical European road rules. For example, many countries require headlights to be turned on at all times, and it's generally illegal to drive while using your mobile phone without a hands-free headset. Seat belts are required by law in Portugal. Ask your car-rental company about these rules, or check the US State Department website (www.travel.state.gov, click on "International Travel," then specify your country of choice and click "Traffic Safety and Road Conditions").

Portugal, statistically one of Europe's most dangerous places to drive, has lots of ambulances on the road. Drive defensively. If you're involved in an accident, expect a monumental headache—you will be blamed. Expect to be stopped for a routine check by the police (be sure your car insurance form is up-to-date). Small towns come with speed traps and corruption. Tickets, especially for foreigners, are issued and paid for on the spot. Insist on a receipt, so the money is less likely to end up in the cop's pocket.

Fuel: Gas and diesel prices are government-controlled and the same everywhere—around $7 a gallon for gas *(gasolina)* and less for diesel *(diesel)*. Unleaded pumps are usually green. Note that your US credit and debit cards are unlikely to work at self-service gas pumps, as well as toll bridges and automated parking garages. It might help if you know your credit card's PIN code, but just in case, be sure to carry sufficient cash.

Navigation: On freeways, navigate by direction (*norte* = north, *oeste* = west, *sul* = south, *este* = east). Also, since road numbers can be confusing and inconsistent, navigate by city names. You can pick up a Michelin map in the US or buy one of the good, inexpensive maps available throughout Portugal.

Tolls: Freeways come with tolls (about $5/hour), but save huge amounts of time. Always pick up a ticket as you enter a toll freeway and then pick up tickets at each opportunity along the way (or risk a fine). Don't use the no-stop-necessary speed lane (labeled *Reservada a Aderentes*, reserved for locals with a monthly pass), or you'll pay for a trip across the country in order to exit—a lesson I learned the expensive way.

Some roads—such as the A-22 along the Algarve—are tolled electronically. Rental cars in these areas often come equipped with an electronic sensor, which automatically registers the tolls (you'll pay when you return the car). If you're driving a car without a sensor, you have five days to pay the toll at any post office, some gas stations, and "pay shops" (small stores and kiosks with a red "pay shop" decal). If you drive into Portugal in a rental car from Spain, France, or another country, you can buy a pass just past the border (3-day pass-€20.62; 5-day refillable pass-€10 minimum).

Parking: Choose parking places carefully. Parking areas in cities generally have a large white "P" on a blue background. Don't assume it's free—check around for meters or ticketing machines. Keep your valuables in your hotel room or, if you're between destinations, covered in your trunk. Leave nothing worth stealing in the car, especially overnight. If your car's a hatchback, take the trunk cover off at night so thieves can look in without breaking in. Try to make your car look locally owned by hiding the "tourist-owned" rental-company decals and putting a Portuguese newspaper in your front or back window. Ask your hotelier for advice on parking. In cities, you can park safely but expensively in guarded lots. While you should avoid parking lots with twinkly asphalt, thieves break car windows anywhere, even at stoplights.

Cheap Flights

If you're considering a train ride that's more than five hours long, a flight may save you both time and money. When comparing your options, factor in the time it takes to get to the airport and how early you'll need to arrive to check in.

The best comparison search engine for both international and intra-European flights is www.kayak.com. For inexpensive flights within Europe, try www.skyscanner.com or www.hipmunk.com.

If you're not sure who flies to your destination, check its airport's website for a list of carriers.

For flights within Portugal, the country's national carrier is **TAP** (www.flytap.com). For flights between Lisbon and other cities in Europe, also try **Iberia** (www.iberia.com), **Vueling Airlines** (www.vueling.com), and **easyJet** (www.easyjet.com).

Be aware of the potential drawbacks of flying on the cheap: nonrefundable and nonchangeable tickets, minimal or nonexistent customer service, treks to airports far outside town, and stingy baggage allowances with steep overage fees. If you're traveling with lots of luggage, a cheap flight can quickly become a bad deal. To avoid unpleasant surprises, read the small print before you book.

Resources

Resources from Rick Steves

Rick Steves' Portugal is one of many books in my series on European travel, which includes country guidebooks, city guidebooks (Rome, Florence, Paris, London, etc.), Snapshot guides (excerpted chapters from my country guides), Pocket Guides (full-color little books on big cities), and my budget-travel skills handbook, *Rick Steves' Europe Through the Back Door*. Most of my titles are available as ebooks. My phrase books—for Portuguese, Spanish, German, French, and Italian—are practical and budget-oriented. My other books include *Europe 101* (a crash course on art

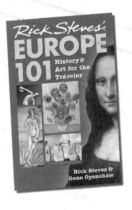

and history), *Mediterranean Cruise Ports* (how to make the most of your time in port), and *Travel as a Political Act* (a travelogue sprinkled with tips for bringing home a global perspective). A more complete list of my titles appears near the end of this book.

Video: My public television series, *Rick Steves' Europe*, covers European destinations in 100 shows, with two episodes on Portugal. To watch episodes online, visit www.hulu.com; for scripts and local airtimes, see www.ricksteves.com/tv.

Audio: My weekly public radio show, *Travel with Rick Steves*, features interviews with travel experts from around the world. All of this free audio content is available at Rick Steves Audio Europe, an extensive online library organized by destination. Choose whatever interests you, and download it via

the Rick Steves Audio Europe smartphone app, www.ricksteves.com/audioeurope, iTunes, or Google Play.

Maps

The black-and-white maps in this book, drawn by Dave Hoerlein, are concise and simple. Dave, who is well-traveled in Portugal, designed the maps to help you locate recommended places and get to local TIs, where you can pick up a more in-depth map of the city or region (usually free).

Better maps are sold at newsstands and bookstores. Before you buy a map, look at it to make sure it has the level of detail you want. Train travelers can usually manage fine with the freebies they get at the local tourist offices. But drivers shouldn't skimp on maps—get one good overall road map for Portugal (a 1:400,000 map, such as Michelin's *Spain & Portugal Tourist and Motoring Atlas* or *Portugal Map,* is a fine bet). Good regional driving maps are available throughout Portugal. An up-to-date map is essential—it can mean the difference between choosing an old, slow road or saving an hour by finding the brand-new highway.

Other Guidebooks

If you're like most travelers, this book is all you need. But if you're heading beyond my recommended destinations, $40 for extra maps and books can be money well-spent.

The following books are worthwhile, though most are not updated annually; check the publication date before you buy. Lonely Planet's *Portugal* is thorough, well-researched, and packed with good maps and hotel recommendations for various budgets. The similar *Rough Guide to Portugal* is hip and insightful, written by British researchers. (If choosing between these two titles, I buy the one that was published most recently.) Students, backpackers, and nightlife-seekers should consider the *Let's Go Spain & Portugal* guidebook (by Harvard students, has the best hostel listings). *Culture Shock! Portugal* provides insights into the culture, customs, and mentality of the Portuguese people.

Dorling Kindersley publishes snazzy *Eyewitness* and *Eyewitness Top 10* guides, covering Portugal, Lisbon, and the Algarve. While pretty to look at, these books weigh a ton and are skimpy on actual content.

Older travelers enjoy Frommer's *Portugal* guide, even though it, like the Fodor's guide, tends to ignore alternatives that enable travelers to save money by dirtying their fingers in the local culture. The popular, skinny *Michelin Green Guide: Portugal* is excellent, especially if you're driving. The Green Guides are known for their city and sightseeing maps, dry but concise and helpful information on all major sights, and good cultural and historical background.

APPENDIX

Begin Your Trip at www.ricksteves.com

At ricksteves.com, you'll find a wealth of free information on European destinations, including fresh monthly news and helpful tips from thousands of fellow travelers. You'll find my latest guidebook updates (www.ricksteves.com/update), a monthly travel e-newsletter (easy and free to sign up), my personal travel blog, and my free Rick Steves Audio Europe smartphone app (if you don't have a smartphone, you can access the same content via podcasts). You can even follow me on Facebook and Twitter.

Our **online Travel Store** offers travel bags and accessories that I've designed specifically to help you travel smarter and lighter. These include my popular carry-on bags (rolling bag and backpack versions), money belts, totes, toiletries kits, adapters, other accessories, and a wide selection of guidebooks, planning maps, and DVDs.

Choosing the right **railpass** for your trip—amid hundreds of options—can drive you nutty. We'll help you choose the best pass for your needs, plus give you a bunch of free extras.

Want to travel with greater efficiency and less stress? We organize **tours** with three dozen itineraries and more than 500 departures reaching the best destinations in this book... and beyond. We offer a 12-day Heart of Portugal tour that hits the highlights of this history-rich country. You'll enjoy great guides, a fun bunch of travel partners (with small groups of generally around 24-28), and plenty of room to spread out in a big, comfy bus. You'll find European adventures to fit every vacation length. For all the details, and to get our Tour Catalog and a free Rick Steves' Tour Experience DVD (filmed on location during an actual tour), visit www.ricksteves.com or call us at 425/608-4217.

English editions are sold in Portugal. The *Time Out* travel guide provides good, detailed coverage of Lisbon, particularly on arts and entertainment.

Portuguese history is mentioned (but not thoroughly covered) in various guidebooks, such as Cadogan, Eyewitness, and the Michelin Green Guide.

Recommended Books and Movies

To learn more about Portugal past and present, check out a few of these books and films.

Nonfiction

For a concise, readable history of this country, pick up *Portugal: A Companion History* (Saraiva), or *The History of Portugal* (Anderson).

For a lively account of the Portuguese sea voyages and discoveries in the 15th and 16th centuries, see *The Portuguese Empire, 1415-1808: A World on the Move* (Russell-Wood). The biography *Prince Henry the Navigator: A Life* (Russell) reveals the man who helped set in motion the Age of Discovery. Other famous Portuguese mariners are described in *Over the Edge of the World: Magellan's Terrifying Circumnavigation of the Globe* (Bergreen) and *Unknown Seas: How Vasco da Gama Opened the East* (Watkins).

To explore Portugal's cuisine, read *Food of Portugal* (Anderson) or Lonely Planet's *World Food Portugal* (Scott-Aitken and De Macedo Vitorino).

Fiction

The Lusiads (Os Lusíadas), by Luís de Camões, is one of the greatest epic poems of the Renaissance, immortalizing Portugal's voyages of discovery; it's considered a national treasure. Also look for the work of Fernando Pessoa, a 20th-century Portuguese poet.

Jose Maria Eça De Queirós, who wrote in part to bring about social reform, is considered by some to be the greatest 19th-century Portuguese novelist. English translations include *The Crime of Father Amaro*, which highlighted the dangers of fanaticism in a provincial Portuguese town.

Nobel prize-winning author Jose Saramago's novel *Baltasar and Blimunda* offers a surrealistic reflection on life in 18th-century Portugal, while his books *Blindness* and *Seeing* are satires on society and politics.

Set in Portugal in 1938 during Salazar's fascist government, *Pereira Declares: A Testimony* (Tabucchi) is the story of the moral resurrection of a newspaper's cautious editor. Another novel by Tabucchi is *Requiem: A Hallucination*.

In *A Small Death in Lisbon* (Wilson), a contemporary police procedural is woven with an espionage story set during World War

II, with Portugal's 20-century history as a backdrop. In *Distant Music* (Langley), Catholic Esperanca and Jewish Emmanuel have an affair that lasts through six centuries and multiple incarnations, and describes Portugal's maritime empire, Sephardic Jews, and Portuguese immigrants in London. *The Last Kabbalist of Lisbon* (Zimler), a thriller, illuminates the persecution of the Jews in Portugal in the early 1500s.

Films

Marcello Mastroianni is the namesake in *Pereira Declares* (1996), inspired by the Tabucchi novel mentioned earlier.

Capitães de Abril (2000) relates the 1974 coup that overthrew the right-wing Portuguese dictatorship, from the perspective of two young army captains.

Amália (2008) tells the story of Portugal's beloved fado singer Amália Rodrigues, who rose from poverty to international fame.

Holidays and Festivals

This list includes selected festivals in major cities, plus national holidays observed throughout Portugal. Many sights and banks close on national holidays—keep this in mind when planning your itinerary. Before planning a trip around a festival, verify its dates by checking the festival's website or TI website (www.visitportugal.com); www.whatsonwhen.com also lists many festival dates.

Jan 1	New Year's Day
Mardi Gras Carnival	Feb 12 in 2013, March 4 in 2014
Holy Week	Week before Easter
Easter	March 31 in 2013, April 20 in 2014
April 25	Liberty Day (parades, fireworks)
May 1	Labor Day (closures)
May 13	Pilgrimage to Fátima
Late May-early July	Festival de Sintra, Sintra (www.festivaldesintra.pt)
Corpus Christi	May 30 in 2013, June 19 in 2014
June 10	Portuguese National Day (Camões Day)
June 13	St. Anthony's Day, Lisbon; Pilgrimage to Fátima
Late June	Festas de Lisboa, Lisbon (last three weeks of June)
June 24	St. João Day, Porto
June 29	St. Peter's Day, Lisbon
July 13	Pilgrimage to Fátima
Aug 13	Pilgrimage to Fátima
Aug 15	Assumption (religious festival)

Aug 19	Pilgrimage to Fátima
Sept 13	Pilgrimage to Fátima
Mid-Sept	Our Lady of Nazaré Festival, Nazaré
Oct 5	Republic Day (businesses closed)
Oct 13	Pilgrimage to Fátima
Nov 1	All Saints' Day
Dec 1	Independence Restoration Day
Dec 8	Feast of the Immaculate Conception
Dec 25	Christmas
Dec 31	New Year's Eve

Conversions and Climate

Numbers and Stumblers

- Some Europeans write a few of their numbers differently than we do. 1 = 1, 4 = 4, 7 = 7.
- In Europe, dates appear as day/month/year, so Christmas is 25/12/14.
- Commas are decimal points and decimals commas. A dollar and a half is 1,50, and there are 5.280 feet in a mile.
- When counting with fingers, start with your thumb. If you hold up your first finger to request one item, you'll probably get two.
- What Americans call the second floor of a building is the first floor in Europe.
- On escalators and moving sidewalks, Europeans keep the left "lane" open for passing. Keep to the right.

APPENDIX

Metric Conversions (approximate)

A kilogram is 2.2 pounds, and l liter is about a quart, or almost four to a gallon. A kilometer is six-tenths of a mile. I figure kilometers to miles by cutting them in half and adding back 10 percent of the original (120 km: 60 + 12 = 72 miles, 300 km: 150 + 30 = 180 miles).

1 foot = 0.3 meter	1 square yard = 0.8 square meter
1 yard = 0.9 meter	1 square mile = 2.6 square kilometers
1 mile = 1.6 kilometers	1 ounce = 28 grams
1 centimeter = 0.4 inch	1 quart = 0.95 liter
1 meter = 39.4 inches	1 kilogram = 2.2 pounds
1 kilometer = 0.62 mile	32°F = 0°C

Clothing Sizes

When shopping for clothing, use these US-to-European comparisons as general guidelines (but note that no conversion is perfect).

- Women's dresses and blouses: Add 30
  (US size 10 = European size 40)

- Men's suits and jackets: Add 10
  (US size 40 regular = European size 50)
- Men's shirts: Multiply by 2 and add about 8
  (US size 15 collar = European size 38)
- Women's shoes: Add about 30
  (US size 8 = European size 38-39)
- Men's shoes: Add 32-34
  (US size 9 = European size 41; US size 11 = European size 45)

Climate

First line, average daily high; second line, average daily low; third line, average days without rain. For more detailed weather statistics for destinations in this book (as well as the rest of the world), check www.worldclimate.com.

J	F	M	A	M	J	J	A	S	O	N	D
Lisbon											
57°	59°	63°	67°	71°	77°	81°	82°	79°	72°	63°	58°
46°	47°	50°	53°	55°	60°	63°	63°	62°	58°	52°	47°
16	16	17	20	21	25	29	29	24	22	17	16
Faro (Algarve)											
60°	61°	64°	67°	71°	77°	83°	83°	78°	72°	66°	61°
48°	49°	52°	55°	58°	64°	67°	68°	65°	60°	55°	50°
22	21	21	24	27	29	31	31	29	25	22	22

Temperature Conversion: Fahrenheit and Celsius

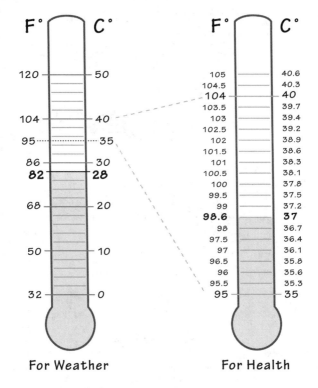

For Weather

For Health

Portugal takes its temperature using the Celsius scale, while we opt for Fahrenheit. For a rough conversion from Celsius to Fahrenheit, double the number and add 30. For weather, remember that 28°C is about 82°F—perfect. For health, 37°C is 98.6°F.

Hotel Reservation

To: _____   _____
                  hotel   *email or fax*

From: _____   _____
                  name   *email or fax*

Today's date: _____ /_____ /_____
                      day   *month*   *year*

Dear Hotel _____ ,

Please make this reservation for me:

Name: _____

Total # of people: _____   # of rooms: _____   # of nights: _____

Arriving: ____ /____ /____   My time of arrival (24-hr clock): _____
              day *month* *year*   (I will telephone if I will be late)

Departing: ____ /____ /____
                day *month* *year*

Room(s): Single____   Double ____   Twin ____   Triple ____   Quad____

With: Toilet ____   Shower ____   Bath ____   Sink only ____

Special needs: View____   Quiet ____   Cheapest ____   Ground Floor____

Please email or fax confirmation of my reservation, along with the type of room reserved and the price. Please also inform me of your cancellation policy. After I hear from you, I will quickly send my credit-card information as a deposit to hold the room. Thank you.

_____
Name

_____
Address

_____
City   *State*   *Zip Code*   *Country*

Before hoteliers can make your reservation, they want to know the information listed above. You can use this form as the basis for your email, or you can photocopy this page, fill in the information, and send it as a fax (also available online at www.ricksteves.com/reservation).

Packing Checklist

Whether you're traveling for five days or five weeks, here's what you'll need to bring. Pack light to enjoy the sweet freedom of true mobility. Happy travels!

- ❏ 5 shirts: long- and short-sleeve
- ❏ 1 sweater or lightweight fleece
- ❏ 2 pairs pants
- ❏ 1 pair shorts
- ❏ 1 swimsuit
- ❏ 5 pairs underwear and socks
- ❏ 1 pair shoes
- ❏ 1 rainproof jacket with hood
- ❏ Tie or scarf
- ❏ Money belt
- ❏ Money—your mix of:
  - ❏ Debit card (for ATM withdrawals)
  - ❏ Credit card
  - ❏ Hard cash (in easy-to-exchange $20 bills)
- ❏ Documents plus photocopies:
  - ❏ Passport
  - ❏ Printout of airline eticket
  - ❏ Driver's license
  - ❏ Student ID and hostel card
  - ❏ Railpass/car rental voucher
  - ❏ Insurance details
- ❏ Daypack
- ❏ Electronics—your choice of:
  - ❏ Camera (and related gear)
  - ❏ Computer/mobile devices (phone, MP3 player, ereader, etc.)
  - ❏ Chargers for each of the above
  - ❏ Plug adapter
- ❏ Empty water bottle

- ❏ Wristwatch and alarm clock
- ❏ Earplugs
- ❏ Toiletries kit
  - ❏ Toiletries
  - ❏ Medicines and vitamins
  - ❏ First-aid kit
  - ❏ Glasses/contacts/sunglasses (with prescriptions)
- ❏ Sealable plastic baggies
- ❏ Laundry soap
- ❏ Clothesline
- ❏ Small towel
- ❏ Sewing kit
- ❏ Travel information (guidebooks and maps)
- ❏ Address list (for sending postcards)
- ❏ Postcards and photos from home
- ❏ Notepad and pen
- ❏ Journal

APPENDIX

If you plan to carry on your luggage, note that all liquids must be in 3.4-ounce or smaller containers and fit within a single quart-size sealable baggie. For details, see www.tsa.gov.

Portuguese Survival Phrases

In the phonetics, nasalized vowels are indicated by an underlined **n** or **w**
As you say the vowel, let its sound come through your nose as well as
your mouth.

Good day.	Bom dia.	boh<u>n</u> **dee**-ah
Do you speak English?	Fala inglês?	**fah**-lah een-**glaysh**
Yes. / No.	Sim. / Não.	seeng / no<u>w</u>
I (don't) understand.	(Não) compreendo.	(no<u>w</u>) koh<u>n</u>-pree-**ayn**-doo
Please.	Por favor.	poor fah-**vor**
Thank you. (said by male)	Obrigado.	oh-bree-**gah**-doo
Thank you. (said by female)	Obrigada.	oh-bree-**gah**-dah
I'm sorry.	Desculpe.	dish-**kool**-peh
Excuse me (to pass).	Com licença.	koh<u>n</u> li-**sehn**-sah
(No) problem.	(Não) há problema.	(no<u>w</u>) ah proo-**blay**-mah
Good.	Bom.	boh<u>n</u>
Goodbye.	Adeus or Ciao.	ah-**deh**-oosh, chow
one / two	um / dois	oo<u>n</u> / doysh
three / four	três / quarto	traysh / **kwah**-troo
five / six	cinco / seis	**seeng**-koo / saysh
seven / eight	sete / oito	**seh**-teh / **oy**-too
nine / ten	nove / dez	**naw**-veh / dehsh
How much is it?	Quanto é?	**kwahn**-too eh
Write it?	Escreva?	ish-**kray**-vah
Is it free?	É gratis?	eh **grah**-teesh
Is it included?	Está incluido?	ish-**tah** een-kloo-**ee**-doo
Where can I find / buy...?	Onde posso encontrar / comprar...?	oh<u>n</u>-deh **paw**-soo ayn-koh<u>n</u>-**trar** / koh<u>n</u>-**prar**
I'd like / We'd like...	Gostaria / Gostaríamos...	goosh-tah-**ree**-ah / goosh-tah-**ree**-ah-moosh
...a room.	...um quarto.	oo<u>n</u> **kwar**-too
...a ticket to ___.	...um bilhete para ___.	oo<u>n</u> beel-**yeh**-teh **pah**-rah
Is it possible?	É possível?	eh poo-**see**-vehl
Where is...?	Onde é que é...?	oh<u>n</u>-deh eh keh eh
...the train station	...a estação de comboio	ah ish-tah-**sow** deh koh<u>n</u>-**boy**-yoo
...the bus station	...a terminal de autocarros	ah tehr-mee-**nahl** deh ow-too-**kah**-roosh
...the tourist information office	...a informação turistica	ah een-for-mah-**sow** too-**reesh**-tee-kah
...the toilet	...a casa de banho	ah **kah**-zah deh **bahn**-yoo
men	homens	**aw**-mayn<u>n</u>sh
women	mulheres	mool-**yeh**-rish
left / right	esquerda / direita	ish-**kehr**-dah / dee-**ray**-tah
straight	em frente	ayn **frayn**-teh
What time does this open / close?	As que horas é que abre / fecha?	ahsh keh **aw**-rahsh eh keh **ah**-breh / **feh**-shah
At what time?	As que horas?	ahsh keh **aw**-rahsh
Just a moment.	Um momento.	oo<u>n</u> moo-**mayn**-too
now / soon / later	agora / em breve / mais tarde	ah-**goh**-rah / ay<u>n</u> **bray**-veh / maish **tar**-deh
today / tomorrow	hoje / amanhã	oh-zheh / ah-ming-**yah**

APPENDIX

In the Restaurant

I'd like / We'd like..	Gostaria / Gostaríamos...	goosh-tah-**ree**-ah / goosh-tah-**ree**-ah-moosh
...to reserve...	.. de reservar...	deh reh-zehr-**var**
...a table for one / two.	...uma mesa para uma / duas.	oo-mah **may**-zah **pah**-rah oo-mah / **doo**-ahsh
Non-smoking.	Não fumar.	no<u>w</u> foo-**mar**
Is this table free?	Esta mesa está livre?	ehsh-tah meh-zah ish-**tah lee**-vreh
The menu (in English), please.	A ementa (em inglês), por favor.	ah eh-**mayn**-tah (ay<u>n</u> een-**glaysh**) poor fah-vor
service (not) included	serviço (não) incluído	sehr-**vee**-soo (no<u>w</u>) een-kloo-**ee**-doo
cover charge	coberto	koh-**behr**-too
to go	para fora	**pah**-rah **foh**-rah
with / without	com / sem	koh<u>n</u> / say<u>n</u>
and / or	e / ou	ee / oh
specialty of the house	especialidade da casa	ish-peh-see-ah-lee-**dah**-deh dah **kah**-zah
half portion	meia dose	**may**-ah **doh**-zeh
daily special	prato do dia	**prah**-too doo **dee**-ah
tourist menu	ementa turística	eh-**mayn**-tah too-**reesh**-tee-kah
appetizers	entradas	ay<u>n</u>-**trah**-dahsh
bread	pão	po<u>w</u>
cheese	queijo	**kay**-zhoo
sandwich	sandes	**sahn**-desh
soup	sopa	**soh**-pah
salad	salada	sah-**lah**-dah
meat	carne	**kar**-neh
poultry	aves	**ah**-vish
fish	peixe	**pay**-shee
seafood	marisco	mah-**reesh**-koo
fruit	fruta	**froo**-tah
vegetables	legumes	lay-**goo**-mish
dessert	sobremesa	soo-breh-**may**-zah
tap water	água da torneira	**ah**-gwah dah tor-**nay**-rah
mineral water	água mineral	**ah**-gwah mee-neh-**rahl**
milk	leite	**lay**-teh
(orange) juice	sumo (de laranja)	**soo**-moo (deh lah-**rah<u>n</u>**-zhah)
coffee	café	kah-**feh**
tea	chá	shah
wine	vinho	**veen**-yoo
red / white	tinto / branco	**teen**-too / **brang**-koo
glass / bottle	copo / garrafa	**koh**-poo / gah-**rah**-fah
beer	imperial	ay<u>n</u>-peh-ree-**ahl**
Cheers!	Saúde!	sah-**oo**-deh
More. / Another.	Mais. / Outro.	maish / **oh**-troo
The same.	O mesmo.	oo **mehsh**-moo
The bill, please.	A conta, por favor.	ah-**kohn**-tah poor fah-**vor**
tip	gorjeta	gor-**zheh**-tah
Delicious!	Delicioso!	deh-lee-see-**oh**-zoo

For many more pages of survival phrases for your trip to Portugal, check out *Rick Steves' Portuguese Phrase Book*

INDEX

INDEX

INDEX

MAP INDEX

Audio Europe

Rick's Free Travel App

Get your FREE **Rick Steves Audio Europe**™ app to enjoy...

- Dozens of self-guided tours of Europe's top museums, sights and historic walks

- Hundreds of tracks filled with cultural insights and sightseeing tips from Rick's radio interviews

- All organized into handy geographic playlists

- For iPhone, iPad, iPod Touch, Android

With Rick whispering in your ear, Europe gets even better.

Find out more at ricksteves.com

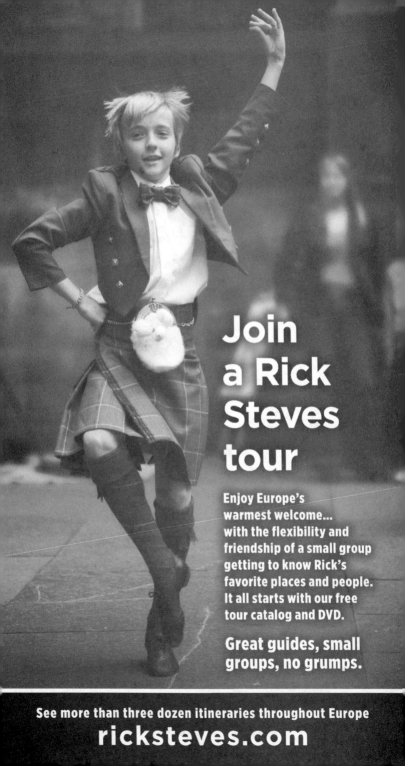

Start your trip at

Free information and great gear to

▶ Plan Your Trip

Browse thousands of articles and a wealth of money-saving tips for planning your dream trip. You'll find up-to-date information on Europe's best destinations, packing smart, getting around, finding rooms, staying healthy, avoiding scams and more.

▶ Eurail Passes

Find out, step-by-step, if a railpass makes sense for your trip—and how to avoid buying more than you need. Get free shipping on online orders

▶ Graffiti Wall & Travelers Helpline

Learn, ask, share—our online community of savvy travelers is a great resource for first-time travelers to Europe, as well as seasoned pros.

Rick Steves' Europe Through the Back Door, Inc.

![Rick Steves](www.ricksteves.com)

Rick Steves

www.ricksteves.com

EUROPE GUIDES

Best of Europe
Eastern Europe
Europe Through the Back Door
Mediterranean Cruise Ports

COUNTRY GUIDES

Croatia & Slovenia
England
France
Germany
Great Britain
Ireland
Italy
Portugal
Scandinavia
Spain
Switzerland

CITY & REGIONAL GUIDES

Amsterdam, Bruges & Brussels
Athens & the Peloponnese
Barcelona
Budapest
Florence & Tuscany
Istanbul
London
Paris
Prague & the Czech Republic
Provence & the French Riviera
Rome
Venice
Vienna, Salzburg & Tirol

SNAPSHOT GUIDES

Berlin
Bruges & Brussels
Copenhagen & the Best of
    Denmark
Dublin
Dubrovnik
Hill Towns of Central Italy
Italy's Cinque Terre
Krakow, Warsaw & Gdansk
Lisbon
Madrid & Toledo
Munich, Bavaria & Salzburg
Naples & the Amalfi Coast
Northern Ireland
Norway
Scotland
Sevilla, Granada & Southern Spain
Stockholm

POCKET GUIDES

Athens
Barcelona
Florence
London
Paris
Rome
Venice

Rick Steves guidebooks are published by Avalon Travel,
a member of the Perseus Books Group.